The
China
Handbook

The

China

Handbook

Edited by

Christopher Hudson

Advisers

Marc Blecher
Oberlin College

Judy Curry
University of Illinois at Chicago

FITZROY DEARBORN PUBLISHERS

CHICAGO · LONDON

FITZROY DEARBORN PUBLISHERS
70 East Walton Street
Chicago, Illinois 60611
USA

or

11 Rathbone Place
London W1P 1DE
England

British Library Cataloguing in Publication Data
The China Handbook. - (Regional handbooks of economic
    development : prospects onto the 21st century)
    1. China - Economic policy - 2. China - Economic
    conditions
    I. Hudson, Christopher
    338.9'51

ISBN 1884964885

Library of Congress Cataloging in Publication Data is available

First published in the USA and UK 1997
Typeset by Print Means, New York, New York
Printed by Braun-Brumfield, Inc., Ann Arbor, Michigan

Contents

Society and Human Dimensions of Development

Appendices

Editor's Note

The China Handbook, the first volume in a series entitled *Regional Handbooks of Economic Development: Prospects onto the 21st Century,* provides an overview of China's development path in the second half of the 20th century, with particular emphasis on the period since 1978— commonly referred to in this book as the "reform period." Chapters focus on China's key economic programs and policies as well as China's handling of important trade and investment relationships with neighboring countries. In common with other volumes in the series, *The China Handbook* is designed to address complex development issues in a manner accessible to academic and non-academic audiences alike. It is our special aim to make China's economic development understandable to college-level students.

The contents of this book were chosen with the help of two advisers, who are listed on page iii. Topics range from current trends in agricultural and industrial policy to the impact market-oriented economic reforms have had on labor, social welfare, and education. Contributors were asked to focus on issues affecting China's modernization efforts in the 1990s, and to consider how China's current economic initiatives may play out in the years to come. The volume opens with two chapters that set China's economic conditions and initiatives within their historical context.

Chapters are presented under four main headings: History; Regional Context; Political Economy and Development Policy; Society and Human Dimensions of Development.

Each chapter has been prepared by a recognized expert in the field and consists of an essay on the topic, a further reading list with annotations, and, in many cases, supplementary materials such as graphs and tables. In-text references to sources listed in "Further Reading" are given as author's last name followed by date; sources not listed in "Further Reading" are given more complete details within the text.

The volume closes with a series of appendices, including a detailed chronology of events; a glossary of terms; biographical entries on key personalities; government administration charts; and an annotated bibliography of secondary sources.

The editor would like to thank the advisers and contributors for their cooperation and efforts. Special thanks belong to Michael Jeffers for his advice in organizing the Regional Handbook series, and especially to Paul Schellinger and Marc Blecher for their invaluable help at every stage of this project.

History

Chapter One

The Maoist Period, 1949–78: Mobilizational Collectivism, Primitive Accumulation, and Industrialization

Victor D. Lippit

When the People's Republic of China was founded on October 1, 1949, following decades of civil war and Japanese invasion, it inherited an economy in shambles. Modern industrial output, which had grown from a minuscule base by an average of 9.4% yearly between 1912 and 1936, showed virtually no growth between 1935 and 1949. Production in most industries had declined sharply from previous peak levels, hyperinflation had wiped out the value of the previous regime's currency, and most transactions were being carried out on a barter basis. In 1949, close to 90% of the population lived in rural areas, and some 65% of national income was generated in the agricultural sector.

By 1978, the communist regime had created a diversified industrial structure, institutionalized the accumulation process through a system of central planning modeled on the Soviet system as well as a uniquely Chinese system of collectivized agriculture, and laid the groundwork for the exceptionally rapid economic growth that was to characterize the reform era that began in 1978. Nevertheless, much of the 1949–78 period was marked by dramatic conflict within the leadership over economic and social policy, and by massive social upheavals. During the last two decades of the period, rural and urban incomes were stagnant, breaking the socialist promise of prosperity for working people, and by 1978 the extreme politicization of everyday life had created a high degree of cynicism among ordinary people. Economic growth was sustained by extremely high levels of capital accumulation, a consequence of the growing inefficiency of the economic system. Because each unit of incremental output required rising levels of investment, the resources available for raising consumption levels were limited severely.

Thus, the period between 1949 and 1978 was a mixed one for the Chinese economy and society. The key divide within the Communist Party leadership lay between Mao and his allies on the one hand, driven by their visionary belief in the virtually unlimited potential for economic construction created by socialist relations of production, and a more pragmatic group of officials on the other, ready to tailor their vision of socialist construction and society to China's limited production capabilities. From 1949 until the mid-1950s, these two groups generally worked in harmony, but from 1955 until Mao's death in September 1976, Chinese policy was marked by an alternating pattern of extreme mobilizational collectivism followed by periods of moderation that were needed to help the economy and society recover from the visionary policies pursued by Mao.

During the period of rehabilitation and reconstruction between 1949 and 1952, output in both industry and agriculture increased rapidly from the sharply depressed 1949 levels; production output in 1952 surpassed previous peak levels in nearly every industry. To avoid the artificial upward bias entailed in basing long-term growth calculations on the 1949 levels of output, most assessments of the Maoist period take 1952 as the base year. Moreover, although Mao died in 1976, the policies of his later years generally were kept in place from 1976 to 1978 (after which the era of reform ushered in a sharp break); thus, the entire period from 1952 to 1978 is referred to in this chapter as the "Maoist period." Table 1.1 indicates the output of major products during both the recovery and Maoist periods.

Table 1.1 also reflects the overwhelming emphasis placed on capital goods production and the relatively slow growth in consumer goods production throughout the Maoist period. Moreover, since the population growth rate over the entire period averaged about 2.2%, and since food was the major consumption item for both rural and urban households throughout the period, the slow growth in agricultural production placed a sharp constraint on the government's ability to improve living standards. Also noteworthy is the fact that gains in agricultural production were minimal despite massive increases in the production of such agricultural inputs as chemical fertilizers and power-driven machinery (see Table 1.1). These inputs were introduced primarily in the 1970s, and the failure of agricultural output to respond commensurately is an indicator of the extent to which the institutional organization of agriculture limited their effectiveness.

Land Reform and the Collectivization of Agriculture

During the civil war period (1946–49), the communist leadership never disputed the desirability of collectivization as an ultimate goal. The strong popular support the party was able to generate among the mass of the peasantry, however, relied first and foremost on its commitment to land reform under the "land to the tiller" policy. Land reform was carried out first in the extensive areas that came under communist rule during the course of the civil war, and in the remainder of the country between 1950 and 1952. Some 40% to 44% of the agricultural land area was redistributed under the land reform, which sought to distribute land holdings equally within each village. The commercial and industrial enterprises owned by rich peasants and small landlords initially were protected from expropriation.

Building on the tradition of mutual aid among peasant households, rural cadres sought to encourage the establishment of new mutual aid teams even before the land reform was completed. The mutual aid teams typically consisted of some seven or eight households that pooled their labor during the busy agricultural seasons and sometimes combined their assets to purchase production equipment. By 1952, 40% of China's rural households were organized in mutual aid teams, up from 11% in 1950; the proportion reached 58% in 1954.

The initial strategy for collectivization envisioned a gradual, voluntary process that would extend over 15 years. Collectivization was based on the Marxist principle that the relations of production (reflected in collectivization) could only be transformed successfully as the development of the productive forces permitted. In the Chinese context of the early 1950s, this was understood to mean that collectivization could only proceed as the industrial sector developed the capacity to provide the machinery and other inputs that would give large-scale units in agriculture decisive productivity advantages. Moreover, the anticipated higher productivity in collective units was expected to ensure peasant support for collectivization by tying collectivization to steadily rising living standards for the members of collective units. Mao himself insisted that at least 90% of collective members should experience higher incomes during their first year of participation.

A variety of economic problems encountered during the early 1950s, however, led Mao to break with this consensus strategy.

The slow growth of agricultural production, which threatened the regime's ambitious plans for rapid industrialization, was compounded by the fact that the poor-peasant beneficiaries of the land reform, preferring to retain output for their own consumption, were much less willing to market their output than were expropriated landlords and rich peasants. Although as much as 50% of agricultural output was marketed in the 1920s and 1930s, by 1953 the marketing ratio had fallen to 28%. This problem was exacerbated by the slow growth rates of crop production in 1953 and 1954 (1.6% and 2.3%, respectively).

Concurrently, China launched its First Five-Year Plan in 1953; investment rose 84% from 1952 levels and the urban population grew by 6 million people or 8.4%. To ensure urban supplies, the state launched a "planned purchase and supply" system in November 1953, requiring peasants to sell agricultural products to the state at below-market prices. This created a further disincentive to increase agricultural production. Since the peasants had a strong preference for increasing their food consumption, the state would have had to raise prices significantly to increase the marketed share of agricultural output, and this in turn would have required a drastic cutback in the regime's industrialization plans. Faced with the contradiction posed by the imbalance between industrial and agricultural growth, Mao sought to resolve the crisis by dramatically accelerating the timetable for collectivization.

In a famous speech in July 1955, Mao criticized the rural cadres for failing to respond sufficiently to peasant demands for collectivization. He argued (incorrectly) that, following the land reform, class polarization had reemerged in the countryside as the poor-peasant beneficiaries of the land reform, lacking the ability to purchase farm implements and other inputs, increasingly were forced to sell or mortgage their newly acquired land to rich peasants. More importantly, he took issue with the Communist Party's Marxist position that collectivization should only proceed in step with the

development of the industrial sector's capacity to provide the needed inputs. Instead, he envisioned new relations of production that would release enormous productive potential in the countryside. Given Mao's great prestige as the leader of the revolution, and fearful of being criticized, rural cadres responded by greatly accelerating the collectivization process and violating the principle of voluntary participation.

In 1954, only 2% of the peasant households were members of the elementary agricultural producer cooperatives (APCs). Based on the natural village or hamlet, the elementary APCs averaged about 30 households and were considered "semi-socialist" because members retained ownership rights over the land and equipment they contributed, and also because the net income was distributed partly on the basis of labor performed and partly on the basis of land and capital contributions. In June 1955, 14% of rural households were members of elementary APCs; following Mao's July speech, that percentage climbed to 59%.

The summer of 1955 marked a turning point not only in agricultural policy but in the overall Chinese approach to economic development. On the one hand, the majority of party leaders advocated a "rationalistic" and pragmatic approach to development, including the use of material incentives (mixed with moral appeals), an emphasis on the development of expertise, and a cautious approach to collectivization. On the other hand, Mao focused on the almost limitless possibilities of collective mass action while turning a blind eye to the negative consequences in his pursuit of rapid socialist modernization.

The pressures to accelerate collectivization continued into 1956. The large return to capital (about 50%) in the elementary APCs limited incentives by reducing the amount available for distribution according to labor performed, and the fully socialist, advanced (as opposed to elementary) APCs were preferred for ideological reasons in any event. Averaging about 200 households, advanced APCs combined several elementary APCs and eliminated the return to property. The proportion of peasant households belonging to advanced APCs increased from 4% at the end of 1955 to 88% at the end of 1956 and 100% by April 1958.

By compressing the collectivization process into such a short span of time, Mao effectively abandoned the principle of voluntary participation and recanted his promise that collectivization would bring shared prosperity. However, by placing the administrative control of agricultural produce in the hands of the state, he was able to assure a much higher proportion of agricultural sales than the peasantry would have made voluntarily. This allowed China to sustain a more rapid pace of investment and industrialization than otherwise would have been possible. In other words, industrialization in the Maoist era was sustained in large measure by a process of "primitive accumulation," based on the extraction of surplus from the agricultural sector.

The Socialization of Industry and the First Five-Year Plan

Under Mao's leadership, the Communist Party adopted in 1947 a strategy for socialist transition. Seeking to isolate the large landlords and the "bureaucratic capitalists" (large-scale capitalists who enjoyed their position as a result of state support), Mao explicitly acknowledged the need to retain a capitalist sector in the economy for a lengthy period of time, and during the 1950–53 period small-scale private businesses actually increased in number. Meanwhile, the Kuomintang regime had seized Japanese businesses at the end of World War II with the ultimate intention of privatizing them; with the resumption of the civil war, however, the conditions for privatization were never realized. Thus, the communist regime inherited a large state sector when it assumed control of the country; 45% of industrial output was under direct or indirect state control in 1949 and 63% was under state control by the end of 1950.

In 1951, the "three-anti" campaign was launched, the first of many campaigns that targeted the abuse of power in the state bureaucracy. Concerned with the legacy of bureaucratic rule in China, Mao sought throughout his leadership to limit actual and potential abuses of power by the bureaucracy. Ironically, Mao staunchly opposed permitting the market to play a central role in the economic and political process based on his belief that marketization inevitably would lead to capitalist restoration. Mao's alternative strategy for restricting the role of bureaucracy was to decentralize the state administration by pushing power downward in the bureaucracy to lower-level units, including many units created especially for this purpose. Rural collectives and later the people's communes are representative of this strategy. The "mass line" instructed cadres to formulate policies based on their understanding of the peasants' and workers' wishes, to test these policies in practice, and to modify them on the basis of their outcomes. Administrative decentralization, however, proved unable to eliminate the problems of bureaucracy and often contradicted the goals of the central planning system. As a result, the leadership alternately sought to centralize and decentralize the state administration throughout the Maoist period.

In 1952, the leadership launched the "five-anti" movement against private enterprises making "excessive profits." The campaign successfully brought the private sector under state control. Many private enterprises were converted into joint state-private enterprises, wherein equal proportions of net profit were allocated to the private entrepreneur, taxes, reinvestment, and worker welfare. By the end of 1952, only 17.1% of industrial output was produced and sold entirely within the private sector. Beginning in 1956 the return to the original owners was reduced to 5% of the capital invested, a payment which persisted until the practice was abandoned altogether during the Cultural Revolution in 1967.

From 1953 to 1957, China launched its First Five-Year Plan. Owing partially to the 156 large-scale projects provided by the Soviet Union, industrial production advanced strongly. From 1952 to 1957, the output of rolled steel increased from 1.1 million metric tonnes to 4.5 million; coal output increased from 64.7 million metric tonnes to 130 million; the output of electric power increased from 7.3 billion kilowatts to 19.3 billion; and the output of cement increased from 2.9 million tonnes to 6.9 million. Despite collectivization, however, the growth of agricultural output lagged far behind that of industry, and the leadership became increasingly aware that rapid industrial growth could not be sustained without measures to improve agricultural performance. To restore incentives in agriculture the regime was compelled in 1957 to ease pressures on the collectives to deliver their output to the state.

The Great Leap Forward and the Organization of the People's Communes

The imbalance between agricultural and industrial growth was reflected in the difficulty the state encountered in increasing grain procurements even as the urban population was growing rapidly (the population in the cities rose from 71.6 million in 1952 to 92 million in 1957 and 130 million in 1960). The imbalance was also reflected in the agricultural sector's inability to provide adequate supplies of raw materials for light industry (mainly consumer goods) during the First Five-Year Plan. During that time, the agricultural sector supplied some 80% to 85% of the raw materials for light industry, and the sluggish growth of agriculture was reflected in the severe underutilization of capacity in the consumer goods sector. Moreover, since China's exports during the same period primarily consisted of processed and unprocessed agricultural products, and since over 90% of China's imports were raw materials and intermediate products, the problems in agriculture also constrained industrial performance via their impact on the foreign trade sector.

In an effort to stimulate the performance of agriculture and light industry, the communist regime pursued a path of administrative decentralization in 1957, handing over extensive decision-making powers to the provinces and localities, and cut back on required grain sales to the state. Nevertheless, the imbalance between industry and agriculture persisted, as did the problem of procuring adequate grain supplies for the cities. Moreover, as peasants flocked to the cities, urban unemployment emerged as a major problem. In order to solve these problems, Mao envisioned a great movement of mass mobilization in which new forms of social organization would provide the basis for overcoming the production constraints imposed by nature. The movement became known as the Great Leap Forward (GLF), and under it China sought to double national income in a short period of time.

The Great Leap Forward spanned the years 1958–60, during which China sought to maintain rapid growth in the modern industrial sector while mobilizing people in rural areas to increase production using labor-intensive techniques. This technological dualism became known in China as "walking on two legs." The leadership hoped that the underemployed labor in the countryside could produce inputs for the agricultural sector without drawing resources away from the modern industrial sector. The most notable example was the movement to create tens of thousands of "backyard steel furnaces" in rural areas during 1958. Labor-intensive capital construction also was used to create agricultural infrastructure, especially in irrigation and other water conservancy projects. The mobilization of this labor was facilitated by the ongoing institutional transformation of the countryside, which culminated in the merging of the advanced agricultural producer cooperatives into people's communes.

During the winter of 1957–58, a number of advanced APCs joined forces to work on large-scale water conservancy projects. The resulting organization, called a people's commune, received high praise from Mao in the spring of 1958. Soon after, a movement was launched to reorganize the entire countryside into people's communes; by September 1958, 98% of rural households had joined. The commune represented a dramatic new form of social organization: initially comprising some 5,000 households and integrating village government into itself, the average commune became an all-encompassing economic, political, and social unit, responsible for capital construction, everyday farming activities, small-scale rural industry, education, health care, and the full range of local government activities.

At first, the communes were expected to speed the transition to communism in the countryside. Communal cafeterias provided meals free of charge, and a range of services from haircuts to communal baths also were provided to members. Adopting the communist principle of distribution according to need required the leadership to break with the socialist principle of distribution according to labor performed. Material incentives were replaced by the enormous social pressures associated with mobilizational collectivism. Local cadres organized the peasants in military fashion to march into the fields at daybreak to "attack" nature. The entire country was exhorted to work hard for a few years to provide the basis for a new era of collective prosperity.

The communes thus represented an institutional response to the same forces generating the Great Leap Forward. Communes were encouraged to initiate local industries to provide farm inputs, and the socialization of household tasks like cooking enabled women to participate more fully in agricultural activities while men spent an increasing share of their time laboring in the new industries.

Owing to a lack of planning and experimentation, both the commune system and the GLF quickly encountered great difficulties. The output of the new industries was typically so poor in quality that it proved unusable—steel manufactured at low temperatures in the small-scale furnaces proved extremely brittle and snapped readily when subject to stress or cold temperatures. Moreover, the diversion of labor from agriculture led to declines in output, and the transport

system, which delivered inputs to rural industries and distributed their output, was often unavailable for transporting agricultural inputs or harvested produce. Many of the water conservancy projects proved counterproductive as irrigation channels were created without adequate provisions for drainage, leaving heavy alkaline residues on the land and resulting in sharp declines in land productivity. The communal dining halls were highly unpopular since the cooking of the evening meal depleted the supply of wood for heating households.

Meanwhile, the extreme politicization of everyday life placed overwhelming pressure on local cadres to report large increases in output that grossly misrepresented actual circumstances. This breakdown of the national statistical system deprived the leadership in Beijing of an accurate means of assessing agricultural output. As a consequence, required sales of grain to the state were increased sharply, ushering in a period of malnutrition and even starvation in the countryside. Despite the bumper harvest in 1958, which was assured prior to the formation of the communes, grain production fell sharply from 200 million tonnes in that year to 170 million tonnes in 1959 and 143.5 million tonnes in 1960. Scholars estimate that between 17 million and 23 million Chinese lost their lives during the ensuing famine.

However, organizational adjustments enabled the communes to survive the calamity of the Great Leap Forward. The regime ceased to promote communal dining halls and the military-style approach to production in 1959, and in the ensuing years China sought to decentralize the responsibility for production while introducing material incentives. The communes were reduced in size to an average of about 3,000 households and came to have four distinct levels, each with different responsibilities. The commune level was designated the administrative center, with the chairman and other leading cadres appointed by the party. The commune level typically administered a middle school, a clinic or small hospital, and a few larger industrial enterprises. Production brigades, consisting of the administrative villages and averaging about 200 households (formerly these were the advanced APCs) were responsible for administering elementary schools; additionally, most rural industrial enterprises and smaller-scale infrastructure projects were organized at this level. Production teams, consisting of the natural villages and averaging about 30 households (formerly the elementary APCs) were responsible for everyday agricultural production and income distribution; sometimes these production teams ran very small enterprises. Finally, households were allocated small private plots for their own use, although administrative interference sometimes curtailed their autonomy over these land parcels.

The Post-Leap Retrenchment

Because reserve stocks of grain cushioned the 1959 collapse in agricultural production, the worst impact on food supplies did not occur until 1960–61. To combat the ensuing crisis, production teams increasingly turned over the responsibility for agricultural production to individual households, although the formal structure of the commune was maintained. The regime recentralized control over industry, closing down the weaker rural enterprises while retaining and consolidating the stronger ones. The party leadership reaffirmed the importance of material incentives, Mao's mobilizational approach to economic activity fell into disfavor, and Mao himself lost the power to direct national policy (he later complained that Deng Xiaoping and other party leaders had even stopped consulting him).

Industrial production did not fare as poorly as agricultural production during the Great Leap Forward and its aftermath. In the first place, one of the favorable conditions for launching the Great Leap Forward was the expectation that several of the major industrial projects aided by the Soviet Union would reach their productive capacity by the end of the decade. Second, the commitment to developing heavy industry and to rapid industrialization was unquestioned among all factions of the Chinese

leadership, and thus resources were always available for this purpose, no matter the consequences to other areas of China's economy. Finally, the failure of Mao's mobilizational approach to development made it increasingly apparent that raising agricultural productivity would require a significant increase in the inputs provided by the industrial sector. Thus, by 1965 China was producing more than nine times as much chemical fertilizer as it had in 1957.

During the Great Leap Forward, industrial production increased from an index of 100 in 1957 to 181 in 1960, yet the increase was unsustainable. Production collapsed to an index of 105 in 1961, stabilized at 111 the following year, and then increased to a new high of 199 in 1965. The excessive accumulation rates of the GLF, which reached 43.8% of national income in 1959, were scaled back to 10.4% in 1962 before increasing again, allowing for improvements in consumption. Agricultural production, which had increased from an index of 100 in 1957 to 103 in 1958, fell to 69 in 1961 and then recovered more slowly to 101 in 1965. Not until 1978 did the per capita production of grain in China surpass the 1957 level on a sustained basis.

The period of recovery from 1961 to 1965 was marked by the recentralization of economic control, by the restoration of planning and the gathering of statistical information that planning required, and by renewed attention to material incentives and living standards. As the recovery gathered steam, the production teams became the main unit of village income distribution (production teams were reorganized so that members received income based on the work-points they earned for performing different production tasks). China's unique efforts to develop rural industry were not abandoned, although rural enterprises were established and supported more selectively; by the mid-1960s these were producing a sizable share of China's cement and chemical fertilizer output. Meanwhile, rural infrastructure projects were designed more carefully, and thus large-scale projects typically were restricted to the winter off-season.

The Cultural Revolution

During the period of recovery, Mao grew increasingly dissatisfied with the marginalized role he had been forced to assume following the collapse of the GLF. Additionally, Mao was disturbed by the emergence of a technology oriented and rationalistically organized society in which the pursuit of individual benefit superseded ideology as the primary motivating force behind economic and social activity. Having lost his dominant role in the party, Mao was compelled to find some outside agency to voice his concerns. He found such a force in the red guards, the millions of activist youths who, with his encouragement, launched the Great Proletarian Cultural Revolution in 1966.

Proponents of the Cultural Revolution sought to transform China's institutions, national consciousness, and social values. They reasoned that, although the economic base of Chinese society had been socialized as a result of the 1949 revolution, the institutional superstructure and patterns of national thought had yet to be transformed accordingly. If the latter were not transformed, they argued, the result might be the restoration of capitalism. Thus, the Cultural Revolution was viewed by its proponents as a struggle between two roads, one leading to socialism and the other to capitalism.

The active phase of the Cultural Revolution lasted from 1966 to 1969 and was marked by a wide range of institutional innovations. The principal slogans included "serve the people" and "fight self," encouraging those in authority to refrain from using their positions for personal benefit. The "two participations" encouraged workers to participate in management and managers to join in physical work. The May 7th Cadre Schools encouraged intellectual workers, ranging from school teachers to senior bureaucrats, to take part in six-month rural retreats, during which participants divided their time between physical labor and academic study of the socialist classics.

Also during the Cultural Revolution efforts were made to improve educational opportunities for peasants, and a system was instituted under which a few production team members received basic health care training for six months to a year; these "barefoot doctors" treated simple ailments and assisted with family planning services. Urban doctors, meanwhile, came under intense pressure to offer their health care services in the countryside, and to train peasants to be "barefoot doctors."

Unfortunately, the Cultural Revolution also resulted in widespread persecution. Jiang Qing, Mao's wife, and the three other members of the "Gang of Four" headed a regime that exerted intense pressure and ordered physical attacks on those who opposed the Cultural Revolution. The Gang of Four set themselves up as a small coterie to approve the ideas that could be disseminated throughout the nation. Furthermore, they distinguished between "socialist-roaders" (themselves) and "capitalist-roaders," including all those who sought material comforts, the preservation of individual liberties, and the preservation of China's traditional culture, and who supported the use of examinations in education, the use of foreign technology, and the use of markets and other rationalistic means of economic management.

Those who opposed the mainstream views often were harassed, attacked, dispatched to the countryside for "re-education," and sometimes killed. Traditional forms of education were scorned: middle school students often were sent to participate in physical labor, universities were closed for several years until a new curriculum could be formed, and graduate education was eliminated in favor of an apprenticeship system.

Additionally, many party leaders and other cadres who had committed their lives to the Communist Revolution came under severe attack during this period (1966–76). Deng Xiaoping, who later would become China's paramount leader, was paraded around Beijing wearing a dunce cap and exiled to the countryside for a prolonged period of re-education; Deng's son suffered paralysis as a result of being pushed out of a fourth-story window. Everyday life was politicized in the extreme, and workers were forced to attend innumerable meetings. Meanwhile, the leadership still refused to provide material incentives for farmers and state industrial workers, living standards stagnated in both urban and rural areas, and a deep cynicism prevailed throughout much of China. Although Hua Guofeng, Mao's successor, attempted to remedy some of the worst abuses of the Cultural Revolution in the two years following Mao's death, not until 1978 did Deng Xiaoping marshal support within the party leadership and break sharply with the Maoist social vision, leading China into the era of reform.

Despite the turmoil that attended the Cultural Revolution, especially during its early phase, output in industry and agriculture continued to rise. This increase was sustained by high rates of capital accumulation, which rose from an average of 24.1% of national income in the 1966–69 period to 33.0% in the 1970–78 period. In urban areas, despite declining housing space and real wages (which declined from an index of 93 in 1965 to 86 in 1976 [1957=100] in the state sector) household incomes increased somewhat as the labor force participation rate (i.e., the proportion of household members who held jobs) rose and the dependency ratio (i.e., the number of unemployed household members per employed member) declined. In the countryside, commune members were forced to use and pay for the massive new inputs provided by the industrial sector even when the sharply higher production costs reduced the value of the work-points they earned. Between 1957 and 1975, real peasant per capita consumption rose by only 22.2%, a figure heavily skewed in favor of suburban communes, and in 1975 fully 42.7% of the nation's production brigades were categorized as poor, where collective incomes averaged less than 50 *yuan* per capita.

Although the gross value of industrial output grew at an average rate of 10.4% between 1965 and 1975, and the gross value of agricultural output grew at an average rate of 4.0% over the same period, the rising share of investment in national income and the 2.4% population growth rate limited gains in per capita consumption. A period of relative moderation followed on the heels of the active phase of the Cultural Revolution as factional fighting was brought to a halt by army intervention, universities were reopened, and the leadership began to explore foreign trade opportunities (major contracts were signed for the import of entire chemical fertilizer plants during 1972–73). Furthermore, after treating its population problems with benign neglect during most of the Maoist era–and allowing population to grow by an average rate of 2.6% during the 1960s–China initiated a major family planning effort beginning in 1970; the natural growth rate of the population fell from 25.8 per thousand in that year to 15.7 per thousand in 1975 and 11.6 per thousand in 1979. Nevertheless, the inefficiencies associated with central planning and the collective organization of agriculture required that the leadership continue to rely on extremely high rates of capital accumulation to sustain industrialization, limiting the possibilities for improvement in popular living standards.

Self-Reliance and Egalitarianism in the Maoist Era

While Mao never claimed to understand macroeconomic policy issues, he did have a vision of the type of society he wished to create in China. Among the values at the core of his vision were self-reliance and equality, and the Maoist era was characterized by wide-ranging efforts to secure these sometimes conflicting goals.

Self-reliance was pursued at every level of Chinese society, often making a virtue of necessity. At the national level, the Western boycott of China led by the United States in the 1950s and 1960s, and the Soviet Union's decisive break with China in 1960, forced China to rely primarily on its own resources. Although China did receive technical assistance and some US$430 million in loans from the Soviet Union in the 1950s, as early as 1956 it became a net exporter to the Soviet Union, remaining so until its debt was repaid in 1965 (in this way China helped finance Soviet development during the period). While China's inability and disinclination to participate in international markets certainly slowed its development, Mao's policy of self-reliance contributed to the development of a relatively diversified industrial base. In an irony that parallels many others of the Maoist era, the policy of national self-reliance, although it limited economic performance during the Maoist era itself, helped lay the groundwork for more successful economic performance during the ensuing era of reform.

In the industrial sector as well, the value of self-reliance helped make a virtue of necessity. Central planning is inherently inefficient because central planners have no way to gauge the real or opportunity cost of their decisions. This problem is magnified in less-developed countries like China, which have limited ability to communicate precise information to the center. One way to address this problem is to increase vertical integration—to require enterprises to assume responsibility for producing or acquiring as many of their own inputs as possible. Another is to increase regional or provincial responsibility for local planning—to make planning more manageable by decentralizing its administration. China followed both of these paths during the Maoist era, with varying degrees of commitment.

While both of these solutions make the process of planning more manageable, neither can address its efficiency costs; there is no reason to assume a priori that having factories produce more of their own parts or acquire them locally will result in least-cost solutions. Moreover, as centrally planned economies grow in size and complexity, their efficiency problems tend to grow disproportionately. Thus, during China's First Five-Year Plan, when investment accounted for 24.2% of material output, industrial output grew at an average annual rate of 15.8%, indicating that $1.53 was required for each

dollar of incremental output. By contrast, from 1970 to 1977 the investment rate reached 32.6% of material product and industrial output grew by an average of 9.7% annually, indicating that $3.26 had to be spent for each dollar of incremental output. Basing growth on rising investment levels limits the resources that can be used for consumption.

In agriculture, Mao's goal of self-reliance was reflected in the management of the commune system. Each commune, for example, was expected to be a self-reliant grain producer. Even communes located in regions that were unsuited for grain production were forced to comply, raising production costs and limiting the gains that might have come from specialization and exchange. Thus, the emphasis placed on self-reliance resulted in significant efficiency costs throughout the economy.

The Maoist regime also promoted egalitarianism with great fervor, but unfortunately its emphasis on self-reliance had serious costs in this regard as well. Although a high degree of equality was attained within most villages and cities, the majority of communes in remote locations were disadvantaged severely, while those located in suburban areas or those that enjoyed favorable growing conditions and ready access to transportation were able to achieve much higher levels of prosperity. Moreover, despite the stagnation in real wages, the falling dependency ratio and rising labor force participation rates in urban households led to a growing gap between urban and rural households. The household registration system prevented peasants from migrating to urban areas or even to more prosperous rural regions, further causing urban-rural and inter-regional income gaps to widen.

Public policy during the Maoist era addressed these problems in a number of ways, but always with limited success. Holding down real wages in urban areas, which included a prolonged period of freezing workers' promotions, represented one attempt. Efforts to increase rural access to medical care through the barefoot doctor system and traveling medical teams during the Cultural Revolution represented another. Further, the central government budget was used to shift resources from the established industrial bases in the coastal and northeastern regions to the new industrial cities in the interior. Nevertheless, urban-rural and intra-rural disparities in income continued to grow.

Conclusion

Mao's vision of a new China incorporated such traditional socialist values as equality, solidarity, and overall social welfare, but it was limited by his commitment to a Leninist vanguard party, precluding genuine worker and peasant control over their own institutions. Mao was well aware of the potential for bureaucratic abuse created by the centralized state (he observed this tendency in the Soviet Union), but critical of the drive for personal material gain that he saw at the heart of capitalism; as such he was unwilling to sanction the use of the market as a way of checking bureaucratic power and accelerating economic development. Although he was well able to articulate the critical internal contradictions in Chinese society, Mao had a limited understanding of macroeconomic issues, and, like Marx and Lenin before him, tended to view the economy as a unit of administration; in so doing, he tended to marginalize or misconstrue the issues of incentives, initiative, innovation, and efficiency.

For Mao, initiative and innovation involved coming up with imaginative solutions to pressing problems rather than a systematic effort to develop new products and processes. Moreover, Mao believed that linking personal prosperity with the general good could substitute for material incentives. According to Mao's vision, the development of new institutions like the people's communes would release the vast productive power of the masses, and the decentralization of bureaucratic control would make it possible both to check bureaucratic power and to mobilize the masses for economic construction. One of the core meanings of the term "mobilize" is "to make ready for

war," and Mao's thinking about economic efforts as parallel to preparation for military conflict is an indicator of the limitations of his ideas on economic policy.

While a broad consensus within the party leadership underlay economic policy during the 1949–55 period, and a consensus remained throughout the Maoist period to pursue rapid industrialization/modernization at all costs, a sharp split emerged in 1955 that separated Mao from most of his colleagues concerning the appropriate means for economic construction and the type of society that China would create in the process. After 1955 the Maoist era was marked by ongoing struggles over Mao's efforts to mobilize the masses and use socialist consciousness and relations of production as the basis for economic construction. Mao's periodic success in shaping economic policy according to his social vision typically resulted in acute economic and social problems, opening the way for a period of moderation until Mao could regather his strength. This occurred following the "socialist high-tide of collectivization" in 1956, the Great Leap Forward of 1958–60 and the active phase of the Cultural Revolution in 1966–69.

The performance of the Chinese economy over the entire Maoist period was mixed. Industrial output grew at an average annual rate of 11.2% over the entire 1952–78 period, and China was able to create a diversified industrial structure, which included the capital goods industry. Concurrently, except for the production calamity associated with the Great Leap Forward, China was able to raise land productivity, normally the first consideration for a poor country with a growing population and little reclaimable agricultural land. Also in the area of agriculture, the commune system permitted the mobilization of labor in the winter to create an extensive supportive infrastructure, ranging from roads and terraces to major water conservation projects; from 1970 to 1978 more than 100 million people worked on such projects each winter. The development of industry, meanwhile, made possible massive increases in agricultural inputs; the total horsepower of agricultural machinery increased from 1.7 million horsepower in 1957 to 14.9 million in 1965, and from 101.7 million in 1975 to 181.9 million in 1979.

Against these gains, a number of serious deficiencies in both industry and agriculture emerged. As the Chinese economy grew and became more complex, decreasing efficiency was inevitable, and this was manifest in the rising investment rates needed to sustain growth, a phenomenon which in turn sharply curtailed the possibilities of raising living standards. Between 1957 and the mid-1970s wage rates stagnated, and the state prohibited promotions within the established wage-grade system for long intervals. Moreover—Maoist rhetoric to the contrary notwithstanding—Chinese enterprises were not marked by active worker control or participation in management. Several factors were responsible for this.

First, within a planned economy a given enterprise must be subordinated to the overall requirements of the plan; the party secretary's role as the most powerful individual within the enterprise assured that party dictates would at all times receive priority (the same arrangement existed in the communes). During the Cultural Revolution, numerous instances were reported in the press of workers volunteering to work on their days off or to work overtime; these typically were portrayed as the result of a heightened social consciousness. The reality underlying such "voluntary" activity was more complex. Since enterprises provided housing, leave permits, work assignments, and even rights to buy consumer goods in short supply, workers could not afford to alienate their superiors. Moreover, anyone displaying "bad character" could be made the object of group criticism. When an enterprise official needed extra help to meet an assigned target, he or she usually could count on the support of a few opportunists eager to curry favor. The remaining workers would then be forced to go along to avoid being singled out as bad characters.

Subject to limited improvements in living standards, forced to attend innumerable meetings, and highly conscious of their own manipulation, China's workers became increasingly cynical and alienated by the end of the Maoist era. In one of the great ironies of the Maoist era, workers deprived of material benefits tended to become more concerned with material goods. From the perspective of the peasantry, workers were regarded as a privileged group; from the workers' perspective, the state imposed unfair burdens on their lives.

Similar to the performance of the industrial sector during the Maoist era, that of the agricultural sector was mixed. While agricultural output grew by 3.2% per year between 1952 and 1978, grain production grew by 2.4% per year, just ahead of the 2.2% population growth rate. Moreover, following the dislocations associated with the Great Leap Forward, grain output per capita did not recover its 1957 level on a sustained basis until 1978. Since the agricultural land area remained roughly constant during the Maoist era at approximately 250 million acres (the limited area of reclaimed land nearly offset the land lost to industrial construction, transport, and housing), and since the population grew from 575 million to 963 million during this period (1952 to 1978), the strong growth in land productivity played a critical role in meeting the nation's food needs. It should be noted, however, that improvements in living standards rely essentially on labor productivity, and that agricultural labor productivity during the Maoist era appears to have declined, limiting possibilities for raising consumption standards in the countryside.

Given the massive increases in agricultural inputs, the extensive infrastructure developed under the communes, and the leadership's belief that the communes would make "rational" land use planning possible, the lack of increase in labor productivity must be explained. The leadership's failure to raise labor productivity was the result of several policy errors that limited agricultural performance and that ultimately may have been responsible for the 1982 decision to dismantle the commune system.

Some will argue that any system of collective agriculture is bound to fail. While these critics may argue correctly, the failure of China's commune system does not prove the point; rather, the system's failure was a consequence of the serious policy errors that undermined it. First, the communes were set up hastily in 1958 before their various features could be tested adequately, including the incentive system and the mechanism for distributing income. Second, the principles of voluntary participation and mutual benefit were violated; peasants were forced to join the communes regardless of their preferences and the impact on their incomes. Third, communes were not allowed to realize the benefits of specialization and exchange: all, for example, were compelled to grow grain regardless of their climate. Fourth, commune members were forced to buy high-priced machinery and other inputs while selling their output at low, state-set prices; thus, commune members were not the beneficiaries of rising output. Finally, commune leaders were selected by and responsible to the party hierarchy, not their members. It is impossible to gauge how the communes and their members would have fared in a market environment and under a different policy regime.

When considering the impact of the communes on the course of Chinese development, their role in rural industrialization also must be taken into account. China's rural, small-scale enterprises were developed largely under the commune system. Able to take advantage of the surplus labor that existed in the agricultural sector, of local resources too limited to be attractive to large-scale state enterprises, and of the ready availability of agricultural inputs, the commune enterprises often made good economic sense. In addition to these advantages, they often were able to provide the agricultural sector with inputs and consumer goods or, benefiting from their lower cost structure, to serve as subcontractors to state-owned firms. In 1979, enterprises at the commune and brigade levels employed 28 million people out of a total rural labor force of some 300 million. Converted into the collectively-owned township and village enterprises (TVEs) after the dissolution of the communes in 1982, these became the most dynamic sector of the economy during the reform era, with employment increasing to some 129 million by 1995.

The early development of the commune industries during the Maoist era—and their subsequent flourishing in the era of reform—parallels the experience of the Chinese economy as a whole. During the Maoist era, numerous preconditions were established for a flourishing economy, but the internal contradictions of Maoist policy forestalled the appearance of that prosperity. Primary education essentially was universalized, and secondary education was developing rapidly prior to the setback it received during the Cultural Revolution. The rural infrastructure established under the commune system, as well as the rapid growth of industries providing agricultural inputs, created the preconditions for a flourishing agriculture once market incentives and a shift of control to the direct producer came into play. The diversified industrial base created during the Maoist era contributed to the subsequent rapid growth once market reforms and international trade and investment opportunities were introduced.

With the exception of the crisis period that followed the collapse of the Great Leap Forward, consumption patterns generally were maintained at low subsistence levels throughout the Maoist era, freeing resources for investment. In this sense the entire Maoist era may be referred to as a period of "primitive accumulation" in which capital construction proceeded not on the basis of the reinvested profits or surplus that a mature capitalism characteristically provides, but on the basis of using the power of the state to redirect resources from the initial creators of the surplus to the state or to others who are prepared to use it for investment rather than consumption. From this perspective, the Maoist era in China failed to usher in an era of general prosperity. It did, however, create the conditions for the ensuing reform policies to do just that.

Further Reading

American Rural Small-Scale Industry Delegation, *Rural Small-Scale Industry in the People's Republic of China,* Berkeley: University of California Press, 1977

An informative account by a group of specialists who visited China in 1975, describing the economic rationale of rural small-scale industry, its relation to agriculture, worker incentives, and the technology employed.

Dernberger, Robert F., editor, *China's Development Experience in Comparative Perspective,* Cambridge, Massachusetts: Harvard University Press, 1980

A collection of essays analyzing China's development experience and relating it to that of other countries.

Lardy, Nicholas R., *Economic Growth and Distribution in China,* Cambridge and New York: Cambridge University Press, 1978

Examines the role of central planning in mitigating the growth of regional inequalities, and of administrative decentralization in mitigating the inefficiencies of central planning.

Lardy, Nicholas R., *Agriculture in China's Modern Economic Development,* Cambridge and New York: Cambridge University Press, 1983

A comprehensive examination of the impact of state policy on peasant behavior and the overall performance of the agricultural sector.

Lee, Hong Yung, *The Politics of the Chinese Cultural Revolution: A Case Study,* Berkeley: University of California Press, 1978

A fascinating account of the Cultural Revolution in its active phase (1966–69), providing insight into its historical development, internal logic, and factional struggles among the red guards and other groups.

Lippit, Victor D., *Land Reform and Economic Development in China: A Study of Institutional Change and Development Finance,* White Plains, New York: International Arts and Sciences Press, 1974

Argues that the rural surplus received by landlords and rich peasants in pre-revolutionary China was transferred to poor peasants by the land reform and then partly extracted by the state to finance industrialization, still leaving the poor peasants as net beneficiaries.

Lippit, Victor D., *The Economic Development of China,* Armonk, New York: M.E. Sharpe, 1987

Examines the impact of class structure on underdevelopment in China prior to 1949 and that of the new class structure on its subsequent development, including an assessment of the extent to which peasant and worker interests have been reflected in that development.

Mao Zedong, *Quotations from Chairman Mao Tsetung,* Beijing: Foreign Languages Press, 1974; San Francisco: China Books and Periodicals, 1990

The little red book brandished by red guards during the Cultural Revolution, it contains selected passages from Mao's writings on the mass line, self-reliance, serving the people, the nature of contradictions, and other topics.

Milton, David, Nancy Milton, and Franz Schurmann, editors, *People's China: Social Experimentation, Politics, Entry onto the World Scene 1966–72,* New York: Random House, 1974; London: Penguin, 1977

A collection of documents, speeches, and articles from the 1966–72 Cultural Revolution period.

Nolan, Peter, *The Political Economy of Collective Farms: An Analysis of China's Post-Mao Rural Reforms,* Boulder, Colorado: Westview Press, and Cambridge: Polity Press, 1988

A thoughtful critical analysis of China's experience with agricultural collectivization by someone previously sympathetic to the process.

Oi, Jean Chun, *State and Peasant in Contemporary China: The Political Economy of Village Government,* Berkeley: University of California Press, 1989

An insightful analysis of the struggle to secure the agricultural surplus that the state, the collective, and peasant families carried out in production teams and villages.

Rawski, Thomas G., *Economic Growth and Employment in China,* Oxford and New York: Oxford University Press, 1979

Examines the structure and growth of the labor force and of labor productivity during the Maoist period.

Riskin, Carl, *China's Political Economy: The Quest for Development Since 1949,* Oxford and New York: Oxford University Press, 1987

The most thorough, insightful analysis of the policy issues and development experience of China during the Maoist era.

Schurmann, Franz, *Ideology and Organization in Communist China,* 2nd edition, Berkeley: University of California Press, 1971

A seminal, sophisticated early work analyzing ideology, government, management, the party, and other subjects.

Selden, Mark, and Victor D. Lippit, editors, *The Transition to Socialism in China,* Armonk, New York: M.E. Sharpe, and London: Croom Helm, 1982

A collection of "re-evaluation" essays focusing on different aspects of the experience of China's economy and society under Mao.

Selden, Mark, *The Political Economy of Chinese Development,* Armonk, New York: M.E. Sharpe, 1993

A collection of thoughtful, insightful essays on collectivization, primitive accumulation, inequality, urban-rural relations, and the overall development process.

In addition to the above sources, the U.S. Congress Joint Economic Committee (Washington, D.C.: U.S. Government Printing Office) publishes every few years a compendium of invited essays by specialists in different areas of the Chinese economy; the most useful works for the Maoist period include: *An Economic Profile of Mainland China* (1967); *People's Republic of China: An Economic Assessment* (1972); *China: A Reassessment of the Economy* (1975); and *Chinese Economy Post-Mao* (1978).

Victor D. Lippit is Professor of Economics at the University of California, Riverside. His books include *Land Reform and Economic Development in China: A Study of Institutional Change and Development Finance* (1974); *The Economic Development of China* (1987); and *Radical Political Economy: Explorations in Alternative Economic Analysis* (1996). He is also coeditor, with Mark Selden, of *The Transition to Socialism in China* (1982).

Table 1.1: China's Macroeconomic Performance: Main Indicators

Item	Unit	1949	1952	1978	Annual Average Growth Rate (%) 1952–78
Gross output of industry	billion *yuan*	14.0	34.3	423.1	11.2
Gross output of agriculture	billion *yuan*	32.6	48.4	145.9	3.2
Major industrial products					
coal	million tons	32.4	66.5	617.8	9.0
crude oil	million tons	0.1	0.4	104.1	23.4
electricity	billion kwh	4.3	7.3	256.6	14.7
crude steel	million tons	0.2	1.4	31.8	12.9
cement	million tons	0.7	2.9	65.2	12.8
chemical fertilizer	thousand tons	6	39	8,693	23.1
cloth	billion meters	1.9	3.8	11.0	4.2
bicycles	thousands	14	80	8,540	19.7
Major farm products					
grain	million tons	113.2	163.9	304.8	2.4
cotton	million tons	0.4	1.3	2.2	2.0
oil-bearing crops	million tons	2.3	3.7	4.6	0.8
hogs	millions	57.8	89.9	301.3	4.8
Farm machinery in use					
large and medium tractors	thousands		0.6	557	30.0
hand tractors	millions			1.4	
power-driven drainage and irrigation machines	million hp		0.1	65.6	27.1

Source: Lippitt, 1987: 106–107

Chapter Two

The Dengist Period: The Triumphs and Crises of Structural Reform, 1979 to the Present

Marc Blecher

The commonplace term for the vast changes that have taken place in China since 1978 is "reform"–an appropriate term insofar as it refers to aspects of the *process* by which these transformations have occurred: change has been pursued gradually and without violence. But "reform" can hardly capture the depth and breadth of the *substance* of China's many changes. Since 1978 China has not merely been tinkering with, perfecting, or toning down Maoist state socialism. Something far more thoroughgoing is afoot. The country has been seeking, often successfully, to excise, root and branch, many of the basic elements of its Maoist polity, economy, society, and political culture. It has questioned almost everything that went before. Its leaders and people have sought to create unprecedented new forms of political authority, economic activity, social organization, and cultural expression. If, as Theda Skocpol argues, revolution is defined as a "basic transformation of a society's state and class structures," then what China has been undergoing is no mere "reform," but rather something that would more aptly be called a peaceful revolution. Another, perhaps less oxymoronic, term to capture China's gradual and peaceful process toward "basic transformation of

… state and class structures" is "structural reform."

Dismantlement of Maoist Leadership and Ideology

At the Third Plenum of the Eleventh Party Central Committee in December 1978, Deng Xiaoping headed a group of leaders who were critical of Maoist radicalism. The Dengists returned to key positions of leadership in the Politburo and its Standing Committee. Modernization replaced class struggle as the main ideological principle guiding politics and policy. Radical advances in rural collectivization were rejected, and the importance of private plots and markets was reaffirmed. Premier and Party Chairman Hua Guofeng's grandiose plans for rapid development of heavy industry were scrapped in favor of a more balanced and measured approach. In short, the way was now cleared for China's program of "reform"–in truth, a riptide of profound restructuring–in pursuit of socialist modernization.

The Dengists had their work cut out for them. They had to root out Maoist ideology, politics, policies, and institutions, and then face the more challenging task of replacing them with something new. Since political change was a precondition of change in ideology, policy, and institutions, and since the political arena was what the Dengists knew best, they began there. Mere days after the Third Plenum adjourned, Wang Dongxing, Mao's personal secretary and a leading protagonist in the political intrigues of the Cultural Revolution, was removed from his key position as head of the Party Central Committee General Office. At the Fourth Plenum in September 1979, many prominent leaders associated with Mao were demoted, while future top leaders Zhao Ziyang and Hu Yaobang were promoted. Deng, preferring to lead from a position less vulnerable than the very top, and hoping to encourage his older colleagues to relinquish their power, shrewdly contented himself with the Chair of the Military Advisory Commission (a post that would prove indispensable in the maelstrom of 1989) and a vice-premiership. Nonetheless, he now was clearly the key figure in Chinese politics and remained so for the better part of the next two decades.

The leadership changes, which continued through 1980, were accomplished not only with surprising swiftness and decisiveness; the Dengists, themselves having been victimized during the Cultural Revolution, now sought not revenge but rather a novel approach that would spare both themselves and their enemies any repeat of their previous agonies, and that also would help normalize and stabilize Chinese politics. Thus, although Mao's chosen successor Hua Guofeng was subjected to serious criticism within the party, no large-scale campaign was launched against him or most other surviving Maoists. Hua's move was presented as a resignation, after which he remained a vice-chair of the Party Central Committee as well as a member of the powerful Politburo Standing Committee. Yet this new approach to fallen leaders would be pursued inconsistently. Hua still was subjected to humiliating attacks at closed party meetings. Moreover, in late 1980 and early 1981 the "Gang of Four" were subjected to a televised trial, their final public condemnation.

The Dengists next turned their attention to ideology. A momentous move already had been made at the Third Plenum, when class struggle was displaced in favor of socialist modernization as the guiding principle of Chinese socialism. Toward the end of that year, Vice-Premier Ye Jianying criticized the Cultural Revolution as having been a calamity. Thornier by far was the question of Mao. More than even a predominant leader, Mao was a founder of the People's Republic of China, the author of its central body of doctrine, and a cult figure. It would not be possible to break with the leadership, policies or institutions of the Maoist period without rethinking Mao's own writing and leadership. Yet reconceptualizing Mao's political ideas had obvious hazards and thus was managed with the greatest sensitivity. After extended preparation and intra-party debate as well as several trial balloons, in June 1981 the Chinese Communist Party (CCP) issued a major document titled "On Questions of Party History," which criticized Mao's political ideas in relation to the Cultural Revolution. The document claims that

> the history of the "cultural revolution" has proved that Comrade Mao Zedong's principal theses for initiating this revolution conformed neither to Marxism-Leninism nor to Chinese reality. They represent an entirely erroneous appraisal of the prevailing class relations and political situation in the Party and state.

The document berated Mao for becoming "arrogant" and elitist during the Cultural Revolution, when he "divorced himself from practice and the masses, acted more and more arbitrarily and subjectively, and increasingly put himself above the Central Committee." Nevertheless, Mao still was hailed:

> Comrade Mao Zedong was a great Marxist and a great proletarian revolutionary, strategist and theorist ... .[I]f we judge his activities as a whole, his contributions to the Chinese Revolution far outweigh his

mistakes. His merits are primary and his errors secondary.

Similarly to its handling of Hua's dismissal, the Dengist leadership chose to deal with political enemies differently than its predecessors had. Although the balanced assessment contained in "On Questions of Party History" no doubt was motivated by a political desire to maintain as broad a base of support as possible during a very risky break from the past, it was nevertheless a refreshing change from the manichaean, polemically-charged approach to problems that has stifled serious debate on key issues of the socialist experience in China.

The Struggle for Structural Reform

As difficult as it was to attack Maoist leaders and ideology while still maintaining a power base, the Dengists soon faced the far more intractable task of replacing Maoist policies and institutions with new ones. The vast state bureaucracy, state-owned industry, and guarantees of a decent livelihood to state officials, functionaries, and workers, proved resilient and resistant to change. Part of the difficulty would turn out to be structural. Reform in many areas proved exceedingly complex, conjuring up old problems (like developmental imbalances and inequalities) while creating new ones (such as powerful inflationary pressures and rampant corruption). Moreover, the Dengists found it difficult to discern or arrive at suitable alternatives for many Maoist-period policies and institutions. For example, competitive markets, which were to replace state planning, often did not develop smoothly or naturally. No substitute for state-owned industry appeared readily on the horizon, and no means could easily be found to replace state-subsidized housing, education, health care, or retirement income. The Dengist leadership also encountered serious political obstacles in reforming Maoist-period policies and institutions. Many very senior and powerful leaders had deep reservations about the rise of the market, the social and economic inequalities, and the

Westernization of Chinese society and culture that the reforms brought in tow. In addition, many ordinary people who felt abandoned by their government found numerous ways to make their opposition felt. For example, farmers often refused to plant the crops the state demanded, or to sell their produce to the state at the prices being offered. Often they resorted to violent protest, including staging uprisings and even killing and maiming tax collectors. Industry began to suffer strikes and slowdowns. Two waves of public protest took place on a national scale, one of which mesmerized the world. The reformers' many struggles to restructure Chinese politics, society, economy, and culture will be addressed throughout the remainder of this chapter and book.

Early Initiatives, Mixed Results: 1979–83

In the glow of the Third Plenum, 1979 dawned with optimism about reform, both in China and abroad. However, Chinese society and its political and economic institutions held surprises in store for both supporters and opponents of the Dengist initiatives. The country's initial four years of grappling with structural reform would produce almost unimaginably deep changes in the countryside. It was all the more startling, then, that during this same period changes in politics and the industrial economy–arenas thought to be most directly under central control–would encounter such unanticipated obstacles and equivocal results.

Rural Reform on the Fast Track

Perhaps the most remarkable early success of structural reform took place in the countryside. Beginning in early 1978, some farmers and local officials, particularly those in poor areas, spontaneously began experimenting with contractual relationships. Under the most extreme form, individual households contracted for use of collective property (usually a piece of land, but also possibly a fish pond, orchard, tractor, or workshop) in return for a payment to the collective in cash or kind. The farmers could keep all profits and were responsible for their losses. This new contractual relationship came to be known as a "responsibility system."

These developments on the ground took place in advance of any policy initiatives from the state. From the top leadership to the villages, the country was divided over the prospect of converting collective agriculture to a contracting system. Thus, Deng Xiaoping—who in 1962 had supported rural contracting with his famous words, "it doesn't matter if the cat is black or white, so long as it catches mice"—had difficulty moving his plan forward. Even the triumphantly reformist Third Plenum of late 1978 forbade responsibility systems. Yet household responsibility systems quickly gained momentum in many poor areas. A fascinating political dynamic of popular initiative and political influence now was set in motion. Step by step, villagers and local leaders in various parts of the country moved ahead in developing contracting systems that were more and more comprehensive and individualistic. Each time they were crossing the boundaries of state policy. Not surprisingly, the results they achieved were usually significant increases in production. Party and government leaders sympathetic to radical rural reform would visit or receive favorable reports about these places, and use these villages' experiences to support their arguments for further reform. In early 1982, they pronounced that the household responsibility system was not only permissible, but consistent with socialism. The political dynamic now shifted. What had been a broad, spontaneous movement toward decollectivization now became a program that leadership actively propagated, and, in many places, even forced on unwilling farmers and recalcitrant leaders (in ways not so dissimilar from those used during the Maoist period to implement radical policies, such as the "high tide" of collectivization in 1956). By mid-1982, almost

three quarters of production teams engaged in household contracting, and the process was virtually complete by the end of 1983.

Two concomitants to this process also moved relatively quickly. First, as decollectivization proceeded, many restrictions on private commerce gradually were lifted. Markets sprang back to life, and the state pulled back its regulation of them. Where it used to set prices for a wide range of goods, now it mostly set maximum prices only (with the exception of some key commodities such as grain and cotton). Even the number of goods with state-set maxima declined gradually. Second, the rural economy was depoliticized. Class labels like "capitalist" and "rich peasant" were abolished so that enterprising and prosperous contractors would not be stigmatized. Economic and political administration were separated institutionally. As the responsibility systems proliferated, farmers began to gain (and communes began to lose) control of concrete production issues such as cropping choices and labor allocation. China's fourth constitution, adopted in late 1982, spoke of town and township governments rather than people's communes, which had been created in 1958 in order, as the slogan had it, to put "politics in command" of agriculture. By the end of 1984, communes were a thing of the past (except in Tibet, where they continued a while longer).

The swift pace of rural institutional reform surprised many people, including its supporters in the top levels of leadership. Yet if they concluded from this success that further transformation of other arenas of China's polity and economy would be a downhill process, they were in for another surprise. Structural reform of politics and the industrial economy has proven far more difficult, and in some cases intractable. Indeed, efforts in this direction have encountered frequent setbacks and have provoked crises that have threatened the very existence of the People's Republic. These processes and dangers are ongoing.

Abortive Political Reform

The Third Plenum began with a simple, bold, and momentous move: it relegated class struggle to the back burner, thereby accomplishing several goals related to political and economic restructuring. The party was attempting to reassure all Chinese people, no matter what their class background, that they would no longer suffer ferocious attacks based on their position in a society that had been overturned three decades before. The change would help create the conditions for social and, therefore, political stability by disposing of an issue that had rent China asunder. The leadership also had its eye on the rise of a new class of entrepreneurs who would help develop China's prospective market-based economy once class struggle no longer was wielded against them. Abandonment of politicized class categories would also help encourage intellectuals, whom the state would need in order to implement its plans for China's technological modernization. The Dengists shrewdly made this simple but profound move, and it met with instant and very broad, if quiet, approval.

However, neither this stunning move nor the rapid changes in central leadership involved structural reform of the political system, such as the introduction of rights, party and government reorganization, and transformations in state-society relations, including the rise of elections and of interest organization and politics. Indeed, the changes that eventually took place hardly merit the simpler term "reform." Although minor changes were made to top-level party organization, the basic ideological and institutional features of the Maoist-period Leninist political system were preserved. The Communist Party continued to dominate political life, firmly resisting the rise of alternative organizations, citizens' political rights, and new forms of state-society relations.

At the outset of the Dengist period, such an outcome was not readily apparent, however. Even before the landmark Third Plenum, structural political reform reached the

political agenda with a loud thump. In mid-November 1978, citizens put up posters on a Beijing street corner just blocks from Zhongnanhai, the residence of the top party leadership. While at first they merely expressed support for Deng Xiaoping, within a week they were raising larger issues of democracy and citizens' rights. "Democracy Wall" became the site of lively political debate among Chinese and, even more novel, between Chinese and foreigners. Some Chinese visiting the wall went so far as to ply Western journalists with questions to ask Deng. Soon some participants, having outgrown the format of the big character poster, moved on to editing and publishing newsletters and magazines, and to forming independent political organizations. Initially, Deng supported the concept of Democracy Wall; after all, many of the writers were directing their critiques against his Maoist opponents. But Deng and most of his colleagues soon began to worry that a good deal of this public discourse, as well as the concept of independent publications and organizations, would erode party authority. By the spring of 1979, Deng emphasized the "four cardinal principles": the socialist road, the dictatorship of the proletariat, the leadership of the party, and Marxism-Leninism-Mao Zedong Thought. Moreover, he referred to some of the people engaged in the pro-democracy activities as "bad elements"—an epithet echoing one of the class-like categories that the leadership had set about abolishing. When a Beijing zoo electrician named Wei Jingsheng criticized Deng's turnabout, he soon found himself sentenced to 15 years in prison. Freedom of speech and association, a potentially crucial element in structural political reform, and certainly an element that could stimulate other changes, was once again removed from the political agenda.

The Dengist leadership was not prepared for such basic transformations of the political system; even its initiatives to make far less momentous political modifications met with very mixed results. As has been shown already, the leadership was equivocal in normalizing the treatment of top leaders ousted from their positions, an issue with serious implications for the manner in which China's leaders conduct themselves while in office. In 1982, the Twelfth Party Congress took up two major questions. The first involved the transfer of top positions from the elderly patriarchs of the Chinese Revolution to the next generation. A new body–the Party Central Advisory Commission–was created to give aged leaders an honorific way to relinquish their direct power and to serve instead as experienced advisers only. Most, however, were unwilling to step down so soon, and they joined only on the condition that the powers of the new Commission be strengthened. (During the 1989 events, the Commission would become a central player in the decision to crack down.) Second, to reduce the power of any one individual at the very top of the party, the Twelfth Party Congress revitalized the office of the central party secretariat to replace the posts of chair and vice-chair of the Central Committee. The General Secretary, it stipulated, was to be constrained by other members of the Secretariat. Then, at the National People's Congress at the end of the year, socialist China's fourth constitution was adopted, emphasizing rationalized institutions and leadership processes that would be regulated by law. The new constitution spelled out and separated more clearly the functions of various bodies, imposed term limits on top leadership positions, and prohibited leaders from holding concurrent posts. But, as soon became clear, none of these measures significantly altered the power of China's political elite or the way the government conducted its business.

The Conundrums of Industrial Reform

Like political and rural economic reform, industrial reform was the subject of lively debate and activity at the outset of the Dengist period. There were good reasons to expect swift, deep changes. After all, a broad consensus existed among the top leadership, most experts on the economy, and many enterprise managers that China's

system of state ownership, planning, and management of industry was technically backward, deeply inefficient, and unable to meet the developmental and consumption needs of the country. Moreover, the fact that industry was too tightly under central political control could perhaps be turned into a powerful lever for change by a reform-minded leadership now exercising that control. Such expectations, however, would prove naïve. Industrial reform quickly revealed itself to be an area of protracted conflict among leaders, experts, and middle-level officials, a quagmire of rhythmic policy reversals, and a roller-coaster of economic outcomes, all climaxing, ultimately, in the 1989 protests that threatened to topple the People's Republic.

Efforts to reform the industrial sector got off to a rousing start in 1979, when a major conference of experts from various state agencies and think tanks met in the prosperous city of Wuxi. Participants criticized China's economic planning system for being overly centralized, and for not allowing enterprises enough space to take initiative. Basing economic planning on political criteria, the participants argued, often had led to the wild pursuit of unrealistic goals, wreaking havoc in the process. Over time central planning had produced structural irrationalities such as excessive emphasis on heavy industry and a price system that did not help producers and consumers make rational choices. Instead, they insisted, planning should be grounded firmly in market-like realities such as actual economic capacities, scarcities, and preferences–i.e., in supply and demand. In fact, state planning should not only simulate markets; it should allow them to develop to complement this new, more realistic planning process.

The ink was barely dry on this marketizing manifesto when sparks began to fly. Critics, led by the prominent Vice-Premier Chen Yun, had a different vision, emphasizing "readjustment" of planning over the development of markets. They worried, presciently, that marketization would cause inflation, since market prices of many commodities, especially essential goods such as foodstuffs, clothing, and many basic industrial and agricultural inputs, surely would be much higher than the low prices set by the state. Critics also feared that the more goods moved outside of planned state channels the more difficult it would be for the state to extract the revenues it needed, thus potentially bringing about financial deficits—a concern that also would come true. They sought mainly to change planning priorities to pay more attention to agriculture and light industry and less to heavy industry. In addition, critics wanted to raise standards of living by allocating a greater share of the country's output to consumption and a lesser share to investment. This meant scaling back the grandiose production plans championed by Hua Guofeng. These critics were open to the possibility that certain peripheral sectors of the economy, such as petty retail trade in nonessential goods, could be conducted on markets. However, they fully opposed the brand of planning that simulated markets, not to mention marketization itself.

The critics initially won out. During the second half of 1980, anxiety about the rise of the Solidarity movement in Poland reinforced the position of those taking a political and ideological hard line. At a central party work conference in late 1980, economic reform was put on hold. In the spring of 1981, experiments with reform of enterprises were halted, while a campaign against "bourgeois liberalization" linked economics and politics by emphasizing the pernicious political and social effects of markets. This tendency—called, strangely, both "conservative" and "leftist" because it sought to conserve key features of the Maoist-period political and economic institutions now that they were shorn of their radical, mobilizational thrust—dominated through the end of 1982.

If the years 1979–82 evinced a cycle of advance and then defeat of industrial reform, a similar movement and countermovement took place, this time at a more rapid pace, within the single year of 1983. After several years of political quiescence and dramatically successful rural reform,

the Dengist leaders were able to go on the offensive early in the year. Party General Secretary Hu Yaobang understood the important role that intellectuals would have to play in economic reform. For example, many supporters of the early, shelved marketizing reform plans had been social scientists. They would need reassurance from the highest levels of leadership to encourage them to participate actively in the politically contentious reform process, especially in light of the closing of Democracy Wall. Toward this end, Hu offered his public support for a reformulation of Marxism, put forward by leading intellectuals, that focused on its early, humanistic phase (as opposed to its later, more overt emphasis on class conflict, from which intellectuals had suffered during the Maoist period).

Concurrently, in June 1983 Premier Zhao Ziyang argued that prices, taxes, and credit had major roles to play in regulating the economy. To reduce further the political control of enterprises, Zhao also introduced a new system of state revenue collection. Instead of requiring enterprises to turn over most of their profits to the ministries that supervised them, they now were required to pay taxes according to a standardized, predictable scale; after-tax profits would be theirs to keep. This clever stroke was intended to increase the power of enterprises vis-à-vis the planning agencies in a way that allayed the conservatives' fears that reform would cause state budget deficits. However, ideologically conservative leaders struck back, launching a campaign against the "spiritual pollution" produced by market society and Westernization that lasted through the end of the year. In response, Zhao Ziyang threatened to resign his office, stating that the campaign was hurting foreign investment.

Thus, five years after the landmark Third Plenum of 1978 announced the dawn of a radically new political direction for China, the country had been through two cycles of political and economic reform offensives, each met by strong counteroffensives from leaders bent on preserving tight political control and major elements of economic planning. Moreover, political disagreements aside, some of the complexities and contradictions of industrial and macroeconomic reform were coming into focus: e.g., the rise of markets versus the dangers of inflation and deficits; the state's need for intellectuals to develop and deploy their skills versus its concern about political liberalization; and the widely shared desire to attract foreign capital versus the concern about the corrosive effects of Western consumer culture. At the end of this period, while the controversies and conundrums of reform had not been resolved, at least the battle lines had been drawn, the boundaries of permissible disagreement had been highlighted, and the structural obstacles had become increasingly clear.

The Rhythms of Market Stalinism

1984–89

In other words, by early 1984 the outlines of Dengist China's political economy were emerging. Over the subsequent decade and more, China's reform policies would score many achievements, engender significant problems, and cause massive crises. As these emerged and came–often painfully–to their successive political resolutions, the political and economic systems' boundaries crystallized. The process took on a two-dimensional rhythm. First, the space for structural economic reform was widened incrementally. Subsequent to each advance came criticism and a temporary stall, followed by yet another advance. Second, the upbeat/downbeat of economic reform stimulated another rhythm wherein demands for deep political change emerged and were met by crackdowns. Dengist China was lurching tortuously toward a new system that may be described as "market Stalinism" (White, 1993: 256; Blecher, 1997: 116n).

The year 1984 dawned with economic reformers back on the offensive. Politically, "leftism" came under attack in the official press. The party made efforts to promote a phalanx of younger leaders. A more permissive atmosphere of cultural expression was

tolerated, including images of Western dress and artistic nudes–precisely the images that the anti-spiritual pollution campaign had attacked. By the end of the year, the value of Marxism itself was openly questioned in the flagship *People's Daily.* In the economic realm, the year began with Deng's highly publicized trip to the Special Economic Zones (SEZs) of south China. Soon after, the factory director responsibility system was promoted as a way to induce enterprises to follow market logic rather than the political wishes of their party committees. In addition, enterprises were given expanded autonomy. In the countryside, land contracts were extended from less than 5 years to 15. Then, amid the euphoria of a bumper harvest, a three-decade-old system of quota grain sales was scheduled to be replaced by a new system of contracts negotiated freely between farmers and the state. In finance, enterprises now were allowed to keep under their own control 70% of their depreciation funds. The system of paying taxes rather than remitting profits was further rationalized. In the area of production planning, the number of products subject to state control was reduced drastically. Enterprises were permitted to make their own decisions regarding all above-quota output, and to negotiate prices for disposing of it. Many of these policies were advanced by a group of young economists who, profoundly influenced by their experience with structural reforms in the countryside, emphasized microeconomic factors (price reform, marketization, and enterprise reform) over the primacy the conservatives placed on macroeconomic issues such as planning balances, investment rates, state finance, and inflation.

Precisely those macroeconomic issues would now be called to the forefront, however, not so much by critics of reform as by the economy itself. Starting in late 1984, double-digit inflation appeared, alarming leaders and ordinary Chinese who had not experienced it for three decades. Many of them linked rising prices not with the abstract issues of structural economic reform but with something more palpable:

the increasing number of small private merchants and workshops. This perception imparted a specific, class-based character to the general unhappiness and worry over inflation. Meanwhile, foreign exchange reserves began to run short owing to profligate imports of foreign equipment and consumer goods. Much of the problem resulted from rising corruption, as relatives of high officials took advantage of their positions to make fortunes on import deals.

As a consequence, the reformist upbeat of 1984 was followed by an equivocal but still detectable downbeat of reaction and retrenchment. The *People's Daily* retracted its critique of Marxism, lamely claiming a misprint. Campaigns against "bourgeois liberalization" resumed. Economically, the central government undertook concerted efforts to bring investment under control and to reduce inflation and the rate of economic growth. When it became clear that the 1985 harvest would decline from the previous year's record high, broad criticism of the contract grain sales system extended to an unprecedented public disagreement between Deng Xiaoping and conservative Vice-Premier Chen Yun at a National Party Conference in September. Chen sounded a nationalist theme, denouncing the reform for making China dependent on foreign markets for its food. Politically, an ongoing party rectification drive shifted its focus from rooting out remnants of Maoism to the problems of corruption and of officials pursuing entrepreneurial goals at the expense of their political duties.

Yet a political countercurrent was also detectable. Deng Liqun, the leading conservative ideologue who had spearheaded the drives against bourgeois liberalization and spiritual pollution, was replaced by Zhu Houze, who, like his patron, Party General Secretary Hu Yaobang, had defended intellectuals against such attacks. This change initiated a period of cultural and intellectual flowering that would last over a year. Further challenges to political boundaries included a series of public outbursts that took place beginning in the spring. Young urbanites who had been relocated to the countryside during the Cultural Revolution held sit-down protests in Beijing, demanding permission to return home. Consumers publicly voiced their dismay over inflation. Students, meanwhile, demonstrated on a wide range of issues, including poor food and dormitory conditions, Japanese imperialism, nuclear weapons testing, African students dating Chinese, and the continued presence of military troops who had moved to campuses in 1967 to quell Cultural Revolution battles. In response, state leaders did not crack down, but instead continued to pursue moderate political changes that directly challenged conservative elders. Several technocratically inclined leaders in their 50s and 60s were promoted to key positions. Moreover, they were receptive to recommendations from the Chinese Academy of Social Science for civil service reform and for further separation of the state from the economy.

Similar to what had happened just a year or so earlier, the progress of reform was slowed not so much by political criticism as by structural factors like the economic downturn and the increasingly apparent contradictions inherent in macroeconomic and industrial reform. The retrenchment policies of 1985 slowed economic growth rates, which bottomed out in early 1986. Opinion surveys showed significant dissatisfaction with the economic inequalities resulting from reform. When the government promulgated new regulations to eliminate lifetime employment and welfare guarantees for state factory workers, putting them instead on contracts, a wave of strikes and factory slowdowns ensued. Economic reform became entangled in a thicket of debate over structural complexities. For example, leaders debated over how to sequence ownership and price reform: if enterprise reform took place without price reform, enterprises would not be able to pursue efficiency through marketized operations. Conversely, if price reform took place first, still unreformed, monopolistic enterprises could make windfalls without improving efficiency. A second debate broiled over the rate at which growth should take place: too high a rate of growth would cause overheating (i.e., inflation and excessive, often unproductive, investment), which in turn would drive down consumption levels; too low a rate of growth recently had produced recession and serious employment problems. Finally, leaders argued over how much attention should be given to large state-owned industries: too much attention would only further encourage many loss-making firms, requiring continued subsidies; too little focus would put the employment and living standards of the large core of China's working class at risk. Several of these issues had significant implications for political reform: e.g., ownership and enterprise reform went to the heart of the state's role in the economy, and brought the issue of corruption in tow. At several major convocations in the fall, no resolution or clear direction emerged.

If this tense stalemate was created in large measure by structural factors, it soon was exploded by a political intervention from one of China's most prominent and outspoken intellectuals. While on a speaking tour in late 1986, astrophysicist Fang Lizhi ridiculed Politburo members by name, denounced socialism as a failure, and called for "complete Westernization," including democracy, individuals' rights, and popular sovereignty. Within days, mass student protests broke out across China, lasting a full month. The leadership waited out the protests, once again eschewing forceful suppression. However, after the protests dissipated in early January 1987, the leadership underscored clearly its commitment to firm political boundaries. Party General Secretary Hu Yaobang was removed from office for having helped create a political atmosphere conducive to anti-government protests. Significantly, Hu also was criticized for contributing to economic overheating (i.e., excessive rates of growth without concomitant increases in productivity, leading to serious inflation). Central authorities launched a new campaign against bourgeois liberalization, a phrase linking political and social ills with their economic roots. Premier Zhao Ziyang, now appointed to replace Hu as Party General Secretary, announced that the campaign would be conducted only within the party and not in the larger society, clearly indicating the continuing lack of consensus among the top leadership.

Perhaps because the leadership believed it had suppressed efforts to reform the political system, it was willing to attempt the most substantial structural economic reforms to date. Deng Xiaoping now decided that the time was ripe for price reform, a move he publicly admitted was sure to spur inflation as well as kindle popular dissent. He also stressed marketization of all the basic factors of production, including labor, capital, and land–they too would have their own versions of price reforms, including floating wages, interest rates, and rent. Structural reforms of ownership and enterprise management, as well as deflationary policies such as constriction of investment and the money supply, were shelved, even though their advocates included Zhao Ziyang and many other influential leaders and economists. On the political front, there was talk of various reforms to control bureaucracy, decentralize, and strengthen the civil service and the role of law. The leadership also spoke of the need for dialogue with the people, who, it was recognized, had increasingly diverse opinions. If all this was intended to allay public concerns, it failed. In the event, none of the rhetoric translated into significant new policies or practices.

Economic crisis ultimately brought a halt to economic reform, this time specifically to Deng's bold plans to marketize not just commodities but also labor, capital, and housing. In this instance, however, the leadership's internal discord, combined with its recognition of the sheer complexity of structural reform, delayed the denouement for many months, during which the country's political and economic troubles only intensified. Inflation began to climb again in early 1988. During the first half of the year, factories experiencing financial difficulties owing to the new economic environment began laying off workers and defaulting on their debts and tax obligations. Some closed up under the pressure. Not surprisingly, all this resulted in popular expressions of discontent; what did shock the leadership was the extent of the outcry. Once again students demonstrated and workers struck. Opinion surveys revealed thunderous disapproval of the country's political institutions. Physical assaults on managers and tax collectors rose. Expressions of dissent reached as far as the Seventh National People's Congress, where in March 1988 more than 10% of delegates, an unprecedented number, voted against the party leadership's choice for vice-premier.

Through all this turmoil, Deng Xiaoping continued to insist that price reforms be implemented. As prices rose, the Chinese people heeded their own economic interests far more than their leaders' appeals, a reaction that should not have surprised a leadership exalting the market principle. Depositors withdrew their money en masse, causing a minor financial crisis, while others went on spending sprees in anticipation of rising prices. Most Chinese remembered that the final demise of the Nationalist government on the mainland in 1949 was precipitated by a hyperinflation that dissolved the last remnants of public acquiescence.

In this frenzied atmosphere, the top leadership headed for its annual conclave at the beachfront resort of Beidaihe. Zhao Ziyang requested the authority to declare martial law while threatening to resign. Deng disavowed his role in implementing price reforms and encouraged his colleagues to blame Zhao. Li Peng, a conservative who had been elevated to the premiership just months before, quarreled with Zhao over the rapid pace of economic growth. Faced with runs on its banks and shops, deep divisions in the leadership, and the prospect of having to call out the army, the leadership capitulated. The price reforms, which had been heralded so long and so loudly by so powerful and prominent a figure as Deng Xiaoping, were shelved. Party General Secretary Zhao Ziyang left the meeting politically wounded. As well, the country's top leadership was bruised badly from its internal battles, the failure of its economic policies, and the damage those policies had inflicted on the Chinese people.

Economic policy now returned to familiar and conservative themes: price freezes and deflationary monetary policy, slower growth, renewed emphasis on state-owned industry, centralization of economic control, and a reduced role for the market in favor of greater state control of the economy. Economic reformers, lacking alternatives, countered by advocating large-scale privatization as a way to undercut the state's power in the economy. In September, Zhao Ziyang attacked "bureaucratic racketeering." Attesting to the triumph of market Stalinism, economic reformers long since had given up on democratic political reform. Their political program was "neo-authoritarianism." According to this model, the political and economic authority of the Chinese state could only be curtailed by the rise of a powerful leader. Ironically and naïvely, some had Mikhail Gorbachev in mind. Odder yet, many people invoked fond memories of Chairman Mao, whom they associated with a time when China was free of inflation, corruption, and crime.

The Movement of 1989

A palpable air of crisis accompanied the dawning of the new year. The deflationary, statist economic policies adopted in the wake of the price reform debacle did nothing to alleviate the deep structural problems of the economy. Inflation continued to soar, and people remained fearful of losing their employment and the social guarantees such as housing, medical care, and education that accompanied it. Ideologically, some looked backward to Mao for inspiration, while others looked outward to Gorbachev or to the West. Unfortunately, these models were neither realistic nor thoughtfully developed. Politically, none of them had any connection to a significant leader, organization, or program. Moreover, the state leadership was known widely to be weak and divided. As it turned out, rather little was required to ignite a conflagration.

Beginning in the final days of 1988, demonstrations and eventually riots erupted on Beijing and Nanjing campuses as thousands of male Chinese students once again attacked African men for dating Chinese women. Coincidentally, leading intellectuals campaigned publicly for the release of China's political prisoners, including Democracy Wall activist Wei Jingsheng. That they sometimes campaigned on the international stage particularly must have rankled the nationalistic top leadership. In February Beijing police prevented Fang Lizhi from attending a dinner to which he had been invited by US president George Bush. In early March a demonstration in Lhasa, the Tibetan capital, resulted in the declaration of martial law.

The pace quickened in April following the death of Hu Yaobang, whom intellectuals and political reformers viewed as their leading supporter in the party's top leadership. Students mourning his death poured into central Beijing's Tiananmen Square. Within just three days of Hu's death, more than 10,000 students took the unprecedented step of demanding entry to Zhongnanhai, the highly-restricted residential compound of China's top Communist Party leaders, to discuss an agenda that included reevaluation of the 1986 protests and Hu's role in them, access to financial records of top leaders and their children, political freedoms, and educational funding. When rebuffed, the students clashed with armed military guards at the gate. Meanwhile, demonstrations spread to many of China's largest cities.

On April 26 the leadership published a manifesto on the editorial page of the *People's Daily.* Drafted on the basis of a statement made by Deng Xiaoping, it denounced the students as "hooligans" led by "evil" people bent on fomenting "turmoil." But the demonstrators were not easily cowed. To the contrary, on that day they formally established the Beijing Students' Autonomous Federation. The next day the number of demonstrators doubled to around 100,000. By early May, the social base of the demonstration broadened to include many office and shop staff, workers, and even journalists. Approximately 150,000 filled Tiananmen Square each day.

The leadership now changed tactics. Zhao Ziyang, with Deng's permission, made a conciliatory statement, calling students' demands "reasonable" and urging a "democratic and legal" response. This approach appeared more deft than the heavy-handed threats of the previous week. The most recent editorial sought to defuse the protests by encouraging those who were tiring of the daily excitement to return home and await the start of a more orderly process of political change. However, by changing course the leadership appeared weak and polarized precisely at the moment when it also seemed to be receptive to popular demands. This only encouraged the more radical protesters, while attracting new and decidedly adventurous groups to their ranks, including lumpenproletarians like pickpockets and gangsters, and out-of-towners with high energy and fewer local networks to restrain them. Reflecting this growing division, by mid-May the number of protesters began to wane at the same time that demonstrators began to employ more provocative tactics. Displaying a sharp eye for political symbolism and the ability to exploit mass media, on May 13, just two days before the planned state visit of Soviet President Gorbachev, the more radical elements among student leadership upped the ante, declaring a hunger strike in Tiananmen Square. The image of 3,000 noble students starving themselves in supplicant self-sacrifice before an intransigent, unpopular, corrupt government elicited deep sympathy from hundreds of thousands of urbanites of all backgrounds. They now flocked to Tiananmen, reversing the previously declining numbers. The resurgent movement, combined with the arrival of Gorbachev, put China on the center stage of international media attention.

On May 16 Zhao Ziyang dispatched an emissary to the square to convey sympathy for the protests and to promise no reprisals if the demonstrations would end. Most participants, wishing to declare victory, were willing to make the deal. However, exercising their rights under the students' consensus rules, a small number of the most uncompromising hunger strikers and their supporters obstructed a settlement. The next day, at a Politburo Standing Committee meeting, Zhao Ziyang proposed a further concession–retraction of the April 26 editorial–in the hopes of swaying enough protesters to the side of compromise. But Deng opposed any further concessions; moreover, he persuaded his colleagues to authorize Premier Li Peng to declare martial law as circumstances warranted.

Before resorting to this extreme measure, however, the leadership made one last attempt at compromise. The following day, May 18, Zhao, Li, and other top leaders paid a highly publicized visit to hospitalized hunger strikers to express their sympathy. In addition, Li and other leaders agreed to a live televised meeting with student representatives. At this meeting, Li Peng, who had become a personal target of the demonstrators, began calmly and diplomatically. The students responded by excoriating him and refusing, when he offered, to shake his hand. Wu'er Kaixi, one of the demonstration's most charismatic and radical leaders, who had come to the meeting replete with an intravenous feeding apparatus, collapsed. The Premier lost his composure and exited angrily. Although he had not been present at the televised meeting, Zhao Ziyang went to the square early on the morning of May 19, where he confessed his inability to find a compromise and bade farewell to protesters and to public life. When dawn came, Premier Li announced the imposition of martial law in the capital.

Like its response to the April 26 editorial, this hard-line leadership offensive backfired. At the bottom of the Chinese polity, tens of thousands of Beijing residents came out to their neighborhood intersections to block the troops' advance. The confrontations were stunning: the urbanites appealed to the bewildered troops not to act against the noble and emaciated young people in Tiananmen. Meanwhile, at the top, Nie Rongzhen and Xu Xiangqian, the only surviving People's Liberation Army marshals,

publicly praised the students' patriotism. Seven other senior generals drafted a statement, signed by over a hundred senior officers, maintaining that the army would not fire on the Chinese people. Astonishingly, the military advance stopped.

Deng Xiaoping now took decisive action. Having shrewdly retained the position of chair of the Party Military Affairs Commission, he was able to call an emergency meeting of the regional military commanders in the central city of Wuhan, far from the madding crowd in Beijing. Zhao Ziyang was sacked as Party General Secretary on May 24. Aware that troops still surrounded the city, and that the numbers of demonstrators again were declining, several top student leaders proposed a way out. The protests would cease on May 30 with a huge victory celebration. In what would prove a fateful, tragic juncture, a minority of extremists once again gained the upper hand, scuttling the plan and vowing to continue on into late June, when the National People's Congress was scheduled to meet next door in the Great Hall of the People. In an inspired tactical gambit using postmodern iconography and media politics, on May 29 students fortified their own spirits and galvanized world attention by erecting the "Goddess of Democracy," a figure that combined aspects of the benevolent traditional Chinese deity Guanyin with the Statue of Liberty. That same day, many radical protesters–mainly workers and lumpenproletarians rather than students–were taken into custody.

In response, autonomous workers' associations began to attract significant support. They had a very different agenda that focused on job security, wages, challenges from burgeoning rural and private enterprises, and attacks on their modicum of power on the factory floor. Whereas intellectuals and other middle-class urbanites tended to view increased economic and political reform as the solution to corruption and authoritarianism, workers were more inclined to believe that excessive reform threatened the gains they had made under state socialism. Whereas students erected the "Goddess of Democracy," workers marched proudly under portraits of Chairman Mao. Thus, the alliance of intellectuals, government and shop staff, other urban dwellers, *and* workers–the leadership's worst nightmare–never came off. In the end, failure to secure this alliance would prove to be one of the protest movement's two most serious shortcomings.

The other deficiency involved the students' inability to reach a clear decision in response to the government's concessions. With Zhao out of the way and the infuriated hard-line leadership now fully in charge, the military crackdown got underway on the night of June 3–4. The death toll could not be ascertained, but sources estimate it to have reached 1,000. The vast majority were not students but workers and other Beijing residents, killed in their encampments at major intersections as they tried to prevent troops from reaching the students in the square. Perhaps several dozen people died in the immediate vicinity of the square, and a few actually in it. The casualties in Tiananmen were not higher because most students left by a pre-negotiated exit route. Although less tangible, damage to the popular reputation of the state and its leadership was colossal.

Although it had climaxed, the movement of 1989 had not yet ended. In another stunning example of how repression only increased the protesters' determination, renewed protests broke out in cities all across China two days later. In Shanghai, protesters blocking a railroad track were run over by a train that refused to stop–an incident which stood in sharp contrast to the dominant image of the earlier Beijing protests: a lone man halting the advance of a line of tanks by stepping in front of them. The train subsequently was attacked and burned, killing several more people. In Chengdu, the capital of Sichuan, up to 300 people were killed during violent demonstrations. Many leading intellectuals now fled the country, while Fang Lizhi, the firebrand astrophysicist who incited his students to anti-government protest, took refuge in the US Embassy. More violence ensued during the last two weeks of June,

this time perpetrated by the state. Dragnets resulted in thousands of arrests, and around 50 persons were summarily executed. Significantly, most were workers and lumpenproletarians. The state, however, took a different approach to disciplining the intelligentsia. It widely distributed a "most wanted" list, which included mostly student protest leaders. Some were arrested and sent to prison, but none was executed. Attesting to the declining capacity of the state to control the Chinese people, many of the "most wanted" managed to flee the country, aided by sympathizers and gangs of smugglers hired by Hong Kong support groups.

Through the summer, the leadership adopted several postures toward its public. First, it attempted to mollify them by launching a new campaign against corruption, which included the expulsion of many party members, fines on several large companies engaged in questionable business deals, and a ban on the children of high officials doing business. Second, the leadership initiated a massive propaganda campaign that included circulation of a video portraying the presence of foreign spies amid the protesters at Tiananmen, as well as violent attacks on troops. Third, it resorted to coercion and retribution. The size of the incoming class at Beijing University and other institutions was reduced drastically, and students were required to undergo an extended period of special military training before enrolling.

Despite this repressive atmosphere, citizens and even some officials continued their attacks on the state. Snipers took occasional potshots at soldiers. Beijing University students protested against cuts in the education budget. At one meeting, middle-level government officials hissed at a senior military officer who had come to explain the Tiananmen events. These small protests, however, could not dilute the overwhelming victory of the political hardliners.

1989–96

During the first decade of the Dengist

period, impulses for structural reform of the polity and the economy had proceeded by ebb and flow. The two dimensions of change often had moved in tandem. But as the events of 1989 drew the decade to a close, it became clear that economic change had advanced more rapidly than political change. Put differently, the leadership had achieved broad consensus on the need to transform the Maoist-period economic system, even as it disagreed on what ought to replace it. By contrast, although the Dengists evinced a broadly shared enthusiasm for abandoning Maoist ideology and radicalism, they also, in the end, were committed to maintaining the basic political institutions of the Maoist period: monopolistic rule by the Communist Party and tight restrictions against both civil liberties and an autonomous political sphere of civil society. In a nutshell, what emerged during the 1980s were the clear outlines of market Stalinism. Although economic retrenchment followed on the heels of the 1989 events, before long the market would reemerge more triumphant than ever, while (and indeed partly because) political reform remained in a deep freeze.

Since leaders most hostile to political reform also tended to take a less radical position on economic reform, it is not surprising that their ascendance marked the beginning of an extended period of economic retrenchment. For more than two years after the crackdown, economic policy emphasized austerity, slowed growth to tame inflation, and circumscription of the market. Tightened credit and fiscal policies served to curtail industrial investment, while investment focused on state-owned enterprises rather than the collective or private sectors. In fact, many rural industries were ordered to close or were choked by restrictive credit and tax policies as well as tighter regulation. Renewed investment priority was given to agriculture, for several reasons. Stagnant agricultural growth since 1984 had alarmed China's conservative leaders, who feared rural discontent and dependence on foreign markets for grain. Food price subsidies—advanced to keep urban prices low

while maintaining higher prices paid to farmers—consumed a huge portion of the state budget, contributing to a growing deficit and looming financial crisis. The situation grew so bleak that state grain purchasing agencies lacked funds to pay farmers; when they resorted to issuing IOUs, they incurred farmers' wrath and also ran the risk that even less human energy and fewer material resources would be put into agriculture. Rural infrastructure such as water conservancy projects was deteriorating, threatening future disasters. Meanwhile, for both producer and consumer goods, price controls were reinstated; to this same deflationary end, the money supply was shrunk. In both the countryside and the cities, the leadership launched propaganda campaigns stressing the need for, and virtues of, plain living.

During the winter and spring of 1990, the leadership extended a few olive branches to the Chinese people by lifting martial law in Beijing and Lhasa, releasing several demonstrators, and permitting Fang Lizhi to leave China. However, no one mistook these measures for a change in the leadership's commitment to strict political control. Laws and regulations restricting demonstrations were promulgated. Ideological campaigns for "socialist spiritual civilization" and against bourgeois liberalization renewed, this time containing ominous overtones that the liberalizers might be class enemies. Yet the leadership also recognized the need for some internal housecleaning. Emphasizing the need to improve its relationship with the masses, the leadership even reinstated time-honored Yan'an and mass-line practices such as periodically sending cadres to the grassroots. Toward this same end, the state renewed anti-corruption drives and promoted ideological study. Intellectuals were reminded of their responsibility to serve the state.

Perhaps these measures' success in achieving two years of political quiescence persuaded the leadership that it could risk reopening the economy. In early 1992 economic reform gained renewed momentum. In January the conservative Premier Li Peng declared that the period of "improving the economic environment and rectifying the economic order" (i.e., economic austerity) was over. A week later, Deng Xiaoping embarked on another widely publicized tour of southern China, during which the economic dynamism of Guangdong–the most marketized province in China–was singled out for special endorsement. Once again Deng's ideological pragmatism was on display as he trumpeted the view that markets were not to be equated with capitalism and that socialism's real nature is to liberate productive forces. This time around, however, in order to broaden the base of political support for the new policies, plans for economic expansion included Shanghai. This coastal city, it was believed, would bring in tow a good part of the huge and economically dynamic lower Yangtze Delta region. In fact, Deng now admitted that it had been a mistake not to include Shanghai earlier, suggesting that disagreement over previous economic liberalizations had had a political dimension. Also, Shanghai's ascendance was no doubt also a result of the rise of many key leaders from the city, including Party General Secretary Jiang Zemin. By the end of the year, the target rate for economic growth was raised from 6% to 9%.

Next, the state initiated price and marketizing reforms. Only 72 products remained under state planning. State prices of basic commodities and utilities were raised; for example, grain prices in state shops rose an average of 50% in most provinces. In the summer of 1992, the state announced a pilot plan to free grain markets completely in 400 counties (out of approximately 2,200); meanwhile, crop planning was cut back. In the fall, the leadership took a big risk by deciding to lift grain price controls in order to stimulate lagging production. Politically, at the Fourteenth Party Congress in October, the Party Central Advisory Commission, a bastion of conservative elders, was abolished, and a younger, better educated group of officials was promoted.

By 1993 these policies had resulted in serious economic overheating. Officially,

inflation reached 16% in China's major cities (actual inflation was probably higher). The state's financial crisis continued unabated, while local governments often had to issue farmers IOUs in return for their crops, despite official condemnation of the practice. Increased political tensions in the countryside now became explosive. For example, in June 1993 spontaneous protests by farmers in Renshou County (Sichuan) against road construction levies led to "beating, smashing and looting . . . [in which] some people . . . stormed the district and township governments and schools, beat up cadres and teachers, smashed public and private property, and illegally detained grass-roots cadres and public security personnel" (*BBC Daily Report,* 14 June 1993). When police responded with tear gas, some officers were taken hostage by the angry crowd, and police cars were set ablaze. A month later, an effort by a county government in Hunan to requisition land along a railway line prompted farmers to seize weapons, including semi-automatic rifles, from the local armory; 35 people were wounded as farmers clashed with several hundred troops and armed police. Meanwhile, crime rates increased nationally, and disaffected national minorities rioted in Tibet and Qinghai. Then, in the wake of the 1993 harvest, grain prices soared–approximately 35% in Beijing in just one week–as farmers and traders worked the market. Yet rising prices had not achieved their main objective: grain production increased only modestly in 1993.

Fearful that inflation, crime, and skyrocketing tensions in the countryside would further destabilize the economy, the leadership became obsessed with the need, in General Secretary Jiang Zemin's words, to "take forceful measures to maintain social and political stability." Thus, economic crisis as much as political criticism from conservatives put the brakes on economic reform. In the summer of 1993, banks were ordered to call in loans, interest rates were raised, and infrastructure investment budgets were slashed. The financial resources thus shepherded were to be used in part to put cash rather than IOUs behind state grain purchases amid repeated warnings that farmers were being dangerously overburdened by high input prices, local government levies, corruption, and low remuneration for their sales. In the fall and winter, the state abandoned the abolition of grain price controls.

These retrenchment measures failed to work, an indication that the economy was starting to spin dangerously out of control. In 1993, gross domestic product grew 13.4%, almost 50% higher than the targeted figure of 9%. Inflation ran around 14% according to official figures, and probably was much higher. The following year, the economy overheated even further: GDP grew by almost 12% and was severely unbalanced between industry (17.4%) and agriculture (3.5%). Inflation spiked to 21.4% by official reckoning, more than double the target rate of 10%. This increase resulted in heightened expressions of discontent in both the countryside and the cities. While visiting Mao's birthplace, Party General Secretary Jiang Zemin was surrounded for nearly an hour by unhappy farmers seeking to give him their petitions. The Ministry of Labor admitted in 1994 that

the number of large-scale labor-management disputes exceeded 12,000. In some 2,500 cases, workers besieged plants, set fire to facilities, staged strikes, or detained bosses or leaders. Such events directly threatened the personal safety of party leaders in various factories and mines. In the Jixi Mining Bureau, enterprise leaders did not dare go to the pits for fear that they might be attacked by the workers.

Adding to the leadership's anxiety over the increasingly destabilized economy and the rising discontent it engendered was the specter that inchoate social protest was showing signs of becoming organized. Unofficial trade unions were forming and, shrewdly, began to engage in legal activities such as running employment services and petitioning the National People's Congress. Even more unsettling to the leadership, intellectuals began working with these organizations, a partnership that resembled the alliance at the heart of Polish Solidarity. Dissidents became more openly active on a number of other fronts as well, including education, law, and anti-corruption work.

In this context, the practice of political repression has remained in place. Wei Jingsheng, an electrician who had emerged from the 1978 Democracy Wall movement as China's most prominent dissident, and who had been released in 1993 after serving 14 years in prison, was rearrested in the spring of 1994. After a much-delayed trial he was sentenced to another lengthy jail term at the end of 1995. Authorities rounded up other dissidents as well. To demonstrate its commitment to shutting down any autonomous political organization, in early 1996 the leadership announced that all places of worship would be required to register with the government; its rationale was that "some people are trying to take advantage of more freedom in religion with the aim of overthrowing the government and dividing the nation," an extremely serious charge. In February, rules regarding police use of firearms were relaxed.

However, the leadership has relied on more than naked force in its efforts to enforce social discipline and political compliance. It also has tried to appeal to popular sentiment on two important matters. First, it campaigned noisily against official corruption. Although overall reduction in abuses was not detectable, a few high-profile cases implied that top leaders were taking the matter very seriously. Perhaps the most notable instance involved Beijing Vice-Mayor Wang Baosen, who committed suicide in April 1995 on the eve of the publication of charges that he embezzled funds worth a quarter of a billion *yuan* (US$30 million). Soon after, Beijing Mayor and central Party Politburo member Chen Xitong was removed from office and then arrested on sensational charges that he collaborated with Wang. Specifically, Chen was charged with embezzling funds worth over a billion *yuan,* keeping several apartments for his mistress, and helping her escape to Hong Kong.

Second, the leadership attempted to win public sympathy by taking an increasingly hard line on nationalist issues. It happily adopted an uncompromising posture toward Hong Kong, even erecting a huge clock in Tiananmen Square to count down the seconds until the very moment of planned reunification. To show its resolve to retain control over Tibet, the leadership reacted forcefully in late 1995 when monks linked to the exiled Dalai Lama chose a new Panchen Lama. When the hapless young boy whom the clerics had identified mysteriously disappeared, other monks were brought to Beijing to choose a successor. The Chinese people were treated to the bizarre spectacle of their communist government publicly, and with great fanfare, anointing its own boy as the reincarnation of the Panchen Lama. The leadership also engaged in several rounds of menacing saber-rattling, replete with war games, in response to elections in Taiwan in late 1995 and early 1996.

Ultimately, the key to maintaining public support for the state lies where Deng Xiaoping always said it did: in the condition of the economy. Evidence did suggest that in 1995 the Chinese economy achieved something of a soft landing from its dangerous altitude during the previous two years. Economic growth slowed to 10.2%, compared with 11.8% the previous year. Overall inflation was reported at 14.8%, less than the 15% target and 21.7% level of 1994 (although urbanites' cost of living rose 22%). Farmers harvested a record 460 million tons of grain, rebounding from the 445 million of 1994, and besting the previous record of 456.5 million tons in 1993. This helped reduce upward pressure on grain prices, which had threatened calamity just two years earlier.

Still, massive economic problems loom. In the countryside, declining arable land, unfavorable prices, and yields that are already nearing their maximum levels cast doubt on China's ability to feed its growing population. In urban areas, state-run industry faces myriad problems, unemployment rates are on the rise, and the gap between the rich and poor grows larger. Nationally, a wide gulf remains between the economically advancing coastal centers and the vast hinterland. This imbalance has produced trade wars and political conflict among the leadership.

These difficulties have engendered social and political tensions. Not surprisingly, the market has corroded family and community institutions in China, contributing to cultural and social alienation. Increasingly, education and health care are available only to those who can afford them. Migration from the countryside to the cities continues apace, causing further crowding and contributing to a rise in crime.

Politically, the top leadership acted more cohesively in the years after 1989. In the spring of 1995, for example, Li Peng announced that the succession of Deng Xiaoping by Jiang Zemin was no longer a matter of debate. Meanwhile, the death of Chen Yun weakened opposition to economic restructuring. Deng's death in early 1997 did not provoke the immediate political crisis that many had feared. China's leaders still subscribe to Leninist norms of party discipline, aware that any sign of disunity among them may encourage widespread popular opposition. However, the Chinese political system still confronts many deep cleavages: between coastal areas and the hinterland over issues of finance, trade, and investment; between civilians and the military over budgets and, more seriously, over nationalistic issues that the leadership was stirring up in the mid-1990s; between the central government and localities over trade, economic authority and resources, and political power; and, finally, between an increasingly restive society and a government bent on maintaining political authority at all costs.

Conclusion

Thus, as of this writing in spring 1997, during its breathless passage through an unprecedented process of change lasting almost two decades, China had once again shown its penchant for swimming against the tide, breaking with its own past, and seeking an innovative course. Starting in 1978 it created something new and quite unexpected: a combination of market forces, state and collective ownership and entrepreneurialism, and political repression. This form of political rule and economic organization, best described as market Stalinism, was forged during a rocky process of repeated policy reversals, and in the crucible of two major crises. As the Chinese Revolution and Maoist state socialism had done, market Stalinism broke with several previous models. It dispensed with Maoist radicalism, Stalinist state economic control and mobilization, and capitalism's insistence on extensive private ownership and marketization. However, it also retained important aspects of each model, recombining them in a way that was both novel and that challenged the view that all aspects of Maoism, Stalinism, and capitalism were incompatible. Whatever one's assessment of market Stalinism, its development was unprecedented and heretical.

Furthermore, this strange hybrid had chalked up some impressive achievements since 1978. Market Stalinism fundamentally transformed Maoist politics, economics, and society, and lasted a good deal longer than might have been expected. It defied western liberals and modernization theorists, who argue that capitalism and markets go hand in hand with individualism and the rise of a middle class, leading in turn to democracy. Market Stalinism also outlasted its nearest cousins in the Soviet Union and Eastern Europe, even though in 1989 it encountered a far greater seismic shock than they. Moreover, it produced repeated spurts of economic growth that often surprised even its promoters. Indeed, its major problem was its tendency to produce too much growth too quickly. Finally, market Stalinism had made China a more influential force on the world stage than at any other time in its history.

Yet, as of 1997, Chinese market Stalinism was plagued by contradictions. The country's quiescence did not necessarily indicate political stability or social peace. Moreover,

China's palpable industriousness and economic dynamism did not necessarily reflect the happy equilibrium of an upward spiral of development. Will China consolidate market Stalinism or break with it? If it makes a break, will the process be smooth and gradual, or rough and sudden? And what would emerge from such a break? The world is too complex, and China's circumstances too unprecedented, to permit easy or sure answers. But to make educated guesses, we need to analyze the many contradictory economic, social, and political forces at play. They are the subject of the rest of this book.

Further Reading

Baum, Richard, *Burying Mao: Chinese Politics in the Age of Deng Xiaoping,* Princeton, New Jersey: Princeton University Press, 1994

A comprehensive, textured, and well-written chronological survey of Chinese politics from 1978 to the early 1990s.

Benewick, Robert, and Paul Wingrove, editors, *China in the 1990s,* London: Macmillan, and Vancouver: University of British Columbia Press, 1995

A comprehensive collection of well-written, well-researched and analytically balanced essays.

Blecher, Marc, *China Against the Tides: Restructuring Through Revolution, Radicalism and Reform,* London: Pinter/Cassell, 1997

For further background and analysis of many of the issues raised in this chapter.

China Review, Hong Kong: Chinese University of Hong Kong Press, annual

An annual edited volume with a wide range of timely articles.

Davis, Deborah, and Ezra F. Vogel, editors, *Chinese Society on the Eve of Tiananmen,* Cambridge, Massachusetts: Council on East Asian Studies/Harvard University Press, 1990

Excellent collection of essays on political sociology by leading scholars.

Fewsmith, Joseph, *Dilemmas of Reform in China: Political Conflict and Economic Debate,* Armonk, New York: M.E. Sharpe, 1994

A carefully-wrought, fine-grained analysis of the political and economic debates that swirled around economic reform after 1978.

Kraus, Richard Curt, *Pianos and Politics in China: Middle-Class Ambitions and the Struggle over Western Music,* New York: Oxford University Press, 1989

An insightful and lively study of a representative arena of ideology and cultural politics.

Meisner, Maurice J., *The Deng Xiaoping Era: An Inquiry into the Fate of Chinese Socialism, 1978–1994,* New York: Hill and Wang, 1996

A thoughtful, balanced historical survey.

Naughton, Barry, *Growing Out of the Plan: Chinese Economic Reform, 1978–1993,* Cambridge and New York: Cambridge University Press, 1995

A highly original and persuasive account of the macroeconomics of reform, this book takes a more optimistic view than many economic analyses.

Perry, Elizabeth J., and Christine Wong, editors, *The Political Economy of Reform in Post-Mao China,* Cambridge, Massachusetts: Council on East Asian Studies, Harvard University, 1985

Excellent collection of essays on political economy by leading scholars.

Riskin, Carl, *China's Political Economy: The Quest for Development Since 1949,* Oxford and New York: Oxford University Press, 1987

An incisive analysis of economic development in the Maoist and early reform periods.

Shirk, Susan L., *The Political Logic of Economic Reform in China,* Berkeley: University of California Press, 1993

A sophisticated analysis of how the institutional structure of the Chinese state shaped economic reform.

Shue, Vivienne, *The Reach of the State: Sketches of the Chinese Body Politic,* Stanford, California: Stanford University Press, 1988

Four thoughtful, provocative essays on the changing nature of the Chinese state and its relationships with local society.

White, Gordon, *Riding the Tiger: The Politics of Economic Reform in Post-Mao China,* London: Macmillan, and Stanford, California: Stanford University Press, 1993

A trenchant study of the political conflicts over economic reform, within the state and between state and society.

Marc Blecher is Professor of Politics and East Asian Studies at Oberlin College, Ohio. His most recent books include *China: Politics, Economics and Society—Iconoclasm and Innovation in a Revolutionary Socialist Country* (1986); *Tethered Deer: Government and Economy in a Chinese County* (with Vivienne Shue, 1996); and *China Against the Tides: Restructuring Through Revolution, Radicalism, and Reform* (1997). The present chapter is based on chapter three of the last-named volume.

Regional Context

Chapter Three

China and Hong Kong: The Political Economy of Reunification

Suzanne Pepper

The historic facts and political uncertainties of Hong Kong's return to Chinese sovereignty are well-known. So too is a favorite analogy those facts and uncertainties have inspired. The prospect of rich capitalist Hong Kong being ruled by one of the world's last remaining communist-led governments inevitably provokes questions about geese laying golden eggs and China's ability to preserve them for the benefit of all. Such questions have been essential to the Hong Kong story since the early 1980s, when China announced its intention to take back the colony in mid-1997. Less well-known, however, are the fundamental political and economic changes that have occurred during the intervening years of transition. This chapter focuses on these transitional changes, beginning with their impact on the political determinants of Hong Kong's present and future. The chapter then assesses the economic foundations upon which that future is being built.

The Political Determinants

As of July 1, 1997, Hong Kong will rejoin China after a hiatus of some 150 years, during which the city and its environs were administered as a crown colony by Great Britain. Initially a frontier area along China's southern coastal province of Guangdong, the territory was acquired to serve as Britain's first permanent trading post in East Asia. Hong Kong's 398 square miles of territory were appropriated incrementally between 1842 and 1898, when inhabitants numbered only a few thousand living in scattered farm settlements and fishing villages. By 1997, that same land area contained just over 6.3 million people as well as Asia's busiest port and one of its most dynamic economies.

Restoring National Sovereignty

Had it not been for accidents of history and geography, however, Hong Kong (as well as other treaty ports and spheres of influence that many foreign powers established along China's coast from the mid-1800s) would long since have been returned to Chinese sovereignty. The circumstances of its birth were not auspicious, and foreign territorial acquisitions in China were resisted from the start. Neither the imperial Chinese government before 1911 nor its republican successors afterward viewed the various treaties and conventions that marked foreigners' passage through Chinese time and space as anything more than temporary humiliation. All such agreements still are referred to as "unequal treaties" imposed upon China by the superior force of Western arms.

Hence, by 1949, when the communist-led government was proclaimed from its new capital in Beijing, only the two oldest territories remained under foreign control: Hong Kong and the neighboring enclave of Macau, which had been ruled by the Portuguese since 1557. It is still not clear why the People's Liberation Army was ordered to halt its southward march at these two remaining colonial outposts. Presumably, communist leaders were distracted by their inconclusive struggle with remnants of the Nationalist (Kuomintang) government and by the ensuing war with the United States in Korea.

In any case, the century-old goal of national reunification was merely suspended, not abandoned. Taiwan, Hong Kong, and Macau became "problems left over from history" to be settled "when the time is right." The time for Hong Kong came in 1982, when Beijing announced its decision to resume sovereignty on July 1, 1997. That date marked the expiration of a lease on some 92% of Hong Kong's total area, which had been added after the original land grants were formalized in 1842 and 1860. The extension, still known as the New Territories, was acquired under a 99-year rent-free lease in 1898 and governed as an integral part of Hong Kong thereafter.

A traumatic but futile search for alternatives ensued during 1982–83, with China reviving all the old arguments regarding opium traders, unequal treaties, and national humiliation. Ultimately, Britain agreed to return the entire colony on the designated date. Unwilling to acknowledge the legitimacy of the land grants or any responsibility accruing therefrom, China nevertheless agreed to a number of guarantees designed to calm a local populace generally fearful of living under Communist rule. These guarantees were written into the equivalent of a new "equal treaty," known as the Sino-British Joint Declaration on the Question of Hong Kong (1984). In this document, China promised a new separate status for the territory: the Hong Kong Special Administrative Region (SAR) of the People's Republic of China.

The SAR, the document stated, would enjoy a "high degree of autonomy"; moreover, its way of life, including its capitalist economy plus all existing rights and freedoms, would remain unchanged for 50 years. The Joint Declaration's promises were summarized in two popular slogans: "one country, two systems" and "Hong Kong people ruling Hong Kong." These guarantees acquired legal status in the Basic Law of the Hong Kong SAR, written by Chinese and Hong Kong drafters with British consultation during 1985–90, and promulgated in 1990 to serve as Hong Kong's post-1997 constitution. Similar arrangements were negotiated with Portugal to govern Macau's return to China in 1999.

Britain's 1992 Reform Program

With all the necessary agreements concluded and anxieties contained, Hong Kong seemed destined for a smooth transition to Chinese rule until a series of unanticipated political contingencies decreed otherwise. This sequence began with the 1989 student-led mass protests headquartered in Beijing's Tiananmen Square, the military action against them on June 4, and the Chinese government's suppression of all related dissent thereafter. Similar uprisings followed in Eastern Europe and the Soviet Union, but to opposite effect. Ironically, only China's communist-led government survived among all those challenged between 1989 and 1991. However, the combined result of international revulsion over Tiananmen and the collapse of communism even in its Soviet heartland was a massive shift in the balance of world power and public opinion against China. Consequences for Hong Kong were threefold, reflecting the public's outrage, London's response, and Beijing's reaction.

Tiananmen inspired an upsurge of mass anxiety and activism in Hong Kong, where some 95% of the population are Chinese, and the majority are either post-1949 migrants from China or their descendants and relations. This majority, predisposed to a free-wheeling capitalist lifestyle, made Hong Kong a predominantly anti-communist town, and the events at Tiananmen confirmed everyone's worst fears. Yet Hong Kong also had been a politically passive town, where the main public pursuits were all economic and government remained the preserve of a business-oriented colonial elite. Thus, the spectacle of an estimated 1 million people marching in solidarity with Chinese student protesters was unprecedented. Advocates for democratic reform in Hong Kong grew in number and influence, along with the belief that only more locally elected offices could guarantee the promised "high degree of autonomy" for Hong Kong.

At first, London responded with caution, and much more boldly only after communism's demise. By then (1991), the Basic Law had been promulgated and Hong Kong's first direct legislative election had been held. The latter conformed to prescriptions in the Basic Law that called for gradual evolution toward a more democratic government. The election resulted in a landslide victory for candidates who sought much faster democratization of Hong Kong to safeguard the SAR's post-1997 autonomy. Of the Legislative Council's 60 seats, 18 were contested by direct election for the first time in 1991, and 17 of those seats were won by pro-democracy partisans.

Evidently emboldened by the dramatic force of political change everywhere, London took advantage of certain loopholes in the Basic Law provisions for the 1995 Legislative Council election by introducing, in 1992, a comprehensive political reform program. This program was drafted without first consulting China and implemented over the latter's strenuous objection. Thus, Hong Kong's political development began in earnest with the 1992 reform program and China's reaction to it.

The centerpiece of Britain's initiative was an electoral reform package. Although British promoters claimed reforms would be modest, the changes extended well beyond the few directly elected seats added to local council chambers. Christopher Patten, a leading British politician, was appointed governor in 1992 and charged with implementing the reform agenda. Patten's 1992–97 tenure as Hong Kong's last British governor became, in effect, a five-year crash course on democratic development for the territory and all its citizens. This eleventh-hour effort was aimed at strengthening the role

of Western-style self-governing institutions in Hong Kong and thereby counterbalance China's influence as the Basic Law evolved in practice after 1997.

To summarize, Britain's 1992 program entailed transforming Hong Kong's various partly appointed, partly elected administrative and advisory bodies into a clearly defined three-tiered system of fully elected government councils. These comprised the 18 neighborhood-level district boards, two municipal councils, and the Legislative Council (Legco, in local shorthand). However, in contrast to the lower-level councils where all seats could and did become directly elected, only 20 out of 60 seats in the first SAR legislature could be similarly filled, owing to an explicit Basic Law provision. According to the Basic Law plan, the first SAR legislature would be the last colonial legislature, since the latter's four-year term of office (1995–99) spanned the 1997 divide. But Britain applied a little creative electoral logic to broaden representation for 19 additional seats. Briefly, Britain's creativity was applied as follows.

The Basic Law and appended regulations contain simple unelaborated guidelines for the transitional (1995–99) legislature. Accordingly, the transitional legislature must be composed of 20 seats filled through direct election from geographic constituencies; 30 seats filled by indirectly elected representatives of functional or occupational constituencies; and 10 representatives chosen by an electoral committee. Britain's 1992 reform plan was designed to keep within the letter of these guidelines but not their spirit, since Chinese Basic Law negotiators had been adamant in limiting directly elected seats to only 20. Britain's plan circumvented this restriction by creating nine new functional constituencies designed to represent not just employers and professionals (as do the 21 already existing constituencies, which were retained), but all employed people in Hong Kong. Only the unemployed, retirees, and housewives were unable to claim a vote within the nine new categories. This meant that most residents actually had two votes, or one each in a geographic and a functional constituency. The British-designed electoral committee, responsible for choosing 10 legislators, was composed of all District Board members, all of whom were directly elected under the 1992 reform plan. The net result was to fill 19 Legco seats by the closest possible equivalent of direct election, given the Basic Law guidelines.

Concurrently, the governor's appointed Executive Council (or cabinet) almost disappeared from public view, anticipating an eventual shift from executive-led government to one with legislative checks and balances. These changes began in 1992 and continued through all council elections in 1994 and 1995. Meanwhile, legislators hastened to exploit their growing power by sponsoring bills designed to promote a wide range of civil, social, and economic rights.

China's Response

If Britain's 1992 initiative was conditional upon the shifting international balance of power and opinion against communism and China, the latter's response continues to be returned in kind. Beijing's defiance thus is based on the timing of Britain's initiative as well as Britain's motivation and assumptions about general communist decline. Additionally, the Chinese perceived multiple dangers within Britain's 1992 reform package, including its implied threat to Chinese sovereignty; practical concerns about post-1997 governance and control of Hong Kong; and the potentially subversive impact of a democratic Hong Kong on China itself.

Moreover, by the early 1990s, Chinese leaders were well-versed in Western electoral politics and understood the significance of directly elected government as the basis for popular sovereignty, autonomy, and independence. They also understood the subtle changes associated with the Hong Kong Legislative Council's shift after 1992 from a purely rubber stamp advisory body to a legislature empowered to debate and amend proposals as important as the electoral reform package itself. Chinese leaders saw a Pandora's box of potential challenges

in the Hong Kong government's new, post-1992 efforts to make itself more open, accountable, and responsive to grassroots demands for long-neglected social reforms. Such matters had been debated at length during the Basic Law drafting process between 1985 and 1990, when paramount leader Deng Xiaoping himself had rendered a judgment against Western-style direct democracy for Hong Kong and for China except as a far distant future goal.

Beijing, therefore, responded to Britain's initiative with a difficult dual maneuver that entailed a categorical rejection of Britain's 1992 agenda and all its prescriptions for faster democratization. These were denounced as a deliberate attempt to infringe upon Chinese sovereignty by rooting Hong Kong's government more firmly in the will of its people. At the same time, however, Beijing proceeded with all measures necessary to implement the Basic Law's more gradual approach toward the same end. These two goals thus became the two central planks in China's platform for Hong Kong. The often acrimonious Sino-British dispute that ensued not only added to the turbulence and uncertainty surrounding Hong Kong's transition. More importantly, Britain's 1992 program and China's two-part response have shifted the balance of Hong Kong's post-1997 political development. As defined by the Basic Law, Hong Kong after 1997 was to have become China's laboratory for a controlled experiment in moderate democratic reform, on the terms and at the pace of Hong Kong's own choosing. The plan was to create a modern big-city equivalent to China's equally modest experiment in rural self-government (an experiment that had been underway since the mid-1980s). By contrast, Britain's 1992 initiative prepared the ground for an immediate confrontation between the forces of Western democracy and Chinese communist dictatorship, anticipating Hong Kong after 1997 as the first point of contact between the two.

Hence, China vowed to dismantle or otherwise negate virtually every item on Britain's agenda. The aim was and remains to return Hong Kong's newly reformed political system to as close an approximation of its pre-1992 state as possible, since that had been the intended starting point for implementing the Basic Law. Toward this end, Chinese leaders adopted the golden egg argument. Lu Ping, the senior Beijing official responsible for Hong Kong affairs, emphasized in a 1994 speech China's economic interests in Hong Kong, and warned that those who were trying to turn Hong Kong into a "political city" would be held accountable for their actions.

The second major plank in China's Hong Kong platform, however, stipulates that Hong Kong must be administered after 1997 in accordance with the Basic Law, which states that half the legislature is to be directly elected by the year 2003. The Law also stipulates (in Articles 45 and 68) that the "ultimate aim" is election of a chief executive and all legislative councilors by "universal suffrage." The logic of China's two-part strategy is thus clear, despite all its complexity in practice.

By early 1997, China's strategy was unfolding as planned. Arrangements to dismantle Hong Kong's newly elected councils already had begun with the creation of a hand-picked provisional legislature to serve in a caretaker capacity from July 1, 1997. Having ruled that the election of the Legislative Council in 1995 violated earlier decisions and that the council would not be allowed to complete its four-year term as anticipated in the Basic Law, Beijing decided to replace Legco with a substitute body until fresh elections could be held sometime in 1998. The two main committees authorized to manage transitional work–the Preparatory Committee and the Selection Committee–were formed on schedule in late 1995 and 1996. The former is empowered to make all decisions and take all actions necessary to form the new SAR government, including the nomination and election of Selection Committee members. The latter's principal task is, in turn, to formalize selection of the first SAR governor or chief executive and the provisional legislators. More important was how the people chosen for

these new bodies emerged, since they are to be the builders of Hong Kong's new administration during its founding 1997–98 years.

In fact, Beijing encouraged its partisans and allies to contest the 1994 and 1995 council elections despite its otherwise categorical rejection of the reformed rules under which the elections were held. The declared aim was "to accumulate experience," gain public exposure, and build popular support, while casting an eye toward the post-1997 future. Results vindicated this approach since pro-China candidates acquitted themselves fairly well. Democratic candidates, supported by the Democratic Party (DP) and like-minded independents, took about 60% of the popular vote for the 20 directly elected seats in the 1995 Legco poll; pro-China candidates and their declared allies won only about 30% of the vote. However, by exploiting Hong Kong's complex election laws and offsetting their liabilities as an unpopular minority by encouraging united front alliances with sympathetic outsiders, pro-China legislators actually won about half the seats in the Legislative Council's 60-seat chamber.

For their part, Hong Kong's democrats eschewed the pragmatic united front approach and opted to boycott the provisional legislature rather than acknowledge its legitimacy, a condition China attached to participation. Hence, the foundation for Hong Kong's post-1997 government is being laid by the same pro-China coalition that was brought together for the first time in the 1994–95 council elections. The key elements of that coalition as they emerged finally in the 1995 Legislative Council comprised seven "old" left members; one representative from each of three new united front groups formed within the business community (three total); six sympathetic independents; ten members from the pro-business Liberal Party; and four democrats who regarded as excessively confrontational the mainstream democratic position on China's political plans for Hong Kong.

Specifically, "old" left refers to the small percentage of Hong Kong's population that has sympathized with the communist cause in China since 1949 and before. Such partisans, who are called "patriotic" in local parlance, founded the main pro-China political party, the Democratic Alliance for the Betterment of Hong Kong (DAB). The DAB won six Legco seats in 1995. In the past, "old" left members kept to themselves, read their own newspapers, sent their children to patriotic schools, and worked in China-owned and China-oriented businesses and trade unions. Among these organizations, the largest was the Federation of Trade Unions (in early 1997, FTU membership totaled more than 200,000). Until the 1980s, this community was effectively excluded from Hong Kong's leading political and intellectual circles, which remained categorically anti-communist and uninterested in post-1949 China. By contrast, "new" left refers to those who have joined the "united front" periphery (i.e., political alliances of convenience among those not actually committed to the communist cause but whose interests and sympathies bring them into close association with it). Many Hong Kong business people are now participating in such groups and activities, but are viewed more as allies than pro-China partisans.

Subsequently, this new coalition grew by a careful process of appointment and selection. Soon coalition members filled all seats in the formative bodies of the new SAR administration. These bodies include the Preparatory Committee, the Selection Committee, the provisional legislature, and the Executive Council or cabinet. Shipping magnate Tung Chee-hwa was named the first chief executive of the SAR government.

The political dividing line has thus been drawn between the democratic inclinations of Hong Kong's voting majority, which emerged during the final years of British rule, and China's design for evolutionary reform led by a business-oriented establishment in the pre-1992 mold. Whether Hong Kong adopts a political system based on a known Western model or one based on the Chinese innovation remains to be seen. Results will only begin to come in once the SAR's political arena is fully operational and the democrats have rejoined it (presumably in 1998).

Meanwhile, a secondary fault line cuts across this main political divide. The second line is best illustrated in the two-part balance sheet drawn up after the 1995 Legco election. Although the chamber was almost equally divided between pro-China and pro-democracy supporters, the populist versus establishment calculation yielded a very different result. One tally showed 37 seats for "labor," including all democrats and "old" leftists combined, with only 18 seats secured for "business and industry." Indeed, the new united front groups allegedly were formed not simply to promote China's cause among Hong Kong's entrepreneurs, but also to counter the dominant labor union orientation of the old left.

Accordingly, Britain's 1992 reform program contained elements that were opposed not only by China, but also by Hong Kong's business community. The colony was built by and for this sector, and its members had dominated the political establishment thereafter. This configuration of power was responsible for the underdevelopment of several key areas of Hong Kong society. Citizens' rights and privileges, including labor protection, unemployment insurance, and retirement benefits, had been held at bay by the colonial government in concert with business leaders. During the 1980s, officials rebuffed growing demands for social reform by evoking the specter of "free lunches." The term is still used routinely in Hong Kong when referring to British-style, welfare-state economics as well as to business fears about the consequences of too much mass participation in politics. Such fears were confirmed after 1992, when candidates, legislators, and the Patten administration began actively addressing grassroots demands for social reform.

This unprecedented fall from grace and power helps explain how Hong Kong's capitalists could shift allegiance so quickly to their future communist sovereign. As a Liberal Party legislator and chairman of the General Chamber of Commerce, James Tien often speaks for Hong Kong's business community. He explained its new loyalties in a 1996 statement angrily denouncing democrats and their British mentors for the new focus on politics. He declared that leaders of business and industry had "never accepted" Patten's electoral reforms. Tien was also highly critical of the consequent proceedings in Legco, which he blamed on the new "labor" representatives elected in 1995. He deplored legislation they had introduced on severance pay, maternity leave, gender discrimination, and disability allowances. Even the government's more limited initiatives in these areas Tien viewed as excessive. Employers, he argued, suddenly were being bombarded with welfare demands that should have taken decades to implement. Not surprisingly, Tien professed himself more than willing to cooperate with the new SAR authorities and the provisional legislature in reestablishing Hong Kong's business-friendly environment.

The Economic Fundamentals

And so it came to pass that the parable of the golden goose eggs was taken over and turned on its head by the pro-China, pro-business coalition. The idea originally gained currency during 1982–83, while Britain bargained unsuccessfully to retain an administrative presence in exchange for acknowledging China's nominal sovereignty. Hong Kong was likened to a goose laying golden eggs for China's benefit, and China's communist leaders were said to be at least astute enough to recognize that managing Hong Kong's capitalist economy lay beyond their capabilities. China's leaders responded that, if forced to choose, sovereignty would take precedence over economics. The imagery thereafter took on a life of its own, invoked everywhere to symbolize the dangers of uniting capitalist Hong Kong with communist China.

By 1997, however, events had combined to change fundamentally the context of reunification, leaving the analogy to lapse at its Hong Kong point of origin for want of a clear target. The changing context is perhaps best described in terms of the cost-benefit equation alluded to above. Britain's post-1992 reform model anticipated substantial

social inputs for which Hong Kong's economy heretofore has escaped responsibility in the interests of maintaining its competitive advantage. By contrast, China promises a return to some approximation of the old status quo, with representatives of business and industry ruling Hong Kong under Chinese sovereignty much as they did before 1992.

Nor are Britain's political and social reforms the only relevant changes that have occurred since the early 1980s. Equally significant for Hong Kong's changing allegiances is the economic integration between Hong Kong and China, which intensified from the 1980s. By 1997, the two were not only each other's largest trading partners; each had become the other's largest investor as well, and integration of the two economies was already well advanced. In terms of its economic fundamentals, then, the relationship had changed dramatically since 1982.

Foundations

Traditionally, Hong Kong played only an entrepôt function in facilitating trade between China, Southeast Asia, and the West, including both Europe and North America. Not until 1949 did Hong Kong begin to assume a more direct supportive role. International embargoes against China during the 1950–53 Korean War offered new opportunities for Hong Kong entrepreneurs, some of whom had just fled China. Many managed to redeem themselves with the new communist authorities, albeit from a safe distance, by circumventing the embargoes. The "patriotic" credentials of some Hong Kong capitalists were established in this manner, and services rendered then still are remembered.

For example, a shipping company founded by the father of Hong Kong's new chief executive designate was one such early contributor to the China coast trade. The family fled to Hong Kong from Shanghai in 1948, just ahead of advancing communist armies, but continued to operate a shipping line between the two cities during the 1950s. This case typifies the contradictory role that

Hong Kong has played vis-à-vis communist China ever since: as a safe haven for migrants fleeing the political and economic rigors of communist rule; and as a source of varied economic benefits for China maintained by those same émigrés from their new home base.

Hong Kong's population grew from about 600,000 during World War II to 2.25 million in 1952; by 1981 it had reached 5.1 million. The new arrivals provided a ready market for Chinese foodstuffs, water, and low-cost consumer goods imported in a trading pattern that was dominated by Hong Kong's patriotic business community. During the first three decades of communist rule, the relative value of this trade grew as other sources of foreign capital atrophied under the strictures of China's experiments in socialist construction. By 1982, goods traded with and through Hong Kong were estimated to account for some 40% of China's total foreign exchange earnings. Without them, it was said, China would have "little hope of pulling itself out of the backwardness and poverty into which it has sunk …".

The Korean War had marked a more important juncture in Hong Kong's economic development, however. With much of its trade cut off and refugees pouring in, the colony needed a new means of livelihood and so began manufacturing goods for export. Entrepreneurs adapted quickly to changing market demands; moreover, low-wage immigrant labor was in plentiful supply, free-market principles reigned supreme, and taxes remained low. The colony used this formula to develop into a leading producer and exporter of light industrial goods, primarily textiles, garments, clocks, plastics, toys, and electronic products. Meanwhile, Hong Kong's entrepôt trade with the Pacific region revived and a full range of supporting business, re-export, and financial services developed as well. Hong Kong's transformation into a world-class manufacturing, trading, and financial center occurred roughly between 1960 and 1980.

Hence, Hong Kong's potential value to China by 1982 actually loomed larger than the simple receipts earned from selling food and water to local consumers, especially given the new order developing in China itself. Mao Zedong had been dead just five years, but his successors were moving swiftly. They already had repudiated his radical Cultural Revolution experiments; furthermore, in 1978 they embarked on a 180-degree course correction. Foreign investment and technologies would be welcomed and new economic zones would grant special incentives to lure foreign manufacturers. The first was established in 1980 at the border town of Shenzhen, adjacent to Hong Kong. China's declared aims were to learn the ways and acquire the means of Western capitalist success. Although the full extent of this new direction was not yet apparent, Hong Kong already had begun calculating its prospects under the new order. For China, the colony was recast as a source of investment capital and ready expertise from all its manufacturing, trade, and financial sectors. Not anticipated, however, was just how extensively Hong Kong's economy would be tapped or the transformation it would undergo in the process.

Hong Kong in China

China's post-Mao economic course was a fortuitous coincidence for Hong Kong. By the early 1980s, Hong Kong's competitive edge was being eroded by, among other things, rising domestic costs, especially of land and labor. Entrepreneurs had two choices: either move out in search of lower costs elsewhere or move up with added inputs of capital and technology. The latter option was never seriously considered, since neither government nor private enterprise was inclined to assume the added risks and responsibilities for research and development. Probably, such unyielding laissez faire convictions have been reinforced by the basic transit-stop view of Hong Kong as a place to rebuild fortunes before moving on.

In any case, Hong Kong manufacturers already were moving some of their labor-intensive operations to neighboring countries; China rapidly became the destination of choice. Entrepreneurs moved first to neighboring Shenzhen, and then further inland as China's restrictions on foreign investment eased. Hong Kong industries also gradually increased the range and level of their China-based production, albeit without changing the basic mix of export-oriented light industrial goods. Additionally, Hong Kong's service sector (including hotels and tourist offices) entered China's market, signing joint venture and management contracts throughout the country. By the late 1980s, all non-manufacturing segments of Hong Kong's economy were represented in some form of mainland endeavor, including property development, infrastructure projects, retail outlets, and banking services.

Thus, the feared reversal of China's new economic course never materialized. Rather, the new economic course was maintained through a steady (if not always smooth) sequence of incremental reforms. Each moved the economy further from its socialist past, toward a decentralized, privatized, market-oriented future. Given its natural advantages of geography, cultural affinity, and language, Hong Kong was able to exploit, if not actually anticipate, China's new course every step of the way. In the process, each side complemented the other's economic needs, trading capital and managerial expertise (Hong Kong) for land and labor (China). The statistical record of Hong Kong's "northward strategy" illustrates its impact.

Since 1979, Hong Kong has remained China's largest source of contracted and utilized foreign investment, averaging about 58% of the total on both measures from all countries. By comparison, the United States and Japan followed in second and third place with only 10% and 8% of total contracted investment for the period 1979–90. According to Hong Kong government estimates, by the end of 1995 utilized direct foreign investment in China totaled US$135 billion, of which Hong Kong had provided US$77 billion, up from US$66 billion the year before. Neighboring Guangdong prov-

ince received a majority share of Hong Kong's contribution, which was concentrated in the aforementioned manufacturing operations. By the mid-1990s, Hong Kong firms had set up thousands of factories and processing outlets in China, employing 3 million workers in Guangdong and about 5 million in China overall. Additionally, some 97,000 Hong Kong residents were working in China in 1996.

Trade between Hong Kong and China also was transformed. Earlier, as noted, the hard currency earned was used to pay for China's imports of grain, capital goods, and industrial raw materials. By the mid-1980s, Hong Kong's pre-1949 entrepôt trade with China had revived, and the value of re-exported goods was beginning to surpass those retained locally. In the early 1990s, re-exports via Hong Kong equaled 40% of all Chinese exports and, as of 1995, those re-exports from China amounted to 48% of all Hong Kong exports.

Similarly, Hong Kong sold few goods to China in the late 1970s, but the latter became Hong Kong's largest market over the following two decades. Much of this trade, however, comprised raw materials and semi-finished components being imported for reprocessing in China's new Hong Kong-run manufacturing sector. This sector's output was destined, in turn, for shipment back to Hong Kong and trans-shipment elsewhere (following the trade winds of export-driven consumer production). In 1995, according to Hong Kong government calculations, about 88% of the colony's re-exports involved China either as a source or a destination. Hence, it was the combined force of Hong Kong's new roles as investor in China and re-exporter of China's goods that established each as the other's largest trading partner. Otherwise, minus Hong Kong's indirect entrepôt and trans-shipment functions, the US, Japan, and Taiwan continued to vie for primacy of place among the various categories of direct trade with China.

Owing to these developments, Hong Kong's domestic economy has undergone significant restructuring. During the latter half of the 1980s and the early 1990s, most of Hong Kong's labor-intensive industrial production relocated inland, primarily to the nearby Pearl River delta region of Guangdong. The colony's manufacturing workforce declined from 860,000 in 1980 to 380,000 in 1996. Meanwhile, the sector's share of Hong Kong's gross domestic product (GDP) fell during that time from 24% to just 9%. Figure 3.1 compares GDP by broad sectors that combine manufacturing, construction, and utilities. The result was a new integrated division of labor between blue collar Guangdong and white collar Hong Kong, where factory headquarters remained to coordinate management, communications, financing, freight transport, marketing, and product design, among other tasks.

Yet growth was such (owing to the new China-related trade and investment opportunities) that Hong Kong succeeded in shifting to a predominantly service-oriented domestic economy with minimal disruption. Near full employment was maintained until the economic downturn of 1995, when the unemployment rate rose suddenly from an average of only 2% for the 1984–94 period to 3.6% in mid-1995. Unemployment fell gradually thereafter but had not returned to its previous low by late 1996. Government statistics record a steady GDP growth rate of 7% annually during the two decades 1975–95 (see Figure 3.2). Annual per capital GDP calculated at current market prices nevertheless doubled between 1989 and 1995, from US$11,800 to US$23,000.

China in Hong Kong

Hong Kong's rapid economic advance into China after 1980 was driven entirely by economic needs and benefits on both sides. China's concurrent economic entry into Hong Kong had the added political incentives of promoting "stability and prosperity"—code words for a smooth transition to Chinese rule. More specifically, China aimed to bolster the ranks of Hong Kong's still small pro-China community; to strengthen its own managerial skills; to boost public confidence thereby; to facili-

tate its control over key segments of Hong Kong's economy; and to raise added capital for investment in China.

China enjoyed long-standing if modest commercial and banking ties in Hong Kong that were dominated by the aforementioned patriotic community from 1949 onward. These ties, which persisted over three decades, centered on four Chinese state-owned enterprises: the Bank of China, China Travel Service, China Merchants shipping company, and China Resources trading company, plus department stores, printing presses, newspapers, and bookstores. Building on these foundations, the scope and scale of Chinese economic activity in Hong Kong increased after 1978 and especially after China's 1982 decision to take back the colony. Chinese companies, including those owned by central, provincial, and local governments, rushed to set up shop and open a window on the new capitalist frontier. By the mid-1990s, such companies actively participated in all sectors of Hong Kong's economy.

Statistical records of these activities (which must be treated as estimates and approximations only) indicate that China returned Hong Kong's favor by becoming the colony's largest "foreign" investor. By 1997 China's investments in Hong Kong were as great as or greater than those of Hong Kong in China. According to official Chinese figures, total assets of approved mainland-funded enterprises in Hong Kong totaled US$42.5 billion at the end of 1994, of which US$25 billion represented direct investment. Western sources estimated a much higher investment figure. They also estimated official Chinese investment in Hong Kong to be growing at about 25% annually (exclusive of "undeclared" inflows) by the late 1990s.

State-owned Chinese enterprises, whatever the level of government claiming ownership, are not supposed to operate in Hong Kong without approval from the central Beijing authorities. In 1996, 1,756 Chinese firms were operating in Hong Kong, some 400 of which belonged to neighboring Guangdong province. However, many lower-level governments had formed Hong Kong companies without official approval, as had individuals and entities that were not required to seek consent, including well-connected private citizens and the Chinese People's Liberation Army. Meanwhile, the old China-owned Hong Kong stalwarts had grown to conglomerate proportions. Consequently, four of them (Bank of China, China Resources, China Merchants, and China Travel Service), plus the newer CITIC-Pacific investment company, accounted for well over half the above-cited total asset figure.

According to Chinese statistics, in 1996 China-funded enterprises controlled between 20% and 25% of several key services, including Hong Kong's total volume of trade; total bank deposits; insurance premium earnings; and cargo handling, plus 12% of all construction projects. China-funded enterprises and individual Chinese also entered the hyper-inflated world of Hong Kong's property market and learned quickly to play the game as only Hong Kong punters can, purchasing commercial and residential real estate for post-1997 use as well as for investment and speculation.

Not until the early 1990s, however, did China begin to experiment with that most capitalist of endeavors, the stock market. Soon after fledgling exchanges were opened in Shanghai and Shenzhen, Beijing leaders authorized Hong Kong as another source of capital formation. Since 1993, state-owned industrial enterprises in China have been listed on Hong Kong's stock market, creating the new "H-share" category. Far more popular, however, were the "red chip" offerings of Hong Kong-registered companies owned by Chinese central government ministries and organizations. As of 1996, the two categories combined included more than 60 companies and accounted for 5% of the Hong Kong stock exchange's capitalization. Leading red chips include CITIC-Pacific, the Hong Kong offspring of the central government's China International Trust and Investment Corporation; China National Aviation Corporation (CNAC), the commercial wing of the Civil Aviation Administration of China; China Resources Enterprise, belonging to the Chinese government's Ministry of Foreign Trade; and China Overseas Shipping Corporation (COSCO), owned by the Ministry of Communications.

Taken as a whole, these varied Chinese investments seem to replicate for Hong Kong the same range of activities its citizens are pursuing in China—with one exception. The political imperatives point to that one additional interest in Hong Kong's economy: the corporate acquisition of its commanding heights, or at least its most strategic assets. Currently emerging key players in this regard are the China-owned, Hong Kong-listed red chip companies working in league with some of Hong Kong's own leading business figures and the conglomerates they control. This alliance of Chinese state capital and Hong Kong private enterprise has devised a series of strategies for fundraising and corporate acquisitions via share issues, loan syndications, proxy takeovers through pro-China Hong Kong business leaders, and interlocking alliances with Hong Kong counterparts eager to trade financial and managerial help for connections and opportunities in China.

China-based corporate interests are thus poised to acquire major stakes in some of Hong Kong's key enterprises, including aviation, shipping, banking, electricity, telecommunications, and the media. Typifying this trend was an aggressive bid in 1996 to break the monopoly of British "colonial" interests in Hong Kong aviation. Ultimately, CITIC-Pacific and CNAC together won a majority share in Hong Kong's second airline, Dragonair. The deal was formed at the expense of Swire Pacific, one of Hong Kong's oldest British firms.

Not by coincidence, 22 of the leading Hong Kong participants in these intricate economic power plays are among the 94 Hong Kong representatives on the 150-member Preparatory Committee, responsible for overseeing the creation of Hong Kong's post-1997 government. Among the 22, four property development tycoons stand out not only for the size of their fortunes, but for the concurrent roles they play as investors in China and facilitators of Chinese corporate investment in Hong Kong. The four are: Li Ka-shing, Lee Shau-kee, Cheng Yu-tong, and Walter Kwok.

Integration and the Post-1997 Future

In many ways, then, Hong Kong has raced ahead, leaving observers and key players alike with concepts and vocabularies that are no longer relevant to reunification. Chinese officials still dream of an "economic city" that is no more, while foreign observers invoke the golden egg principle unaware of the new meanings it has acquired in Hong Kong. By 1997, even the hallowed "one country, two systems" promise enshrined in the Basic Law's preamble seemed out of date.

Together these concepts and vocabularies reflected the challenge of uniting Hong Kong capitalism and Chinese socialism as perceived circa 1982. Fifteen years later, the chasm that divided them is no longer so wide; moreover, the challenge of bridging the chasm has changed accordingly, even if the political dangers seem almost as great. In fact, the political and economic lines of Hong Kong's progression toward 1997, although related, have responded to different imperatives and evolved each in its own way. The opportunities for post-1997 success or failure, therefore, will be multidimensional, deriving from both the political and economic realms, as well as from the connecting points between them.

The politics of transition were enlivened first and foremost by Britain's 1992 reform program, which aimed to hasten the pace of democratization. The ensuing Sino-British dispute clarified the alternatives between, on the one hand, Britain's version of direct elections with human rights protection and more open accountable government and, on the other, the arrangements approved by China and spelled out in the Basic Law. China resents not only the aims of popular sovereignty that Britain's program openly promotes, but also the possibility that such aims may inspire a future democratic move-

ment in China itself.

Even within the Basic Law's more modest arrangements, however, there remains ample scope for a future Hong Kong-inspired political reform agenda that might undermine the current determination of Beijing leaders to control China's political evolution overall. Contributing to that possibility will be Hong Kong's ongoing political development, a process that is taking place in a literate, urban community where the Chinese-language press is hyper-active, the public well-read, and a significant proportion of the population is politicized (calculate 1 million; that is, the number estimated to have marched in 1989 and also the number who voted in the 1995 Legco election); where every issue on Britain's reform agenda has acquired a local constituency both for and against; and where millions of trips are made back and forth to China each year. Accordingly, the time frame will be long-term and the possibility of turbulence great. However, it is also likely that Hong Kong will serve as an urban precedent, reinforcing the influence of China's ongoing experiment with rural self-government reform.

Economically, integration was so far advanced by 1997 that its most important impact probably had been registered already. Hong Kong's economic entry into China during the 1980s paralleled and helped pioneer the implementation of post-Mao market reforms. But by the late 1990s, with that course set and the foundations laid, China's main challenge was to build upon reforms with policies the economy could absorb and its people accept. For Hong Kong, meanwhile, the new 1990s recognition of interdependence and mutual benefit was being challenged by the need for even newer terms of reference.

Similar to Hong Kong's initial economic entry into China, this latest challenge is not directly related to political reunification. Specifically, Hong Kong faces a two-part test, one related to its existing presence in China and the other, conversely, to China's role in Hong Kong. The colony has reached an economic crossroads that just happens to coincide with and be complicated by 1997.

The first test, currently being debated by economic and political leaders alike, concerns Hong Kong's newly "hollowed out" economy. With manufacturing capacity relocated to China and the new service industry tied to its China-based assembly line operations, Hong Kong is now vulnerable to the same development process it helped set in motion. The threat is inevitable as China begins to upgrade its own production lines and service capabilities. Thus, Hong Kong's impressive achievements during the 1990s have been accompanied by the downward drift of some key economic indicators. For example, the decline in Hong Kong's overall GDP growth rate (see Figure 3.2) is a function of the structural shift from manufacturing to re-export servicing. Calculated differently, Hong Kong's economic growth averaged 7.4% between 1964–74, 8.5% between 1974–84, and only 5.5% between 1984–94. Hong Kong's own domestic merchandise exports have stagnated since 1989 (see Figure 3.3). The comparative record of China's industrial production and Hong Kong's re-exports suggests an increasing divergence. China's 1993 and 1995 production increases were not correlated (as they had been previously) with Hong Kong's re-export growth, which has been declining since 1992 (see Figure 3.4).

Hong Kong, therefore, has embarked upon a search for a new post-integration, post-industrial course in response to the anticipated deterioration of its roles as a China-based producer and re-exporter of light industrial goods. The current debate tends to pit manufacturers against financial managers. The former are lobbying for the development of a high-tech manufacturing capacity and the latter for a similar "quantum leap" in Hong Kong's service sector with special emphasis on the financial component thereof.

Chief executive designate Tung Cheehwa has sided with the manufacturers who are calling upon government to appropriate funding for research and development. Representatives of the outgoing Hong Kong government reject the idea (as they always

have) as being "un-Hong Kong," or interventionist, counterproductive, and wasteful. Presumably, the plan for upgrading services could be financed by nongovernment sources, since World Bank representative Pieter Bottelier is among its advocates. They subscribe to the "Manhattan-ization" line of reasoning, which holds that Hong Kong should redirect its economy as did New York City under similar circumstances. According to this argument, Hong Kong's only natural advantage henceforth will be its ties to global money markets, and its greatest value to China will be as a source of capital formation. Such a course would also leave ample scope for the development of other specialized services beyond the existing low-profit re-export business.

Arguing against the financial center proposal, opponents reason that it will not be sufficient to sustain growth. Moreover, social consequences could be long-term, expensive, and destabilizing as the old workforce is replaced by one with requisite skills. Such consequences include growing unemployment, greater income disparity, rising social tensions, larger government welfare budgets, and increased educational investment. Such consequences also would compound those of Hong Kong's economic evolution to date. Social dislocation has been contained and unemployment remains low; nonetheless, as of 1995, some 650,000 people were living in "absolute poverty." Of that number, about 500,000 received no public welfare assistance, although an unidentified proportion lived in subsidized public housing (as does just over half of Hong Kong's total population, unable to afford the cost of private sector housing).

The need for further economic restructuring thus anticipates some major changes in Hong Kong's way of doing business, at a time when the shift to Chinese rule will heighten political uncertainties and complicate the search for economic solutions. Among those added complications are an expected rise in corruption, speculation, and influence peddling. There are clear indications that business practices already curbed in Hong Kong but rampant in China's climate of "nascent" capitalism are destined for re-export back to Hong Kong. This course of events was made all the more likely when Beijing announced its aim to use the territory as a source of investment capital, including both global and locally generated.

For example, the red chip China-funded enterprises in Hong Kong have two formal functions: to make "due contribution" to the local community and invest in mainland Chinese development projects. CITIC-Pacific alone is estimated to have contributed US$1.2 billion toward the latter end since 1993. However, an unknown proportion of Hong Kong's total investment in China represents "round-tripping" or recycled Chinese capital. Often undeclared on arrival in Hong Kong and managed by shell companies set up for just this purpose, such funds may be enhanced by a run through the property market or stock exchange, and then hastened on their return journey to China by the incentives offered to woo "foreign" investors.

Hence, the difficulties of preserving Hong Kong for posterity have been compounded many times over. The colony evolved into a modern capitalist success story by exploiting its unique combination of scarce resources to maximum advantage. Those resources always combined external and internal factors, such as a colonial administration, laissez faire economic convictions, and proximity to communist China, together with Hong Kong's own land, labor, and the attributes of its émigré population. Similarly, the strategy always entailed the careful balancing of external and internal accounts: maximum return for minimum cost in the merchandise export trade, while developing domestic land and property into a major source of capital formation. As factor costs rose accordingly, the late 20th-century globalization trend showed the way, which for Hong Kong entrepreneurs was just a short train ride across the border. There the supply of factory space and low wage labor was so plentiful that virtually all Hong Kong's manufacturing capacity had relocated to China by the mid-1990s.

Now, standing on the threshold of a new sovereign and a new future, Hong Kong has become the "first 21st-century economy." With light industry gone and no later stage equivalents to replace it, the territory must again look for ways to guarantee its livelihood. Difficult decisions must be made about industrial and human capital development in order to promote growth and maintain social order. Yet these are ultimately political as well as economic decisions, which helps clarify further China's opposition to Britain's 1992 political reform package, and in turn entrepreneurial Hong Kong's support for China's stand.

That governments must make such decisions also helps clarify why the "freest" economies are not necessarily governed by the freest polities. This contradiction was highlighted in a recently issued "index of economic freedom," which ranked Hong Kong, Singapore, and Bahrain, respectively, as the world's freest economies. Economic growth also correlated positively with economic freedom defined as the least possible government regulation, taxation, etc. The need for regular validation by an electorate evidently forces governments to address public needs to a greater degree than economics would otherwise require—a basic fact of political life long known to Hong Kong entrepreneurs. Their fear of free elections (and free lunches) was confirmed in 1995, when victorious legislative councilors from across the political spectrum immediately began putting together majorities for enhanced labor protection and social security benefits. In this way, China's political leaders and Hong Kong's business community have found common cause in their opposition to faster democratization for Hong Kong.

In the short run, then, the immediate cost of Britain's 1992 political reform program and the dispute it provoked has been to remove Hong Kong's most popular democratic advocates from the process of forming its new SAR government. This has given China a much freer hand to reestablish the corporate power structure in as close an approximation of its pre-1992 form as possible. Over time, however, forces already at work will make past assumptions untenable. Economically, Hong Kong will continue to evolve, along with its function as the point of first direct contact between Western-style capitalism and Chinese-style socialism. The gulf between them will continue to narrow as the integration of private enterprise and state-owned corporate capital proceeds. However, what is good for business in the old narrow sense will not be sufficient to maintain either prosperity or stability. Meanwhile, a democratizing Basic Law government also will have slipped into China across the 1997 divide.

Since 1990, former communist states across the Eurasian continent have experienced a similar fundamental reordering of their political and economic systems. For China, however, these changes are occurring under the existing communist government rather than after its collapse. Whether Chinese leaders can remain on this evolutionary path is a question only history can answer. Hong Kong, meanwhile, will contribute toward that historic end as a uniquely transparent experiment in democratic institution-building and 21st-century economic growth under Chinese communist rule.

Further Reading

Bueno de Mesquita, Bruce, David Newman, and Alvin Rabushka, *Red Flag over Hong Kong,* Chatham, New Jersey: Chatham House, 1996

Presents a complex mathematical formula used to predict Hong Kong's future under Chinese communist rule, accompanied by a clear and informative overview summarizing the authors' critical assumptions as well as Hong Kong's current political and economic problems, potential flashpoints, and likely post-1997 scenarios.

Chan, Ming K., and Gerard A. Postiglione, editors, *The Hong Kong Reader: Passage to Chinese Sovereignty,* Armonk, New York: M.E. Sharpe, 1996

A collection of useful articles on the impact of Hong Kong's transition to Chinese sovereignty, including essays on politics, education, economics, and migration. All are reprinted from the multi-volume series, "Hong Kong Becoming China: The Transition to 1997." The series, published jointly by M.E. Sharpe and the Hong Kong University Press, was launched in 1991 and is written for an international readership by Hong Kong academics under the overall editorial direction of Professors Chan and Postiglione.

Cradock, Percy, *Experiences in China,* London: John Murray, 1994

As a former British ambassador to China and the Prime Minister's advisor, Sir Percy Cradock played a key role in the negotiations over Hong Kong's return to Chinese sovereignty. Part three of this volume recounts that controversial period about which Cradock, now in retirement, has become undiplomatically outspoken and defensive against critics who accuse Britain of failing to extract from China sufficient guarantees for Hong Kong's post-1997 autonomy.

Enright, Michael J., Edith E. Scott, and David Dodwell, *The Hong Kong Advantage,* New York and Hong Kong: Oxford University Press, 1997

Commissioned by the head of Hong Kong's Trade Development Council to counteract prevailing doomsday scenarios in Western media accounts, this book deliberately emphasizes Hong Kong's economic assets over its political liabilities. While conclusions are predictably positive, the authors present a well-researched general introduction to Hong Kong's strengths and weaknesses as a generator of wealth and entrepreneurial talent.

Hong Kong 1996: A Review of 1995 and a Pictorial Review of the Past Fifty Years, Hong Kong: Government Information Services Department, 1996

The Hong Kong government publishes an annual report that includes a comprehensive survey of the colony's development and provides the most readily available source of official statistics. The report began to appear in yearbook form shortly after normal life resumed in the colony following Japan's occupation during World War II, with 1996 marking the 50th commemorative edition.

Miners, Norman, *The Government and Politics of Hong Kong,* 5th edition, New York and Hong Kong: Oxford University Press, 1995

This standard text on the structure of Hong Kong's government was first published in 1975, several years before China's decision to resume sovereignty was announced and political life was enlivened by popular participation. Successive editions thus trace Hong Kong's recent political evolution from a "living fossil" of British colonial administration that had remained essentially unchanged for more than a century, through the democratic reforms introduced in 1992 and implemented thereafter.

The Other Hong Kong Report, 1996, Hong Kong: Chinese University of Hong Kong Press, 1996

Published annually, this report series began in 1989 as a critical counterpoint to the Hong Kong government's official yearbook. The "other report" is widely used by Hong Kong students as a current events reference source and contains chapters on all aspects of the colony's development contributed mainly by local academic writers. The 1996 volume includes essays on budget issues, financial and monetary affairs, labor, corruption, consumerism, and the environment.

Roberti, Mark, *The Fall of Hong Kong: China's Triumph and Britain's Betrayal,* New York: Wiley, 1994

Written in the style of "hard hitting" investigative journalism, this book recounts the decade-long negotiations between Britain and China over Hong Kong's return to Chinese sovereignty. Despite his tendency to over-dramatize, Roberti's presentation is the best documented of those arguing that Britain betrayed Hong Kong's interests during the 1980s negotiations. That argument undoubtedly influenced Britain's unilateral decision to promote more aggressively democratic political reform in Hong Kong during the 1990s.

Sung, Yun-wing, *The China-Hong Kong Connection: The Key to China's Open Door Policy,* New York: Cambridge University Press, 1991

Professor Sung provides one of the few monographic accounts available in English on economic relations between China and Hong Kong during the 1980s. His study begins in 1978, with the new post-Mao economic policies in China, focusing on the new roles they created in turn for Hong Kong as China's trading partner and source of development capital. These 1980s opportunities also laid the foundations for economic integration between Hong Kong and China that became increasingly evident in the 1990s.

Sung, Yun-wing, Pak-wai Liu, Yue-chim Richard Wong, and Pui-king Lau, *The Fifth Dragon: The Emergence of the Pearl River Delta,* New York: Addison Wesley, 1995

This volume begins where Professor Sung's 1991 study on Sino-Hong Kong economic relations left off, to focus on their main consequences. These include the integration of Hong Kong's economy through trade and investment with the neighboring Pearl River Delta region of China's Guangdong province. A second major consequence was the dynamic growth of the region at a rate exceeding that of the original four Asian economic "dragons": Taiwan, Singapore, South Korea, and Hong Kong itself. Sung and his coauthors analyze all facets of the Delta's economic growth as well as its impact on the global market.

Tsang, Steve Yui-sang, *Democracy Shelved: Great Britain, China, and Attempts at Constitutional Reform in Hong Kong, 1945–1952,* New York and Hong Kong: Oxford University Press, 1988

Thoroughly researched and written in solid academic style, this study provides the scholarly underpinnings and historical background for Hong Kong's current political controversies. The author examines colonial Britain's equivocations over democratic reform in Hong Kong, tracing them back to the immediate post-World War II years when proposals toward that end were effectively scuttled.

Suzanne Pepper is a Hong Kong based American writer and a Research Fellow at the Institute of Asia-Pacific Studies, Chinese University of Hong Kong. She is the author of *Civil War in China: The Political Struggle* (1978) and *Radicalism and Education Reform in 20th-Century China* (1996). She has also contributed chapters to vols. 13, 14, and 15 of *The Cambridge History of China,* and has written numerous monographs and journal articles on Chinese politics and education. Her current research topic is political reform in China and Hong Kong. She was coeditor of *China Review* (1995 and 1996).

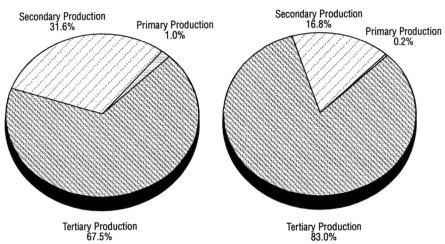

Figure 3.1: Gross Domestic Product by Broad Economic Sector

1980

Secondary Production
31.6%

Primary Production
1.0%

Tertiary Production
67.5%

1994

Secondary Production
16.8%

Primary Production
0.2%

Tertiary Production
83.0%

Definitions: Primary production: agriculture, fisheries, mining, quarrying
Secondary production: manufacturing, construction, utilities (that is, electricity, gas, and water)
Tertiary production: wholesale, retail, import/export trades, restaurants, hotels, transport, storage, communications, financing, insurance, real estate, property ownership, etc.

Source: *Hong Kong 1996* (Hong Kong Government Printer, 1996): 50

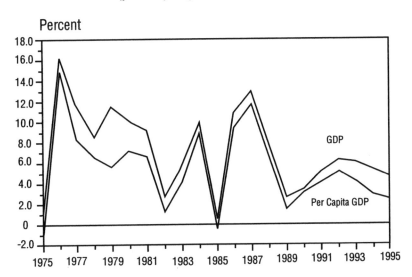

Figure 3.2: Gross Domestic Product
(year-on-year growth rate in real terms)

Percent

GDP

Per Capita GDP

Over the past two decades, the Hong Kong economy has been expanding rapidly, with GDP growing by 7% per annum and per capita GDP 6% per annum in real terms.

Source: *Hong Kong 1996* (Hong Kong Government Printer, 1996): 49

Figure 3.3: Growth in Hong Kong's Visible Trade
(year-on-year growth rate in real terms)

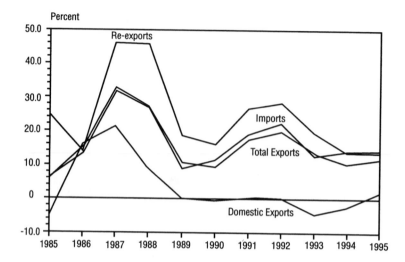

Re-export growth in 1995 was faster than in 1994. Domestic exports also resumed a positive
   growth. Imports continued to grow markedly.

Source: *Hong Kong 1996* (Hong Kong Government Printer, 1996): 56

Figure 3.4: Chinese Production and Hong Kong Re-exports
(1984–95)

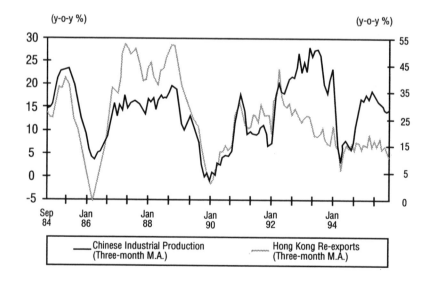

Source: "Hong Kong: Post-97 Economy, Part II," United Bank of Switzerland Globan Research (May 1996): 5

Chapter Four

Growing Interdependence: Economic Relations Between China and Taiwan

Elizabeth M. Freund

Introduction

Since the early 1980s, China and Taiwan have enjoyed vigorous trade and investment relations, resulting in the partial integration of their economies. Economic integration and the ensuing economic interdependence of China and Taiwan lead to possibilities for cooperation as well as conflict: integration may lead to the cooperation needed for Taiwan's reunification with the Chinese mainland; it also may lead to conflict across the Taiwan Straits as each side uses its economic clout as a tool to coerce the other side into political concessions.

For China, integration with Taiwan's economy has economic and political implications. China uses Taiwanese trade and investment to aid in the development of its own economy and also as a bargaining chip to encourage and facilitate reunification. For Taiwanese investors, trade with and investment in China is a matter of survival. Economic cooperation with China particularly helps many of Taiwan's small- and medium-sized firms, which, having been forced out of the domestic market by spiraling business costs, can take advantage of the mainland's lower labor and real estate costs. A presence in the mainland market also gives Taiwanese investors an economic interest in a possibly reunited China. The Taiwan government also sees economic interdependence as a first step toward eventual reunification, but is concerned that China may use its growing economic and military power to

force Taiwan to join the mainland under a Communist government.

A reunited China is the official goal of both the PRC (the mainland People's Republic of China) and the ROC (Republic of China) governments. Since the 1949 split between the mainland and Taiwan, both the PRC and ROC governments consider their respective regimes to be the sole legitimate government of China. The ROC lays claim to the 34 provinces of mainland China as well as the island province of Taiwan. The PRC considers itself the one and only China, and regards Taiwan as a renegade province. While the ROC government seeks reunification of China under a democratic government, the PRC since 1949 has advocated a policy of incorporating Taiwan under the existing Communist government. In the years immediately following the split, China proclaimed that it would "liberate" Taiwan by military means. Although it has never renounced the right to use force to recover Taiwan, China in 1979 adopted a policy of peaceful reunification. In 1984, China adopted a "one country, two systems" policy, allowing Taiwan the autonomy to maintain its own government, military forces, and economic system. The PRC government believes that the "one country, two systems" formula is the most effective way to recover Taiwan and reunify China. Taiwan's one-China policy promotes separation until the mainland catches up with Taiwan economically and politically.

The 1979 change in China's Taiwan policy eased tensions across the Taiwan Straits. In 1987, Taiwan abandoned martial law, allowing its citizens to visit the mainland and Taiwanese entrepreneurs to deal indirectly with the mainland. Since 1987, cross-straits trade and investment have grown steadily, partially integrating the two economies. Cross-straits economic relations chilled, however, in June 1995 after Taiwan's president visited the United States over the objections of the communist mainland. Beijing interpreted President Lee Tung-hui's visit as an attempt to promote Taiwanese independence, and claimed that the visit violated the principle of "one China."

Although talks between Taiwan and China on reunification have stalled, Taiwanese firms continue to do business in China. With US$25 billion worth of Taiwanese investments in the mainland, the ROC government is becoming increasingly concerned that Taiwan is growing economically dependent on China, and politically vulnerable to the mainland government. Taiwan's economy was proven to be vulnerable to the PRC's machinations when, in July 1995, the PRC government retaliated against Taiwan, first by cutting off official talks on eventual reunification, then by engaging in war games in the Taiwan Straits. Nervous Taiwanese investors responded to Beijing's "missile diplomacy" by seeking offshore havens for their investments. By late August 1995, 25% of Taiwan's wealth had fled the island. The Taiwan stock market plunged again in March 1996 when the PRC again engaged in military exercises and missile tests only a few miles away from Taiwan's two major ports, Keelung and Kaohsiung. These military activities were designed to influence Taiwan's first direct presidential elections and discourage Taiwan's independence movement.

From Taiwan's perspective, the integration of the two economies threatens Taiwan's national security. Taiwan's growing economic dependency on China could leave Taiwan vulnerable to China's military threats, economic sanctions, influence in the international community, and to China's attempts to isolate Taiwan from international markets.

To reduce the pace of economic integration, and thereby eliminate the threat of political dependency on the hostile mainland, the ROC government in the mid-1990s encouraged its investors to slow the pace of economic activities with China. The government's influence on investors has been limited, however, because many of Taiwan's China-bound investments are less than US$5 million and therefore do not need government approval, and because many companies have moved abroad to avoid government restrictions. Despite the government's warnings about the potential threat that the PRC could nationalize Taiwanese firms in the mainland or confiscate their assets, Taiwanese investors want to capitalize on Chinese markets while the opportunity still exists. To reduce economic dependence, and hence political vulnerability, the ROC government will need to convince investors that feverish investing in China involves risks as well as opportunity. To date, it has largely failed at that task.

Cross-Straits Economic Relations

Cross-straits economic relations date back to the 16th century, when traders from the mainland provinces of Fujian and Guangdong exchanged Taiwanese sugar, rice, deer hides, and crushed deer horns for mainland cotton cloth, silk, paper, and timber. Profitable cross-straits trade relations continued throughout the 18th century as well as throughout Japan's occupation of Taiwan (1895–1945). Links between mainland China and Taiwan were severed following the Nationalists' (Kuomintang, or KMT) retreat to Taiwan during the years 1947–49. Immediately following the split, the communist Chinese proclaimed that they were going to "liberate Taiwan by military means," and the Nationalists threatened that they would "fight back and destroy the Communist regime." In 1971, after the PRC took the ROC's seat in the United Nations, China changed its Taiwan policy by stating that it would pursue voluntary reunification.

Following the economically and socially damaging Cultural Revolution (1966–76), Deng Xiaoping consolidated power in 1978 and began an ambitious program of political and economic reforms designed to modernize China and develop its economy. Because China's financial resources were limited, Deng needed to attract investments from foreign countries. In 1979, Deng embraced an "open door" policy, which encouraged foreign investment in China and welcomed exports to the mainland. Of particular interest to China was access to the West's modern technology and progressive management practices. In 1978, China called for closer ties with Taiwan, and a year later Deng Xiaoping adopted a policy of peaceful reunification. The change in policy eased cross-straits tensions, and, as a result, indirect trade with Taiwan began to flourish. In 1980, indirect cross-straits trade via Hong Kong jumped 248% over 1979. It is difficult to determine the actual amount of cross-straits trade and investment flows because there is an enormous gap between official PRC and ROC statistics. Taiwan's figures do not include indirect trade that is not approved by the government, and therefore are much lower than China's figures, which include all trade and investment from Taiwan. Much of Taiwan's trade and investment in the mainland is conducted by small firms that engage in direct investment by sidestepping government prohibitions (for a discussion of the gap between China's and Taiwan's statistics, and of unapproved direct investment in China, see Leng Tse-kang, 1996: 108–11).

Eager to cash in on China's development, Taiwanese investors flocked to the Chinese mainland. Taiwanese investment in China increased dramatically after the ROC government lifted martial law in 1987 and rescinded the ban on travel to China. Impelled by investors' interest in the mainland, the ROC government the following year discarded its anti-communist posture. The Mainland Affairs Council (MAC) was established in 1990 to research and formulate Taiwan's China policy. In the absence of direct government-to-government relations, the civic Straits Exchange Foundation (SEF) was established in 1991 to handle all government-related communication between Taiwan and China. In 1991, the SEF sent an 18-member delegation to make the first formal visit to China.

In 1988, the ROC government officially permitted indirect trade with the mainland via a third area, and in 1990 allowed entrepreneurs to travel to the mainland for business dealings or to participate in trade shows. Also in that year, the ROC government permitted indirect exports, investments, and technological cooperation with the PRC via a third area. These policy changes resulted in an outbreak of "mainland fever": more contracts were signed in 1988 for Taiwanese China-bound investments than over the previous five years.

Indirect Cross-Straits Trade

Until the implementation of Deng's open door policy in 1979, cross-straits trade consisted largely of goods smuggled from Taiwan to China, and of illegal labor smuggled from China to Taiwan. In 1980, China began to encourage Taiwanese imports to China by abolishing tariffs on goods with Taiwan certificates of origin. China abandoned this policy in 1981 after fraudulent Taiwan certificates of origin flooded the mainland. Still, import and tariff controls imposed on Taiwanese goods were less stringent than those placed on goods from other sources. The change in tariff policy led to a drop in Taiwanese exports to China in 1982 and 1983. China's economic recovery in 1984 and 1985 fueled an increase in Taiwanese imports. Taiwanese exports to China declined again in 1986 when import restrictions were re-introduced by China to stop the sharp decline in its foreign exchange reserves.

Cross-straits trade grew steadily after Taiwan lifted martial law and, in 1988, officially allowed indirect trade with China. Because Taiwan continues to prohibit direct cross-straits contact, all China-bound goods and services must be transported through a third country. Most of this trade is transshipped through Hong Kong. According to ROC official statistics, indirect cross-straits trade in 1988 reached US$2.7 billion, an increase of 79.5% over the previous year. From 1989 to 1992, indirect trade grew steadily at an annual growth rate of 28.8%. In 1991 alone, indirect cross-straits trade totaled US$5.79 billion, a 40% increase over the same period in 1990. By 1995, trade via Hong Kong reached US$9.8 billion.

Taiwanese Investments in Mainland China

China today is the world's hottest emerging economy. Its economic boom is largely export-driven, and foreign-invested firms are playing a larger role in the growth of China's exports. Exports of foreign firms in China rose more than 45% in 1993, but China's total exports rose only 8%.

Foreign investment in China began after passage of the 1979 joint venture law. To encourage foreign investment in the mainland, China established four Special Economic Zones (SEZs) in the southern coastal provinces of Guangdong and Fujian. The SEZs encourage foreign investment by offering foreign firms preferential tax treatment, reductions in land-use fees, and favorable labor policies. Guangdong's SEZs, Shenzhen and Zhuhai, are adjacent to Hong Kong and Macau, respectively. In Fujian, the Xiamen SEZ faces Taiwan 90 miles across the straits. The fourth SEZ, Shantou, is close to Hong Kong and home to many overseas Chinese. In 1984, China extended preferential policies to 14 coastal cities to attract technology-intensive investment.

To encourage investment and eventual reunification, China enticed Taiwanese entrepreneurs to invest in the SEZs by implementing generous preferential trade and investment policies such as tax holidays and exemptions. In 1988, Fujian set up 10 Taiwanese investment zones and Xiamen issued special preferential policies for Taiwanese investors; Hainan Island in southern China set aside a special export processing zone for Taiwanese investors. Moreover, since 1988 investors have been allowed to

buy and sell real estate in the mainland. Chinese entrepreneurs from Taiwan also were able to take advantage of preferential treatment granted to all overseas Chinese. For example, Guangzhou granted special tax breaks to overseas Chinese investors, Fujian granted overseas Chinese a 50% reduction on land-use fees, and Shanxi offered overseas Chinese the right to apply for preferential treatment. Although Taiwanese no longer enjoy these privileges, they were able to take advantage of the special treatment to gain a solid foothold in China's markets and establish strong networks throughout the mainland. Common cultural, ethnic, and linguistic affinities, as well as kinship ties, have made the Chinese mainland a natural destination for Taiwanese investors.

The location of the SEZs in relation to Taiwan, Hong Kong, and Macau is no accident. Hong Kong and Macau will revert to mainland China in 1997 and 1999, respectively, and China seeks Taiwan's eventual reunification as well. China views creation of the SEZs as a way to facilitate reunification with Taiwan. Currently, few Taiwanese want to reunite with China, considering the tremendous gap in living standards, business environment, and political liberties between China and Taiwan. However, China can bridge this gap by establishing living and business conditions in the SEZs similar to those in Hong Kong. If China can make the SEZs into "mini-Hong Kongs," then it believes that it can smooth reunification with Hong Kong, Macau and Taiwan. Thus, China is using the SEZs as testimony that it can exist as "one country, two systems."

Since the late 1980s, Taiwan has become more important to China as a source of foreign investment. In 1989, Taiwan firms had invested US$1 billion in China; in 1993, Taiwan surpassed the United States and Japan to become the second largest source of foreign investment in China, behind Hong Kong. Hong Kong's investment in China in 1994 amounted to US$19.8 billion, followed by Taiwan's US$3.4 billion and Japan's US$3.6 billion. (These figures, which come from mainland sources, are much higher than Taiwan's official figures because they include investment that has not been approved by the ROC government. They indicate that approved investment accounts for only a fraction of Taiwan's total investment in China.)

In 1991, the ROC officially sanctioned Taiwanese indirect investment in China. In accord with Taiwan's "three nos" policy (no commercial, no navigational, and no postal links between Taiwan and China), Taiwan firms wanting to invest in the mainland must do so through a branch of a Taiwan company or a foreign company outside China, or through indirect remittance. All Taiwanese investments on the mainland require government approval. In 1991, Taiwanese investments in China were restricted to 3,679 product categories. Furthermore, to protect Taiwan's national security and domestic economy, the government prevents the transfer of some high technology; it also limits investments to labor-intensive projects to which China could supply raw materials and to areas that have low inter-industrial linkages.

Taiwanese investment flew to China in the late 1980s and early 1990s for several reasons. The appreciation of the New Taiwan dollar and a sharp rise in wage costs and land rent costs forced many of Taiwan's sunset industries either to relocate to China or close shop. An increasingly vocal labor movement prompted many firms to move to China or Southeast Asia, where labor was less organized and more compliant. The deterioration of social order in Taiwan, a desire to expand export markets, and the use of PRC export quotas to get around international trade restrictions also made China attractive to Taiwan investors.

Taiwanese investment in mainland China is concentrated heavily in the southern provinces of Guangdong and Fujian. Substantial investment by Taiwanese entrepreneurs has changed the economic structure of the Guangzhou, Fujian, and Xiamen economies. The economic base of those areas has shifted from agriculture to manufacturing and services. In Guangdong and Fujian, there has been an increase in banking, insurance and financial services, transportation and telecommunication facilities, as well as an expansion of tourism and a rise in real estate transactions.

The Xiamen SEZ: An Example of China-Taiwan Interdependence

The Xiamen SEZ provides a good example of China-Taiwan integration and interdependence. Xiamen in the early 1990s attracted the most Taiwanese investment in China, accounting for approximately one-fifth of total projects and half of total pledged and invested capital. In 1991, one-third of Xiamen's foreign investment came from Taiwan. Investors in Xiamen provided raw materials, capital, technology, management expertise, and export markets; Xiamen supplied cheap labor and land.

During the 1980s, the bulk of Taiwanese ventures were small-scale and labor-intensive. They manufactured light industrial and consumer goods such as shoes, apparel, toys, umbrellas, handicrafts, luggage, and sports equipment. During the 1990s, single investments by small- and medium-sized companies gave way to joint investment by conglomerates. Taiwanese-invested firms in Xiamen also lengthened their terms of investment from less than 20 years to more than 20 years. In addition, Taiwan investors began to lease or buy land to develop industrial parks rather than merely rent or buy factories. Since 1991, Taiwanese investors in Xiamen have focused their efforts less on manufacturing and more on the service sector. In 1992, investors began to turn their attention to real estate projects. Two-thirds of Xiamen's property developers came from Taiwan.

Taiwan's largest companies have shown great interest in investment opportunities in Xiamen. During the late 1980s, more than half of Taiwan's top 100 companies sent delegations to Xiamen to discuss investing there. These visits resulted in the signing of nearly a dozen contracts. The average capitalization was US$3.469 million per project, far exceeding the US$1.35 million average for non-Taiwanese foreign investment. By mid-1991, Taiwanese investors had 417 ventures with a total investment of US$1 billion.

Taiwanese investment has helped cultivate Xiamen's private sector. Xiamen's state-owned sector since the early 1990s has been shrinking while the private sector has expanded. In 1991 the exports of some 200 Taiwanese firms in Xiamen accounted for more than 22% of Xiamen's totals. During the early 1990s, foreign firms were exempt from many of China's state-mandated labor policies. Thus, Xiamen's state industrial firms found it difficult to compete with Taiwanese and other foreign firms (for example, the Xiamen Mechanical Engineering Plant, one of Xiamen's leading state firms, was forced to close in 1991). Not surprisingly, because foreign firms are not subject to restrictive and costly state regulations on terms of employment and remuneration, some Taiwanese firms used less capital per unit of labor than Chinese state-owned firms.

In sum, through the creation of the Xiamen SEZ China has attempted to bring to fruition the principle of "one country, two systems" and thereby facilitate reunification with Taiwan. China's strategy has been to replicate Hong Kong's living and business conditions using Taiwanese capital, thus closing the gap in economic conditions between the two sides of the Taiwan Straits. This, it is hoped, will allay Taiwanese fears that reunification with the mainland would stifle or harm Taiwan's economic well-being.

Competition for Taiwanese Investments

Taiwanese enthusiasm for doing business with the mainland has led to a tug of war between Taiwan and China for Taiwanese investment capital. Since the early 1990s, China and Taiwan have been vying for Taiwanese investments. After Deng's 1992 tour of southern coastal China (where the aging leader encouraged more rapid economic development) the average value of individual Taiwanese investments in China doubled from US$365,000 during the years

1990–92 to US$779,000 in 1993. In 1995, the average value of Taiwan-listed companies reached more than US$6.6 million.

According to ROC government statistics, Taiwan investment in China exceeded US$910 million during the first eight months of 1996, up 23% from the same period the previous year. The province of Jiangsu emerged as the front-runner in the race to attract Taiwanese capital in 1996; investments there totaled US$420 million, an increase of more than 60% from the same period in 1995. Guangdong ranked second among provinces by attracting US$190 million worth of Taiwanese investment capital, up 34.2%. The ROC government has warned that such large capital flows from Taiwan to China may weaken the island's economy. Particularly worrisome has been the flight to China of Taiwan's manufacturing and petrochemical industries. Formosa Plastics canceled a proposed US$5 billion petrochemical complex near Xiamen only after the Taiwanese government offered the company lucrative incentives to build domestically.

Mainland China is the most popular location for Taiwan's overseas manufacturing investments. According to ROC government statistics, Taiwan's manufacturing sector has invested a total of US$5.733 billion in China. By early 1996, one in three Taiwan-listed companies had significant manufacturing interests in China. According to Taiwan's Ministry of Economic Affairs, by September 1996 Taiwan's manufacturing sector had invested more than US$9 billion overseas, including US$5.73 billion, or 61.84%, in China. The outflow of capital from Taiwan to China has alarmed the ROC government because it represents a hollowing of Taiwan's domestic economy. Previously, Taiwanese manufacturers in China had to depend on raw materials, parts, and semi-finished products from Taiwan. In recent years, however, this dependence has decreased significantly. Investment in China by Taiwan's small and medium downstream manufacturers originally was intended to create a market for the large enterprises that supply them with industrial parts. Instead, Taiwanese parts manufacturers have followed the downstream manufacturers to the mainland, thereby decreasing Taiwan's exports of industrial parts.

To stem the outflow of Taiwanese capital, Taiwan's central bank in October 1996 eased lending for the fifth time that year by cutting bank reserve requirements. Unfortunately, this move failed to spur interest in domestic investment. Taiwanese firms continue to invest in China, and very few repatriate their earnings.

The massive transfusion of Taiwanese capital to China has further tied the Taiwanese economy to the mainland economy. Taiwan currently has a trade surplus with China. Although Taiwanese traders benefit financially from doing a brisk trade with China, Taiwan's trade surplus has made it economically dependent on China. Attesting to this, Taiwan's international trade surplus in 1995 totaled US$8.1 billion; discounting its trade surplus with China, however, Taiwan would have an overall trade deficit. In an effort to slow trade with China, Taiwan's President Lee in 1996 announced a "go slow" policy designed to encourage Taiwanese firms to be more prudent in their trade relations with China.

The growing interdependency of the two economies was evident during the 1996 "missile crisis" in the Taiwan Straits. In March 1996 China attempted to influence Taiwan's first direct presidential election by threatening to launch 20 to 30 short-range ballistic missiles within a few miles of Kaohsiung and Keelung, Taiwan's busiest ports. Although China launched only four missiles, the threat of a missile strike undermined investor confidence. Stocks plunged and billions of dollars left Taiwan following the March tests. Taiwanese investors, anxious to protect the billions of dollars they had invested in the mainland, urged the ROC government to resume talks with China, a move that alarmed government officials. The ROC government believed that Beijing was trying to win over Taiwanese entrepreneurs, hoping that investors would pressure the ROC government to broaden cross-straits economic relations despite the fact that political talks had not moved forward.

The 1996 missile crisis had only a temporary effect on Taiwanese investment in China. Cross-straits tensions eased following Taiwan's presidential elections, and Taiwanese investors returned to China. In July 1996, Taiwanese investment in China totaled a record US$230 million, a 99% increase from June. The average value of each project also increased, reaching US$6 million—the highest level since 1991. Immediately after his election in March 1996, President Lee offered to resume a dialogue with China (talks had broken off after Lee's 1995 visit to the United States). Despite Taiwanese conglomerates' huge capital-intensive and technology-intensive investment in China, the PRC refused to resume official talks with Taiwan. In the summer of 1996, the ROC government initiated efforts to discourage China-bound investments, its purpose being to pressure China into resuming political talks.

In early August 1996, President Lee warned Taiwanese entrepreneurs that increasing reliance on China, as well as creeping inflation and slowing growth on the mainland, posed a risk to investors. He ordered a review of the government's mainland investment policy, and urged local enterprises to focus on domestic projects. Attempting to stem the flow of large-scale investments to the mainland, Lee also proposed to cap Taiwanese investment in China to one-fifth of Taiwan's total overseas investment. Moreover, in a speech to KMT legislators on August 14, Lee proposed limiting a company's investment in China to 20% of its investment in Taiwan. The move revealed the consequences of Taiwan's economic interdependence with China. The day after Lee proposed these measures, the Taiwan stock market fell 1.4%. Lee's comments were intended to strengthen his position for future talks with the mainland government. Instead, the ROC government appeared impotent to persuade domestic firms to stay home.

Try as it may to control the pace and

scope of Taiwanese investment in China, the ROC government cannot control Taiwanese investors in the long run. Although President Lee may influence investors in the short term, his influence is blunted by investors' unquenchable pursuit of profits. Exhortations by the ROC government to avoid economic dependence on China have been ill-received by the Taiwanese business community. Small companies largely have ignored the ROC government's warnings not to invest in China, and have skirted laws by operating off the books. Rather than limit investments in the mainland, Taiwanese entrepreneurs are expanding operations there, and indirect, as well as unofficial direct, cross-straits trade is flourishing. For the Taiwanese, trade with and investment in China is not merely an opportunity, it is a necessity. Previously, Taiwan producers needed China's cheap labor as wage costs increased at home. Now, even capital-intensive industries recognize the need to exploit China's market.

Even large conglomerates that maintain friendly ties with President Lee have agreed to take his advice only in the short term. Immediately following Lee's August 14 remarks, Taiwanese petrochemical conglomerate Formosa Plastics Group announced that it would suspend a planned US$3 billion power plant project in China's Fujian province. The company expressed its desire to "comply with government policy" by suspending the deal, but curiously allowed a government agency to announce the decision on its behalf. If the plan had been executed, it would have been the largest Taiwanese project, and one of the largest foreign investments, in Chinese history. In September 1996, Taiwanese food giant President Enterprises Group bowed to government pressure and canceled plans to invest US$100 million in China. The company, Taiwan's leading investor in China, shelved its plans to build two power plants on the mainland after reports surfaced that President Lee was upset by a meeting between President Enterprises' vice-chairman Kao Chin-yen and PRC president Jiang Zemin earlier that month. Instead, the company

pledged to invest more than US$1.1 billion in domestic projects over two years. Furthermore, the company stated that it would spend the same amount to build two shopping malls and to enter medical manufacturing in Taiwan (the pharmaceutical project alone would cost US$33 million). Abandonment of such major projects by Formosa Plastics and President Enterprises temporarily cooled plans by other Taiwanese firms to invest in China.

Lee's primary concern that Taiwan's corporate chiefs effectively could become spokespersons for Beijing may be well founded. On a visit to Beijing in late August 1996, a Taiwanese trade delegation called for immediate talks between China and Taiwan for the purpose of improving economic relations. Meanwhile, Chang Yung-fa, chairman of EVA Airways and the Evergreen shipping conglomerate (the world's largest container fleet), criticized as out-of-date a government policy that forbids direct links with China. Chang, who is a good friend of President Lee, requested that ROC authorities allow direct transportation links with mainland China. Direct navigation, he argued, would be a big boon to Taiwanese shipping companies and manufacturers who had invested in the mainland. Many Taiwanese investors in China were compelled to transport goods from their mainland factories to Hong Kong, then ship them to Taiwan. Direct cross-straits transportation, Chang noted, would save these investors time and money, as well as promote closer commercial ties between Taiwan and China.

Lee need only look as far as Hong Kong to find an example of how economic exuberance by corporate chiefs has led to unfavorable political circumstances. Hong Kong entrepreneurs, eager to invest in China, have turned a blind eye to China's attempts to determine the political future of their city. In December 1996, the PRC government selected Tung Chee-hwa, a Hong Kong shipping magnate, to head Hong Kong's government after it reverts to China in July 1997. Tung has been amenable to China's plans for the future of Hong Kong, even defending China's plans to roll back existing civil rights laws.

The ROC government will need more than moral persuasion to encourage Taiwanese investors to resist the powerful lure of China's hot economy. While Taiwanese investors such as President Enterprises and Formosa Plastics are willing to abide by government policy in the short term, they are planning for the long term by continuing to expand their operations in China. In September 1996, President Enterprises announced that it would reapply for government approval to build power plants in China. Meanwhile, the company, which already has US$200 million invested in 15 mainland companies, has gone ahead with its existing mainland operations. Similarly, Formosa Plastics announced in September 1996 that it would resubmit plans to build a US$3 billion power plant in southern China. If the government refuses to approve the company's plans, Formosa Plastics could invest in China through its US subsidiaries.

By late August 1996 President Lee had back-peddled from his hard-line stance, stating that the government would not restrict corporate investments in China. In fact, the Ministry of Economic Affairs approved all 19 applications for US$95.9 million worth of investments in China. Around this time, China announced plans to permit direct shipping from Taiwan to the mainland ports of Fuzhou and Xiamen.

Unfortunately for the government of Taiwan, China appears to have the upper hand in encouraging Taiwanese entrepreneurs to shift allegiances from Taiwan to mainland China. While the ROC government and Taiwanese entrepreneurs debate over the correct mainland policy, China again is wooing Taiwanese investors by offering them treatment more generous than that offered to other foreign investors. The province of Fujian has created a special economic zone designed particularly for direct investment by Taiwanese firms. In early 1996, Tianjin, a coastal city in northern China, established an investment zone targeting Taiwan businesses.

President Lee's position was compromised further when PRC president Jiang Zemin proposed a measure allowing direct navigational and postal links between China and Taiwan for the first time in 46 years. To Lee's surprise, Jiang soon thereafter offered to resume political talks with Taiwan.

Conclusion

For China, economic interdependence with Taiwan has its advantages as well as disadvantages. Taiwanese capital helps to fuel China's economic steam engine and cushions economic downturns. In 1996, a slight economic slowdown would have been steeper without Taiwanese capital inflows. Taiwanese-invested projects have introduced much needed foreign technology and management expertise to China, and have increased China's foreign exchange through export earnings. Taiwanese capital also is funneled into capital construction projects necessary for China's modernization.

Conversely, economic interdependence has resulted in Chinese trade deficits with Taiwan; cross-straits trade and investment is asymmetrical, with Taiwan enjoying large trade surpluses with China. Until the ROC government relaxes restrictions on mainland trade and investment in Taiwan, China will continue to suffer trade deficits with its neighbor. Furthermore, if Taiwanese investors become discouraged by increasing crime, corruption, and intrusive government regulations in the SEZs and other foreign investment zones, they may move operations elsewhere, perhaps to Southeast Asia where land and labor is also plentiful and cheap. Any significant movement of Taiwanese investment from the mainland would affect China's economy adversely, particularly the SEZ economies.

Thus, economic interdependence presents opportunities and problems for both China and Taiwan. Cross-straits interdependence is likely to increase as China continues to seek sophisticated technology and management practices from Taiwan, and as Taiwan seeks regular access to the mainland market. Although political tensions at times may curb cross-straits economic activities, interdependence between China and Taiwan will continue well into the 21st century.

Further Reading

Cheng Tun-jen, Chi Huang, and Samuel S.G. Wu, *Inherited Rivalry: Conflict Across the Taiwan Straits,* Boulder, Colorado: Lynne Rienner, 1995

Discusses the effect of domestic politics on the China-Taiwan relationship, stressing the importance of external forces, especially the United States, in foreign policy alternatives. Includes chronicle of major events of cross-straits rivalry.

China Quarterly 136 (December 1993), special issue on Greater China

Introduction moderates the alarmist interpretations of Greater China. Eleven articles discuss the economic, political, and social interactions among China, Taiwan, Hong Kong, Macau, and Chinese overseas. Contributors tend to focus on political reform and economic integration within Greater China.

Howell, Jude, *China Opens Its Doors: The Politics of Economic Transition,* Boulder, Colorado: Lynne Rienner, and Hemel Hempstead: Harvester Wheatsheaf, 1993

Explains and documents the relationship between politics and economics of China's open door policy from 1978 to 1992, with particular emphasis on sociopolitical changes that it has engendered. Cross-straits trade and investment is illustrated in a case study of the Xiamen Special Economic Zone.

Leng Tse-kang, *The Taiwan-China Connection: Democracy and Development Across the Taiwan Straits,* Boulder, Colorado: Westview Press, 1996

Explores the transitional role of the state in Taiwan's economic development, focusing especially on the impact of trade with mainland China.

Noland, Marcus, *Pacific Basin Developing Countries: Prospects for the Future,* Washington, D.C.: Institute for International Economics, 1990

Examines economic and trade policies undertaken in the newly industrializing countries (NICs) of Hong Kong, Singapore, Taiwan, and Korea, as well as the less developed countries of Malaysia, Thailand, the Philippines, and Indonesia.

Shambaugh, David L., editor, *Greater China: The Next Superpower?* Oxford and New York: Oxford University Press, 1995

Clear and comprehensive analysis of the growing links between China, Hong Kong, Taiwan, Macau, and Chinese overseas in the areas of economics, culture, and politics.

Shirk, Susan L., and Christopher P. Twomey, editors, *Power and Prosperity: Economics and Security Linkages in Asia-Pacific,* New Brunswick, New Jersey: Transaction, 1996

Analyzes the effect of cross-straits trade and investment relations on the China-Taiwan political relationship. Includes some discussion of economic interdependence and the link between economics and security.

Wachman, Alan, *Taiwan: National Identity and Democratization,* Armonk, New York: M.E. Sharpe, 1994

Examines the history of democratization of Taiwan from the perspective of the national identity problem. Discusses effect of development of national identity on prospects for Taiwan independence and reunification with the Chinese mainland.

Wang, Nian-Tzu, editor, *Taiwan's Enterprises in Global Perspective,* Armonk, New York: M.E. Sharpe, 1992

Discusses Taiwan's economic performance in global comparison and Taiwan's economic relations with China through a series of enterprise field studies.

Elizabeth M. Freund is Assistant Professor of Political Science at Mary Washington College, Fredericksburg, Virginia. She is the author of "Downsizing China's State Industrial Enterprises" in *Adjusting to Capitalism: Chinese Workers and Their State,* edited by Mark Selden (1996). She has contributed articles on Chinese economic issues to the *American Asian Review, Asian Affairs,* and *The Employment Report of the Asian Law Journal,* among other periodicals. She formerly taught at Lingnan College in Hong Kong and at the University of Virginia.

Chapter Five

China in East Asia: Changing Relations with Japan and Korea

Quansheng Zhao

From the perspective of the People's Republic of China, the combined area of East and Southeast Asia remains one of the most important areas of consideration for Chinese foreign policy, not only in military and political terms but also in economic terms. Economic relations with this region have direct implications for China's modernization drive.

Data from Table 5.1 reveal that China's foreign trade with Asian countries in 1994 totaled more than China's foreign trade with all countries outside Asia combined. The rankings of China's trading partners (according to region) were as follows: Asia (US$142.2 billion), Europe (US$43.8 billion), North America (US$38.6 billion), Latin America (US$4.7 billion), Oceania (US$4.6 billion), and Africa (US$2.6 billion). Moreover, trade with East and Southeast Asia constituted 55% of China's total foreign trade in Asia; trade with "Greater China" (including Taiwan, Hong Kong, and Macau) also figured prominently. As other chapters in this section deal with China's relations with Southeast Asia, Taiwan, and Hong Kong, this chapter will focus on Northeast Asia, namely China's relations with Japan and Korea.

In addition to trade relations, security issues—and more specifically the arms race—within the Asia-Pacific region are of paramount concern to Beijing. According to a US Pentagon study released in early 1995, Asia will become the world's leading importer of arms by the end of the decade. Between 1994 and 2000, East Asia will

account for 30% of global demands for arms, while South Asia will account for 5%. The study estimates that the Asian market as a whole will be worth US$76–87 billion over the six-year period. Taiwan is expected to be Asia's leading buyer, followed by Japan and South Korea. In response, the United States has decided to maintain its troop strength in East Asia at approximately 100,000 men, rather than reduce its military presence as previously planned.

The first section of this chapter examines economic relations between China and Japan and assesses how security issues have affected these relations. The second section similarly examines China's relations with Korea.

China's Interdependence with Japan

Chinese foreign policy toward Japan has been influenced by Beijing's changing perception and interpretation of Japan. Throughout the Maoist years, Chinese policy toward Japan was determined largely by the Cold War, and by China's perception of Japan as a "running dog of American imperialism." However, diplomatic relations between the two countries have improved vastly since China first attempted to normalize relations with Japan in 1972. Today, Chinese authorities use very different phrases to describe Japan, including "good neighbor" and "good friend," despite sporadic problems between the two countries.

China's new perception of Japan is perhaps most evident in the economic realm. Since 1972 economic cooperation between the two countries has helped grow their economies and also has promoted stability in the Asia-Pacific area. Moreover, bilateral exchanges in trade, foreign investment, joint ventures, technology transfer, and personnel exchanges have ushered in a major new period of Asian history. In 1993, for example, Japan was China's foremost trading partner, far outdistancing the US in terms of total value. Japan has a large share of Chinese markets in virtually every field except aircraft technology, which is dominated by US companies. Table 5.2 indicates that China-Japan trade, particularly China's export to Japan, has increased steadily since 1989, and that China has enjoyed a favorable balance in its trade with Japan.

Furthermore, Japan has been a major source of capital, technology, and manufactured imports to China. Entering the 1990s, Japanese direct investment in China also has gained momentum both in terms of actual value and numbers of projects (see Table 5.3). In the first six months of the 1994 fiscal year, for example, Japan invested US$1.14 billion (a 63.5% increase from the same period the previous year), ranking China as the second largest destination for Japanese overseas direct investment (the US ranked first at US$6.6 billion).

Japanese official development assistance (ODA) to China, initiated in 1979, is another important facet of economic cooperation between the two countries. ODA includes government loans, grants, and technical aid. Despite China's late entry to Japan's list of aid recipients, Japanese aid to China grew substantially during the 1980s and well into the 1990s (see Table 5.4). Japan remains the largest ODA donor to China among members of the Development Assistance Committee (DAC), an international committee under the Organization of Economic and Cooperative Development (OECD) whose 21 members include all European donors, plus Japan, Australia, Canada, and the United States. In 1990 and again in 1991, Japan's shares of aid to China

totaled more than half of all ODA disbursed to China (see Table 5.5). Not surprisingly, China ranks among the top recipients of Japanese ODA.

As part of its ODA disbursements, the Japanese government has offered four major loan packages to China, known as "soft loans." Prime Minister Masayoshi Ohira pledged the first government-to-government loan of 350 billion *yen* (US$1.5 billion at the time) during his visit to China in December 1979. These monies were used to implement China's five-year plan for the years 1979–84. The second loan package of 470 billion *yen* (US$2.1 billion) was offered by Prime Minister Yasuhiro Nakasone in March 1984 for the five-year period 1985–90. During his visit to Beijing in August 1988, Prime Minister Noboru Takeshita promised a third package totaling 810 billion *yen* (US$5.4 billion) to be disbursed over the years 1990–95. The fourth Japanese aid package to China, agreed upon in December 1994, amounted to 580 billion *yen* (US$5.8 billion) for the three-year period 1996–98.

Obstacles to Sino-Japanese Economic Relations

Large-scale bilateral economic exchanges and government aid from Japan has fostered economic interdependence between the two countries. However, this interdependence has not precluded political and strategic tensions between Beijing and Tokyo. One such tension involves an ownership dispute over islands the Chinese call "Diaoyu" and the Japanese call "Senkaku," a cluster of unpopulated, rocky islands located between Taiwan and the Ryukyu Islands that are reported to lie in an area possessing significant oil deposits. This territorial dispute has lasted since 1972.

Another obstacle to the development of full bilateral relations is the issue of "Japanese militarism." Owing to the bitter memory of the Japanese invasion during World War II, China's misgivings about Japanese militarism are enduring. Yet Beijing has demonstrated a propensity either to play down or to emphasize those misgivings according to the dictates of its changing policy agenda.

During the 1960s and 1970s, Beijing's wariness of Japanese militarism was fueled primarily by international events. Following the 1969 Sato-Nixon joint communiqué, which stated that "the maintenance of peace and security in the Taiwan area was also a most important factor for the security of Japan," then-Premier Zhou Enlai accused Eisaku Sato's government of increased militarism and of pursing Japan's wartime goal of a Greater East Asia Co-Prosperity Sphere. During a visit to North Korea in the spring of 1970, Zhou argued vigorously that "Japanese militarism has revived and has become a dangerous force of aggression in Asia." However, Mao Zedong eventually came to view Japan and Western Europe as intermediate zones between the "revolutionary forces" of the Third World countries and the two "reactionary" superpowers (the US and the Soviet Union), and China sought to cultivate friendly relations with Japan and Western European countries.

Beijing's need of development assistance also prompted it to seek closer ties with Tokyo and to stop the Chinese media's criticism of Japanese militarism. Such criticism disappeared completely after Kakuei Tanaka became Japanese prime minister in 1972. At that time, China, believing that the transition from Sato to Tanaka presented it with the best opportunity to conduct direct relations with the Japanese government, launched a new campaign calling for "Sino-Japanese friendship" and "normalization of relations." By the late 1970s, China actively was seeking an international coalition to counter Soviet expansionism, and had not only ceased opposition to Japan's rearmament, but actually sought closer defense relations with Japan.

During the early 1980s, Beijing's misgivings were sustained by a rising nationalism in China, an ideological current strengthened by the drive toward modernization. In 1982, Japan's Ministry of Education was criticized sharply by Japan's Asian neighbors (including China, Thailand, Hong Kong, and North and South Korea) for revising the description of Japan's wartime behavior in school textbooks. The change in wording–that Japan had "entered" as opposed to "invaded" China and other parts of Asia–provoked protests throughout East and Southeast Asia. Beijing launched a full-scale campaign attacking Japanese militarism, and protests continued until Tokyo promised to review the disputed term prior to Prime Minister Zenko Suzuki's visit to Beijing to mark the tenth anniversary of normalized relations between China and Japan. Suzuki reportedly spent a considerable portion of his visit reassuring the Chinese leaders of Japan's position.

The "textbook controversy" resurfaced in 1985 and 1986, when Japan's Ministry of Education published new editions of textbooks describing Japan's actions in World War II. The problem was exacerbated by Prime Minister Nakasone's official visit to the Yaskuni Shrine to honor those killed in World War II. The shrine contains the remains not only of Japanese soldiers but also of a number of Japanese war criminals, including General Hideki Tojo, commander-in-chief of the Japanese army in China during the war. Following Nakasone's visit, China's news media launched a new wave of criticism against Japanese militarism, triggering student demonstrations in Beijing, Shanghai, and other major Chinese cities.

China's response to Japanese "militarism" is an example of how the international environment and domestic pressures have influenced China's foreign policy. In the early 1970s, China's primary purpose for criticizing Japan's "revived militarism" was to challenge Prime Minister Sato's conservative position toward China; Chinese leaders hoped that a pro-Beijing leader would replace Sato, thereby accelerating Sino-Japanese rapprochement. Before 1972 Beijing perceived Japan as an aggressor and also an important member of the Cold-War rivalry camp. Increasingly after 1972, however, China viewed Japan as a friendly country, and the issue of militarism in bilateral relations became much less important. In the

1980s, the issue of Japanese militarism spurred by the textbook controversy offered China's leaders the opportunity both to promote nationalism at home and to pressure Japan into making political and economic concessions. A slogan used by Chinese student demonstrators indirectly linked the militarism issue with the Sino-Japanese trade imbalance: "Down with the Japanese economic invasion."

More recently, the Chinese navy-sponsored magazine *Xiandai Jianchuan* (Modern Naval Vessels) published an article stating that Japan's navy was no longer exclusively defense-oriented and that Japan's capability of exerting military power should be monitored carefully. Citing the addition of Japanese armed forces to UN peacekeeping operations as well as Japan's dispatching of mine sweepers for operations in the Persian Gulf area, the article suggested that "Japan is probing world opinion regarding its embarkation on a new militaristic path" ("China Snipes at 'Offensive' Maritime SDF," in *The Japan Times* 13–19 June 1994).

During the APEC summit meeting held in Jakarta in November 1994, Chinese President Jiang Zemin held a 45-minute meeting with Japanese prime minister Tomiichi Murayama. Jiang issued a clear warning, stating that "militarism sometimes comes to the surface inside Japan." Jiang referred to the repeated gaffes made by Japanese ministers as they attempted to whitewash Japan's wartime history. At the same time, Japan had become increasingly wary of China's military development. In October 1994, Japanese Defense Agency chief Tokuichiro Tamazawa told US Defense Secretary William Perry that Japan is "anxious about [the increase in] the transparency" of China's defense budget. However, the fact that Japan is China's foremost trading partner and that China's markets will become increasingly important to Japan ensures that Sino-Japanese relations will remain close. It is widely recognized that the relationship between China and Japan comprises the most important bilateral relationship in East Asia.

China's Relations with the Two Koreas: A Balancing Act

Political, security, and economic interests all have played a major role in China's policy toward the Korean Peninsula. In the 1950s, the PRC, spurred by the perceived threat of Western invasion, provided substantial military support to North Korea during its war with the South. Since then, Beijing has made substantial adjustments to its Korea policy in response to changing international and domestic environments. Despite its stated alignment with Pyongyang, China long ago ceased to support a North Korean military attack against South Korea. Moreover, owing to its vested interest in the creation and maintenance of a stable situation in the Korean Peninsula, Beijing consistently has expressed its desire to avoid another major military conflict in the region. However, some scholars believe that, from a security standpoint, China does not support the reunification of Korea, preferring a divided Korea on which it can exert its military influence more readily.

Perhaps the nadir of relations between Beijing and Pyongyang took place in 1969 at the peak of China's Cultural Revolution, when Chinese and North Korean forces clashed along their border. Since the beginning of the 1980s, Beijing gradually has strengthened its ties with Seoul, while there were signs in the mid-1990s that Beijing's relationship with Pyongyang had cooled. In July 1995, for example, a North Korean official told a visiting American delegation that if the US wished to counterbalance China's growing power in the region it should reestablish diplomatic relations with North Korea. Moreover, according to an unpublished study by the American Enterprise Institute's Nicholas Eberstadt and three other scholars, China's food exports to North Korea dropped from US$149 million in 1993 to US$55 million in 1994, while its coal and oil exports fell from US$264 million to US$194 million.

Nevertheless, the PRC has managed to maintain a workable relationship with North Korea. High-level bilateral visits have taken place virtually every year since 1978. Furthermore, political developments in China and the disintegration of communist regimes in Eastern Europe during the late 1980s brought Beijing and Pyongyang closer together. North Korean leader Kim Il Sung openly supported Deng Xiaoping's military suppression of student demonstrations in 1989.

Partly owing to its lukewarm relations with China, Pyongyang was able to play its relationship to Beijing against its relationship to Moscow, effectively preventing China from moving closer to Seoul. However, when the Soviet Union established diplomatic relations with South Korea in 1990, the PRC answered by expanding its relations with South Korea. First, China and South Korea agreed to set up nongovernmental trade offices in Seoul and Beijing, respectively. Two years later in September 1992, China significantly altered its policy toward South Korea, agreeing to establish official diplomatic relations. Beijing's reasons for resuming normalized relations with Seoul included wanting to gain increased leverage with regard to the Korean conflict (and East Asia as a whole). As one US official suggests, "Having good relations with both [Koreas] puts China in the best possible situation" with regard to world politics and regional affairs.

Beijing also sought to normalize relations with Seoul in order to access South Korea's growing economy. Chinese leaders recognized that the PRC's modernization programs could not be realized without extensive external support from industrialized countries, including advanced technology, capital, markets, and managerial training. Establishing economic ties with South Korea served to diversify China's pool of resource suppliers.

South Korea has become an increasingly important trading partner for China. Table 5.6 indicates that Sino-South Korean trade had bypassed Sino-North Korean trade by the mid-1980s. In 1994 China's trade with South Korea reached US$11.6 billion, exceeding trade with North Korea many times over. As a newly industrialized country and a close neighbor, South Korea also has provided China with valuable economic development strategy, especially with regard to "export-led" industrialization.

In addition, South Korean businessmen have conducted direct investment and joint ventures in China (see Table 5.7). Owing to geographic proximity as well as social affinity, South Korea has concentrated its investment in the Bohai Sea area (Shandong, Tianjin, Beijing, and Hebei) and the northeast region (Liaoning, Jilin, and Heilongjiang); Shandong province has the highest concentration of South Korean investment (see Table 5.8).

In sum, economic cooperation between China and South Korea is likely to continue, despite their differing political systems and levels of economic development. During a state visit to South Korea in November 1995, President Jiang Zemin reemphasized the importance of China's ties with South Korea and projected expanded bilateral economic relations for the future. Moreover, in addition to recognizing their mutual economic interests, each side regards the other as a counterweight to the increasing economic and military strength of Japan. This was in evidence when China's Jiang Zemin and South Korea's Kim Young Sam jointly condemned Japan's history of militarism during Jiang's 1995 visit.

Beijing's Response to North Korea's Nuclear Development Program

In the spring of 1994, the International Atomic Energy Agency (IAEA) under the UN unearthed fresh evidence of North Korea's clandestine nuclear program. IAEA Director Hans Blix reported that a facility which Pyongyang had described as a radio-chemical laboratory was actually "the most proliferation-sensitive facility" of North Korea's seven nuclear installations. In response, the US and South Korea exerted pressure on Pyongyang to open its nuclear installations for international inspection, threatening economic sanctions if their demands were not met. Beijing's response was twofold. First, Chinese officials reached a consensus with the US, Japan, and Russia on prohibiting nuclear development in the Korean Peninsula. Second, at a meeting with South Korean President Kim Young Sam and Foreign Minister Han Sung Joo in Beijing, Chinese leaders clearly stated their opposition not only to economic sanctions but also to a UN Security Council resolution calling for inspection of North Korea's nuclear facilities. Instead, Beijing wished to exert its own influence on Pyongyang, and therefore demanded that the UN Security Council downgrade its call for inspection of North Korea's nuclear installations from a resolution to a nonbinding "statement" (a resolution would have required China to go on record with either a veto or an abstention; a statement, which requires no vote, allowed China to side with North Korea and also with South Korea and the international community). In this manner, China advanced its own security interests while also preserving favorable relations with important trade partners.

The death of Kim Il Sung in July 1994 did not alter China's policy toward the Korean Peninsula. During an official visit to Seoul in October-November 1994, Chinese premier Li Peng assured South Korean president Kim Young Sam that China supported the Geneva nuclear accord signed by North Korea and the US in September of that year. Meanwhile, President Jiang Zemin also expressed "strong support" for the accord to US president Bill Clinton at the APEC summit in Jakarta. However, Beijing indicated that it also supported replacing the Panmunjom armistice with a permanent treaty, a position shared by Pyongyang (but not Seoul). These actions further demonstrated China's strategy to maintain favorable relations with both North Korea and South Korea.

Conclusion

East Asia remains a pivotal region for China's external relations. The dynamics of the political economy among China, Japan, and the two Koreas has far-reaching political and strategic implications. It is believed that China's relations with Japan and the two Koreas will assume increasing importance in Asia as both US presence and Soviet ambitions in the region fade in the post-Cold War era. As long as China pursues its goal of economic modernization, the trend toward economic interdependence in the East Asian region will continue to play a significant role in China's external relations both economically and politically.

Further Reading

Cotterell, Arthur, *East Asia: From Chinese Predominance to the Rise of the Pacific Rim,* London: John Murray, and New York: Oxford University Press, 1993

Examines the dramatic transformation around the Pacific Rim, providing a historical context that extends from the dawn of Chinese civilization to Japan's emergence as the first East Asian nation to develop an industrial economy.

Howe, Christopher, editor, *China and Japan: History, Trends, and Prospects,* Oxford: Clarendon Press, and New York: Oxford University Press, 1996

Fifty years after the end of their conflict in the Pacific War, China and Japan are emerging as two of the key countries in the post-Cold War era. This multi-disciplinary study represents an ambitious attempt to summarize the relationship between them in terms of its historical background, modern development, contemporary trends, and meaning for the rest of the world.

Kim, Samuel S., editor, *China and the World: Chinese Foreign Relations in the Post-Cold War Era,* 3rd edition, Boulder, Colorado: Westview Press, 1994

In this informative volume, Chinese foreign policy is analyzed in two ways: in terms of bilateral relations and of thematic topics. The book examines China's most important bilateral relations with the United States, Japan, Russia, and the third world. It also studies key issues in Chinese foreign relations, such as the use of the military, economic interdependency, human rights, and international organizations.

Lardy, Nicholas R., *China in the World Economy,* Washington, D.C.: Institute for International Economics, 1994

Examines the implications of China's emergence as a major player in the world economy and analyzes China's integration into the international economic order and the problems posed for the rest of the world.

Lee, Chae-Jin, *China and Japan: New Economic Diplomacy,* Stanford, California: Hoover Institute Press, 1984

This original in-depth analysis concentrates on salient cases of Sino-Japanese economic interaction: a multibillion-dollar steel complex at Baoshan, the joint offshore oil development in the Bohai Sea, and Japanese loans provided to fund China's important construction projects.

Lee, Chae-Jin, *China and Korea: Dynamic Relations,* Stanford, California: Hoover Institute Press, 1996

The first volume in English to analyze comprehensively China's policy toward Korea from the Korean War to the present day. Timely and thought provoking, this book illuminates China's shift from ideological and revolutionary exhortation to diplomatic and economic cooperation.

Taylor, Robert, *Greater China and Japan: Prospect for an Economic Partnership in East Asia,* London and New York: Routledge, 1996

Explores the ambiguous economic and political relationship between Greater China and Japan. It analyzes the mutual suspicions: the Chinese fear of a Japanese military revival and the Japanese concern over Chinese territorial ambitions.

Whiting, Allen Suess, *China Eyes Japan,* Berkeley: University of California Press, 1989

Provides a comprehensive examination of the perceptions of China and Chinese foreign policy toward Japan. Examines key issues of these bilateral relations, including the textbook controversy, the anti-Japanese student demonstrations, and economic cooperation.

Zhao, Quansheng, *Japanese Policymaking, the Politics Behind Politics: Informal Mechanisms and the Making of China Policy,* New York: Praeger, 1993; Hong Kong and New York: Oxford University Press, 1993

This study probes the politics behind the formal screen of Japanese diplomacy. The book offers new insights into Sino-Japanese relations and draws broader lessons for Japan's international relations through four case studies of Japanese policies toward China. These include the watershed 1972 Sino-Japanese rapprochement and Japan's foreign aid policy toward China before and after the Tiananmen tragedy of 1989.

Zhao, Quansheng, *Interpreting Chinese Foreign Policy: The Micro-Macro Linkage Approach,* New York and Hong Kong: Oxford University Press, 1996

This book uses the "micro-macro linkage" model to interpret China's past and present policies toward Taiwan, the United States, the former Soviet Union, Japan, the Korean Peninsula, and Southeast Asia. It provides a comprehensive, enduring, and useful framework for understanding Chinese policy decisions and behavior patterns.

Quansheng Zhao is Associate Professor and Asia Coordinator at the School of International Service of the American University, Washington, D.C.; he is also Associate-in-Research at the Fairbank Center for East Asian Research at Harvard University. He is the author of *Japanese Policymaking, the Politics Behind Politics: Informal Mechanisms and the Making of China Policy* (1993) and *Interpreting Chinese Foreign Policy: The Micro-Macro Linkage Approach* (1996). He is also coeditor, with Robert Sutter, of *Politics of Divided Nations: China, Korea, Germany, and Vietnam* (1991). The author would like to thank Ying Guo and Brian Klein for research assistance in the preparation of this chapter.

Table 5.1: China's Major Trading Partners (1994)

(US$ million)

Region and Selected Countries	Export	Import	Total Value
Asia	73446.70	68765.15	142211.85
Japan	21573.12	26320.77	49893.89
Within Greater China	35273.16	23673.45	58946.67
Hong Kong	32364.51	9456.62	41821.16
Macau	666.50	132.00	798.50
Taiwan	2242.15	14084.83	16326.98
North Korea	424.52	199.22	623.74
South Korea	4402.30	7318.34	11720.65
ASEAN	6379.01	6829.85	13208.85
Brunei	16.26	0	16.26
Indonesia	1051.70	1588.37	2640.07
Malaysia	1117.66	1622.67	2740.32
Philippines	475.69	272.40	748.09
Singapore	2558.42	2482.02	5040.44
Thailand	1159.28	864.39	2023.67
Burma	369.11	143.28	512.39
Cambodia	35.27	1.00	36.27
Laos	35.97	4.38	40.35
Vietnam	341.66	149.19	490.85
Africa	1749.05	893.98	2643.03
Europe	18803.98	25040.20	43844.19
EEC	14580.23	16938.76	31518.99
United Kingdom	2414.00	1769.90	4183.91
Germany	4761.45	7136.73	11898.23
France	1424.36	1939.01	3363.37
Italy	1590.66	3068.06	4658.72
Former USSR	1946.55	4662.58	6609.13
Russia	1581.14	3495.75	5076.89
Latin America	2454.75	2247.38	4702.13
North America	22860.16	15801.30	38661.46
Canada	1396.94	1830.75	3227.69
USA	21461.48	13970.42	35431.90
Oceania	1723.84	2915.61	4639.45
Australia	1487.87	2451.81	3939.68

Source: *China's Latest Economic Statistics* (February 1995): 19–23

Table 5.2: China's Trade with Japan (1989–95)

(US$ million)

	1989	1990	1991	1992	1993	1994	1995
IMPORTS	8,477	6,145	8,605	11,967	17,353	18,687	21,934
% of Total	10.3%	6.8%	8.1%	10.2%	12.7%	11.8%	11.3%
Exports	11,083	12,057	14,248	16,972	20,651	27,569	35,922
% of Total	17.1%	17.7%	19.1%	22.3%	24.7%	28.1%	29.0%
Balance	(2,606)	(5,912)	(5,643)	(5,005)	(3,298)	(8,882)	(13,988)

Data compiled from: International Monetary Fund, *Direction of Trade Statistics Yearbook,* 1996

Table 5.3: Japanese Investment and Number of Projects in China (1986–95)

Year	Value of Japanese Actual Investment (US$ million)	Number of Projects
1986	201	94
1987	220	113
1988	515	237
1989	356	294
1990	503	341
1991	533	599
1992	710	1805
1993	1324	3488
1994	2075	3018
1995	3108	2935

Source: Eric Harwitt, "Japanese Investment in China: Strategies in the Electronics and Automobile Sectors," *Asian Survey* 36, no. 10 (October 1996): 982

Table 5.4: Japan's ODA Disbursements to China

(US$ million)

Year	Grant Aid	Technical Assistance	Loan Aid	Total
1979	0.0	2.6	0.0	2.6
1980	0.0	3.4	0.9	4.3
1981	2.5	9.6	15.6	27.7
1982	25.1	13.5	330.2	368.8
1983	30.6	20.5	299.1	350.2
1984	14.3	27.2	347.9	389.4
1985	11.6	31.1	345.2	387.9
1986	25.7	61.2	410.1	497.0
1987	54.3	76.0	422.8	553.1
1988	52.0	102.7	519.0	673.7
1989	58.0	106.1	668.1	832.2
1990	37.8	163.5	521.7	723.0
1991	56.6	137.5	391.2	585.3
1992	72.1	187.3	791.2	1,050.6

Source: Gaimusho, *Japan's Official Development Assistance*, various volumes

Table 5.5: DAC Countries' Shares of Total ODA Disbursed to China

(US$ million)

Year	Top Donor	Second Donor	Third Donor	Other Donors	Total Bilateral	Total Multilateral
1990	Japan 723.02 (51.1%)	Germany 228.94 (16.2%)	Austria 102.84 (7.3%)	361.57 (25.5%)	1,416.37 (100%)	659.80
1991	Japan 585.30 (50.1%)	France 138.46 (11.9%)	Germany 107.09 (9.2%)	337.04 (28.8%)	1,167.89 (100%)	782.95

Source: Gaimusho, *Japan's Official Development Assistance*, various volumes

Table 5.6: China's Trade with South Korea and North Korea (1980–94)

(US$ million)

Year	South Korea	North Korea
1980	188	677.5
1981	280	531.0
1982	139	585.4
1983	120	527.7
1984	434	498.2
1985	1161	488.3
1986	1289	509.8
1987	1679	513.3
1988	3087	579.0
1989	3143	562.7
1990	3821	482.7
1991	5812	610.4
1992	8218	696.5
1993	9078	890.0
1994	11660	623.7

Source: Chae-Jin Lee, *China and Korea: Dynamic Relations*, Stanford, California: Hoover Institution, 1996: 140, 146

Table 5.7: South Korean Investment in China (1988–93)

Item/Year	1988–89	1990	1991	1992	1993	Total
Number of cases approved	11	35	107	260	630	1,043
Amounts approved (US$ million)	13.8	50.0	121.9	220.9	570.3	976.9
Actual Investment (US$ million)	12.8	48.3	91.0	168.6	153.9	474.6

Source: Chae-Jin Lee, *China and Korea: Dynamic Relations*, Stanford, California: Hoover Institution, 1996: 140, 146

Table 5.8: Geographic Distribution of South Korean Investment in China (By the end of 1993)

	Number of cases approved	Percentage	Total amount (in thousands of dollars)	Percentage
Bohai Sea Area				
Shandong	293	28.1	374,331	38.3
Tianjin	109	10.5	131,053	13.4
Beijing	69	6.6	62,362	6.4
Hebei	27	2.6	23,553	2.4
Subtotal	498	47.7	591,299	60.5
Northeast region				
Liaoning	221	21.2	125,155	12.8
Jilin	99	9.5	46,186	4.7
Heilongjiang	79	7.6	76,990	7.9
Subtotal	399	38.3	248,241	25.4
Central China				
Jiangsu	44	4.2	45,897	4.7
Shanghai	19	1.8	18,612	1.9
Zhejiang	11	1.1	6,676	0.7
Subtotal	74	7.1	71,186	7.3
South China				
Guangdong	40	3.8	42,609	4.4
Fujian	10	1.0	16,195	1.7
Hainan	2	0.2	800	-
Subtotal	52	5.0	59,604	6.1
Other regions	20	1.9	6,594	0.7
TOTAL	1,043	100.0	976,923	100.0

Source: Chae-Jin Lee, *China and Korea: Dynamic Relations*, Stanford, California: Hoover Institution, 1996

Chapter Six

China and Southeast Asia in the 1990s: Prospects for Economic Cooperation

Guangzhi Zhao

Introduction

During the 1980s and early 1990s, China and most of the Southeast Asian countries experienced impressive and steady economic growth. As shown in Table 6.1, Gross Domestic Product (GDP) growth in China and the ASEAN (Association of Southeast Asian Nations) countries has far outpaced GDP growth in the United States and West Europe. In contrast to the sluggish economic growth in the industrialized economies, the average GDP growth between 1980 and 1994 was 11.6% in China and 6.0% in the major ASEAN countries (Indonesia, Malaysia, the Philippines, Singapore, and Thailand). More importantly, rapid economic growth is projected to continue in the region. If current trends continue, the world's four largest economies in the year 2010 will be similar in size: Japan, China, the European Union (EU), and the United States. The ASEAN countries will comprise the fifth largest economy.

In addition to strong GDP growth rates, both China and the major ASEAN countries have experienced rapid economic growth as a result of increased participation in international trade. This trend has included the significant development in recent years of trade among Asian countries. The share of exports shipped within Asia has increased by over 10% in the past eight years. This increase suggests that a new era of economic cooperation in Asia is taking shape, an era in which countries like China and the major ASEAN members play an increasingly important role.

Security issues, however, may determine how fully China and Southeast Asia will pursue common economic interests. The peaceful environment currently enjoyed by all countries in the region belies the fact that the power structure in Asia has changed dramatically since the ending of the Cold War. During the Cold War, China sided with the US, albeit marginally, to guard against the expansionist aspirations of the Soviet Union. However, the end of the Cold War, the peacefully negotiated settlement of the Cambodia problem, the collapse of the former Soviet Union, and the retreat of the United States' military presence have created a vast power vacuum in the region. These circumstances have fueled speculation that China will assume an increasingly powerful role in the region.

Another factor that may hinder further efforts at economic cooperation is an historical mistrust that still exists between China and the Southeast Asian countries. This mistrust derives not only from ideological differences, but from dissension over policies relating to the ethnic Chinese in Southeast

Asia and the territorial dispute over the Sprately Islands in the South China Sea (China, Vietnam, the Philippines and Malaysia all claim ownership of the islands). The strategic and economic values of the Sprately Islands and the surrounding areas have compounded this dispute.

In sum, economic dynamism, its changing power structure, and the historical mistrust between these countries have prompted observers and scholars to raise the following questions: which economic path will a strong and prosperous China take? Will China be more assertive in regional affairs and assume a leadership role in the region? Or will China pose a direct threat to its neighbors? In an attempt to answer these questions, this chapter examines the historical development of China's and Southeast Asia's economic relationship, current trends in regional relations, and the factors that will influence the future development of these relations.

Historical Transformation of the Relations Between China and the Southeast Asian Countries

The relationship between the PRC and its neighbors to the southeast may be broken down into three major periods. The initial period was characterized by "comrade-to-comrade" relations, wherein leaders emphasized shared ideology among countries in the region. This brand of foreign relations was later transformed into "people-to-people" relations. Finally, China and Southeast Asian countries developed mature "state-to-state" relations based upon the principle of state sovereignty.

The period during which regional relations were based on shared ideological identity spanned the years 1949–71. During this period, political diversity in the Southeast Asian region prevented China from adopting a single Chinese policy toward all countries in the region. Instead, China adopted three major policies toward different countries in the region, each designed to serve China's national interests. Most importantly, China formed political alliances with

communist countries and gave political, organizational, and military support to indigenous communist movements in the region. For example, China offered political, economic, and military support to North Vietnam and assisted communist parties in Indonesia, Thailand, and Malaysia. In so doing, China sought to project its influence in the Asian region and in the international communist movement.

China's second major policy was reflected in its attempts to neutralize all pro-socialist or newly independent nationalist governments in the region. For example, during his visit to India and Burma in June 1954, Chinese premier Zhou Enlai proposed the adoption of the Five Principles of Peaceful Coexistence. The five principles included respect for sovereignty and territorial integrity, a commitment to nonaggression, non-interference in domestic affairs, mutual benefits, and peaceful coexistence. Through this policy China sought to develop cordial relations with countries of different ideologies, thus breaking its own diplomatic isolation in the international community. This proved to be a highly unstable policy. As China's domestic politics became more ideology-oriented in the mid-1960s, China often reverted to assisting indigenous communist movements or rebellions in Southeast Asian countries.

China's third distinctive policy toward Southeast Asia was a hostile policy toward those countries aligned with the United States. China adopted this policy toward Thailand and the Philippines, the two members of the Southeast Asian Treaty Organization (SEATO).

During this period of comrade-to-comrade relations between China and the Southeast Asian countries, economic activities were based on political needs. Economic transactions, therefore, often took the form of economic aid. Table 6.2 reveals the number of commercial agreements signed by the governments of China and the Southeast Asian countries between 1952 and 1979. It clearly displays the relationship between each country's ideological orientation and the volume of its economic activities with China.

The second phase (1972–80) of relations between the PRC and the Southeast Asian countries comprised a transitional period wherein ideological influences in Chinese foreign policy dwindled and a foreign policy based on state sovereignty began to emerge. During this period, improved relations between China and the Western powers (US president Richard Nixon made his historic visit to China in 1972) afforded China the opportunity to reconcile its relations with the countries of Southeast Asia. Not surprisingly, economic interaction became an important medium through which to initiate friendlier political relations. For example, in 1971 Malaysia sent its first delegation to China to attend the Spring Export Commodities Fair in Guangzhou. The Philippine government also used foreign trade contacts to explore the possibilities of further political dialogue with China. As shown in Table 6.2, China and the Southeast Asian countries during this period forged an increasing number of governmental commercial agreements. China established diplomatic relations with Malaysia in 1974, with the Philippines in 1975, and with Thailand in 1975.

China began to pursue state-to-state relations with Southeast Asia starting in the 1980s. This period coincided with China's own modernization drive. Not surprisingly, China's foreign policy became more pragmatic in serving the needs of its modernization. China ceased assisting the indigenous communist movements both inside and outside Southeast Asia. Moreover, the Vietnamese invasion of Cambodia spurred other Southeast Asian countries—especially Thailand—to form a de facto alliance with China against Vietnam. The last major stumbling block to ensuring a peaceful environment in Southeast Asia was removed when the conflict in Cambodia ended and Vietnam reconciled with China and the ASEAN countries. China and Indonesia normalized diplomatic relations in the early 1990s.

This confluence of events created an environment conducive to cultivating new possibilities in economic cooperation. Owing to a relaxed external political environment and a shared goal of economic development, economic relations between China and its Southeast Asian neighbors have experienced unprecedented development.

The Nature of the Economic Relationship Between China and the Southeast Asian Countries

The last two decades have been important years for the development of economic relations between China and the countries of Southeast Asia. As noted earlier, China and the ASEAN countries are among the fastest growing economies in the world. Their economic growth largely depends upon their external-oriented economic activities. In other words, foreign trade has become of utmost importance to their economic success.

Since the 1980s, trade between China and the Southeast Asian countries has grown impressively and steadily. In 1995, the amount of China's exports to the ASEAN countries reached US$9 billion, an increase of thirteenfold over 1977. Meanwhile, exports from the ASEAN countries to China jumped from US$370 million in 1977 to US$8.5 billion in 1995, or 21 times the 1977 figure. Tables 6.3 and 6.4 clearly reveal the rapid growth trend in trade.

The development of economic relations indicated by the rapid growth in trade suggests that economic cooperation has benefited all countries in the region. From China's perspective, the ASEAN market is extremely important. As shown in Table 6.3, exports to the ASEAN countries consistently have accounted for 5% or more of total exports since the early 1980s. While exports to each of five major ASEAN countries may not constitute a large share in China's total exports, combined they ranked fourth in China's total exports in 1995. Meanwhile, although the ASEAN countries were initially more important to China as an export market than as a source of imports, this situation has begun to change in recent years. During the early 1980s, imports from the ASEAN countries accounted for only 2.5% of China's total imports. Since the mid-1980s, however, imports from these countries have increased steadily, reaching 6.4% of China's total imports in 1995. Among the ASEAN countries, Singapore is China's largest trading partner. Traditionally, Singapore composed the bulk of China-ASEAN trade, as shown in Table 6.3. For example, in 1986 Singapore had 57.1% of the total trading amount of the ASEAN countries with China. In 1995, this figure decreased to 35.8%, whereas trade with other ASEAN countries had risen rapidly; that is, trade with Thailand, Malaysia, Indonesia accounted for 19.4%, 18.6%, and 18.9%, respectively, of total trade between China and the ASEAN countries.

Also important to China is the fact that the ASEAN countries remain profitable markets for Chinese products. Although in recent years ASEAN countries have increased significantly their export to China (see Table 6.4), the overall balance of trade remained in China's favor. Southeast Asia has been an important outlet for China's products, ranging from food stuff to machinery tools, and thus an important source for China's foreign exchange.

From the perspective of Southeast Asia, a market-oriented and prosperous China offers clear economic opportunities to the developing economies of the region. Since 1980, China's economic modernization drive toward an increasingly market-oriented economy has allayed fears in the region over China's motivations, and economic relations with China have developed as a result. Additionally, market-oriented reform in China has made China's economic system more compatible with the economic systems of the ASEAN countries and has opened the door for ASEAN countries to access China's immense market of 1.2 billion consumers.

For both China and the ASEAN countries, improved economic relations have served to diversify each country's pool of trading partners. As mentioned earlier,

ASEAN countries' economic success has relied heavily upon an export-oriented economic system. However, their export markets have over-concentrated on the developed countries, especially the United States and Japan. This overdependence has made their economies vulnerable to any disruptions of these markets. For this reason, ASEAN countries have shown great interest in exploring the Chinese market as an alternative.

China and Southeast Asia have worked jointly in other areas as well. An important example is the proposed development of the Upper Mekong Corridor. The upper Mekong flows through Yunnan province in China, Burma, Laos, and Thailand. In recent years, state officials from the participating countries have expressed interest in developing this region cooperatively. These officials share a common belief that poor infrastructure among the countries of the region comprises a major obstacle to economic development. The cooperative development of transportation and communication infrastructure appears to be a top priority.

Other joint infrastructure projects have been proposed. For instance, China, Thailand, Burma, and Laos have agreed to build a circular road linking Jinhong in southern Yunnan with Chiang Rai in northern Thailand. This circular road will pass through Kengtun in northeast Burma and Luang Namtha in the north of Laos. Making the upper Lancang-Mekong River navigable has also been proposed. Markedly different from the lower Mekong River, the upper Lancang-Mekong River flows through deep river valleys and contains submerged rocks and reefs which make water transportation dangerous, especially during the dry season. Nevertheless, the river provides a possible linkage among the countries in the region and would provide a cheaper transportation alternative once it is navigable. Joint explorations and surveys have been made by the countries in the region to make navigation on the river possible.

China and the countries of Southeast Asia also have expressed interest in cooperatively developing power generation projects in the region. Many sites along the Lancang-Mekong River, selected by the Mekong Committee, are ideal for building dams and hydropower stations, and proposals to develop in this region have gained momentum. The Manwan Hydroelectric Station in Yunnan is the first completed major dam on the upper Mekong River, while a new dam, the Dachaoshan Dam, is under construction. Others, such as the Xiaowan Dam, the Jinghong Dam, and the Nuzhadu Dam in Yunnan, are under consideration. Thailand is particularly interested in participating in these projects in hopes to import power from Yunnan to meet the electricity demand in northern Thailand.

Despite the complementary nature of the economic relationships between China and Southeast Asia, these countries compete with each other, thus complicating relations. First, political restraints still exist between China and Southeast Asian countries. Despite its efforts at economic decentralization, China remains a communist country, and the ideological differences between China and most of Southeast Asia still exist (nor has the historical mistrust fully disappeared). Many of the Southeast Asian countries are concerned that an economically powerful China will engage in a new round of ideological crusades in Southeast Asia. This concern looms in the economic relationship between China and Southeast Asia.

Second, most of the countries in the region are facing similar problems and have similar needs, owing to their status as developing economies. Because they compete with each other in increasing trade to the world market and in attracting foreign investment, economic relations are sometimes strained.

As an economy develops, it will increase its share of value-added manufactured goods to the world markets. As shown in Table 6.5, the same trend of development in exports exists in China and the major economies in Southeast Asia. The share of manufactured goods has increased significantly between 1980 and 1993. As mentioned pre-

viously, the Western, developed economies traditionally have comprised the export markets for China and the Southeast Asian countries. This highly dependent concentration in export markets might easily lead to competition and rivalry. Table 6.6 shows the composition of manufacture exports to the Organization of Economic and Cooperative Development (OECD) countries in 1993. The patterns of exports are similar between China and Southeast Asia. This situation may not necessarily lead to absolute confrontation; on the contrary, if handled properly, the competition can be viewed as a benign race instead of a war. Nevertheless, these circumstances reveal the competitive side of the economic relationship between China and the Southeast Asian countries.

Third, the chronic trade imbalance in favor of China presents new problems in the economic relationship between China and Southeast Asia. As shown in Tables 6.3 and 6.4, China has enjoyed a high volume of trade surplus from which it has benefited. However, if the trade imbalance is allowed to continue, further economic interactions between China and Southeast Asia will be hindered as a result. Fortunately, recent evidence suggests that the trade imbalance is starting to reverse.

Prospects for Economic Cooperation

As the Chinese and the Southeast Asian economies boom, the need to strengthen economic ties will likewise grow. However, the future development of relations between China and Southeast Asia will be influenced, to a certain extent, by a variety of factors.

The outcome of China's economic reform is perhaps the most important factor. At the core of China's economic reform is the policy of international openness and economic marketization. This policy is also the basis of economic relations between China and Southeast Asia. Any reversal of China's economic reform path undoubtedly will shake the foundation of these relations. While the positive economic results of market reforms have provided political legitimacy for the communist regime, thus making a reversal of reform unlikely, the possibility exists that the current regime will do whatever it can, including re-centralizing China's economy, to hold on to its power. This possibility has increased as China enters an era of political transition from the old revolutionary guards to the new generation of technocrats.

Meanwhile, the success of China's economic reform will not guarantee the elimination of competition in its current economic relations with Southeast Asia. Many of the current problems may be intensified as a result of the success of China's economic reform, largely owing to the fact that the competitive nature of economic relations with neighboring countries derives from China's economic strength. The success of China's economic reform will strengthen China's economic status and make China more assertive in its economic transactions with other countries, including its Southeast Asian neighbors.

Another phenomenon associated with China's growing economic strength is the emergence of Chinese nationalism and Han chauvinism, reflected in a recently published book, *China Can Say No,* written by several young scholars in China. Although the book targets the relationship between China and the United States, the countries of Southeast Asia were nonetheless sensitive to its nationalistic rhetoric given the geographical proximity of Southeast Asia to China and the presence of a large number of overseas Chinese and people of Chinese origins within Southeast Asia. These countries may choose to slow down or even terminate economic interactions with China in order to prevent the influence and penetration of rising Chinese nationalism. By no means, however, does this imply that further cooperation between China and the Southeast Asian countries is exhausted.

Second, contending territorial claims, especially claims over the Sprately Islands and Paracels Islands in the South China Sea, may jeopardize the economic relationship between China and the Southeast Asian countries. Although these islands are mainly uninhabitable and many of them submerge during part of the year, they are strategically important to the claiming countries. First, the islands are located in the sea lanes from the North Pacific to the South Pacific, and from the Pacific to the Indian Ocean. Second, in the recent years oil and natural gas deposits were found on the continental shelves around these islands. These resources are widely considered an important economic asset to the claiming countries.

Vietnam, Malaysia, and the Philippines make claim to part of the Sprately and/or Paracels Islands, while China claims full sovereignty over the whole region. In early 1992, China's National People's Congress promulgated a Law of the People's Republic of China on Territorial and Adjoining Waters, which clearly and explicitly set the range of China's territorial water, reasserting its claim to the disputed islands in the South China Sea. The law also suggested that military forces would be used if necessary to protect China's territorial integrity. Later that year, both China and Vietnam invited foreign oil companies to explore for oil in the Sprately Islands. Both governments promised to protect the interests of these foreign companies (with naval forces, if necessary). In 1995, China had a direct confrontation with the Philippines over reefs claimed by both countries.

At the moment, no direct or imminent crisis looms. On various occasions, China has made conciliatory gestures, expressing its willingness to participate in talks on security in the South China Sea and to solve the problem through consultation with the countries involved. In July 1995, for example, China agreed for the first time to multilateral discussion on the South China Sea disputes. China also agreed that the 1982 Law of the Sea could form the basis for these discussions. These "concessions" are considered to be positive signs in the efforts to seek a peaceful solution to the dispute.

Third, policies toward ethnic Chinese in the Southeast Asian countries will have a strong impact on the economic relations between China and the Southeast Asian countries. For China, the links between China and ethnic Chinese are assumed to be essential and hence affect external relations between China and Southeast Asian countries. A major component of China's relationship with overseas Chinese is economic: overseas Chinese are an important source of investment for China. Not surprisingly, Southeast Asian countries are wary of China's vigorous efforts to attract investment from ethnic Chinese in Southeast Asia.

For the indigenous countries of Southeast Asia, how to deal with ethnic Chinese is one of the major concerns in developing relations with China. On the one hand, many Southeast Asian countries doubt the loyalty of ethnic Chinese to Southeast Asian governments. On the other hand, ethnic Chinese dominate the capitalist sector of most Southeast Asian countries, and thus contribute to local economic development. Although Thailand and the Philippines have successfully implemented policies for the integration of citizens of Chinese origin, the presence of ethnic Chinese in Southeast Asia will continue to be a factor influencing the political and economic relationship between China and Southeast Asian countries.

In general, the prospects for economic cooperation between China and the Southeast Asian countries are promising. A relatively stable environment of economic relations will likely be sustainable. So long as China moves along the path of non-ideological development and contributes to the peace and security of the Asia-Pacific region, the further development of economic relations between China and Southeast Asia will benefit the entire region.

Further Reading

Chia, Siow Yue, and Bifan Cheng, editors, *ASEAN-China Economic Relations: Trends and Patterns,* Singapore: Institute of World Economics and Politics, 1987

This volume offers an in-depth analysis of the economic relations between China and the ASEAN countries, including detailed descriptions of the bilateral relations between China and the countries in Southeast Asia.

Denoon, David B.H., and Wendy Frieman, "China's Security Strategy: The View from Beijing, ASEAN and Washington," in *Asian Survey* 36, no. 4 (April 1996)

Examining China's security strategy from the perspectives of China, ASEAN and the United States, the authors take a pessimistic view on the future relations between China and the countries in Southeast Asia, predicting that Chinese leaders will become more assertive, more nationalistic, and less conciliatory.

Ellings, Richard J., and Sheldon W. Simon, editors, *Southeast Asian Security in the New Millennium,* Armonk, New York, and London: M.E. Sharpe, 1996

A collection of essays treating security issues in Southeast Asia. The projection of China's role in this region is optimistic. As one of the authors argues, China will not constitute a direct military threat to the security of the region but will engage in more positive political and economic involvement.

Grant, Richard L., editor, *China and Southeast Asia: Into the Twenty-first Century,* Honolulu: Pacific Forum/CSIS, and Washington, D.C.: Center for Strategic and International Studies, 1993

This collection of essays examines China's relations with the countries in Southeast Asia from two perspectives—the economy and security. The authors explore how a strong and prosperous China will interact with the smaller Southeast Asian countries.

Gurtov, Melvin, *China and Southeast Asia, the Politics of Survival: A Study of Foreign Policy Interaction,* Baltimore: Johns Hopkins University Press, 1975

A classic work analyzing the interactions between the People's Republic of China and the Southeast Asian countries between 1949 and 1973. The book includes a series of detailed case studies, followed by some general conclusions.

Suryadinata, Leo, editor, *Southeast Asian Chinese and China: The Politico-Economic Dimension,* Singapore: Times Academic Press, 1995

The authors examine the role ethnic Chinese play in the economic systems in Southeast Asia, offering a historical perspective as well as a context for understanding China's current drive toward economic modernization and its impact on Southeast Asia.

Taylor, Jay, *China and Southeast Asia: Peking's Relations with Revolutionary Movements,* New York: Praeger, 1976

Covers China's relations with Indochina, Burma, Indonesia, and the so-called allied states of Thailand, Malaysia, Singapore, and the Philippines. The author gives a carefully measured appraisal of how much revolutionary factors weigh in China's foreign policy toward Southeast Asian countries.

Wong, John, *The Political Economy of China's Changing Relations with Southeast Asia,* London: Macmillan, and New York: St. Martin's Press, 1984

Offers a balanced perspective on the evolution of the political and economic relationship between the People's Republic of China and the Southeast Asian countries between the 1950s and the 1970s. Analyzes China's trade with Indonesia, Malaysia, the Philippines, Singapore, and Thailand.

Guangzhi Zhao is an Instructor at Northern Illinois University, DeKalb. He is coauthor, with Brantly Womack, of "The Many Worlds of China's Provinces: Foreign Trade and Diversification," in *China Deconstructs: Politics, Trade, and Regionalism,* edited by David S.G. Goodman and Gerald Segal (1994).

Figure 6.1: Export to the Developed Economies

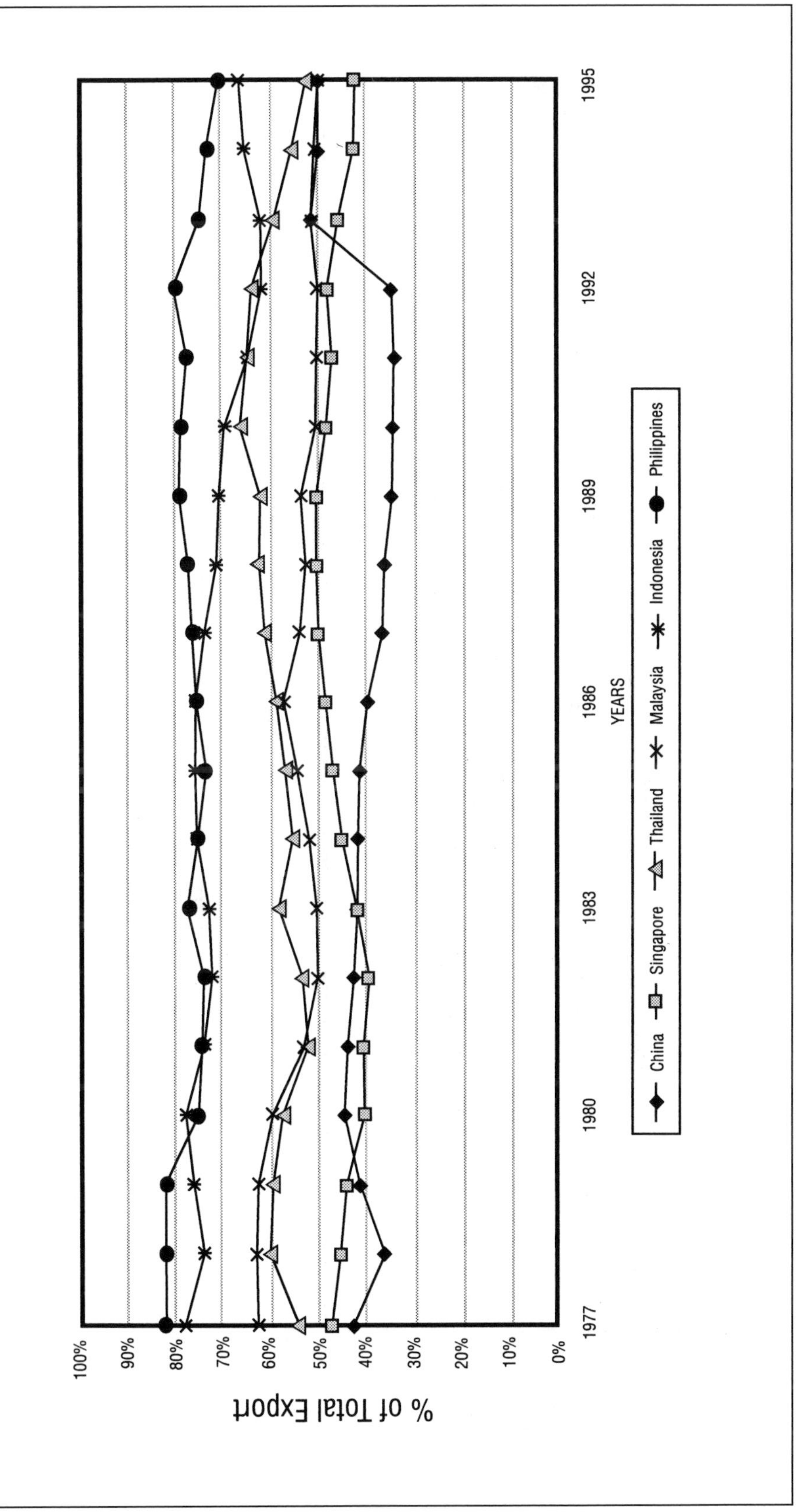

Legend: China — Singapore — Thailand — Malaysia — Indonesia — Philippines

Y-axis: % of Total Export (0% to 100%)

X-axis: YEARS (1977, 1980, 1983, 1986, 1989, 1992, 1995)

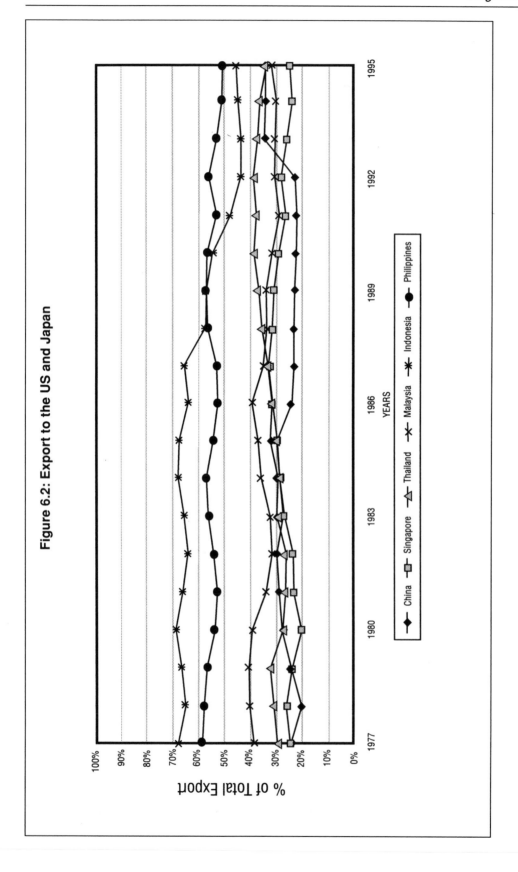

Figure 6.2: Export to the US and Japan

Table 6.1: Comparison of GDP Growth 1980–94

	1980–89	*1990–94*
China	10.2%	12.9%
Singapore	6.4%	8.3%
Thailand	7.6%	8.2%
Malaysia	5.2%	8.4%
Indonesia	6.1%	7.6%
Philippines	1.0%	1.6%
U.S.A.	3.0%	2.5%
Britain	3.2%	0.8%
France	2.4%	0.8%
Germany	2.2%	1.1%

Source: World Development Report 1996

Table 6.2: Commercial Agreements between China and Southeast Asian Countries (1952–79)

	Vietnam	*Laos*	*Cambodia*	*Indonesia*	*Malaysia*	*Philippines*	*Thailand*	*Burma*
1952–55	5	0	0	1	0	0	0	4
1956–60	12	0	7	3	0	0	0	2
1961–65	14	2	9	8	0	0	0	4
1966–70	20	0	3	0	0	0	0	0
1971–75	16	5	5	0	1	3	3	2
1976–79	2	1	3	0	2	4	4	2

Source: Peter Cheng, *A Chronology of the People's Republic of China from October 1, 1949*, Totowa, New Jersey: Littlefield, Adams, 1972; Peter Cheng, *A Chronology of the People's Republic of China   1970–1979*, Metuchen, New Jersey: Scarecrow Press, 1986

Table 6.3: China's Export to ASEAN Countries 1980–95 (US$ million)

	1980	1981	1982	1983	1984	1985	1986	1987	1988	1989	1990	1991	1992	1993	1994	1995
Total Export	18139	21476	21865	22133	24824	27329	31367	39464	47663	51751	62876	71940	85492	91611	120822	148755
Ex./ASEAN	1196	1386	1279	1140	1979	2803	1879	2312	2789	2898	3846	4124	4250	4673	6368	9001
% of total	6.59%	6.45%	5.85%	5.15%	7.97%	10.26%	5.99%	5.86%	5.85%	5.60%	6.12%	5.73%	4.97%	5.10%	5.27%	6.05%
Singapore	421	658	648	567	1239	2063	1217	1323	1464	1642	2016	2014	2031	2245	2563	3500
	2.32%	3.06%	2.96%	2.56%	4.99%	7.55%	3.88%	3.35%	3.07%	3.17%	3.21%	2.80%	2.38%	2.45%	2.12%	2.35%
Thailand	312	228	168	195	251	116	159	301	512	477	854	848	894	750	1159	1752
	1.72%	1.06%	0.77%	0.88%	1.01%	0.42%	0.51%	0.76%	1.07%	0.92%	1.36%	1.18%	1.05%	0.82%	0.96%	1.18%
Indonesia	21	54	46	49	70	124	143	188	236	208	401	481	471	693	1052	1438
	0.12%	0.25%	0.21%	0.22%	0.28%	0.45%	0.46%	0.48%	0.50%	0.40%	0.64%	0.67%	0.55%	0.76%	0.87%	0.97%
Malaysia	184	191	181	186	196	186	203	255	309	332	370	528	645	704	1118	1281
	1.01%	0.89%	0.83%	0.84%	0.79%	0.68%	0.65%	0.65%	0.65%	0.64%	0.59%	0.73%	0.75%	0.77%	0.93%	0.86%
Philippines	258	255	236	143	223	314	157	245	268	239	205	253	209	281	476	1030
	1.42%	1.19%	1.08%	0.65%	0.90%	1.15%	0.50%	0.62%	0.56%	0.46%	0.33%	0.35%	0.24%	0.31%	0.39%	0.69%

Source: International Monetary Fund, *Direction of Trade Statistics Yearbook* (Washington, D.C.), various issues

Table 6.4: ASEAN's Export to China 1980–95 (US$ million)

	Singapore			Thailand			Malaysia			Indonesia			Philippines		
	Total	To PRC	% of Total	Total	To PRC	% of Total	Total	To PRC	% of Total	Total	To PRC	% of Total	Total	To PRC	% of Total
1980	19377	307	1.58%	6501	124	1.91%	12960	217	1.67%	21909		0.00%	5788	45	0.78%
1981	20970	179	0.85%	7027	186	2.65%	11773	88	0.75%	23810	8	0.03%	5721	78	1.36%
1982	20787	240	1.15%	6946	307	4.42%	12044	110	0.91%	22929	14	0.06%	5020	105	2.09%
1983	21832	213	0.98%	6164	107	1.74%	14135	206	1.46%	21146	27	0.13%	4932	22	0.45%
1984	24047	243	1.01%	7414	183	2.47%	16563	165	1.00%	21881	8	0.04%	5343	60	1.12%
1985	22812	333	1.46%	7122	271	3.81%	15408	161	1.04%	18597	84	0.45%	4614	81	1.76%
1986	22501	571	2.54%	8864	276	3.11%	13977	163	1.17%	14809	139	0.94%	4807	101	2.10%
1987	28696	737	2.57%	11563	388	3.36%	17934	279	1.56%	17170	343	2.00%	5696	88	1.54%
1988	39318	1193	3.03%	15956	475	2.98%	21096	415	1.97%	19376	492	2.54%	7034	67	0.95%
1989	44769	1199	2.68%	20028	576	2.88%	25049	481	1.92%	21936	534	2.43%	7754	50	0.64%
1990	52753	799	1.51%	23072	269	1.17%	29420	619	2.10%	25681	834	3.25%	8194	62	0.76%
1991	59219	858	1.45%	28811	335	1.16%	34405	639	1.86%	29186	1191	4.08%	8840	128	1.45%
1992	63475	1113	1.75%	32472	386	1.19%	40709	772	1.90%	33977	1396	4.11%	9829	114	1.16%
1993	74021	1905	2.57%	37158	430	1.16%	47128	1204	2.55%	36843	1249	3.39%	11271	167	1.48%
1994	96376	2098	2.18%	46044	930	2.02%	58748	1933	3.29%	38214	1419	3.71%	13433	164	1.22%
1995	118172	2759	2.33%	56662	1642	2.90%	73990	1962	2.65%	43285	1866	4.31%	17249	216	1.25%

Source: International Monetary Fund, *Direction of Trade Statistics Yearbook* (Washington, D.C.), various issues

Table 6.5: Exports of Manufactures in Total Export

	1980	*1993*
China	48%	81%
Indonesia	2%	53%
Philippines	37%	76%
Thailand	28%	73%
Malaysia	19%	70%
Singapore	50%	80%

Source: World Bank, *From Plan to Market–World Development Report 1996*, Oxford: Oxford University
Press, 1996

Table 6.6: Composition of Exports of Manufactured Goods to the OECD Countries in 1993

	Textile Clothing	*Chemicals*	*Machinery Electronic*	*Transport Equipment*	*Other*
China	32.2%	3.6%	11.8%	0.8%	51.6%
Indonesia	32.6%	2.2%	5.6%	0.7%	59.0%
Philippines	28.4%	1.4%	35.8%	0.7%	33.7%
Thailand	18.5%	1.8%	19.0%	1.0%	59.6%
Malaysia	10.7%	2.2%	47.1%	1.3%	38.7%
Singapore	3.6%	4.3%	23.0%	1.7%	67.4%

Source: World Bank, *Workers in an Integrating World–World Development Report 1995*, Oxford: Oxford
University Press, 1996

Political Economy and Development Policy

Chapter Seven

Plan Versus Market: China's Socialist Market Economy

Joseph Fewsmith

Few topics are more central to the reform of socialist societies than the relationship between plan and market, and how to move from the former to the latter. The topic of plan and market in socialist societies is critical because it is central to ideology, the role of the state, and the distribution of resources in society.

Nothing is more central to Marxism than the notion of ownership. Indeed, socialist revolution is justified largely on the basis that expropriating the means of production from the capitalist class will end the exploitation of workers. In other words, changing the ownership of property is seen as key to managing an economy in the interests of the whole society. Apart from the theory of Marxism, however, political leaders of socialist societies share a common belief that they, as a modernizing or at least nationalist elite, can better utilize scarce resources on behalf of society than can the millions of individuals who make up society. In the case of China, this concept corresponds with a deep historical bias that certain vital goods should be centrally controlled. Furthermore, over time, as socialist institutions take hold and develop, an implicit social contract usually develops between the state and workers wherein both parties are expected to fulfill certain responsibilities. One of those expectations is that the state will play a paternalistic role, taking care of the workers that have been recruited to work in enterprises owned by the "whole people." For all of these reasons, reform of

socialist systems is politically difficult and socially dangerous.

Economic and financial reasons also make it difficult to reform centrally planned socialist economies, the state's dependence on the revenues provided by state-owned enterprises. Socialist societies impose centralized planning because it allows them to mobilize resources and concentrate their use in the hands of the state. Traditionally, China had a dispersed agricultural economy, and it is notoriously difficult for developing states to collect taxes from such an economy. In the case of China, economists estimate that the state never managed to collect more than about 4% of China's Gross National Product (GNP) in the years before the Chinese Communist Party (CCP) came to power. Within only five years of attaining power, China's Communist government was able to collect some 30% of China's GNP.

China invested such revenues in the construction of large, state-owned factories. This development strategy made little sense in terms of China's comparative advantage (i.e., its ability to produce a good at a lower cost than another country). Although China may have been better advised to channel its enormous labor force into labor-intensive industries, it chose instead to develop the sort of capital-intensive heavy industries—such as steel and machine building—that were associated with being "industrialized." China's industrialization strategy was based not only on a model of modernization (one that was about to be superseded), but also on an intense concern over national security. Given the threats–both real and imagined–that China faced in the 1950s, it is understandable that China concentrated on developing heavy industry. As a result, the Chinese state soon found itself almost wholly dependent, in fiscal terms, on the large, state-owned enterprises that it had created. By the late 1970s, the 1,000 largest state-owned enterprises produced 70% of China's industrial output and paid 80% of the taxes and revenues collected by the central government. Today, this dependence makes reform difficult because any miscalculation could have disastrous ramifications for the state itself.

Another consequence of China's developmental strategy was that an enormous bureaucratic apparatus rose to manage the state-run economy. Ministries were established to administer every major sector of the economy–metallurgy, machine-building, petroleum, and water resources, among others. The State Planning Commission presided over this bureaucratic apparatus and guided the overall development of the economy, primarily by devising and implementing one-year and five-year plans. The implication for the reform of the Chinese economy was that a powerful bureaucratic constituency had little interest in market-oriented reform. After all, if enterprises responded to the market rather than to the state, what role would the various ministries play?

Thus, by the late 1970s there were many reasons–ideological, financial, and bureaucratic–that the shift from plan to market would be difficult. Indeed, in the Soviet Union and other socialist countries, precisely such forces repeatedly stalled the introduction of meaningful economic reform even as economic efficiency declined and the need for reform became increasingly clear.

So why did China succeed, at least to the extent it has? Five basic factors have led to the successful introduction of market mechanisms in China's economy. First, China's planning system was never as comprehensive or as bureaucratized as that of the Soviet Union. China's state plan never covered more than about 600 goods, and only one-third of these were managed in detail, whereas the Soviet Union's state plan covered more than 60,000 items. The difference reflected the less centralized nature of China's system. Repeated efforts to decentralize the Chinese economy, starting with the Great Leap Forward (1958–61), had diminished the scope of the planning system, as had political campaigns that targeted technical expertise and bureaucratic behavior. The Cultural Revolution (1966–76) compounded the effect of previous campaigns by undertaking a major decentralization of industry in 1971 and by paralyzing most of China's industrial bureaucracy (at one point, the State Planning Commission was reduced to just over 20 officials). Although the late Maoist leadership attempted to restore a degree of centralized control following the Cultural Revolution, it could not restore the highly centralized system that had prevailed during the 1950s. Moreover, many leaders considered a highly centralized system undesirable.

As a result of administrative and economic decentralization, central authorities determined to reform the tax system beginning in 1980. This task presented central authorities with a basic dilemma: on the one hand, they needed desperately to increase revenues to the central government; on the other hand, they lacked the political muscle to impose a recentralization of the fiscal system on their own terms. The result was a negotiated system in which localities were given various incentives to increase their tax payments to the center. While various forms of incentives were given, the thrust was the same: the more revenues the localities collected the more they could keep for themselves. In the case of Guangdong, a southeastern province abutting Hong Kong, the central government agreed to a system in which the province delivered 1 billion *yuan* per year in taxes. This tax burden was to remain fixed for the following ten years. Such tax systems, which became known as fiscal contracting, spurred localities to develop local industry and thus raise greater revenues.

A third factor contributing to the transition from plan to market involved China's opening to the outside world and also China's interaction with the highly successful Chinese community of Hong Kong. By the time China initiated its "open door" policy in the late 1970s, Hong Kong was a thriving commercial community. Hong Kong developed in the 1960s and 1970s as a center of labor-intensive export goods, such as toys. By the late 1970s, however, Hong Kong had succeeded to the point where the rising cost of local labor was making labor-intensive export processing unprofitable. The opening of China, a country with a seemingly limitless pool of labor, was just what Hong Kong needed. Hong Kong manufacturers, many of whom had family ties across the border in Guangdong (which spoke the same Cantonese dialect), began looking for places to build manufacturing plants. China accommodated these manufacturers by establishing Special Economic Zones in Shenzhen (directly adjacent to Hong Kong), Zhuhai (near Macau), and elsewhere. A decade later, the number of Guangdong workers working for Hong Kong-invested firms in Guangdong far exceeded those working in Hong Kong. Meanwhile, China had found a source of capital, managerial expertise, and marketing know-how.

Reform of the agricultural economy, which began informally in the late 1970s, also contributed to China's transition from plan to market. The implementation of household farming, which vastly increased incentives to farmers, and the subsequent dissolution of the communes freed vast numbers of underemployed agricultural workers for work in the emerging township and village industries. The creation of township and village enterprises, formerly known as brigade industries, was a result of Mao Zedong's efforts to decentralize industry and mobilize labor during the Great Leap Forward. Despite official encouragement, such industries developed slowly. Moreover, contrary to expectation, these were concentrated heavily in relatively capital-intensive industries such as cement production. By the end of the Maoist era, these industries employed approximately 28 million workers and produced only 9% of China's total industrial output. However, owing to reform of the rural economy, township and village industries enjoyed a ready supply of labor and faced fewer restrictions in product marketing. Additionally, the reformed tax system encouraged local governments to aid in the development of such industries. As a result, by the early 1990s rural industries employed more than 120 million workers and produced over half of China's industrial output.

Ironically, the irrational price system also spurred the growth of township and village industries. Because China established fixed prices in the 1950s to support its implementation of the planning system, price ratios (that is, how much one good costs in terms of another) were distorted by the late 1970s. Consumer goods, which had been undervalued by the planners, were expensive relative to their cost of production. Moreover, state-owned enterprises produced an insufficient supply of consumer goods, focusing instead on the production of heavy industrial goods. Township and village enterprises were able to take full advantage of this neglected market.

In short, as China embarked on a path of economic reform in the late 1970s and early 1980s, a number of powerful ideological and bureaucratic forces were hostile to or at least cautious about the pace and scope of reforms. Most of these forces were concentrated at the central level, where the political stakes and the financial risks were the greatest. Arrayed against such forces were powerful economic pressures operating at the local level. The reform of the tax system, the distorted price structure, the unfolding agricultural reform, the abundance of labor, and the influx of outside capital and labor all contributed to an explosion in the growth of township and village enterprises. In retrospect, the convergence of market-oriented factors seems inevitable; at the time, however, no one foresaw the changes that would take place in China's economy.

Debating Plan Versus Market

The factors outlined above account for the lines of conflict that emerged after the adoption of reform, and also explain why incremental reform of the economy continued despite conflict. When Deng Xiaoping and other reform-minded leaders returned to power at the end of 1978, they focused their attention on two related topics: social stability and economic development. Chen Yun, a senior party leader and economic specialist, fretted over the prospect of rural violence. If the livelihood of the peasants did not improve, Chen warned, peasants would flood into the cities to demand food. Deng Xiaoping dismissed the previous 20 years of Chinese history–the period since the Great Leap Forward–as "wasted."

The Dengist leadership's views were influenced by the emergence over the previous two decades of several economic power-houses in Asia: Japan, South Korea, Taiwan, Hong Kong, and Singapore. Even Deng Liqun, who emerged as a leading critic of reform, marveled at the economic progress and social order in Japan. That such nations had grown their economies while China had destroyed itself in internecine conflict only increased the leadership's resolve to pursue reform.

Thus, the leadership sought to jump-start the economy in the late 1970s. In addition to reforming the tax system in 1980, they increased the grain price paid to farmers by the state by 20% and the price of above-quota grain by 50%. Combined with tacit approval for the household responsibility system that was just beginning to emerge in the countryside, these measures fired peasants' enthusiasm. As a result, grain production increased a remarkable one-third between 1978 and 1984.

However, initial enthusiasm for reform in general terms soon foundered owing to differences of opinion within the Communist Party. Some leaders, notably Chen Yun, emphasized the primacy of the plan, pro-

posing a limited, supplementary role for the market. Although Chen favored the introduction of some market forces in the late 1970s (as he had done in the 1950s, prior to the Cultural Revolution), he soon became concerned with controlling the forces his ideas had helped unleash. Other leaders, however, believed that market forces had to play a greater role in the Chinese economy. In their opinion, even planning needed to be based, to a greater or lesser degree, on market considerations. Such arguments were anathema to more conservative Communist Party leaders.

Not surprisingly, the introduction of market forces into China's economy proved difficult. China's planned economy was designed so that its various parts would work together, albeit at a low degree of efficiency, and thus the introduction of market forces was disruptive. For instance, as reformers gradually allowed some enterprises to produce some of their products for the market and to retain some earnings, these enterprises naturally devoted more of their energies to cultivating the market. Given the distorted price structure under which China was operating at the time, some enterprises made windfall profits. Others, however, faced an adverse price structure and, if given the choice, preferred to cut back production and minimize losses. The difference between the suddenly prosperous enterprises and those that began to reduce their output (and hence the taxes they paid) did not necessarily reflect their respective efficiency or managerial capability; it simply reflected a function of the price structure they faced. Without a level playing field that market forces provide, central leaders found it difficult to ascertain which enterprises were more efficient. Thus, the introduction of limited market forces did not necessarily stimulate efficiency, at least in the beginning.

Moreover, enterprises that sold their products on the market began to operate in ways that were considered unorthodox under the old system. For instance, salespersons who traveled around the country either to procure raw materials or to sell the enterprise's products frequently gave small gifts (often as simple as a pack of cigarettes) to the officials they were courting. In the eyes of some, these practices were a form of corruption. Indeed, China's social morés came increasingly under attack during this period of economic change.

These economic and social disruptions prompted critics of reform to call for anticorruption campaigns and a return to the planning system. One major effort to tighten planning occurred in late 1980. In part because of the investment program of Hua Guofeng and in part because of the disruptions caused by the limited introduction of market-oriented reforms in industry, Chinese officials headed by Chen Yun introduced a major period of retrenchment. Retrenchment was intended to reduce inflationary pressures by cutting investment and to rein in market forces by reestablishing the primacy of the plan. In fact, these two goals ran counter to each other. What happened was that as the state cut investment, many enterprises found themselves with excess production capacity. Rather than lay idle and run up deficits, these enterprises decided to sell more of their product on the market. Contrary to the planners' intention, the retrenchment policies provided a major boost for the marketization of the economy.

"Growing Out of the Plan": The 1984 Decision on Economic Restructuring

The conservative planners who initiated retrenchment in 1980 estimated that the country would need at least three years of tight monetary and fiscal controls as well as slow growth in order to readjust important aspects of the economy, particularly the ratio between light and heavy industry and between industry and agriculture. In fact, a great deal of dynamism was pent up in the Chinese economy because of the constraints placed on it during the Cultural Revolution. Owing to the change in political atmosphere and the beginning of reform, the economy soared. The agricultural sector experienced marked increases in production. Soon after,

market-oriented reforms spread to industry, particularly smaller-scale industrial enterprises. Finally, township and village enterprises proliferated. In short, reform during the first few years of the Dengist period proved remarkably robust, and the economy grew faster than conservative planners had anticipated. By 1983, there were new demands to deepen reform by extending it into the cities.

In response to these demands, the CCP adopted the Decision on the Reform of the Economic Structure in 1984. This comprised the single most important document adopted by the Communist Party during the entire reform period, not only because the document constituted an important endorsement for continued economic reform, but because it laid out a broad conception of the reform process that accorded well with Chinese realities. First, it confronted an important ideological issue. For years, Chinese authorities had based their economic plans on the basic structure of Stalin's 1952 work, "On the Economic Problems of Socialism." Stalin held that commodities could play a role in a socialist economy, but only among so-called "collective enterprises" and between them and state-owned enterprises. Although this was an ideological issue, it had important ramifications for the management of the economy. The term "commodity" in the Marxist lexicon denotes the transfer of ownership. Since state-owned enterprises were understood to be owned by "all the people," the transfer of a "product" from one enterprise to another could not be regarded as a change in ownership. This Stalinist legacy thus maintained that a so-called "product economy" was compatible with socialism (because products were exchanged among various state-owned enterprises), but that a "commodity economy" was not compatible. The practical implication of this was that state-owned enterprises were not regarded as profit maximizers that had their own independent interests. Instead, state-owned enterprises were supposed to be owned by the whole society, having no interests of their own separate from those of society as a whole. Commodities could exist in such a society, but only between lower levels of ownership (collectives); the society as a whole could not be described as a "commodity economy" for commodities were only subordinate to products.

While the issues of Marxist ideology had long been debated in China, conservatives had always rejected the idea of a commodity economy as "unsocialist." In 1984, however, the CCP finally decided to pursue a commodity economy. The practical effect of this was to remove many of the ideological and political obstacles to the creation of a modern economy. Reformers no longer feared (or at least not so much) being accused of deviating from socialism.

Second, the Decision on the Reform of the Economic Structure sketched a general direction for reform, namely that market forces would supplant planning measures as the engine behind the economy: as the economy grew, the importance of the plan (in proportion to the whole economy) would shrink. In short, China would attempt to "grow out of the plan" (this phrase is borrowed from Barry Naughton, *Growing Out of the Plan*, 1995).

Third, the 1984 decision indirectly contributed to the implementation of price reform. Chinese economists had long realized that China's distorted, irrational price structure in turn was distorting the distribution of goods and resources. The Decision on the Reform of the Economic Structure specifically stated that price reform would be the "key" to economic reform, although it did not offer a plan on how to reform prices. At the time, conventional wisdom suggested that prices be reformed one sector at a time. That is to say, as production in one sector increased to meet market demand, then prices in that sector could be freed to regulate supply and demand. The problem with this approach, as reforms in Eastern Europe had demonstrated, was that shortages were endemic to planned economies, and thus price reform could never be completed.

Attempting to solve this problem, reformers established a so-called "two-

track" price system, which called for the adoption of two separate prices (in actuality there were sometimes more) for the same product. In other words, a product such as iron would have an "in plan" price set by the state that dictated the price at which iron was sold to state-owned enterprises. Concurrently, iron that factories produced in excess of state-set quotas could be sold at a different, higher price (the "out-of-plan") that would better reflect supply and demand. Because demand was perpetually greater than supply, enterprises had no trouble selling all their above-quota production at the higher out-of-plan price. This gave enterprises a tremendous incentive both to expand production to sell more produce at above quota prices and to begin developing new products that would meet market demand. In other words, the two-track price system induced many state-owned, and especially collectively owned, enterprises to act as economic creatures and to produce for the market.

Although state-owned enterprises responded to these new incentives, enterprises that benefited the most were township and village enterprises. The decision to "freeze" the plan meant that township and village enterprises would neither be incorporated into the plan as they grew nor shut down as they began to compete with state-owned enterprises. The decision of China's authorities to allow township and village enterprises to compete with state-owned enterprises was critical in the development of economic reform and in the transformation from plan to market. Many township and village enterprises developed around the large cities where state-owned enterprises were located. State-owned enterprises, frequently unable to expand production because of constraints on land acquisition and costs (such as hiring new laborers and providing full benefits), found that it was more cost-effective to subcontract part of the production process to nearby township and village enterprises. In any case, as the township and village enterprise sector grew, their products increasingly challenged those of state-owned enterprises, cutting into the profit margins of the latter (which had been artificially high because of their monopoly position).

In short, following the promulgation of the Decision on the Reform of the Economic Structure, economic reform began to take root.

Deepening Debates Over the Course of Economic Reform

The fundamental difficulty of moving from a planned economy to a market economy derives from the interconnection between the distorted price system, the close administrative relationship between enterprises and their governing administrative units (including both central ministries and local governments), and the difficulty of maintaining a stable price level. Theoretically, the overall price level of goods should not change in the course of price reform because the prices of some goods should go down while those of others should go up. In practice, however, inflationary price increases are difficult to avoid in a period of reform, owing to intense bureaucratic pressures against prices going down. Enterprises whose goods are overvalued by the distorted price structure resist price decreases and the relevant administrative units support their opposition for fear that tax revenues will decline. Therefore, prices can go up but not down, making the process of reform inflationary and thus politically risky.

Given this situation, reform of a centrally planned economy is a threefold task. First the price system must be reformed to provide a level playing ground for all enterprises. Second, ownership reform must weaken and eventually sever the link between enterprises and their supervising administrative units so that the enterprises do not rely on administrative support to avoid competing on the market. Finally, reformers must attempt to accomplish the above two goals within a general context of stable prices. A reform that sets off inflationary pressures faces bureaucratic resistance from officials whose job it is to maintain

price controls and stable prices; moreover, inflationary pressures may lead to social unrest, if consumers take to the streets to protest rising prices.

Because prices, ownership, and price levels are all interconnected in the planned economy, it is difficult to start the reform process in any one area. Confronted with this scenario, reformers in the Soviet Union attempted "shock therapy," which seeks to accomplish everything at once by carrying out a process of privatization and a simultaneous freeing of previously fixed prices. Shock therapy, however, neglects the creation of markets, and without markets there is a strong tendency for demand to dry up and for production to shrink, as indeed happened in the Soviet Union. China's incremental reform process avoided this problem but could not avoid the frictions that arose from partial price reform, partial ownership reform, and the resulting inflationary pressures.

During the late 1980s, Chinese policymakers debated these issues. These debates occurred both among reformers and between reformers and conservatives, the latter preferring a more limited reform program. Meanwhile, pro-reform economists were divided over which reforms to implement first: price reform or ownership reform. Still others argued that both needed to be done, albeit at a slower pace in order to maintain macroeconomic stability. Each of these different approaches rose to the fore at one time or another during the late 1980s as the reform process encountered difficulties.

At the other end of the spectrum, conservatives fretted that the whole reform process was misguided. Although they favored some reforms, they effectively sought to return China's economy to the "golden age" of the 1950s. As conservative policymakers watched the economic reforms unfold, they focused their attacks on three major problems. First, they blamed reform for unleashing inflationary pressures that threatened the stability of the economy and society. In fact, the rates of inflation that China suffered during those years were far more modest than those encountered by other developing and reforming countries. China, however, had long been accustomed to no inflation at all, and fairly modest rates were viewed as intolerable by many. Second, conservatives worried that the growth of township and village enterprises was eroding the profit margins of large- and medium-sized state-owned enterprises, threatening both the fiscal stability of the central state and the ability of state-owned enterprises to develop as the "pillars" of the socialist economy. Third, conservatives criticized the corruption that emerged alongside economic reform, arguing that the two-track price structure adopted in the mid-1980s permitted abuses of the system. Indeed, enterprise officials, recognizing the wide gap between in-plan and out-of-plan prices, often used their control over in-plan goods to divert them to the market to make large profits. Sometimes these profits were used to benefit the organization as a whole, but frequently such gains found their way into the hands of individuals. By the late 1980s, corruption had become endemic.

These problems generated intense political conflict and formed the critical background to the bold but misguided effort to adopt radical price reform in 1988. This initiative, which Deng Xiaoping appears to have sponsored, was intended to solve China's economic dilemmas in a single stroke. If price reform were enacted, some argued, the "dual track" price system would no longer exist because all prices would be unified on the basis of market prices. As a result, enterprise officials would no longer be tempted to direct in-plan goods toward the market. Unfortunately, this initiative failed miserably, owing to lack of preparation and foresight on the part of the leadership and also to poor timing. At the time that Deng announced his intention to oversee radical price reform, inflationary pressures were building up in the Chinese economy. Chinese consumers reacted rationally, withdrawing their money from banks (since interest rates were lower than the rate of inflation) and purchasing durable goods (such as washing machines and televisions)

that they hoped would hold the value of their money. This resulted in a purchasing panic such as China had not seen since the late 1940s.

In the face of such consumer panic, the government also panicked. Responsibility for economic management was stripped from Zhao Ziyang, the reform-minded general secretary who had guided economic reform throughout the 1980s, and given to Li Peng, the conservative premier. A program of retrenchment, which conservatives had long sought, was implemented. Political tensions among the leadership reached new heights, just as dissatisfaction among the populace was coming to a boil. These contributed to the events at Tiananmen Square and across China in the spring and summer of 1989, when hundreds of thousands took to the streets in protest; a divided government responded at first ineptly and then brutally.

The Economy Under Retrenchment

Following the adoption of retrenchment policies in the fall of 1988, and the ouster of Zhao Ziyang in the wake of the Tiananmen crackdown, conservative policymakers had more complete control over the direction of economic affairs than at any time since the early 1980s. Initial efforts focused on bringing inflation under control. This was accomplished by a combination of economic and administrative measures. Policymakers offered savings accounts (similar to certificates of deposits) that were indexed to the rate of inflation to encourage people to put their money into banks (instead of continuing to purchase consumer goods, which drove up prices). The government also relied heavily on a variety of administrative measures to bring demand under control and reduce inflation. It curtailed bank lending and investment and required enterprises to have their investments approved by the responsible administrative authority. Moreover, policymakers attempted to revive planning by introducing a so-called "double guarantee" system. Applying to approximately 250 key state-owned enterprises, the double guarantee system stipulated that the government would guarantee inputs at in-plan prices, in return for which these enterprises would guarantee to supply their output at in-plan prices to the government.

Overall, the efforts of conservative officials to turn back the clock failed. Their attempts to reduce inflationary pressures actually brought about a period of deflation, while their efforts to implement the double guarantee system and to otherwise restore the role of planning in the economy lessened the competitive pressures on state-owned enterprises. At the same time, tight monetary and fiscal policies left state-owned enterprises short of cash and finding little demand for their products. The outcome was twofold. First, the profits of large state-owned enterprises collapsed, dropping by over 50% in 1990 alone. Second, inter-enterprise debt—the money owed by enterprises to each other for the supply of raw material or the purchase of goods—escalated. By June 1991, inter-enterprise debt reached some 300 billion *yuan*, a figure large enough to raise serious concern about the liquidity of the economy.

Revival of Economic Reform

In January and February 1992 Deng Xiaoping made an important trip to the Shenzhen Special Economic Zone (SEZ) in Guangdong province. Deng had approved the establishment of Shenzhen and other economic zones in 1979, and in 1984 he had traveled to Shenzhen to declare the success of the SEZs. Now, nearly a decade later, the 88-year-old patriarch was returning to Shenzhen to revitalize the economic reform program. The aging and officially retired leader peppered his remarks with some of the harshest language he had ever used against his conservative critics. He told the left (that is, the conservatives) to "go to sleep" and declared to his audiences that the left was more dangerous than the right (the latter had been under official assault since Tiananmen). He called for faster economic growth and urged Guangdong province to catch up to the "four small dragons" (Hong

Kong, Taiwan, Singapore, and South Korea) within 20 years. With Deng leading the charge, economic reform took off once again. At the Fourteenth Party Congress in Beijing in October 1992, the CCP adopted the most reform-oriented platform in its history. The goal of reform, the party now declared, was to build a "socialist market economy," a system that far exceeded in scope the commodity economy that had been pursued by the leadership in 1984.

Not surprisingly, Deng's trip to Shenzhen and the Fourteenth Party Congress ushered in a new period of rapid economic growth. In 1992, the economy grew over 14%, followed by growth rates of 13.5%, 11.8%, 10.2%, and 8.0% in 1993, 1994, 1995, and 1996, respectively. At the same time, China began attracting unprecedented amounts of foreign investment. China currently attracts more foreign investment that any other economy in the world. Owing to this upsurge in economic activity, China virtually completed the transition from a planned economic system to a market-oriented economic system, in the sense that most prices by the end of the period were set by the market. Township and village enterprises, which had accounted for only 9% of industrial production in 1978, accounted for nearly 60% of such production in 1996. Only about 7% of producer prices were still controlled by the plan. Even the problem of dual-track prices largely was resolved as the market set the prices for a wider array of goods.

Problems

China's transition from plan to market has been a highly contentious process, fraught with economic upturns and downturns as well as political conflict. It also has proceeded contrary to the conventional wisdom of Western economists. While most observers agree that reform has succeeded in an overall sense, the transition from plan to market has not been completed. Moreover, there remain serious problems in the economy as well as heated debates over how to move forward.

The most important problem currently facing the leadership is how to manage the large- and medium-sized state-owned enterprises that have not been able to orient themselves to the market economy and now confront serious losses. In 1996, some 43% of state-owned firms incurred losses, and the amount of losses was five percentage points greater than the year before. These losses now total 61.6 billion *yuan* (US$7.4 billion), while another 150 billion *yuan* (US$18 billion) are tied up in excessive inventories. The situation has reached a critical mass, and Beijing must determine either to transform these enterprises or shut them down.

The decision regarding the fate of state-owned enterprises will be difficult to make because these enterprises employ roughly two-thirds of urban workers. Forcing them into bankruptcy would cause massive unemployment and undoubtedly result in social disorder. Indeed, even laying off enough workers to make state-owned enterprises economically viable would be impossible. Economists estimate that between 20% to 40% of workers (totaling 25–40 million) in state-owned enterprises are redundant and could be laid off without any loss of efficiency. Since enterprises historically have provided for the welfare of their workers in retirement, China simply does not have a well-established social security system. Efforts to establish a welfare system are underway, but still far from complete.

Conversely, allowing state-owned enterprises to remain inefficient also is dangerous. As noted above, these enterprises are incurring losses at an unsustainable rate. Moreover, owing to reform efforts in the 1980s, state-owned enterprises now are supported primarily by loans from state-owned banks rather than by state financial allocations. This measure, originally intended to pressure state-owned enterprises to become more efficient, has shifted the burden onto state banks. At present, approximately one-third of all loans extended by Chinese banks are nonperforming, that is, they will not be paid back. In other words, loss-making state-owned enterprises are now creating troubles for the financial sector, making it difficult for reformers to undertake significant financial reform.

Furthermore, without significant financial reform Chinese enterprises will never be subject to the discipline of hard-budget constraints; that is, they will never be forced to survive solely on the income they earn from selling their products and whatever loans banks are willing to extend under the expectation that these will be repaid. Financial reform is essential to the efficient operation and the full opening up of the Chinese economy. Although the Chinese economy has made remarkable strides in opening up to the outside world, becoming the tenth largest trading nation in the process and the largest recipient of direct foreign investment in the world, it has not made its currency fully convertible. In 1996, China made its currency convertible for the current account, but that does not allow the Chinese people to buy and sell foreign currency, as can citizens of any country with a fully convertible currency. If China were to take that step today, a large-scale sell-off of Chinese assets and purchase of foreign assets would ensue, denominated in dollars, *yen,* and other foreign currencies. Thus, fully convertible currency is not likely to become a reality in the foreseeable future.

Hovering over these and other problems are continuing political disputes over the role of state-owned enterprises in China. While some policymakers seem willing to contemplate a substantial privatization of the Chinese economy, others clearly are not. Some officials, most notably Premier Li Peng, have stated publicly that state-owned enterprises are an essential component of socialism. Presumably, these officials fear that the CCP would lose political control if it permitted the bankruptcy or the privatization of state-owned enterprises.

Current policy appears to be a compromise. On the one hand, policymakers have allowed smaller state-owned enterprises either to go bankrupt or to be sold, leased, or merged with other enterprises—de facto privatization. On the other hand, policymakers appear determined to bolster the behemoths that make up the core of the old planned economy by supplying them with sufficient resources and managerial expertise. This, it is hoped, will make them run more efficiently, thus avoiding the necessity of privatization.

Although this compromise policy delays the inevitable decision on how to deal with large state-owned enterprises, and thus the full marketization of the Chinese economy, the policy may be a reasonable step for the moment, given the unpalatable alternatives. China's leadership is hoping that enough large state-owned enterprises can be reformed and restructured to become viable, while the continued growth of the economy allows the state to continue subsidizing their operation. Inevitably, over time, many of these state-owned enterprises will be privatized in piecemeal fashion—by selling off certain assets to other enterprises that are viable or by merging with foreign companies that are willing to undertake restructuring in the hopes of making profits. Thus, China may grow out of these economic problems just as earlier it grew out of the plan.

Further Reading

Bachman, David M., *Chen Yun and the Chinese Political System,* Berkeley: Institute of East Asian Studies, University of California, 1985

A good treatment of the most senior economic specialist within the top party elite after 1949. Chen Yun is credited with bringing inflation under control after the communist victory, managing the First Five-Year Plan, and restoring the economy after the disasters of the Great Leap Forward and the Cultural Revolution. In the 1980s, Chen emerged as a leader of the "conservative" camp and was frequently critical of Deng Xiaoping's more reform-minded policies.

Byrd, William A., and Qingsong Lin, editors, *China's Rural Industry: Structure, Development, and Reform,* Oxford and New York: Oxford University Press, 1990

An important aspect of China's economic reforms has been the unexpected rise of Township and Village Enterprises. The essays collected in this volume provide a good understanding of the way in which these enterprises emerged, their unique characteristics, and the problems they face.

Crane, George T., *The Political Economy of China's Special Economic Zones,* Armonk, New York: M.E. Sharpe, 1990

One of the most important innovations in China's economic reforms was the creation of Special Economic Zones, first in the southeastern provinces of Guangdong and Fujian, then, under the guise of Economic and Technical Development Zones, in 14 coastal cities, and finally in the island province of Hainan. This book looks at the creation and development of Special Economic Zones, including their sometimes rocky relations with the central government.

Fewsmith, Joseph, *Dilemmas of Reform in China: Political Conflict and Economic Debate,* Armonk, New York: M.E. Sharpe, 1994

How to proceed with reform remained a controversial issue throughout the 1980s, and this book traces the debates among economic specialists, many of whom advised the party leadership. The book lays out the dilemmas faced by reform advocates as they tried to design policies that were feasible and would avoid criticism from the party elite.

Lardy, Nicholas R., *Foreign Trade and Economic Reform in China, 1978–1990,* Cambridge and New York: Cambridge University Press, 1992

This book describes carefully the evolution of China's foreign trade system since the inauguration of economic reform in 1978. It makes clear both how far China has come and how far it has to go.

Lardy, Nicholas R., *China in the World Economy,* Washington, D.C.: Institute for International Economics, 1994

This is the clearest and most authoritative account of such important issues as the size of China's economy, the real trade balance between the United States and China (it is not as large as usually thought), the nature of Sino-US trade disputes, including intellectual property rights, and China's possible participation in the World Trade Organization (WTO). It is brief and highly readable.

Naughton, Barry, *Growing Out of the Plan: Chinese Economic Reform, 1978–1993,* Cambridge and

New York: Cambridge University Press, 1995

Perhaps the most readable account of the process of economic reform from the perspective of an economist. Naughton's thesis is that China not so much engaged in economic reform as allowed the economy simply to outgrow the old planned economy.

Pearson, Margaret M., *Joint Ventures in the People's Republic of China: The Control of Foreign Direct Investment Under Socialism,* Princeton, New Jersey: Princeton University Press, 1991

Joint ventures have become an important part of China's economic reform and of opening to the outside world. Pearson looks at the ways the Chinese government has sought to control this influx of capital.

Vogel, Ezra F., *One Step Ahead in China: Guangdong under Reform,* Cambridge, Massachusetts, Harvard University Press, 1989

China's southeastern province of Guangdong (across the border from Hong Kong) has pioneered many of China's economic reforms. Vogel's book gives a highly readable account of how reform has progressed in Guangdong, "one step ahead" of other regions.

Young, Susan, *Private Business and Economic Reform in China,* Armonk, New York, and London: M.E. Sharpe, 1995

One of the most controversial aspects of economic reform in China has been the emergence of a private economy. This book looks at the size of the private sector, the ways in which it has emerged, and its likely future.

Joseph Fewsmith is the Director of the East Asian Interdisciplinary Studies Program and Associate Chairman of the Department of International Relations at Boston University. He is the author of *Party, State, and Local Elites in Republican China* (1985) and *Dilemmas of Reform in China: Political Conflict and Economic Debate* (1994). He has written numerous articles on the politics and economics of contemporary China and is editor of *Chinese Economic Studies,* a journal of translations.

Chapter Eight

China's Urban Industry

Chun Chang and Yijiang Wang

1 Introduction

Although China traditionally has been an agricultural economy, industrialization has been a national goal since 1949 and rapid industrial growth an important feature of the economy. From 1979 to 1994 China's Gross Domestic Product (GDP) growth rate averaged approximately 10% annually. Significantly, while the average growth rate for agricultural output during this period was 6.2%, that for industrial output was more than 14%. These figures reflect the importance of China's industrial sector to the larger economy. Moreover, owing to China's size and wealth of resources, as well as to the market-oriented reform measures, continued industrial growth in the future appears likely.

Because industrialization has been the centerpiece of China's economic development strategy, both under the old regime, which sought to coordinate industrial growth through careful central planning, and under the new regime, which has supported market-oriented reform, analyzing China's industrial policies over the years will reveal much about the nature of China's economic institutions. Under the central planning system, the generation of Chinese leaders led by Mao Zedong pursued industrialization as a way for China to reemerge as a world power after more than a century of humiliation inflicted by the Western industrial powers and Japan. To expedite the process of industrialization, China's communist government adopted

the Soviet model of central (or state) planning. According to this system, the state suppresses the market mechanism for resource allocation so that state planners can channel more resources to factories and thus increase the rate of industrial development, especially the development of heavy industry (the term "heavy industry" denotes the production of basic materials that in turn are used for construction and to produce consumer goods). The Maoist leadership believed this approach effectively would develop China's industrial sector. Some observers and scholars have suggested that this decision to promote heavy industry at the expense of other sectors of the economy is the root of many problems in the current Chinese economic system.

After Mao's death, the second and third generations of Communist Party leaders gradually have introduced market-oriented reform measures aimed at making China more competitive in the world economy, raising the living standards of the Chinese people, and thus preserving the Communist Party's hold on power. Although the success of agricultural reforms during the early 1980s contributed greatly to improved living standards, the aforementioned growth figures suggest that China's sustained economic growth during the past two decades was owing mainly to the expansion of the industrial sector. As a result of this sustained high growth, China has become a major trader in the world economy; the total volume of China's foreign trade increased from around US$20 billion per annum in the late 1970s to ten times that amount by the mid-1990s. The importance of China's industrial development to the welfare of its people and to the world economy cannot be over-estimated.

This chapter provides an overview and analysis of China's urban industry during the Maoist period, the 1980s, and the 1990s. In doing so, this chapter examines the "structure" of the industrial sector (defined here as the degree of competition within the sector as measured by the market share of the four largest industrial producers). The chapter then examines the relationship between the structure of the industrial sector and the "conduct" of industrial firms, including their pricing, output, investment, and decisions regarding research and development. Finally, it analyzes how industrial firms' conduct has affected their economic performance. The chapter also examines how the major institutional features of the planned economy affected the conduct and performance of China's industry.

2 China's Urban Industry Before 1979

2.1 Size and Ownership Structure

Prior to 1956, the private sector produced more than half of China's industrial output. However, the campaign to reform industry and commerce launched by the Chinese Communist Party (CCP) in 1956 dramatically changed the ownership structure of China's industrial sector. By the time market-oriented reforms were introduced in the late 1970s, China's industry was concentrated in urban areas and owned mostly by the state. Thus, over the course of the period 1956–78, the terms "industry," "urban industry," and "state-owned industry" became increasingly indivisible.

During the late 1950s and 1960s, state-owned enterprises (SOEs) accounted for about 90% of the country's industrial output. The percentage dropped to slightly less than 80% during the late 1970s, owing to increased production on the part of collec-

tively-owned industrial enterprises, most of which were located in urban areas. Until the mid-1980s, the industrial output of native-owned private businesses and foreign-owned firms was negligible. Overall, the industrial sector in 1978 employed 43.5 million people, 72% of whom worked in the state sector; moreover, 91.8% of the industrial sector's 242.37 billion *yuan* in fixed assets belonged to the state.

The state's industrial assets derived from three sources. First, after the civil war ended in 1949, the communist government confiscated and nationalized the properties of the "bureaucratic bourgeoisie" (i.e., those with close ties to the exiled National-ist, or Kuomintang, government). Second, the properties of the "national bourgeoisie" (native industrialists not affiliated with the Nationalist government) were managed by the state in the 1950s; the state paid a fixed fee (*ding xi*) to the owners as compensation. These, too, were nationalized in the mid-1960s at the peak of the Cultural Revolution. However, continuous heavy invest-ment by the state accounted for the majority of industrial sector assets. Owing largely to the state's financial commitment to heavy industry, the industrial sector's total assets in 1979 were nearly 30 times its 1950 assets and nearly three times its assets in 1969. Not surprisingly, this increased the industrial sector's production capacity. As a consequence, during the years 1954–78 industry output growth averaged 12% annually (see Table 8.1. It should be noted that the high growth rates of the early 1950s were not the result of Maoist indus-trial policy; instead, they reflect economic recovery from the Japanese invasion and the civil war).

2.2 Heavy Industry Policy Under the Planning System

China adopted the Soviet-style comprehen-sive planning system in the 1950s. Under this system the state planning committee determined how financial, material, and human resources should be allocated among different sectors of the economy.

The state set prices for producer and consumer goods regardless of their actual market value. These prices served no other purpose than to keep records of resource flows in the economy (although consumers still responded to price signals with their consumption choices). The state employed five-year plans to implement its economic development strategy. Adjustments were made annually during each five-year plan to recalibrate resource allocation.

Aided by technical and financial support from the Soviet Union, China built 156 "key" large-scale industrial projects during the First Five-Year Plan (1953–57). These projects played an important role in the development of China's industrial sector during the following two decades. Following the break in relations with the Soviet Union, the Chinese government implemented four more Five-Year Plans. The only three years during this period not covered by a comprehensive five-year plan were 1963–65, when the government adopted policies to consolidate and adjust the economy following the disastrous Great Leap Forward of 1958–60.

As previously mentioned, the Maoist leadership adopted the planning system in part to channel resources and capital to heavy industries, believing that a strong heavy industry would spur and sustain China's industrialization process. Owing to this development strategy, the growth rates of heavy industries during the Maoist period were much higher than those of light industries (i.e., industries that produce consumer goods). This is reflected in the changes in the heavy-light industry ratio over time. In 1949, heavy industry produced slightly more than one-quarter of China's industrial output. Its output rose steadily through the 1950s and has maintained a 50–60% share of total industrial output since the late 1950s (see Table 8.1).

2.3 Performance

Taken out of the larger context, the growth rates of China's mostly state-owned urban industry appear impressive; they suggest that China's approach to industrialization

might serve as a model for other developing, centrally-planned economies. An average annual growth rate of 14% for industrial output over a period of nearly three decades would be an astonishing achievement in a market economy. China's increased heavy industry output from roughly one-quarter to more than one-half of total industrial output suggests that the Maoist leaders succeeded in implementing their heavy industry policy through the planning system.

However, if the ultimate goal of industrialization was to produce a great volume of higher quality products that in turn would improve the living standards of the Chinese people, then the planning system failed miserably. On the eve of the reform era, China's urban industry suffered from low efficiency levels, using obsolete technologies to produce unwanted products at high costs. Not surprisingly, the average productivity of capital had declined substantially during the Maoist period. In 1957, 100 *yuan* worth of capital produced 139.3 *yuan* worth of industrial output. In 1977, the same amount produced only 95.5 *yuan* worth of industrial output, so that by 1977 the average productivity of capital had decreased some 30%. Studies also found stagnating total factor productivity. Owing to growing inefficiency in China's urban industry, the government was compelled to increase inputs in order to sustain industrial growth, particularly that of heavy industry. Unfortunately, this increased state investment in industry came at the expense of agriculture and Chinese consumers (see Louis Putterman, "Dualism and Reform in China," in *Economic Development and Change* 40, no. 3 [April 1992] for a discussion of the "dual" economy of industry and agriculture). Thereafter, state planners struggled to strike a balance in resource allocation between the industrial and agricultural sectors, and between heavy and light industries.

Beginning in the late 1970s, China opened its doors to the outside world. Through increased contacts with industrialized and newly industrialized countries, Chinese leaders began to realize that the planning system had produced high costs and low efficiency and had resulted in low living standards for the Chinese people. Thus, policymakers sought to reform China's economic system, including the urban industrial sector.

3 Reforming the Urban Industrial Sector

This section discusses the circumstances that led to the introduction of market-oriented reforms beginning in 1978, the reform measures adopted, and their effects on urban industry during the 1980s.

3.1 The Causes of Inefficiency

Scholars and observers generally attribute the failure of the Maoist economic system to two major shortcomings of the command economy. First, without the benefit of market indicators to ascertain consumer demand, neither central planners nor producers in the economy had the relevant information regarding production needs. This gap resulted in the underproduction of some goods and overproduction of others. Moreover, because political considerations often influenced production decisions, mistakes were frequent and costly. The most apparent example of this took place in the 1950s, when China's supreme leader Mao Zedong, believing that China could match the industrial strength of the United Kingdom within ten years and that of the United States within 15 years, launched the Great Leap Forward, an all-out campaign for rapid industrialization characterized by heavy industry growth. As a result of this misguided belief, the total assets of state industry increased from 45% to 66% over the period 1957–60 (see Tables 8.1 and 8.3). The campaign impoverished the agricultural sector and pushed current consumption of the population to an unacceptably low level. Consequently, the campaign was abandoned in the early 1960s. Central planners scaled back industrial output (the industrial sector did not reach its 1958 output level until 1964); in particular, the weight of heavy industry was scaled back to

approximately 55% of total industrial output (see Table 8.1).

The second major shortcoming of the command system was that state planners could not appropriately measure performance and reward the most efficient firms. Under the planning system, firms were provided the necessary financial resources and material inputs regardless of whether their production technology was cost-efficient or their investments financially sound. This problem, common in socialist economies, is known as "soft-budget" constraints. Under such a system, firms had little incentive to reduce production costs, introduce new products, or utilize their financial resources responsibly.

3.2 Major Reform Measures and Their Effects

In 1979 and during the early 1980s, the Chinese government introduced reform measures to improve the efficiency of the industrial sector. These measures focused on expanding enterprise autonomy, increasing incentives, and introducing markets to complement or replace the planning system. The rationale behind these measures was twofold. On the one hand, retained profits would provide firms with more funds to invest in response to market signals (this arrangement by itself represented expanded enterprise autonomy). On the other hand, retained profits could be used to reward workers and managers for reducing production costs, introducing new products, and increasing the productivity of their enterprises.

A second wave of reforms was initiated in 1984. The most notable reform measure introduced during this round was the contract responsibility system (*chengbaozhi*), which provided additional incentives to managers. Under this system, managers of most state-owned enterprises signed multiyear contracts with government agencies in charge of their enterprises (i.e., an industrial bureau); these contracts specified financial and nonfinancial objectives to be achieved by the manager, thus linking managers' compensation with performance.

In the late 1980s, the rise of inflation and the ensuing political unrest slowed the progress of economic reforms. By the early 1990s, however, reforms gathered renewed momentum. Firms gained even greater management autonomy and the economy became increasingly marketized.

Taken as a whole, these reform measures significantly altered the environment in which SOEs operated and the manner in which they were managed. Firms quickly started to respond to market signals to determine what goods to produce. In 1981, 30% of retail goods were produced according to market demand. This figure rose steadily throughout the 1980s and most of the 1990s. In 1994, 90% of retail goods and 80% of producer goods were allocated by markets (see Table 8.2). Meanwhile, industrial output continued to grow by 15% annually. However, in contrast to Maoist state industry, industrial growth during the reform period was characterized by technological efficiency as measured by total factor productivity (see Gary Jefferson and Thomas Rawski, "Enterprise Reform in Chinese Industry," in *Journal of Economic Perspectives* 8, no. 2 [Spring 1994] for a summary of studies on total factor productivity of Chinese industrial enterprises).

Unfortunately, other factors have limited the effectiveness of these reform measures. For example, owing to increased enterprise efficiency, one-quarter to one-third of all workers in the state industrial sector now are considered redundant. Despite SOE managers' increased autonomy, most find it politically expedient to keep redundant labor on the payroll. Also, both managers and the government have tended to renege on contracts, thus diminishing the effectiveness of the contract responsibility system. These problems have prevented SOEs from becoming financially responsible for their operational decisions. These problems are addressed in greater detail later in this chapter.

3.3 Entry of New Firms

Notably, the reform of China's industrial sector spurred the entry of new firms of different ownership types, including collectively-owned urban enterprises, rural enterprises, private enterprises, and foreign-owned enterprises. Most impressive has been the proliferation of rural enterprises, known as township and village enterprises (TVEs). TVEs grew in numbers at an average annual rate of 30% during the 1980s. By the mid-1990s TVEs produced nearly half of China's industrial output and employed nearly 100 million workers. As a result of this massive entry of new firms, SOEs' share of total output has declined from nearly 80% in 1979 to less than 40% in 1994 (see Table 8.3).

4 China's Industry in the 1990s

The liberalization of consumer and producer prices and the intensified competition owing to new entries in the 1990s significantly affected China's SOEs. Moreover, they will continue to affect the future course of Chinese industry. This section examines the performance and the ownership structure of the industrial sector in greater detail.

4.1 Performance of the State Industrial Sector

During the reform period, the state industry sector continued to grow at pre-reform levels (see Table 8.1). The average growth rate of total industrial output from 1979 to 1993 was 14%, while the average growth rate of fixed assets investment for the same period was 15.5%. Labor employment in 1993 was 1.43 times that in 1978. Despite these positive trends, the financial situation of SOEs actually has worsened during the reform period. Over the past 15 years, both the number of SOEs losing money and the average loss have increased steadily (see Table 8.4). Currently, the state industrial sector heavily burdens state resources.

To the dismay of central authorities, the financial troubles of SOEs have set off a chain reaction in China's economy. Many SOE employees now receive only minimum subsistence pay and at times are paid in-kind with their employer's own product, which they in turn must sell for cash. Owing to fears on the part of state officials that growing dissatisfaction among state workers may lead to severe social unrest, state banks have continued to issue loans to SOEs despite the fact that repayment of the loans is unlikely. Meanwhile, to maintain liquidity in the economy, the government has had to increase state bank credit quotas, which in turn have created inflationary pressures. Also, because SOEs are the main source of fiscal revenue, their financial difficulties have resulted in declines in government revenues. These effects suggest that the financial problems facing the state industrial sector are a major contributor to China's macroeconomic instability.

Explanations abound as to why SOEs have performed so poorly. One explanation is that massive entries of new firms have increased product market competition, which in turn has reduced the monopoly profits that many SOEs previously had enjoyed. Another explanation is that most SOEs cannot compete with the newly entered firms because they have to support a large number of retired workers.

Policymakers and observers in China, however, claim that poor management is the primary reason that SOEs continue to perform poorly. This argument has some merit. In spite of increased marketization across the remainder of China's economy, financial resource allocation to SOEs for the most part continues to be determined bureaucratically. For example, state banks continue to issue loans to SOEs at the behest of government officials. Consequently, few loss-making SOEs are bankrupted. In other words, the fundamental problem of soft-budget constraints still prevails in the state industrial sector. Because SOEs are not subject to stringent market discipline, stakeholders within SOEs are freer to pursue their own private interests. Managers may find it more worthwhile to start underfunded and risky projects, to produce beyond the profit-maximizing quantity of output for "empire building" (i.e., increasing the size or capacity of an enterprise at the expense of economic efficiency), or to

please workers by distributing generous bonuses or building more worker housing. In response to these abuses, the government repeatedly has decreed that SOEs should start fewer new projects or abandon those in progress, reduce output levels, and curb excessive bonuses to workers.

Thus, high industrial output growth rates mask serious deficiencies in the urban industrial sector. Although on the surface statistical increases in output, projects, and bonuses paid to workers suggest a healthy sectoral economy, the financial difficulties of SOEs pose a serious threat to macroeconomic stability in China.

4.2 Ownership Structure

As described earlier, economic reforms pertaining to China's urban industry have altered the ownership structure of the sector. Most notably, the state's share in the sector has decreased while township and village enterprises have assumed a much greater share. Furthermore, the industrial sector has enjoyed massive in-flows of direct foreign investment, making China the world's second largest recipient of foreign direct investment behind the US. Chinese cities received a total of US$81.43 billion in foreign investment between 1990 and 1994. Not surprisingly, this direct foreign investment also has contributed to the changing ownership structure of China's urban industrial sector. By 1993 fully foreign-owned businesses and joint ventures (firms operated jointly by foreign and Chinese businesspersons) already had produced 11% of China's total industrial output and employed more than 10 million workers. In addition to their financial input contributions, these firms imported more up-to-date production technology and improved managerial skills, spurring other enterprises in the sector to follow suit.

Finally, although still relatively small, private businesses established by native Chinese have begun to impact the ownership structure of China's urban industry (at the outset of the reform era, Chinese entrepreneurs hesitated to start their own businesses, fearing a new round of persecution by the state; however, many soon became convinced that the government's reform efforts had created a much more amiable environment for private business). In 1985 the private sector's industrial output exceeded 1% of total industrial output for the first time since the late 1950s. Subsequently, private-owned firms grew rapidly, producing more than 8% of the nation's industrial output in 1993.

In sum, SOEs' share of China's urban industry shrank from nearly 80% in 1979 to less than 40% in 1995, and their growth rates have been accompanied by deepening financial problems. Today, more than 60% of China's industrial output is produced by non-state enterprises, including urban collectives, TVEs, foreign-owned firms, and native-owned private businesses. Meanwhile, the SOEs' profound financial difficulties call into question the viability of state-owned industry in an increasingly competitive market environment; they also exacerbate the redundant labor problem in state-owned industry. Fortunately, TVEs, foreign-owned firms, and native-owned private businesses introduced dynamics for sustainable long-term growth of China's urban industry.

Significantly, the erosion of the planning system has not led to decreases in the size of China's heavy industry sector. In the mid-1990s, heavy industry still accounted for more than 50% of the nation's industrial output. Many firms in this sector still are plagued with obsolete equipment and technology and unwanted products. Their continued operation is made possible by heavy state subsidies, which they often receive in the form of low interest loans from state banks.

5 The Future of China's Urban Industry

Barring dramatic political events, the gradual trend toward marketization of China's economy is likely to continue, and TVEs, urban collective enterprises, foreign-invested enterprises, and private businesses are likely to flourish in the foreseeable future. Meanwhile, the Chinese government is committed to reforming SOEs, and therefore those that are profitable will continue to grow. However, the SOE sector as a whole will grow much more slowly than other types of firms.

The financial difficulties of SOEs pose a serious challenge to China's leaders. Having largely abandoned the contract responsibility system, the CCP in a 1994 resolution called for the establishment of a "modern enterprise system." The resolution recognized that reforming SOEs and improving their performance would require more than simply increasing SOE management autonomy and retained profit, or providing SOEs with better technology and using incentive contracts like the contract responsibility system to increase SOE productivity. Although the party's resolution failed to define a "modern enterprise system," scholars and policymakers in China increasingly have recognized that financial market discipline is needed to improve the performance of SOEs. However, financial discipline is difficult to achieve within the existing ownership and industrial structure, and thus SOE ownership needs to be restructured in some way. In 1996 the government endorsed a policy of "keeping large ones and letting go of small ones." That is, the government will retain large SOEs for restructuring while allowing small SOEs to be privatized.

Regardless of whether China's leadership attempts to restructure ownership of SOEs, if the reform-era trend is any indication the SOEs' dominance in China's industrial sector will continue to decline. This decline does not minimize the importance of improving SOE performance—after all, SOEs in the mid-1990s still produce 40% of the nation's industrial output and employ more industrial labor and have greater assets than all other sectors combined. Moreover, SOEs' investment behavior and financial difficulties will continue to affect China's macroeconomy. Both in the near and intermediate future, how to relocate redundant SOE workers will remain a politically and socially thorny question for

China's policymakers. However, for the industrial sector as a whole, the declining relative size of SOEs does suggest that the trend toward rapid and sustained industrial growth combined with a more balanced product structure is likely to continue.

Further Reading

Broadman, Harry G., editor, *Policy Options for Reform of Chinese State-owned Enterprises: Proceedings of a Symposium in Beijing, June 1995*, Washington, D.C.: World Bank, 1996

Part of a series of such publications by the World Bank, this book contains five policy option papers by Chinese officials on such topics as SOE performance, corporatization, asset management, and organizational and debt restructuring–each followed by the commentary of a World Bank official. One paper presents the World Bank's recommendations for reform of SOEs.

Chang, Chun, and Yijiang Wang, "The Nature of the Township-Village Enterprise," in *Journal of Comparative Economics* 19 (1994)

This article describes the ownership and control structures of township-village enterprises in China and explains why such a unique ownership arrangement exists.

Chen, Derong, *Chinese Firms Between Hierarchy and Market: The Contract Management Responsibility System in China*, New York: St. Martin's Press, and London: Macmillan, 1995

Introduced in 1987, the CMRS is an important component of enterprise reform by seeking to increase SOE autonomy from the government. Applying a sociological institutional approach to the case of four Beijing SOEs, the book traces the formation and implementation of contracts, concluding that while the CMRS did allow managers more flexibility, more substantial reform is called for.

Chinese Economic Studies, special issues on "Deficits in Chinese Industrial Enterprises" 26, nos. 1 and 2 (Fall/Winter 1992)

This journal performs the valuable service of translating into English Chinese documents and articles of contemporary and historical significance on topics relating to economic issues. These two journal numbers contain studies presenting problems and countermeasures for industrial enterprise deficits in the late 1980s. The first volume's three articles provide an overview while the second volume contains more focused case studies.

Folta, Paul Humes, *From Swords to Plowshares? Defense Industry Reform in the PRC,* Boulder, Colorado: Westview Press, 1992

China stands as an international model for the transformation of military facilities to civilian production. In the process, the military has become a major economic power in China. Examining the period from 1978 to 1990, the analysis argues that military enterprises initiated many of the management and production reforms but that the problems of inefficiency and lack of autonomy remain. The appendices present statistical tables and organizational charts.

Hay, Donald, Derek Morris, Guy Liu, and Shujie Yao, *Economic Reform and State-Owned Enterprises in China, 1979–1987,* Oxford: Clarendon Press, and New York: Oxford University Press, 1994

Part of a series of joint studies by economists from the Chinese Academy of Social Sciences, Oxford University, and University of California, San Diego, this book presents an examination of the first decade of SOE reform. Issues addressed include the extent to which greater autonomy and incentives were given to SOEs and the impact of changes in the external environment on enterprise behavior. At times the text is highly technical but the authors present the significance of their models and findings in accessible language.

Jefferson, Gary H., and Thomas G. Rawski, "Enterprise Reform in Chinese Industry," in *Journal of Economic Perspectives* 8, no. 2 (1994)

This article first reviews the economic conditions that existed prior to the reform initiatives of the late 1970s and then describes the impact of reform policies on the structure, conduct, and performance of SOEs during the 1980s. It also examines the growth of industry outside the state sector.

Naughton, Barry, *Growing Out of the Plan: Chinese Economic Reform, 1978–1993,* Cambridge and New York: Cambridge University Press, 1995

A comprehensive study of China's economic

reforms from late 1978 to 1993. The book focuses on industry and macroeconomic policy as a way to view reform strategy as a whole.

Tam, On Kit, editor, *Financial Reform in China,* London and New York: Routledge, 1995

This collection of papers examines some of the more macro financial structures affecting institutional reform. The subjects covered include monetary management, central bank controls, financial institutions, rural finances, foreign exchange, and the interbank money market.

Warner, Malcom, *The Management of Human Resources in Chinese Industry,* London: Macmillan, and New York: St. Martin's Press, 1995

In breaking the "iron rice bowl," China must reform its labor and personnel system. Section one presents a historical and conceptual overview while section two includes discussion of reforms at the city and enterprise level, illustrated with case studies from SOEs in four major northern Chinese cities. The book also discusses the impact of the recent labor law reform on urban industry, arguing that the iron rice bowl remains surprisingly resilient.

Woo, Wing Thy, Wen Hai, Yibiao Jin, and Gang Fang, "How Successful Has China's State Enterprise Reform Been?" in *Journal of Comparative Economics* 18 (1994)

The authors show that documented total factor productivity gains in China's SOEs may be owing to underdeflation of output and overdeflation of intermediate inputs. They also argue that increases in total factor productivity do not necessarily improve SOEs' financial performance.

Yingyi Qian, "Enterprise Reform in China: Agency Problems and Political Control," in *Economics of Transition* 4, no. 2 (1996)

The author argues that China needs to transform its enterprise ownership structure through a combination of privatization, denationalization, and pluralization; through a state assets management system to limit political influence from the government; and through corporatization to establish effective corporate governance, which may take a variety of forms.

Chun Chang is Associate Professor in the Carlson School of Management, University of Minnesota.

Yijiang Wang is Assistant Professor in the Industrial Relations Center, Carlson School of Management, University of Minnesota.

Professor Chang and Professor Wang have coauthored articles on Chinese urban industry in *Journal of Economic Behavior and Organization, Journal of Comparative Economics,* and *Research in Labor Economics,* among others.

Table 8.1: Industry Output Growth Rates and Heavy-Light Industry Ratios 1949–93

Year	Growth Rate	Light Industry	Heavy Industry
	(% per year)	*(As % of Industry Output)*	
1949		73.6	26.4
1950	36.4	70.7	29.3
1951	38.2	67.8	32.2
1952	29.9	64.5	35.5
1953	30.3	62.7	37.3
1954	16.3	61.6	38.4
1955	5.6	59.2	40.8
1956	28.1	57.6	42.4
1957	11.5	55	45
1958	54.8	46.4	53.6
1959	36.1	41.5	58.5
1960	11.2	33.4	66.6
1961	-38.2	42.5	57.5
1962	-16.6	47.2	52.8
1963	8.5	44.8	55.2
1964	9.6	44.3	55.7
1965	26.4	51.6	48.4
1966	20.9	49	51
1967	-13.8	53	47
1968	-5	53.7	46.3
1969	34.3	50.3	49.7
1970	32.6	46.2	53.8
1971	14.7	43	57
1972	6.9	42.9	57.1
1973	9.5	43.4	56.6
1974	0.6	44.4	55.6
1975	15.5	44.1	55.9
1976	2.4	44.2	55.8

Table 8.1: Industry Output Growth Rates and Heavy-Light Industry Ratios 1949–93

Year	Growth Rate	Light Industry	Heavy Industry
	(% per year)	*(As % of Industry Output)*	
1977	14.6	44	56
1978	13.5	43.1	56.9
1979	8.8	43.7	56.3
1980	9.3	47.2	52.8
1981	4.3	51.5	48.5
1982	7.8	50.2	49.8
1983	11.2	48.5	51.5
1984	16.3	47.4	52.6
1985	21.4	47.4	52.6
1986	11.7	47.6	52.4
1987	17.7	48.2	51.8
1988	20.8	49.3	50.7
1989	8.5	48.9	51.1
1990	7.8	49.4	50.6
1991	14.5	48.9	51.1
1992	27.5	47.2	52.8
1993	28	44	56

Resources: *Statistic Year Book of China's Industry Economy 1994*: 25
Note: Ratio = Heavy Industry Output/Light Industry Output

Table 8.2: Shares of Three Pricing System for Retail Goods in China (1990–94)

	State-Fixed Price	State-Directed Price	Market-Adjusted Price
1990	29.80%	17.20%	53.00%
1991	20.90%	10.30%	68.80%
1992	5.90%	1.10%	93.00%
1993	4.80%	1.40%	93.80%
1994	7.20%	2.40%	90.40%

Resources: Almanac of China's Economy 1995: 21

Table 8.3: Industry Output of Four Kinds of Economies in China 1979–94

Year	State-Owned	Collective	Private	Others	SOE's Output Shares
	(billion *yuan*)				
1979	367.36	100.77	0	0	78%
1980	391.56	121.336	0.081	2.449	76%
1981	403.71	132.938	0.19	3.14	75%
1982	432.6	144.242	0.34	3.94	75%
1983	473.94	166.314	0.75	5.04	74%
1984	526.27	226.314	1.48	7.67	70%
1985	630.212	311.719	17.975	11.741	66%
1986	697.112	375.154	30.854	16.306	63%
1987	825.009	478.174	50.239	27.877	61%
1988	1035.128	658.749	79.049	49.532	58%
1989	1234.291	785.805	105.766	75.844	58%
1990	1306.375	852.273	129.03	104.756	57%
1991	1495.458	1008.475	160.91	159.958	56%
1992	1782.415	1410.119	250.68	263.357	52%
1993	2272.467	2021.312	440.205	535.206	48%
1994	2620.084	3143.404	885.323	1042.135	39%

Resources: Statistic Year Book of China's Industry Economy 1995: 26

Table 8.4: Total Loss from SOEs 1979–93

Year	Total Loss from SOEs (billion yuan)
1979	3.638
1980	3.430
1981	4.596
1982	4.757
1983	3.211
1984	2.661
1985	3.244
1986	5.449
1987	6.104
1988	8.192
1989	18.019
1990	34.880
1991	36.700
1992	36.930
1993	45.260

Resources: Statistic Year Book of China's Industry Economy 1994: 56

Chapter Nine

The Impact and Prospects of Rural Enterprise

Michelle S. Mood

Introduction

Rural enterprises have been part of Chinese village life throughout this century, but only after the reforms of the late 1970s did they become a significant economic presence across much of rural China. Overall, rural industrial output grew nearly 17% per year from 1978 through the early 1990s. By 1994, nearly 20 million non-state rural enterprises employed 113,296,984 peasants (or 24% of all rural labor), produced one-half of the national industrial output value, paid one-quarter of national taxes, and brought in about one-third of the nation's foreign exchange from exports. Following the reorganization of the countryside in the early 1980s and the loosening of many economic strictures via the reforms, rural enterprises have become a key way for villages and towns to fund local projects, employ villagers, maintain a social safety net, and develop their local economies.

Rural enterprises encompass many types of non-farming activities and all ownership forms. Such enterprises include small kiosks selling beer and cigarettes, hotels and restaurants, construction or transportation teams, and handicraft, processing, and industrial factories. They are owned by individuals (*getihu, getiqiye, siying qiye*), household alliances (*lianhu*), townships and towns (*xiangbanqiye*), villages (*cunbanqiye*), shareholders (*gufenqiye*) and cooperative liaisons and joint ownership of every imaginable type (*lianbanqiye, liany-*

ingqiye, hezuoqiye, heziqiye). Liaisons may include partnerships between government or administrative offices, individuals, and foreigners (*sanziqiye*), among others. Collective township and village enterprises (*xiangcun jiti suoyouzhi qiye*) are those owned 51% or more by townships or villages. Although some sources include *lianyingqiye* in the "collective" category, perhaps to shore up the numbers of collective enterprises or to stamp alliance enterprises with the respectability of a "collective" label, this chapter does not consider *lianyingqiye* collective enterprises because just 0.6% of *lianyingqiye* involve villages or townships. Officially, these types of rural enterprises together are called *xiangzhenqiye*, which is translated as rural enterprises or township and village enterprises (TVEs).

This chapter provides an overview of the economic and political details of this burgeoning sector. In so doing, two main conclusions are drawn. First, dynamics at the village level—and not central directives—have determined most characteristics of rural development during the reform era. Second, contrary to the West's expectations, the degree of marketization does not always correlate with the degree of privatization of the economy.

Rural Enterprise Growth Trends

Table 9.1 charts the development of rural enterprises by sector since 1983. Overall numbers of TVEs increased markedly in

1984 when Central Committee Document Number One legitimized TVEs, and again in 1985 when Central Committee Document Number Four legalized non-collective enterprises. Most strikingly, the numbers of construction, transport, service, and food enterprises skyrocketed in 1985. Either these types of enterprises "sprung up like bamboo shoots after a spring rain," or, more likely, they already had existed, operating semi-covertly, but had not been counted until they were legal. Table 9.1 also indicates clearly that service and food-related enterprises hire very few workers per enterprise. In 1994, service and food enterprises accounted for 33% of all TVEs but hired only 13.7% of TVE workers. By contrast, rural construction teams numbered 4.5% of TVEs but hired 14% of the workers, while industrial factories, accounting for 37% of TVE enterprises, hired 62% of the workers.

Table 9.2 shows the changes over time in the ownership structure of the TVE sector. Although collective enterprises currently comprise only 8.8% of all TVEs, they hire 52% of TVE workers. Because many collective enterprises are factories, which hire greater numbers of employees, China's rural collective sector enjoys a higher labor productivity and has more capital-intensive production. By comparison, individual enterprises comprise 87% of TVEs but hire only 42% of the employees. After jumping dramatically in number during the mid-1980s, individual enterprises steadied in 1988, hovering at about 16 million until 1992, when Deng's trip South reinvigorated the sector. Despite the central leaders' consistent promotion of collective TVEs, however, the number of collective township and village enterprises continued to fall in 1991, when other sectors were rebounding after the 1989–90 economic slowdown.

Rural enterprises cooperatively managed with, jointly owned with, or fully owned by foreigners (*sanziqiye*) numbered 29,371 in 1994, or just 0.16% of all TVEs. Of these *sanziqiye*, 14,146 were jointly funded by China and foreign investors (*heziqiye*). Notably, 10,212 (or 35%) of all *sanziqiye* were newly established in 1994.

This may indicate that foreign investment and foreign management are important new trends in TVE development.

Total output value of TVEs in 1994 exceeded 4.25 trillion *yuan* (in fixed 1990 prices), or 40% of China's gross social output value. Agriculture produced 1.35% of China's gross social output value, industry 75.9%, construction 9.5%, and service and food 8.04%. Industry, not surprisingly, was the most productive sector, as indicated by its employing almost two-thirds of TVE workers yet producing three-quarters of the output value. Construction suffered particularly low labor productivity, employing 14% of TVE workers while producing only 9.5% of the output value. Individual enterprises, which account for 87% of all TVEs, produce just 26.5% of the output value despite employing 42% of TVE workers. Collective enterprises are by far the most productive; collective township enterprises and village enterprises produced 35.3% and 32.5% of TVE output value, respectively, despite employing only 26% of TVE workers apiece and in total comprising 8.8% of all TVEs.

The macroeconomic indicators in Tables 9.1 and 9.2 mask the fact that the distribution of TVEs is very uneven. In 1994, the eastern provinces (Beijing, Fujian, Guangdong, Guangxi, Hebei, Jiangsu, Liaoning, Tianjin, Shandong, Shanghai, Zhejiang) produced 69% of the TVE output value, while the central region (Anhui, Henan, Heilongjiang, Hubei, Hunan, Jilin, Jiangxi, Neimenggu, Shanxi) produced just 23% and the western region (Gansu, Guizhou, Ningxia, Qinghai, Shaanxi, Sichuan, Yunnan, Xizang, Xinjiang) only 6.4% of the TVE output value. Although 6.4% represents only a small fraction of TVE output value, the western region is experiencing the most rapid growth; in 1991 it had accounted for only 3% of TVE industrial output value. Variation in population densities explains some of the regional disparity, although in 1989 the eastern region had just 41% of the population, the central region 36%, and the western region 23%. Ownership forms also vary by region. In general, there are more private enterprises in poorer interior areas and more collective enterprises in the richer coastal areas; however, Guangzhou and coastal Fujian are exceptions, since they are wealthy yet have many private enterprises. Variation is present at the local levels as well; one village may have no private enterprises while a neighboring village has 30.

TVE Policy Developments

TVEs are an easy target in a reforming command economy because, although legal, they operate in the ideologically gray areas outside the state-controlled sector. Until recently, during every reform-era political disturbance and macroeconomic setback, some part of the TVE sector had been attacked. A bit of policy history will serve to illustrate the vulnerability of TVEs and the resultant fluctuations in their economic indicators as seen in Tables 9.1 and 9.2.

Originally, TVEs served as handmaiden to agriculture and to state enterprises. Additionally, collective ownership has been the ownership form most acceptable to the central leadership. The effects of this early orientation linger on more strongly in some areas than in others. In Tianjin during the early 1990s, for example, 40% of TVEs still processed for state enterprises, while fully 25% of TVEs were collective (almost three times the national average). Nationally, as treatment of TVEs swung from support to tolerance to repression and back again, enterprises creating agricultural inputs (e.g., fertilizer, agricultural machinery), processing agricultural goods (e.g., pickled vegetables, cotton thread, vegetable oil), or processing for state enterprises (e.g., quarrying rocks, making spare parts, supplying chemical dyes) have survived the fiercest crackdowns.

Of course, TVEs have outgrown their handmaiden role to agriculture and state industry, and, by doing so, have become vulnerable to censure. As China's economic reforms accelerated in the early 1980s, TVEs expanded into producing their own products, often light consumer goods independent of the state and agricultural sector. After

the poor crop harvest in 1985, TVEs came under attack for this diversification. Central authorities blamed low agricultural output on local authorities neglecting agricultural production in favor of TVE development. Consequently, leaders institutionalized rural enterprise support for agriculture in the form of subsidies to resident farmers and levies to the local government to be spent on agricultural modernization (*yigong bunong* and *yigong jiannong*, respectively) These subsidies totaled up to 20% of pre-tax profits.

After the anti-bourgeois liberalization drive got underway following the 1986 student demonstrations, collective enterprises explicitly were promoted over non-collective enterprises. Within a year, however, the trend to restrict private TVEs and to interfere in collective TVE affairs was reversed after the Thirteenth National Party Congress in October 1987, when leaders chose to deepen rural reforms and increase reliance on markets. On a trip researching TVEs at the end of 1987, Zhao Ziyang noted that it was entirely possible that coastal China would base its economy on TVEs, and that TVEs could possibly account for the major share of the nation's total exports. At the beginning of 1988, China's top leadership emphasized TVE exports and TVE staff training, while officially accepting large private enterprises. By the end of the year, however, the Agriculture Minister He Kang and Politburo Member and State Council Vice-Premier Tian Jiyun had reversed the swing toward industrialization, privatization, and market liberalization in favor of returning to an increase in administrative control over rural industry. This pro-agriculture and anti-inflation crackdown on "excessive growth in industrial production" targeted high-growth enterprises in coastal areas and those rural and urban collective industries and industries run by townships and villages that competed with state enterprises for raw materials. As He Kang admitted, by the end of 1988, "TVEs [had] taken the brunt of curbs placed on the supply of credit, energy and raw materials."

Economic overheating, political unrest,

and fears that state enterprises would suffer as a result of competition from TVEs precipitated a successful campaign to "readjust, consolidate, transform, and upgrade" enterprises by continuing to suppress industrial enterprises in 1989 and 1990. Scholar David Zweig notes that "conservative leaders . . . attacked rural enterprises as part of their broad strategy to restrengthen their own base of policy support–the state sector" (David Zweig, "Internationalizing China's Countryside: The Political Economy of Exports from Rural Industry," in *China Quarterly* 128 [1991]: 736). Central directives declared that all TVEs that consume too much "energy, produce shoddy goods, pollute, or compete in a major way with state enterprises for material should be closed down, suspended, merged or forced to shift to other production lines" (737). By restricting loans by half, drying up credit sources, and denying the establishment of all but select enterprises (those exporting, processing agricultural products, supplying big industry, and producing energy, raw materials, daily necessities in short supply, or agricultural machines and tools), curbs were made on most sectors, particularly on industrial TVEs. Loans were issued only to exporting TVEs, and TVE production overall slowed by 10% during the first half of 1989. Unfortunately, these were the very TVEs that produced most of the agricultural subsidies.

By the end of 1989, official figures claimed that up to 3 million "unqualified" rural enterprises in all sectors had been closed or merged. Not surprisingly, growth in industrial enterprises was curtailed sharply, as were the numbers of construction enterprises (see Table 9.1). Construction enterprises, although officially tolerated, are in practice often targeted because the sector creates "nonproductive" construction such as apartment complexes and retail stores, not just "productive" factories. Construction enterprises also bring into the cities substantial numbers of peasants who live in on-site shacks and are a potential source of turmoil.

Because 3 million enterprises closed in 1989, some scholars believe that township

and village collective enterprises (TVCEs) are operating under hard-budget constraints (see Martin L. Weitzman and Chenggang Xu, "Chinese Township-Village Enterprises as Vaguely Defined Cooperatives," in *Journal of Comparative Economics* 18 [1994]: 135). While it is safe to assume that TVEs operate on far harder budgets than state enterprises, other scholars have shown that very few TVEs operate on hard-budget constraints. These scholars point out that in 1989 the original three-year tax holidays for TVEs elapsed, bankrupting many economically unsound TVEs. TVCEs, meanwhile, operate on "flexible" budgets. For example, rural credit cooperatives allow debtors to default, and as a result debtors sometimes delay their payment of overdue loans indefinitely. Additionally, electricity and other inputs sometimes are offered to TVCEs at low government prices.

The January 1991 National Rural Enterprises Political Ideology Work Conference initiated a bizarre policy twist engineered by central-level conservatives. Seeking to increase party leadership over political and ideological work related to TVEs, this conference ordered Communist Party members to set up party branches in each enterprise. Deputy Minister of Agriculture Chen Yaobang noted in his speech that "the teachings of political ideology should permeate enterprise production, management, administration, service and [profit] allocation." Since this concern over party influence took place in 1991 rather than in the wake of the urban demonstrations of 1989, proponents of the initiative most likely were responding to the crisis in the USSR rather than to immediate internal threats. During 1991, the center also persisted in tightening credit and discouraging competition with state enterprises. Consequently, because TVCEs are particularly dependent on loans, the number of collective TVEs continued to fall in 1991 despite recovery in other sectors. By the end of 1991, however, flooding disasters had reminded China's leadership that TVEs are a strong and reliable source of income, less subject to the uncertainties of nature than agriculture, and thus the ideological drive to interfere with TVEs quietly and completely was dropped.

A confluence of other events also reinvigorated the TVE sector after 1991. Deng's trip to the South in January 1992, the Fourteenth Congress of the Chinese Communist Party in October 1992, and the expiration after three years of the administration provisions related to the post-June 4, 1989 economic rectification campaign served to re-legitimize TVE development in all sectors and all ownership forms. The resulting accelerated development was facilitated by a renewed commitment to the market and an openness toward new and complex forms of ownership, such as stock systems and different kinds of contracting. In 1993 the number of TVEs increased 17%, the highest increase since the rapid growth of the mid-1980s (see Tables). Industrial enterprises, free from central pressure for the first time since 1988, increased 15% while private enterprises increased by almost 18%.

Why, then, did TVE numbers decline by almost 6 million enterprises and by more than 10 million workers in 1994? After all, the late 1993 Decision of the CCP Central Committee on Certain Questions Regarding the Establishment of a Socialist Market Economic System favored the market more than ever and emphasized the position of TVEs as "an important pillar of the rural economy" to, among other things, "promote the transfer of the rural surplus labor force." The most salient explanation for the fall in TVE economic indicators during a liberalizing environment is that the new 1994 tax laws stifled development. The elimination of favorable adjustment taxes hampered those TVEs operating on the hardest budgets—private TVEs. Accordingly, declines in private TVEs accounted for the great majority of total TVE losses (see Table 9.2). However, not all private enterprises closed; private entrepreneurs likely found it more profitable to operate illegally than to pay taxes or close their doors. The concentration of private enterprises in the service sector explains the 45% drop in service enterprises and their workers. Relatedly, the increase in enterprise deficit, indirectly the result of fiscal reform, may explain the many capital-intensive industrial TVE closures in 1994 (over 2 million enterprises). Fiscal reform has profoundly affected TVE development.

Varying Roles of Local Government in TVE Development

This section examines the relationship between TVEs and grassroots government and explores the variations in local development paths. The findings discussed herein support the conclusions that the course of TVE development is determined largely at the village level and that rural collective enterprises remain economically viable even as local economies become increasingly marketized.

Several government offices have authority over rural enterprises. The Agriculture Ministry's Bureau of TVE Administration (*Xiangzhenqiye Guanli Ju*), devoted to managing rural enterprise, has branches at each administrative level down to the county level. At the township level, the local government's Economic Commission (*Jingji Weiyuanhui*, or *Jingwei*) is the most influential in guiding TVE development. Economic Commissions must approve the establishment of township TVCEs, and can use loans to manipulate TVE development at both the township and village levels. Township Economic Commissions are directly subordinate both to their township governments and to the County Economic Commission TVE Administration Department (*Xiangzhenqiye Guanli Bu*). At the village level, all three "leading bodies"—the Communist Party, the villagers' committees, and an economic institution (sometimes the Economic Commission, but other times a village Agricultural, Industrial, and Commerce General Corporation [*Nong Gong Shang Zonggongci*])—may play a role in directing the local economy. These village-level economic institutions are subordinate to Township Economic Commissions. Tax and finance offices at the county and township level also shape rural enterprise development in their localities. The Industry and Commerce Bureau (*Gongshang Xing-zhen Guanli Ju*) is responsible for registering and administering private and individual enterprises.

Although the 1988 National TVE Work Conference report noted that each level of the offices that administer TVEs should be regarded as the TVE government department at that level, in practice all TVE offices are subordinate to the government offices at their level. This reduces TVE offices to an advisory role with regard to the economy because they cannot make, implement, or enforce policy onto the government at the same level. Ultimately, in terms of enforcement, the Agriculture Commission (*Nongye Weiyuanhui*, or *Nongwei*) at the prefecture, city, municipal, or provincial level wields the most authority since it can force counties to compel township governments to comply. However, the Agriculture Commission rarely interferes, allowing villages to develop in accordance with local dynamics.

Collective TVEs, the economic heavyweight among rural enterprises, have an unusual relationship to local governments owing to their ownership form. Local residents own TVCEs, but they cannot transfer, sell, or inherit TVCE assets. Participation in collective ownership is determined by residency, which in turn is determined by birth or (for women) marriage. Weitzman and Xu note that "the typical resident waits passively to receive or to enjoy the benefits, of which the major part is not in monetary form but in the form of communal social investment, which is shared by everyone in the community" (Weitzman and Xu, 1994: 133–34). Owing to the nature of the collective ownership form, non-locals (*waidiren*) do not enjoy collective ownership benefits. Although TVEs hire them, "outsiders" receive less remuneration overall than resident "owners." On the other hand, local governments can force villagers to donate money to a TVCE or to make a personal investment in a TVCE as a precondition to being hired (*yizi dailao*); non-locals are not subject to these impositions.

Since the populations of townships and villages are too large to act in concert as owners, the Economic Commission at the township level and the village economic corporation or village Communist Party branch at the village level act as the de facto owners. Thus, cadres and officials can exercise control over contracting enterprises, granting loans, determining expenditures on capital projects and investment of all kinds, allocating jobs and other inputs, and determining remuneration and other distribution of factory profit. Although this arrangement provides the opportunity for cadre corruption, it also benefits TVCEs by offering them channels through which to access limited resources (particularly loans) and protection from changes in central or middle-level policies (see Chun Chang and Yijiang Wang, "The Nature of the Township-Village Enterprise," in *Journal of Comparative Economics* 19 [1994]: 443–44).

In practice, the degree to which local officials micro-manage their enterprises varies from full involvement to complete disregard. The quality, characteristics, and effectiveness of this leadership also vary. Scholars are still exploring the reasons for these variations as well as fluctuations in the concentration of different ownership forms; they attribute these variations to central policies, geography, level of infrastructure, the lingering effects of traditional or communist norms, kinship networks, the degree of market penetration, level of resource endowment and economic development, access to capital, and employment pressure and labor quality, among other causes.

In the mid-1980s, Chinese scholars identified several "models" (*dianxing*) of TVE development. Southern Jiangsu (the Sunan model) was cited for its emphasis on collective TVEs and for its efforts to coordinate township and village governments. Wenzhou City (the Wenzhou model) was singled out for its emphasis on private and household alliance enterprises in all sectors of the economy and on the hands-off approach of its grassroots governments. Other variations among rural political economies have emerged: township and villages may seek to influence TVE development using indirect measures (via registration, licensing, providing access to limited resources) or direct measures (e.g., coordinating or micro-managing day-to-day TVE affairs), or they may choose to avoid involvement altogether. Moreover, rural political economies are distinguished not only by the scope and style of township and village leadership or by the size of the private sector; they also differ according to the method in which top positions in TVCEs are filled, employees are hired and remunerated, and TVCE profit is allocated. These variations lend credence to the assertion that local governments are determining the political economy of TVE development.

The fact that certain of these above-mentioned characteristics tend to cluster together suggests that TVE development is structured according to a complex dynamic of political, economic, and social forces which close off some routes and reinforce institutions consistent with the locally dominant path. A discussion of the three main types of local political economies will serve to illustrate this point.

Areas that have been deeply penetrated by the market and have large private sectors comprise the first type of local political economy (the Wenzhou model falls into this category). This type functions very much like classic laissez-faire capitalism. The bulk of economic activity occurs in private factories, and even collective TVEs operate more on hard-budget constraints than elsewhere. TVCE profits are reinvested for the purpose of increasing productivity and efficiency. In addition, TVCEs hire and fire workers without regard for ensuring local employment. Managers' contracts hold managers responsible for any losses incurred under their tenure, and reward successful managers for profitable returns. Competent workers also are rewarded or punished according to their contribution, and a fairly equal opportunity exists for upward mobility (although blockage of female advancement is widespread). These villages tend not to provide communal goods, and the condition of their roads, schools, and clinics is sometimes abysmal.

Because profits are reinvested in the factories or used as incentives to spur increased productivity, social relief is not available. The local political economy allows some villagers to rise to wealth while others become destitute.

While familiar to Westerners, the characteristics of this system are fairly new to rural China. They contradict the Communist Party's historical commitment to full employment, egalitarian remuneration, and a locally-funded rudimentary safety net in the countryside. Although the 1993 decision to pursue a "socialist market economy" may have sealed the central leadership's commitment to a market-based TVE economy, many locales still resist tossing villagers unprotected into a market economy.

Highly marketized local economies where the private sector is blocked from developing and where TVCE profits are used to protect villagers from laissez-faire capitalism (even as TVCEs operate within the market) comprise the second main type of local political economy (the Sunan model fits this type). In this type all entrepreneurial activity is channeled through local cadre organizations such as the village Communist Party branch or villagers' committees. However, firm administrative control over enterprise development in these locales does not imply that the TVCE sector is administered by incompetent bureaucrats. Instead, village leaders are highly skilled, market-savvy entrepreneurs who are held accountable for their job performance (leaders are voted out of office if they prove incompetent). TVCE managers also are held to a high standard of capability. Remuneration for white collar and blue collar workers is based on productivity, and upward mobility is open to all competent employees. Enterprise profits are allocated for reinvestment and for providing communal goods, including free schooling and health care and a well-maintained transport and irrigation infrastructure. These villages provide social relief while also avoiding the problem encountered in non-marketized areas of staffing economic leadership positions with inept bureaucrats (see next type).

Thus, such villages are able to develop their local economies without sacrificing the basic needs of villagers.

There are also villages lacking both market penetration and a private sector. In these villages, cadres manage or coordinate most economic activities. Village leadership tends to be stagnant, and villagers' committees are either nonexistent or moribund. Despite their lack of expertise in economics, marketing, or technology, cadres micro-manage TVCEs, choosing factory management (generally from among fellow cadres), eliminating manager autonomy, and sometimes even hiring workers. Managerial contracts usually accord with the collective contract responsibility system, wherein managers are not responsible for profits and losses. Profits are not used for maximizing production or profit but for satisfying cadre consumption (vehicles, government buildings, banquets, etc.). Although a minimal safety net exists in these villages, the economy is stagnant and upward mobility is not available to workers.

In the less marketized areas, villagers enjoy at least a crude job security and social safety net. However, since cadres siphon money for bureaucratic consumption, TVCEs benefit village leaders more than the villagers themselves. Furthermore, because cadres limit advancement to factory and village management to other party cadres (and do not institutionalize advancement based on merit), these villages are not able to take advantage of younger, better educated, and more market-savvy talent. Not surprisingly, this style of economic management prevents villagers from receiving the full benefits of marketization, while hindering the economic development of the village.

From the perspective of the rural Chinese, marketized villages that allow private factories benefit entrepreneurs, unmarketized villages benefit cadres, and villages with enlivened markets but no private sector benefit the remainder of the rural population. Generally speaking, the evidence so far indicates that the average villager fares better overall if local authorities are supporting collective TVEs because income

inequality is the smallest if collective enterprises dominate over private enterprises (see Ho, 1994; Mood, "Political Implications of Economic Transitions: Grassroots Politics of Industrial Reform in China," Ph.D. diss., Cornell University, 1996). However, income equality is undesirable if TVE profits and overall income are low because of incompetent cadre management.

These examples, while painting in broad strokes the variation in rural China today, illustrate the point that rural development paths largely are determined by local factors. While scholars disagree on the determining factors, it is clear that central and provincial level leaders find village political economies beyond their reach. These circumstances open the way for local politics to help determine the degree of marketization and the size of the private sector.

The Future

Are collective TVEs an anomaly left over from Maoist China? Will they disappear with the advancement of the market? Most scholars outside China assume that a typical market economy is inevitable throughout China. Since the ownership of TVCEs is based on place of residence, the collective structure of TVCEs would have to change or disappear if ever a free labor market and free movement of labor were permitted in China. If allocation of profits reflected investment alone, then the extracting of capital from TVCEs for public goods would by definition also disappear. Previously, some scholars assumed that the explosive growth of the 1980s would not be sustained because of "the tendency for non-state enterprises to cluster at the low end of the scale and technology spectrum and the somewhat artificial nature of the domestic cost advantages" which were temporary (Gary H. Jefferson and Thomas G. Rawski, "Enterprise Reform in Chinese Industry," in *Journal of Economic Perspectives* 8, no. 2 [Spring 1994]: 62). So far, however, the enlivened markets found in rural China have only strengthened the collective ownership form, as measured by number of firms, employees, taxes, exports, and production. Employment growth in the TVCE sector was six times greater over the period 1991–95 than it was during the years 1986–91 (450,000 versus 3,020,000 new jobs). Growth in TVCE employment comprised 18% of all urban and rural combined non-agricultural employee growth from 1991–96, an increase from 6.4% during the years 1986–91.

Additionally, TVCEs may continue to thrive because localities have a vested interest in their development. At the grassroots level, informal institutions are being strengthened and reinforced by TVCE wealth. Local interests become entwined with the established political economy and resist change. For example, despite accelerated marketization, local governments are not accordingly stepping out of the economy. In fact, interpenetrations of local power structures, villagers, and the economy are emerging and sticking. Therefore, non-economic factors also play a role in directing the development of TVEs.

Nevertheless, TVEs of all ownership forms suffer constraints on their development. Limited access to energy is the greatest constraint on China's development and TVE development in particular. Additionally, the lack of start-up capital, human capital, infrastructure, and raw materials also limit TVE growth to a smaller degree, as do prohibitions on use of arable land. TVEs may founder because of these structural restrictions.

One significant new policy trend emerging in the 1990s is that Chinese leaders repeatedly have advocated promoting TVEs to stabilize ailing agriculture. Although 1993 had brought a record-breaking grain harvest, 1994 production dropped by 2.5%, stirring fears of overall rural instability just as TVEs were suffering the effects of fiscal reform measures. At the 1995 Third Session of the Eighth National People's Congress, Li Peng advocated developing TVEs in order to increase agricultural output and raise farmers' income, while Chen Jinhua, Minister in Charge of the State Planning Commission, noted that TVEs were

necessary to fulfill agricultural goals. Agricultural crises, which at times during the 1980s had led to backlashes against TVEs, have become the very reason to maintain support for TVEs. However, following the record-breaking grain harvests in 1995 and 1996 (a 1.9% increase over 1993, and then an additional increase of 4.5%), the central leadership's concern over grain production dropped sharply, as did its support for TVEs.

The Draft Outline of the Ninth Five-Year Plan emphasized a long-term focus on agriculture, and exhorted TVEs to help stimulate rural income and employment in order to raise financial investment for farming and to secure future agricultural growth. If TVEs of all sectors are deemed potential sources of agricultural investment, then all rural enterprises, especially highly productive and profitable industrial factories with independent products, will remain legitimate in the eyes of policymakers. However, recent history indicates that, without some kind of economic crisis, the central leadership does little more than sloganeer with regard to TVEs. TVEs will remain vulnerable to attack as long as they compete with state enterprises for energy, materials, and markets, and compete with agriculture for labor and land.

Future trends indicated by recent policy developments also include the central state abandoning diversity in implementation (*yindizhiyi*) in favor of an increasingly rationalized legal structure; homogenized laws across regions, ownership structures, and economic sectors; and greater use of indirect economic controls to manipulate development via credit and tax policy. The question remains whether the institutions will be built to implement these strategies effectively. China's leaders have encountered far less difficulty in tearing down the barriers of the command economy than in building new institutions to replace the old ones.

Some observers may argue that a strong central leadership could enforce central interests over local ones. This scenario is unlikely for two reasons. First, if the past is any indication, central leaders will avoid taking a strong stance on TVEs, despite the recent high-level support for TVEs as a means to ensure agricultural production. Instead, TVE policy and the position of TVEs will likely continue to fluctuate according to the changing central agenda. Second, local governments impede implementation of policies that run counter to local interests. Grassroots search for profits precludes effective regulation of much of TVE behavior because the enforcers of policy–township and village governments–are also TVE owners who want to minimize central control, maximize local income, and otherwise guide the development of their local economies.

Further Reading

Bhalla, A.S., *Economic Transition in Hunan and Southern China*, New York: St. Martin's Press, and London: Macmillan, 1984

Based on field research conducted in 1980 and 1981, this book provides an early and not very well organized look into the macroeconomic reforms in Hunan (with some focus on the South-Central region, which includes Guangxi–the subject of relatively little study); the book contains one chapter on rural industrialization.

Byrd, William A., and Qingsong Lin, editors, *China's Rural Industry: Structure, Development, and Reform*, Oxford and New York: Oxford University Press, 1990

The fruits of an extensive research collaboration between the World Bank and the Chinese Academy of Social Sciences from original fieldwork in the mid-1980s, this is still the seminal work on almost all aspects of TVEs with regard to economics (efficiency, finances, factors of production and labor, etc.), local government involvement, and the resultant varying TVE development patterns.

Dong, Fureng, *Industrialization and China's Rural Modernization*, New York: St. Martin's Press, and London: Macmillan, 1992

This senior economic policy advisor to the Chinese government has compiled a concise if at times slanted history of the changes in the rural economic structure, focusing on policy related to the rural non-farming sector and the implications for neoliberal rural modernization. Dong concludes that the government-controlled TVE pattern of growth found in southern Jiangsu is the preferred path.

Findlay, Christopher C., Andrew Watson, and Harry X. Wu, *Rural Enterprises in China*, New York: St. Martin's Press, and London: Macmillan, 1994

Based on some of the assumptions of development economics, this is a thorough, well-documented and lucid presentation of the role of TVEs in structural economic change, focusing on growth, capital, labor, and efficiency, and mainly using State Statistical Bureau data, supplemented by primary survey research data. The present chapter draws much of its statistical information from this source.

Ho, Samuel P.S., *Rural China in Transition: Non-agricultural Development in Rural Jiangsu, 1978–1990*, Oxford: Clarendon Press, and New York: Oxford University Press, 1994

A thorough and enriching study based on collaborative fieldwork in 1986–88 documenting and explaining all aspects of the political economy of rural non-agricultural development in Jiangsu (the province with the largest, most productive and profitable TVEs) and extending that study to generalize about TVEs nationally.

Huang Shu-min, *The Spiral Road: Change in a Chinese Village Through the Eyes of a Communist Party Leader*, Boulder, Colorado: Westview Press, 1989

Bird's eye view of the effect of economic reforms on a Fujian village with an insider's look at rural politics, including cadre corruption, manipulation, and *guanxi* involved in running township and village enterprises.

Kraus, Willy, *Private Business in China: Revival Between Ideology and Pragmatism,* translated by Erich Holz, Honolulu: University of Hawaii Press, and London: Hurst, 1991

Based mainly on pre-1989 information and a rather unreflective acceptance of Chinese views of the state, collective, and private/individual sectors, this book gives a straightforward and nicely detailed presentation of the impact of the private sector (both urban and rural) on the macroeconomy, society, and politics over time, using national, provincial, and some city statistics as well as anecdotal evidence.

Naughton, Barry, *Growing Out of the Plan: Chinese Economic Reform, 1978–1993*, Cambridge and New York: Cambridge University Press, 1995

Combines narrative with sophisticated analysis of the main events of the reform process relating to industry and macroeconomic policy. The book clarifies concepts deliberately obfuscated by the Chinese and unveils many traps into which foreign observers of Chinese economics fall; it also argues against the prevailing view that economic success is due mostly to non-state enterprises.

Odgaard, Ole, *Private Enterprises in Rural China: Impact on Agriculture and Social Stratification*, Brookfield, Vermont: Ashgate, and Aldershot, Hampshire: Avebury, 1992

Based on original research for a doctoral dissertation, this is a careful and well-grounded study describing and explaining private rural enterprises' role in ameliorating resource deficiencies during decentralization, particularly with regard to rural income distribution.

Vermeer, Eduard B., editor, *From Peasant to Entrepreneur: Growth and Change in Rural China*, Wageningen, Netherlands: Pudoc, 1992

These excellent papers originating from the second (1991) European conference on Chinese agriculture and rural development are careful, well-supported studies of a broad range of issues relating to rural entrepreneurship, including the effects of developments in technological innovation, rural marketing, finances, employment, migration, and the growth of rural towns, as well as the effects of economic stagnation and various rural policies on entrepreneurship.

Wong, John, Rong Ma, and Mu Yang, *China's Rural Entrepreneurs: Ten Case Studies*, Singapore: Times Academic Press, 1995

Based on collaborative research between Singapore's Institute of East Asian Political Economy and several Beijing institutions, this is a good source of basic information, with little commentary, on seven town-owned and three village-owned factories (not entrepreneurs) in southern Jiangsu and eastern Shandong, drawn from interviews not only with factory white- and blue-collar workers, but also with numerous township, county, and prefecture leaders.

Michelle S. Mood is Assistant Professor of Political Science at Providence College, Rhode Island.

Table 9.1: TVE Growth Patterns By Sector

	1983	1984	1985	1986	1987	1988	1989	1990	1991	1992	1993	1994
TOTAL TVEs (million)	1.35	6.07	12.2	15.2	17.5	18.9	18.7	18.5	19.1	20.1	24.35	18.7
Agricultural	0.27 20%	0.25 4.1%	0.22 1.8%	0.24 1.6%	0.23 1.3%	0.23 1.2%	0.23 1.2%	0.22 1.2%	0.23 1.2%	0.25 1.2%	0.28 1.1%	0.25 1.3%
Industrial	0.74 55%	4.81 79%	4.93 40%	6.36 42%	7.08 41%	7.74 41%	7.37 39%	7.22 39%	7.43 39%	7.94 39%	9.18 37%	6.99 37%
Construction	0.06 4.2%	0.08 1.3%		0.89 5.9%	0.90 5.2%	0.96 5.1%	0.97 5%	0.90 4.9%	0.89 4.7%	0.99 4.7%	1.22 5.0%	0.83 4.5%
Transport	0.09 6.8%	0.13 2.4%	6.28 58%	2.62 17%	3.25 19%	3.73 20%	3.80 20%	3.81 21%	4.00 21%	4.37 21%	4.86 20%	n/a
Service	0.18 14%	0.8 13%									1.49 6.1%	0.84 4.5%
Food				5.05 33%	6.03 34%	6.23 33%	6.37 34%	6.34 34%	6.53 34%	7.37 35%	6.56 27%	5.50 30%
Other											0.95 3.8%	0.57 3.1%
WORKERS (million)	32.4	52.1	69.8	79.4	88.1	95.5	93.7	92.7	96.1	106	124	113
Agricultural	3.09 9.6%	2.84 5.5%	2.52 3.6%	2.41 3%	2.44 2.8%	2.50 2.6%	2.39 2.6%	2.36 2.5%	2.43 2.5%	2.68 2.5%	2.85 2.3%	2.61 2.3%

Table 9.1: TVE Growth Patterns By Sector (continued)

	1983	1984	1985	1986	1987	1988	1989	1990	1991	1992	1993	1994
Industrial	21.7 67%	36.6 70%	41.4 59%	47.6 60%	52.7 60%	57.0 60%	56.2 60%	55.7 60%	58.1 61%	63.7 60%	72.6 59%	69.6 62%
Construction	4.83 15%	6.84 13%	8.0 11%	12.7 16%	13.8 16%	14.9 16%	14.0 15%	13.5 15%	13.8 14%	15.5 15%	18.3 15%	16.2 14%
Transport	1.1 3.4%	1.29 2.5%	1.14 1.6%	5.41 6.8%	6.32 7.1%	6.84 7.2%	7.00 7.5%	7.11 7.7%	7.32 7.6%	8.00 7.5%	9.32 7.6%	n/a
Service											3.49 2.8%	1.89 1.7%
Food	1.65 5.1%	4.55 8.7%	16.9 24%	11.3 14%	13.0 15%	14.2 15%	14.0 15%	14.0 15%	14.4 15%	16.7 16%	14.1 11%	13.9 12%
Other											2.85 2.3%	1.86 1.6%

Source: ZXN, 1978–87: 570–74; 1990: 122–25; 1991: 134–36; 1993: 142–44; 1994: 152–59 and 161–68; 1995: 87–94. Raw figures are rounded off; percentages are calculated from full figures.

Table 9.2: TVE Growth Patterns by Ownership Form

	1984	1985	1986	1987	1988	1989	1990	1991	1992	1993	1994
TOTAL TVEs (millions)	6.065	12.23	15.15	17.50	18.88	18.69	18.50	19.08	20.92	24.53	18.67
Township & Town	0.402 6.6%	0.420 3.4%	0.426 2.8%	0.420 2.4%	0.424 2.4%	0.406 2.2%	0.388 2%	0.382 2%	0.397 1.9%	0.434 1.8%	0.425 2.3%
Village & Team	1.462 24%	1.430 12%	1.302 8.6%	1.163 6.6%	1.167 6.2%	1.130 6%	1.066 5.6%	1.060 5.7%	1.131 5.4%	1.251 5.1%	1.216 6.5%
Alliance	0.906 15%	1.121 9.2%	1.093 7.2%	1.188 6.8%	1.20 6.4%	1.069 5.7%	0.979 5.2%	0.849 4.4%	0.902 4.3%	1.039 4.2%	0.791 4.2%
Individual	3.296 54%	9.254 76%	12.33 81%	14.73 84%	16.09 85%	16.08 86%	16.302 87%	16.789 88%	18.49 88%	21.81 89%	16.24 87%
WORKERS (millions)	52.08	69.79	79.37	88.05	95.46	93.67	92.65	96.1	106	123.5	113.3
Township & Town	18.79 36%	21.11 30%	22.75 29%	23.98 27%	24.90 26%	23.84 26%	23.33 25%	24.31 25%	26.29 25%	28.81 23%	29.61 26%
Village & Team	21.03 40%	22.16 32%	22.66 28.5%	23.21 26%	24.04 25%	32.37 25%	22.59 24%	23.36 24%	25.47 24%	28.87 23%	29.38 26%
Alliance	5.349 10%	7.714 11%	8.341 11%	9.236 11%	9.766 10%	8.838 9%	8.143 9%	7.263 7.6%	7.710 7.3%	9.137 7.4%	7.304 6.5%

Table 9.2: TVE Growth Patterns by Ownership Form (Continued)

	1984	1985	1986	1987	1988	1989	1990	1991	1992	1993	1994
Individual	7.020	18.81	25.62	31.63	36.75	37.63	38.58	41.16	46.78	56.64	47.01
	14%	27%	32%	36%	39%	40%	42%	43%	44%	46%	42%

Source: ZXN, *1978–87: 570–74; 1992: 137–38; 1993: 145–46; 1994: 150, 160; 1995: 87, 88*

Chapter Ten

The Political Consequences of China's Agricultural Reforms

Scott Wilson

Since 1978, Chinese agriculture has benefited from technological advances and burgeoning rural markets. These and other developments have combined to raise overall agricultural production, improve significantly China's level of food consumption, free up labor for industrial employment, and make China the most efficient producer of grain per land unit. For these reasons, Chinese agricultural reform is considered an economic success story among socialist and post-socialist countries.

Against the backdrop of these breakthroughs, however, agriculture in China faces a looming crisis. Rising food consumption standards have increased demand for grain, pressuring China's farmers to produce ever greater yields. Current data suggest that China soon will be forced to import significant amounts of grain to meet its growing demand, perhaps outstripping the world's productive capacity. Moreover, China's highly successful rural industrialization program has siphoned off capital as well as key natural resources (including land and water) from agriculture. How China will meet its future food demands is unclear.

This chapter begins by giving a brief account of late Maoist-period attempts to improve agricultural production. The following sections recount the agricultural reforms of the last two decades and analyze their economic and political consequences. Finally, the author argues that Chinese rural areas are in a paradoxical situation: the success of decollectivization and rural industrialization has both enriched the countryside and limited the potential for future agricultural growth.

1 Late Maoist Agriculture

Agricultural production during the late Maoist period was organized collectively (stated differently, the state owned all productive assets such as land and implements). Farmers were organized into production teams (*shengchan xiaodui*), basic administrative units that consisted of approximately 30–50 households. Each production team was responsible for assigning work, evaluating each member's work performance, managing productive assets, and, after meeting its obligations to sell grain and other products to state procurement organs, allocating each member a modicum of cash and a share of the product retained by the production team (these were allocated according to work-points earned by members). Production brigades (*shengchan dadui*), which coordinated procurement of grain and allocation of resources and labor, stood above several production teams in the administrative hierarchy. Finally, communes (*gongshe*) were the highest level of local administration and the lowest unit in the state hierarchy. Communes collected taxes, received and disseminated production quotas, interpreted state policies, and coordinated labor transfers for large capital construction projects such as irrigation ditches.

The collective form of agricultural organization gave local administrators vast powers over production and production teams. Officials at all three levels of local administration exerted influence over local plans for cropping, grain sales to the state, and work organization. During Maoist political campaigns, local administrative powers often became politically charged as pressures increased to distribute goods in an egalitarian manner. Under pressure from central and provincial governments to uncover and punish political opponents, local officials often gave preferential treatment to impoverished production team members and their families. Wealthy citizens often were forced to do the most menial tasks and received fewer work-points for their endeavors.

The marketing of agricultural goods was organized according to "unified purchase and sales" (*tonggong tongxiao*). Each production team was required by the state to sell grain to state procurement organs at prices fixed below the true market value. Any grain sold above the fixed quota brought a price set 30% higher than the quota price. Under this system the state established a virtual monopsony (single purchaser) for most agricultural items. The state also operated as a monopolist (single seller) through its unified sales regime, setting the selling price for grain and other agricultural items and using a ration system to allocate the subsidized items to urban consumers. State organs set prices for, sold, and distributed nearly all agricultural products, rendering rural producers and urban consumers dependent on the state for their livelihood.

Furthermore, production and marketing systems combined to restrict the scope of farmers' autonomy. Local officials, especially production team leaders, made the majority of decisions regarding production. Moreover, the quota and state pricing system compelled farmers to produce specific items determined by the state and to sell them at depressed prices. Central authorities promoted grain production at the cost of harvesting other important crops, thus reducing the scope of comparative advantage. Emphasis on grain production impov-

erished areas that could not produce grain as well as other crops.

Finally, local officials coordinated large-scale capital construction projects (these projects included opening irrigation ditches, land reclamation, and digging wells, among others). Although these projects were designed to raise the productive capacity of land and to take advantage of unemployed rural labor during the slack season, they often generated political conflict, primarily because prolific production teams and production brigades were forced to transfer labor and resources to their struggling counterparts. Farmers viewed such labor transfers as unfair because the work usually was uncompensated and distracted them from their own off-farm projects.

Overall, agriculture during the late Maoist period (1966–76) was characterized by slow growth that barely kept pace with China's expanding population. Critics of Maoist agricultural organization point out that the radical egalitarianism of the period suppressed demand and failed to provide material incentives to producers, resulting in a paltry growth rate for agriculture under Mao. During the period 1957–78, per capita grain output rose just 0.2% per annum despite efforts on the part of the central government to maximize production.

2 1978–84: Deng's Early Agricultural Reforms

In 1978, Chinese reformers initiated a great reversal of the Maoist agricultural organization. Reforms were marked by decentralization of state control over production and the introduction of certain aspects of marketing.

The process of government-sanctioned agricultural reform began when central leaders raised agricultural procurement prices in 1978 in order to improve production incentives as well as narrow the pricing gap between industrial goods and agricultural goods (under Mao, the state set the prices of industrial goods near or above the market price while setting prices for agricultural products below their market value. This practice comparatively undervalued agricultural products, placing an unwelcome burden on farmers). Grain procurement prices were raised by 20.9%, oil-bearing crops by 23.9%, and cotton by 17% (see Table 10.2). The state also raised the bonuses for above quota procurement from 30% of the state fixed price to 50%.

During the years 1980–86, central authorities circumscribed state intervention in agricultural marketing and production by reducing the number of agricultural goods under direct state pricing control from 113 to 17 (prices for 11 other agricultural goods were subject to state "guidance"). Moreover, the state gradually replaced the old state pricing system, which had changed little under Mao, with a two-tiered pricing mechanism. The government continued to set basic procurement prices for essential agricultural products including grains, vegetable oils, and cotton; however, state officials also set "negotiated prices" (*yijia*), or prices more accurately reflecting market value, for products sold above fixed quotas. Finally, state officials slowly increased the number and type of goods that farmers could sell at local markets at floating prices independent of state control. Initially, only nonessential agricultural products could be sold at local markets, but the state quickly removed this restriction.

The most widely celebrated agricultural reform, however, was not initiated by central authorities. This reform, referred to as the "agricultural responsibility system," was instigated by villages in Sichuan and Anhui that, without official sanction, began to divide collective agricultural fields, thus rejecting egalitarian aspects of the Maoist work-point remuneration system. The responsibility system initially took three forms. "Contracting output to the group" (*baochan daozu*), the least radical departure from Maoist agricultural organization, involved assigning quotas to small work groups within production teams. Work groups received work-points from their production teams for completing tasks and could earn extra points for surpassing quotas. This model continued to link remuneration to the overall productivity of the production team, but did allow for some devolution of work organization and less egalitarian distribution of work-points. However, this system only partially resolved the conflict between individual incentive and the collective distribution of rewards; thus, local authorities quickly abandoned this method of organization in favor of more fundamental reforms.

A second model, "contracting output to households" (*baochan daohu*), provided greater individual incentives than contracting output to teams. Under this regime a household contracted to meet a production quota in exchange for work-points. Although contracting output to households reduced the potential for shirking duties, it still tied work-point remuneration to the output of the entire production team. Moreover, the collective retained control over crop selection, agricultural inputs, and remuneration.

A third model, "contracting everything to the household" (*baogan daohu* or *da baogan*), took the most radical steps toward dismantling the Maoist collective organization. Under this model most collectively held assets–including implements, draught animals, and land–were divided among villagers for individual use. Families were allowed to use these productive assets so long as they met a few obligations. First, the contracting families were required to sell a fixed quota of grain and other products (usually cotton and/or oil-bearing crops) to the state at stipulated prices. Second, they had to pay a state agricultural tax (this was a small obligation because the tax rate had not been changed since its initial determination in 1952). Finally, local officials could require contracting parties to pay a small set of fees to maintain the few remaining local collective operations. Once farmers met these obligations, they could dispose of the remainder of their crop in any way they saw fit. Farmers also had greater control over crop selection and marketing (for a discussion of the three models see Riskin, 1987: 286–90).

Not surprisingly, the allocation of land to households generated some political conflict in villages. Owing to concerns that land be allocated equitably with regard to quality and proximity to one's home, villagers carefully monitored and sometimes challenged the distribution of land under the new system. In some cases, farmers claimed that village and team officials distributed the land unfairly. In many other cases, however, the distribution of land parcels followed a transparent and fair process in which land was evaluated according to its quality and convenience and then distributed by drawing lots. Each family received an allocation of land parcel(s) according to its number of members (in some instances, age and gender of family members also were factors).

Pressures to distribute land equitably according to quality and convenience led to the practice of fragmenting village landholdings. What had once been large tracts of land soon resembled a patchwork quilt. The state contributed to land fragmentation by distinguishing types of land: "grain ration land" (*kouliang di*), "responsibility land" (*zeren di*), "contracted land" (*chengbao di*), and private plots (*ziliu di*)–along with other local variations, each carrying a different set of obligations and fees. Some locales gave each family a separate parcel of each type of land, causing fragmentation of holdings. A national survey revealed that the average Chinese farm consists of 9.7 plots totaling 8.35 *mu* (or roughly 0.13 hectares). This extensive land fragmentation strongly resembles the pre-revolutionary landholding pattern, noted for its inability to make more than incremental technological improvements in production. In some instances, villagers cannot use mechanical inputs such as tractors and plows on small tracts of land without damaging neighboring fields.

It is also noteworthy that the state made a concerted effort to increase the application of fertilizer to fields in the early stage of Deng's reforms. Although new high-yielding seeds were disseminated during the late Maoist period, lack of fertilizer and irrigation prevented harvests from reaching full potential. In response, the state increased the application of chemical fertilizers 10.7% per annum

for the period 1979–85, and land productivity increased as a result. Moreover, when fertilizer application slowed after 1985, so too did agricultural production.

3 1985 to the Present: Continued Attempts to Reform Agricultural Prices

The initial round of reforms achieved two fundamental goals: it improved farmers' incentives to produce and addressed some of the organizational problems associated with collectives. Nevertheless, problems still existed within the agricultural sector, most notably the pricing mechanism for agricultural commodities. On the procurement side, prices remained discouragingly low; on the distribution side, the state still subsidized urban consumers by artificially deflating prices.

Agricultural reforms since 1985 have focused on altering the method of procurement while further reducing the number of state price controls. Beginning in 1985, the state, which had persisted with unified purchase and sales (*tonggou tongxiao*) through 1984 for grain and other essential products, advanced a new method of procuring essential products called "contracted fixed procurement" (*hetong dinggou*). Under this system, local state agents would offer to buy essential products from farmers at a fixed price; meanwhile, farmers could opt to sell their goods to state agents or to the free market. Following steady agricultural growth during the period 1978–84 (including bumper grain harvests in 1983 and 1984), state planners were confident that they could abolish mandatory quotas and state price controls over grain without inducing rampant inflation. This move to decentralize even grain procurement was representative of the radical shift away from state control over marketing that was undertaken by state planners.

Unfortunately, falling grain production accompanied reduced price controls. Formerly, when production had exceeded demand, state prices provided a price floor for grain. Now that prices no longer were guaranteed, however, farmers turned to more profitable "cash crops" such as vegetables and livestock. The state further eroded farmer confidence in its ability to market grain by announcing that in 1985 the government would guarantee only purchases of contracted grain production, effectively abandoning its previous commitment to buy all grain offered for sale to the state. As a result, grain production dropped by 6.9% and cotton production by 33.7% in 1985. The state responded by quickly reimposing price and procurement controls to increase grain sales to the state.

The state had not abandoned its goal of fundamental price reform, however. In 1992 the state again banned price and procurement controls over grain, opting to allow markets to determine the prices paid to farmers and prices paid by urban residents. To cushion the inevitable inflation for urban consumers, local state agents provided small monthly subsidies to city residents. Unfortunately, these efforts could not counteract the high inflation of the mid-1990s, and many urban consumers became increasingly dissatisfied with their government.

Overall, the state has made great efforts to modify the pricing mechanism for agricultural goods. Free floating prices have provided farmers with clear information on changing consumer demands and have encouraged farmers to alter production to meet these demands. In contrast, farmers received unclear signals regarding consumer tastes when the state partially controlled agricultural procurement prices, and the outcome was that farmers produced a surplus of some agricultural products and a shortage of others. Price reform has allowed farmers to increase their incomes by switching to more lucrative crops and has improved consumption standards by adjusting the product mix to meet consumer demand.

4 The Fruits of Agricultural Reforms

4.1 Greater Production

Although observers agree that rural China experienced an economic growth surge between 1978 and 1984 and that growth subsequently slowed, the causes of these two trends are much disputed. Critics charge that reform measures have diminished China's ability to be a self-sufficient grain producer. They argue that, although grain production increased 33.6% in the early period of Deng's reforms, production dropped and only slowly improved after 1984, rising only 9.3% for the decade 1984–94 (see Table 10.1 for a summary of production data). Moreover, per capita grain production remained virtually unchanged during the latter period. Proponents of the reforms point out that production of other important agricultural items, including silkworm cocoons, fruit, livestock, and fish, has made impressive gains since 1984, with production increasing in some cases more rapidly than during the first six years of agricultural reforms (see Table 10.1). They argue that relative declines in grain production are the result of farmers choosing to produce more lucrative crops.

National data on procurement prices for agricultural products support the latter argument: the rise of grain procurement prices outpaced the rise of prices for other agricultural products during the 1978–84 period; however, since 1984 procurement prices of non-grain products have risen more rapidly.

In addition to pursuing higher returns, farmers switched to production of nonessential cash crops for two reasons. First, as the state allowed prices of agricultural products to reflect market value more accurately, farmers gained a clearer picture of the basket of goods sought by consumers. No longer forced to sell fixed quotas of grain to the state at state-set prices, farmers opted to produce goods that were in greater demand. Second, as standards of living have risen so too have consumer tastes. In the Chinese (and East Asian) context this pattern has included a decreasing demand for grain and a growing demand for vegetables, fish, and meat.

Also relevant to agricultural production is the fact that the quantity of land under cultivation in China dropped 4.5% over the period 1978–94. China's burgeoning population and demand for a more abundant and higher order diet only magnify this decrease in cultivated land. Although central leaders blame peasant housing construction for much of the land loss, national data indicate that housing construction was brought under control around 1988. Rather, development of rural industry and capital construction projects is responsible for most of the land loss in recent years.

4.2 Higher Rural Incomes and Greater Inequality

Increased production and higher procurement rates have translated into higher rural incomes. The national average net annual income for the rural population in 1980 was just 191 *yuan*. By 1994 net income had risen to 1,221 *yuan* (not adjusted for inflation). Although inflation has caused part of the rapid income growth since 1978, improved rural diets and housing reveal a qualitative rise in the rural standard of living.

However, although rural per capita income has improved in the aggregate, the distribution of income has been far from equal. Without production teams to limit income differences through the work-point system, intravillage income stratification has increased. Moreover, the individualization of many types of property rights (including rights to manage production and to receive income flows) has allowed institutional mechanisms for class cleavages to reemerge.

Comparing data on provincial rural per capita net income reveals significant differences. In particular, coastal provinces compare favorably to inland provinces. Putterman (1993) shows that the ratios of the highest provincial rural per capital net income to the lowest rose steadily from 1.83:1 in 1980 to 2.68:1 in 1988. Recent data indicate the provincial gap has expanded, climbing to 3.07:1 in 1994.

The main concern here is whether regional and provincial income inequality relates to agricultural production. A cursory glance at the data in Table 10.3 suggests that a positive relationship does exist between rural poverty and rural employment in traditional agricultural tasks (the same relationship does not exist between rural poverty and rural employment in industry). The five provinces with the highest rural per capita net incomes in 1993 were Zhejiang, Guangdong, Jiangsu, Fujian, and Liaoning. In these five provinces 23.1% of the rural population were able to secure work in factories; only 42.2% remained in farming and related activities. The five provinces with the lowest rural per capita net incomes in 1993 were Ningxia, Shaanxi, Yunnan, Guizhou, and Gansu. In these five provinces only 9.4% of the rural workforce found work in manufacturing, while 66.1% were employed as agricultural workers. Statistical comparison suggests that provinces whose economies are rural industry-based have a distinct income advantage (for more discussion, see Riskin, 1987: 251–54).

Data on regional inequality confirm the link between dependence on agricultural production and low income. Excluding the centrally administered cities and autonomous regions from the analysis, the eastern region had the highest rural per capita net income in 1993, followed by the central and western regions. Conversely, the west's rural workforce has the highest percentage of workers employed in traditional agricultural activities, followed by the central and eastern regions; the eastern region's workforce relies most heavily on rural industrial employment. Moreover, factoring in the centrally administered cities (located in the eastern region) and autonomous regions (located mainly in the rural western section) would only strengthen the correlation. The aforementioned data give strong support to the argument that dependence on agricultural production explains at least part of regional and provincial rural income variation.

4.3 Political Cleavages

Implementation of agricultural reforms has proceeded smoothly considering how radically the reforms have transformed the countryside. The initial jump in rural incomes owing to raised procurement prices helped ease the transition. Nevertheless, reforms have caused some political turbulence. For example, applications for party membership in the countryside are down compared to earlier periods and the state has encountered recalcitrant farmers who oppose some central policies.

Not surprisingly, the political tensions in villages are caused in part by increasing income differentials. Intravillage stratification has pitted wealthy families against poor ones and entrepreneurs against officials. Known as "red eye disease" (*hongyan bing*) to villagers, some local cadres, envious of the newly wealthy, have tried to collect arbitrary fees from local entrepreneurs. Conversely, the emerging new stratum of wealthy villagers has attempted to defy local officials and thwart policy implementation. Some members of the new elite have developed ties to higher-up officials in order to gain a measure of protection against village leaders' attempts to solicit illegal fees and curb entrepreneurial activities.

An example of a central policy opposed by many farmers is the one-child policy. Farmers want to violate the one-child policy in order to increase the family labor pool, mainly for off-farm employment. Consequently, many village officials have found strictly implementing the one-child policy very difficult and sometimes have taken great measures (including coercing women to have abortions) to gain compliance with this national policy. Improved village incomes, however, have weakened the effect of economic sanctions imposed on violators and have provided the means for some violators to leave the village and join the "floating population" in cities.

4.4 Assessing the Reforms

Reform proponents usually emphasize the improved incentives and greater rationality associated with the rapid and fundamental reorganization of agricultural production. Unlike the collective organization of Chinese agriculture, the household responsibility system unleashed farmers' entrepreneurial spirit. The result of the great transformation was a remarkable agricultural take-off. The improved pricing mechanism for agricultural products merely enhanced farmers' incentives.

Scholars who are more skeptical of the household responsibility system challenge several claims made by proponents of the reforms. First, some have argued that the introduction of the most radical reform, contracting to the household (*da baogan*), did not coincide with the agricultural takeoff. The contracting system first was undertaken in 1978; however, many locales did not undertake the contracting system until the early 1980s. Bramall (1993) shows that Sichuan, a leader in agricultural reform among provinces, did not formally endorse the universal introduction of the household contract system until 1983. Other authors have found that some locales with previously high production rates did not implement the household contracting system until 1984. According to Bramall, China's rapid agricultural development began prior to the full implementation of the household responsibility system, and authors who claim that agriculture prospered with the sudden introduction of the household responsibility system in 1978 overstate their case. Thus, the reorganization of production only partially explains the development pattern through 1985.

Instead, Bramall argues that increases in technical and capital inputs such as fertilizer and irrigation allowed farmers to take advantage of improved seeds developed under Mao. Moreover, the new decentralized system of production has wrought political decentralization and thus has reduced the number of administrative tools that village heads and party secretaries possess to mobilize labor for capital construction projects.

Hinton (1989) also laments the productive advantages lost with the dismantling of collectives. In addition to a reduced capacity to utilize irrigation, Hinton notes that land fragmentation under the household responsibility system has prevented the use of important technological and mechanical inputs such as tractors. Although Hinton acknowledges that the household responsibility system has greatly improved land productivity, he suggests that labor productivity lagged far behind. Corn and wheat regions of China could make good use of tractors, but land fragmentation prevents their application and blocks potential improvements to labor productivity.

5 Further Reform or Retrenchment?

Although Bramall and Hinton underscore some of the positive contributions of collective agriculture, neither likely would suggest a full-scale return to Maoist organization. Indeed, most economists, recognizing that collective organization of agriculture and emphasis on egalitarianism failed to provide incentives to farmers and reinforced a pricing system that transferred rural capital to industry, agree that it was imperative that the state implement agricultural price reforms.

Some economists have suggested that further price reforms, linking domestic agricultural commodity prices to international markets, would be useful (see Huang, in Garnaut, Guo, and Ma 1996: 34). Their argument is as follows: if domestic production of an agricultural commodity is so expensive that its price rises above the international market price, then China would be better off importing the item; similarly, if a commodity sells for less in China than the world market price, then Chinese farmers could earn more money by selling abroad than at home. Their argument is based on the theory of comparative advantage.

However, political circumstances make it unlikely that further price reforms will be enacted. Since the founding of communist rule, the central government has spent extraordinary sums of money subsidizing urban food consumption in order to ensure political stability in China's cities. Attempts to remove price restrictions on agricultural commodities have led to periodic urban unrest since 1978. Although trading agricultural commodities on international markets

may be alluring to some central officials, most would likely be unwilling to risk further political dissatisfaction in the cities.

In addition to contributing to higher consumer food prices in the cities, international trading of agricultural commodities would hurt rural China. Areas with low land and factor productivity concentrated in the poor western and central regions of China would be hit hardest by lower priced agricultural products from abroad. Some of these areas, especially Tibet and Xinjiang, have been prone to separatist movements, and central officials do not wish to sour relations between the center and such peripheral political hotbeds. Again, political logic places limits on further reforms that might improve Chinese agricultural development.

Ironically, the clearest long-term threat to the future development of agriculture is rural industrialization, which is the greatest source of wealth in the countryside. Rural enterprises are the fastest growing industry in China and a source of many exportable items. Central leaders have an obvious interest in maintaining and encouraging rural industry; moreover, rural industry is a source of pride for Chinese leaders and helps balance China's foreign trade. From a local perspective, villagers earn higher wages in industry than in the fields, and local officials can more easily earn bonuses for surpassing their production quotas. Additionally, it is easier to provide communities that rely on rural industry with collective welfare than communities that rely on traditional farming activities.

Although rural industry has made a significant contribution to China's rural economy, it threatens the viability of Chinese agriculture. Township and village factories take land out of agricultural production, use scarce water, and pollute the environment. As Brown (1995) notes, these problems imperil Chinese food production. To meet its rapidly growing demand for food, China likely will require imports of grain. Moreover, rural industry is concentrated in the coastal region where land is most fertile: as industry continues to take up valuable land, greater food production demands will be placed on China's least productive regions.

In sum, China has taken great strides toward developing its agricultural sector since 1978. However, the reforms also have had negative consequences. The dismantling of collective farming has circumscribed China's ability to exploit mechanical inputs in agriculture. Growing income stratification among rural communities has led to new political challenges to local administration. In addition, the conflict between urban consumers and rural producers over the prices of agricultural goods remains problematic for central authorities. Although reforms have vastly improved China's agricultural production, they also have placed technological and political limits on the further expansion of agriculture. Ironically, the reform that has most enriched the countryside—the deregulation of rural industry—also diminishes China's ability to feed itself.

Further Reading

Bramall, Chris, *In Praise of Maoist Planning: Living Standards and Economic Development in Sichuan Since 1931,* Oxford: Clarendon Press, and New York: Oxford University Press, 1993

Analyzes rural development in Sichuan, one of the pioneering provinces in rural reforms. By examining the timing of Deng's reforms and improvements in agricultural production, the author pokes holes in much of the prevailing wisdom on the contribution of the household responsibility system to agricultural growth.

Brown, Lester R., *Who Will Feed China? Wake-Up Call for a Small Planet,* New York: Norton, and London: Earthscan, 1995

Provides an analysis of the looming crisis in Chinese food lproduction. The author draws interesting and compelling comparisons between Chinese agricultural development and food consumption patterns and those in Japan, Taiwan, and South Korea. Based on the paths taken by earlier East Asian developers, which China seems to follow, China (and the world) must brace itself for a much

greater demand for food and strain on world resources, Brown concludes.

Chan, Anita, Richard Madsen, and Jonathan Unger, *Chen Village under Mao and Deng,* 2nd edition, Berkeley: University of California Press, 1992

Analyzes the political and economic transformations of a village in Guangdong province since 1949. In addition to being a good concise source on village political movements under Mao, it also includes interesting information on the breakdown of collectives under Deng.

Garnaut, Ross, Guo Shutian, and Ma Guonan, editors, *The Third Revolution in the Chinese Countryside,* Cambridge and New York: Cambridge University Press, 1996

In addition to a good opening set of articles on the historical development of Chinese agricultural policy, the book contains detailed analyses of topics relating to Chinese agriculture. The contributors are knowledgeable and the topics chosen are important. Several chapters in the book offer an economic argument for further reform and liberalization.

Hinton, William, *The Great Reversal: The Privatization of China 1978–1989,* New York: Monthly Review Press, 1989

Drawing on various on-site inspections and interviews in different areas of China, Hinton develops a leftist critique of the reform era. Although Hinton does not present much statistical information to back many of his claims, his profound knowledge of rural development in Chinese locales gives a certain force to his arguments. A good, provocative book to read alongside more standard economic accounts of Chinese reforms.

Huang Shu-min, *The Spiral Road: Change in a Chinese Village Through the Eyes of a Communist Party Leader,* Boulder, Colorado: Westview Press, 1989

Offers an interesting view of the Maoist and Dengist rural policies through the eyes of a local leader.

Oi, Jean Chun, *State and Peasant in Contemporary China: The Political Economy of Village Government,* Berkeley: University of California Press, 1989

Considered by most scholars to be required

reading on political and economic organization under Mao and the breakdown of collectives under Deng. The author examines the formation of clientelist networks in a single locale. The book provides a good understanding of the intertwining of political and economic power under the collective system. Its cut-off date of 1986 makes it somewhat more limited on the Deng era.

Potter, Sulamith Heins, and Jack M. Potter, *China's Peasants: The Anthropology of a Revolution,* Cambridge and New York: Cambridge University Press, 1990

An account of Zengbu Brigade in Guangdong province during the Mao and Deng eras. Provides an excellent account of the interface of socialist institutions and local culture. Economists may want to skip the more anthropological chapters, but will take interest in the discussion of the implementation of Maoist organization and Dengist reforms.

Putterman, Louis G., *Continuity and Change in China's Rural Development: Collective and Reform Eras in Perspective,* New York: Oxford University Press, 1993

Provides a good detailed account of the economic transformations in rural China since 1949. The author relies primarily on data from a single township but integrates it with other data sets and a broader discussion of Chinese rural development. Economic students will find the book particularly useful, but others may have more difficulty following some of the statistical analysis.

Riskin, Carl, *China's Political Economy: The Quest for Development Since 1949,* Oxford and New York: Oxford University Press, 1987

Although this book does not specifically cover agriculture, most chapters have a discussion of agricultural development. It provides good detailed analyses of rural economic organization, policy processes, and economic outcomes.

State Statistical Bureau, *China Statistical Yearbook 1995,* Beijing: China Statistical Information and Consultancy Service Center and International Center for the Advancement of Science and Technology, 1995

Zhu Ling, *Rural Reform and Peasant Income in China: The Impact of China's Post-Mao Rural Reforms in Selected Areas,* New York: St. Martin's Press, and London: Macmillan, 1991

The author draws on a sample of nine villages near Luoyang City in Henan province to address the issue of farmer income during the Deng era. The analysis covers not only the roots of income growth but also rural poverty, an understudied topic in the Deng era.

Zweig, David, *Agrarian Radicalism in China, 1968–1981,* Cambridge, Massachusetts: Harvard University Press, 1989

The author gives a close account of the radical impulses in rural political and economic organization during the collective era. The book is most helpful as a source on the Maoist egalitarian goals, their implementation, and the resulting practice.

Scott Wilson is Assistant Professor of Political Science at the University of the South, Sewanee, Tennessee.

Table 10.1: Percentage Change in Output of Selected Major Agricultural Products

Product	1978–94	1978–84	1984–94
Grain	46.0	33.6	9.3
Oil-bearing crops	281.3	128.2	67.1
Cotton	100.3	188.8	-30.6
Tobacco	80.2	44.0	25.1
Silkworm cocoons	256.4	56.3	128.0
Tea	119.6	54.5	42.1
Fruit	432.7	49.9	255.5
Slaughtered pork[a]	44.2	14.9	25.5
Poultry[a]	140.5	70.8	40.8
Fishery products			183.2

Calculated using State Statistical Bureau 1995: 347–48
a. Figures use 1980 as a baseline

Table 10.2: Percentage Increases in the Purchasing Price of Selected Farm and Sideline Products

Product	1978–94	1978–84	1984–94
Grain	448.1	98.1	176.7
Oil-bearing crops	353.9	51.8	199.0
Cotton	376.5	56.9	203.7
Tobacco	140.8	47.5	63.3
Silkworm cocoons and silk	434.8	26.4	323.1
Tea	229.2	35.2	143.5
Fruit	224.9	50.7	115.6
Livestock for slaughtering	459.5	32.0	323.9
Aquatic products	535.4	38.5	358.8

Calculated from State Statistical Bureau 1995: 247–48

Table 10.3: Provincial Rural Per Capita Net Income and Distribution of Rural Capital Workforce

Province	Per Capita Net Income (in yuan)	Rural Workforce Employed in:	
		Rural Industry (in percentage points)	Farming, Forestry, Animal Husbandry, and Fishing (in percentage points)
Zhejiang	2225	25.4	44.4
Guangdong	2182	20.0	41.0
Jiangsu	1832	25.3	43.2
Fujian	1578	16.7	51.3
Liaoning	1423	27.9	31.2
Heilongjiang	1394	19.6	36.9
Shandong	1320	15.6	55.9
Jilin	1272	18.5	46.0
Jiangxi	1218	12.8	56.1
Hubei	1173	15.9	53.9
Hunan	1155	11.2	62.8
Guangxi	1107	7.2	68.0
Hebei	1107	17.0	53.9
Anhui	973	11.4	61.6
Sichuan	946	10.0	64.6
Henan	910	11.5	62.3
Shanxi	884	19.3	44.0
Qinghai	869	11.4	60.0
Ningxia	867	10.8	60.0
Shaanxi	805	12.4	60.4
Yunnan	803	6.0	76.5
Guizhou	787	6.8	74.8
Gansu	724	11.0	59.0

Column 2 is taken from State Statistical Bureau 1995: 281;
columns 3 and 4 are calculated from State Statistical Bureau 1995: 86

Table 10.4: Regional Rural Per Capita Net Income and Distribution of Rural Capital Workforce

Region	Per Capita Net Income (in yuan)	Rural Workforce Employed in:	
		Rural Industry (in percentage points)	Farming, Forestry, Animal Husbandry, and Fishing (in percentage points)
Eastern region[a]	1596.8	19.4	48.6
Central region[b]	974.7	12.5	59.5
Western region[c]	835.5	9.6	65.0

a. Includes Guangxi, Guangdong, Fujian, Zhejiang, Jiangsu, Shandong, Hebei, and Liaoning provinces.
b. Includes Ningxia, Shaanxi, Shanxi, Henan, Hubei, Anhui, Jiangxi, Hunan, and Guizhou provinces.
c. Includes Gansu, Qinghai, Sichuan, and Yunnan provinces.
   Column 2 is taken from State Statistical Bureau 1995: 281;
   columns 3 and 4 are calculated from State Statistical Bureau 1995: 86

Chapter Eleven

The Private Sector in China's Economic Reforms

Susan Young

In present-day China, public ownership of the means of production is in an absolutely dominant position and labor force is no longer a commodity. Generally speaking, individual economy will not engender capitalism because in the scope of management, the supply of raw materials, price and taxation, it is subject to control and restriction by the public economy and by the state organs concerned.

–Beijing Review, August 18, 1980

The state should create conditions for economic sectors under different kinds of ownership to compete in the market on equal terms, and should deal with the various types of enterprise without discrimination.

–Central Committee decision, November 14, 1993

Beginning in the early 1950s, the Chinese Communist Party set about systematically eliminating private business in China. By 1978 the private sector consisted of about 150,000 individual peddlers, craftspeople, and repairers making a precarious living under a haze of political disapproval. Through the 1980s and 1990s, the reversal of this extermination policy was reflected in the rapid growth of private businesses. Today, a dynamic private sector is active throughout the Chinese economy, closely integrated with other ownership sectors, and of increasing economic and political significance. Government statistics list nearly 26 million businesses which provide 10% of jobs and make up nearly 90% of wholesale and retail trading outlets, 30% of retail sales volume, and over 10% of gross industrial output value.

The two quotations at the beginning of this chapter illustrate the dramatic change in official attitudes toward the market and the private sector in China's reform process. Private business was first revived in the late 1970s as a "quick fix" measure, a cheap, simple way of filling up a few of the gaps left by the ailing planned economy. Small private businesses could easily make life a little better for the Chinese public by providing employment and improving services available to consumers. By the 1990s, China's reforms had gone far beyond cosmetic surface changes, and the private sector was no longer viewed as something to be limited to a subordinate and supplementary role, but as a significant and dynamic part of the economy in its own right. This change has been reflected in a new confidence and a surge of growth in China's private sector in the 1990s; however, the private sector has been affected significantly by the conditions of its growth and remains sensitive to political constraints. This chapter examines the reasons behind the rapid and unexpected transformation of the private sector in China, and assesses how the history of its development through the 1980s affected its nature and role.

Size and Scope of the Chinese Private Sector

Chinese authorities divide the private sector into two categories: the "individual economy" of *getihu*, which consist of individual or family businesses with not more than seven outside employees, and "private enterprises," or *siying qiye*, which are private businesses with over seven outside employees and, in most localities, a minimum capital requirement as well. This line is a political division, chosen to mark the point at which a business might start to generate enough surplus to turn capitalist, and initially was intended as a limit beyond which private business would not be allowed to expand. Even after larger businesses became acceptable (how and why they did is discussed below), the line remained, so marking the division between the perception of *getihu* as traditional, low-tech, non-expansionist businesses, and more development-oriented, expansionist enterprises.

The private sector is more significant in the rural economy than in the cities. Nationally, registered private businesses made up roughly 13% of gross output value of industry in 1995, but at the village level the private sector's share was 45.8%. Registered private businesses (mostly very small) comprised 87% of enterprises in China's rural townships and villages in 1994, and provided 41% of off-farm jobs. The relative strenght of the private sector in the rural economy is related to the way individual households became the main economic unit in the agricultural reforms (see Chapter 8 for a discussion of "contracting to households"), as opposed to the cities where state-run units continued to dominate. Of the *getihu*, 66% are located in rural areas, whereas a majority of registered *siying qiye* (57%) are located in urban areas, mainly in the more developed eastern coastal provinces. The greater marketization of these areas offers more economic opportunities for larger private businesses, while diminishing the need for bureaucratic assistance. As discussed below, entrepreneurs in rural and inland areas are more likely to work within the collective categories, which provide them with more security and government assistance.

For many years, the popular perception of China's private sector focused on the more visible *getihu*: the roadside sellers of fried dough, noodles, and poor-quality clothing, the bicycle repairers who set up shop with a foot-pump and a few spanners,

and tailors and hairdressers. Indeed, the *getihu* developed the most rapidly in commerce, food service, and other services, benefiting from the ease of entry and the massive pent-up demand resulting from neglect of these sectors in the planned economy. Since the mid-1980s, the private sector also has demonstrated strong growth in transport and construction, largely in response to the boom in demand as rural industries and rural-urban marketing took off. Among larger private enterprises, more than 60% are industrial and about 25% commercial, with smaller percentages in transport, construction, food service, and various service trades.

Experiments in reforming the structure of ownership have been an important feature of the post-Mao reforms. By the mid-1990s property rights in China ranged from individual ownership through a variety of co-operatives, partnerships, shareholding companies, public ownership at all levels of government, and joint ventures among different combinations of all these. Rural reforms offered peasants opportunities to run nonagricultural enterprises. Private leasing of state and collective firms also led to a privatization of management and, in some cases, assets of state or collective enterprises. Including these arrangements in a discussion of the private sector is problematic, because many are not fully private; however, leaving them out would give an inadequate picture of the scope and opportunities for private entrepreneurship in China. In fact, an interactive relationship developed between the recognized private sector, which was strongly affected by ideological constraints, and the extensive opportunities created by increased flexibility in the state and collective sectors. Eventually this brought about an erosion of ownership boundaries and helped create the conditions for the increasing legitimacy and importance of private enterprise in the Chinese economy. The following discussion explains this process, looking first at the politics of the simultaneous promotion and limitation of the recognized private sector, then at the manner in which the wider context of the reform process enabled the private sector to overcome the limitations upon it.

The Development of China's New Private Sector

Unlike former socialist countries of Eastern Europe, China has not attempted a sudden transition from a planned economy to a market economy. Instead, it has undergone an evolutionary process. There has been no change of government, no rejection of communist ideology, no official adoption of privatization as a desirable goal. Not until 1993 did the Chinese Communist Party (CCP) officially declare that it was aiming for a market economy (for some years the official phrase had been "commodity economy"), albeit a socialist market economy. Studies of the private sector under reform programs in Eastern Europe and the Soviet Union before 1989 have highlighted the precariousness and marginality of private business under Communist Party rule. In general, private sectors in reforming socialist countries have been highly insecure and peripheral, vulnerable to extortion by officials, and forced to rely extensively on personal connections, bribery, and other types of informal or illicit behavior to survive.

In China, too, the private sector initially was envisaged as having only a peripheral role. Having spent 30 years working to eliminate the private sector from the Chinese economy, the CCP was reluctant to admit in the late 1970s that it needed at least some private business after all. Accordingly, the initial revival of the private sector was undertaken on a small-scale, experimental basis at local levels, and worked into public central policy only gradually. When reformers publicized the policy of reviving private business in 1980–81, they emphasized that only very small, simple businesses would be allowable, and that these would be limited by state regulations and their dependence on the now well-established socialist public economy. The framework envisaged in this policy still consisted of the traditional hierarchy of state, collective, and individual ownership, with state enterprises viewed as politically and economically superior.

In line with these ideas, private sector policy at the beginning of the 1980s was aimed at allowing a limited amount of private business to take on some of the small-scale tasks that were difficult for the planning system to perform effectively. Private operators usually were not issued licenses if their businesses competed with local state or collective businesses. In addition, licenses initially were restricted to people who did not have other employment prospects, such as retired people without adequate support or former *getihu* who had lost their businesses during the Cultural Revolution. In August 1980, however, a major Central Committee-sponsored work conference on employment recognized that private businesses could provide an employment option for the approximately 17 million people who had been sent to the countryside as educated youth in the 1960s and 1970s and were now returning to the cities, plus the additional 5 million or so who were leaving school each year. This measure was followed by new central government initiatives that encouraged private sector growth, such as allowing bank loans to *getihu* and lowering *getihu* taxes. Provincial governments followed up by enacting regulations on the individual economy, and the policy of promoting a limited private sector finally was confirmed by the State Council's issuing of national regulations on the urban, nonagricultural individual economy in July 1981.

These regulations affirmed the role of the individual economy as a "necessary supplement" to the state and collective sectors, and promised state protection and support toward this end. At the same time, the regulations placed limits on the size and scope of these businesses. Operators were permitted to engage in "small-scale handicrafts, retail commerce, catering, services, repairs, nonmechanized transport and building repairs," so long as these were "beneficial to the national economy" and did not involve the "exploitation of others." The regulations specified that *getihu* should be limited to unemployed youth or retirees with certain skills to pass on, and should employ at most two assistants and five apprentices. Provincial and local regulations often included further limits on the trades open to private operators, the size and technological level of their equipment, and their mobility.

Barriers to Private Business

Although China's private sector quickly exceeded these politically determined limits, private operators experienced many of the same problems as their counterparts under reforming socialist economies elsewhere. Initially, even the development of small-scale private businesses met with considerable opposition and obstruction. Some local officials interpreted "appropriate development" to mean hardly any development at all and refused to license more than a very few *getihu* in their localities. Others placed all sorts of constraints on private operators, requiring, for example, that all private restaurants have at least five rooms (not easy in China's crowded spaces), or fining transporters who crossed district boundaries, or removing *getihu* shop signs on the grounds that they were unsightly (they were no more unsightly than the state shops' signs).

Simply put, an inescapable contradiction existed between the promotion of private business and Communist ideology. This made it difficult both for reformers to declare support for the private sector clearly and openly and for private entrepreneurs to rely upon that support. Thus, the ambivalence of central policy toward private business (promoting its revival but discriminating against it in favor of collective enterprises) was reflected in uncertainty at lower levels (see Linda Hershkovitz, "The Fruits of Ambivalence: China's Urban Individual Economy," in *Pacific Affairs* 58, no. 3 [1985]). Private sector policy left the detailed decision making to administrators at lower levels, who in turn based their decisions partly on their interpretation of central politics. These local officials interpreted leftward shifts or calls to slow down the pace of reforms as a signal to repress private business. Such signals resulted in tighter limits, increased inspections, higher fees and taxes, and even widespread arbitrary closures of private businesses. Declines in the private sector growth rate or in absolute numbers of registered businesses correlated to all the major political or economic retrenchment phases: the moves to limit inflationary pressures and control market activity in late 1980–81, the campaign against "spiritual pollution" in 1983, the credit squeeze and political problems culminating in the fall of Hu Yaobang in 1986, and, most dramatically, the drive to "restore economic order" in 1988–89 and the repression of the Tiananmen protests. Following the latter campaign private sector numbers fell by more than 14%.

Private businesspersons also experienced economic problems owing to their marginal position in a system only beginning to change from a planned, collectively organized economy and society to an increasingly market-based economy. In the planned economy, business premises, labor, raw materials, equipment, energy, and finance were supplied to enterprises administratively; thus, private businesses, excluded from the plan, often found it difficult to obtain these resources. State-run wholesalers often refused to sell to private businesses, or required them to buy unwanted items along with their order. Private businesspersons complained at having to pay retail prices instead of wholesale, but from the state enterprises' point of view this was not unreasonable, since private enterprises required only small quantities of goods. Banks and rural credit societies generally discriminated against private businesses, charging higher interest as a matter of policy and refusing them credit altogether in many cases. Central regulations allowed private businesses to operate an enterprise bank account (with associated credit and transfer facilities not available on a personal account) from 1983, but some localities retained this barrier for many years.

Although more raw materials became available on the market as the reforms continued, many key inputs remained controlled. Other resources were simply difficult to find: private operators had to obtain them through carefully cultivated connections in a state factory or bureau that had access to such supplies. Connections had to be maintained not only by paying good prices, but also with bribes, commissions, gifts, and favors. Surveys of larger private enterprises, which normally have more complex input requirements than the small *getihu*, often have found that these spend as much as 20–30% of gross income on developing and maintaining the *guanxi* (connections) necessary for their business (see Young, 1995: chapter 3). Officials also used their control over key inputs as leverage over private entrepreneurs. Local governments could force private entrepreneurs to hand over their enterprises to collective ownership by threatening to cut off inputs such as electricity or raw materials not easily available on the market, blocking licenses or approvals, cutting off access to credit, or by adding new restrictions on the enterprise's activity (see Odgaard, 1992: chapter 6). Nearly all private enterprises had to rely on the cooperation of officials to obtain inputs and approvals, and the insecure political status of private entrepreneurs combined with bureaucratic influence over many areas of economic activity to pressure entrepreneurs into buying support from both officials and the wider community. Private entrepreneurs often donated conspicuously to local projects such as schools or tree-planting programs, provided free services for the local poor, or otherwise contributed to local welfare. A 1987 survey of 97 private enterprises found that they contributed on average more than 5% of gross profits in this way.

Advantages for Private Business

China's new private sector thus faced all the standard barriers to private business under Communist Party rule. In China's case, however, further reforms began to change the economic and administrative environment in ways that enabled the private sector to overcome these barriers.

First, the economic conditions of the early reform period were highly favorable to the growth of small private enterprises. Much of the early growth of private businesses occurred in consumer goods retailing and services. These trades required little in the way of special skills or capital, and were in great demand. China's enormous population, combined with the rising income levels resulting from the reforms to urban wages and agricultural purchase prices in the late 1970s, offered an immense market for retailing and consumer services like restaurants and repair shops. Furthermore, these trades had been neglected under the planning system. Operating without competition, state shops were notorious for their indifference to consumer preferences, and the formation of large-scale organizational units to suit the planning system had led to a drastic decline in the ratio of shops to population. In a nation that did its shopping on foot or bicycle, the loss of the corner store posed a great inconvenience; private traders recognized that they could make high profits by bringing the goods to consumers. Private businesses also quickly took advantage of the state system's neglect of variety by producing and marketing many small consumer items. In Wenzhou, for example, which became famous for its development of an economy dominated by the private sector, individual families produced small and varied consumer items such as buttons, which then were marketed all over China by a network of individual traders.

Rural reforms both stimulated and benefited from private sector growth. Beginning in 1979 peasants were allowed to sell produce directly to urban residents in free markets, and, although private trade across district boundaries was not initially permitted, in fact private operators soon began to buy meat and vegetables from peasants in the countryside to sell at a profit in the cities, and to market urban consumer goods in the countryside. The raising of agricultural produce prices and the spread of the household responsibility system in agriculture raised incomes and gave peasants choices as to how they wished to allocate their labor. Given that industry and commerce offered workers higher incomes relative to agriculture, this arguably has resulted in a neglect of agriculture, but it was undeniably a major factor in rural private sector growth. Increases in rural savings provided the financial basis for new private businesses, which also benefited from the release of a vast supply of cheap labor. Private transporters, builders, carpenters and suppliers of building materials appeared at the same time that rising incomes and rural enterprise development created an increased demand for rural housing and business construction.

The increasing marketization of the economy naturally reduced the constraining effect of the state-run economy. Reforms to reduce the role of central planning and make state enterprises more profit-oriented made these enterprises more willing to interact with private businesses. This increased marketization both eased private sector supply problems and created new opportunities as state enterprises bought from private producers or subcontracted production to them. A 1993 nationwide survey of larger private enterprises (*siying qiye*) found that nearly all manufacturing and processing enterprises listed state enterprises as their main suppliers and consumers. Even commercial and service enterprises frequently sold directly to state enterprises or other state units.

The second way in which reforms enabled private businesses to excel was by altering the administrative and organizational environment of China's economy. Reformers emphasized economic development as the foremost goal of the reform process, and administrators were evaluated according to this criterion. At the same time, the centrally promoted policy of "seeking truth from facts" created an atmosphere conducive to experimentation and increased the discretion of local administrators over the specifics of enterprise organization. Reform-era policies tended to combine clear and detailed economic demands (for example, specific quotas for creating new jobs, new enterprises, or increasing industrial income) with much less detailed political constraints on what kinds of economic activity and organization were

permissible. This encouraged officials to exceed these constraints if it was economically advantageous to do so.

Organizational changes also increased the relative powers of local governments. During the early 1980s, fiscal contracting schemes were introduced in which local governments (down to the township level) contracted to deliver a certain amount of revenue up to the next level of government and claimed a proportion of the surplus revenue. Local governments were expected to use this surplus for local expenses or for investing in local economic development. Naturally, this investment was channeled to local collective enterprises or agriculture rather than to the private sector. In addition, however, local governments could charge fees from private businesses to pad their local coffers. Although private entrepreneurs often resented these locally determined, random, and sometimes excessive charges, this arrangement actually benefited private sector development: local administrators now had an immediate interest in seeing private businesses grow.

In this environment, administrators who previously were encouraged to limit private sector growth now were given strong incentives to use any and all means available, including private enterprise, to spur economic growth in their localities. In addition, most limits that had been placed on private enterprises, including restrictions on mobility and mechanization, were removed. The limit on the number of employees, however, was a political assertion of the non-capitalist nature of the private sector under socialism, and was retained.

"Private" Enterprise within the Collective Sector

The previous section described how favorable economic conditions for private business development were combined with the localization of economic administration, together with strong pressures on local administrators to promote local economic growth. These factors would be expected to encourage local government support of private business development; however, owing to the leadership's socialist orientation, collective enterprises still received preferential policies over private businesses. Officials sought to rectify this problem by incorporating the would-be private entrepreneurs into collective-sector categories. This enabled private entrepreneurs to obtain the tax breaks, credibility, and local government assistance aimed at promoting collective rather than private enterprise. In a system with extensive government involvement in the economy, and a political bias against private enterprise, it made good sense to establish connections with local officials. Not only did this solution expedite local economic affairs, it also minimized risk by making local officialdom an interested party in the private sector's survival and growth. For administrators, it meant that they could utilize the available entrepreneurial talent in developing their local economies by assisting these entrepreneurs in obtaining credit or land that otherwise would be unavailable to them. This arrangement enhanced the power of local officials both in relation to entrepreneurs and to higher levels of government.

Thus, throughout the 1980s, the majority of entrepreneurs who expanded their enterprises chose to do so within the collective category. Fortunately for them, collective status was not hard to obtain. Some enterprises merely paid a fee, usually a small percentage of gross income, to a state or collective enterprise or government organization to be registered as a collective subsidiary or spin-off of the larger unit. Since reform policies included the promotion of such enterprises in many guises—for example, rural township and village enterprises, collectives created by state enterprises to employ the children of their own employees, and state enterprise spin-offs created under a variety of formal ownership arrangements to work outside state-sector constraints in research and development, marketing, and finance activities—it was easy enough for a wholly independent enterprise to find a niche. Others took steps to create

collective-sector characteristics in their enterprise, and with the connivance of local administrators this could be as simple as calculating year-end bonuses as a percentage of profits.

In fact, rural policies specifically encouraged a generous interpretation of collective status. Early policies encouraging peasants to engage in nonagricultural production and become "specialized households" provided one avenue for the development of private businesses. The framework for specialization could include manufacturing, construction, commerce, or transport, as well as the more usual rural sidelines like raising chickens. Peasants also were encouraged to form joint or cooperative ventures of two or more families. Under some regulations these were subject to the same employment limits as *getihu*, but some localities chose to view them as part of the peasant collective economy; for example, some localities offered these ventures the tax-free period granted to new collective enterprises. Although private enterprises employing more than seven people were perceived as a threat to traditional socialist organization, the major policy documents for rural work in 1983 and 1984 suggested that, so long as these enterprises demonstrated at least some cooperative or collective characteristics, such as distributing some of their profits to workers on a share basis or reinvesting rather than taking the bulk of profits as personal income, they could be included in collective categories.

Beginning in 1983 entrepreneurs could gain collective status for their business pursuits by leasing collective enterprises. Many village leaseholders enjoyed independent management rights, paid a set rent to the village and claimed the rest of the profits. Since many village enterprises were small workshops that originally were founded by only two or three people, this development served to recognize the property claims of the original founders rather than to "privatize" collective assets. Although leaseholders of larger enterprises did not always enjoy a high degree of autonomy, they still were able to extract profits from the enterprise. Leasing a state or collective enterprise, therefore, provided another way for entrepreneurs to build up capital, which they in turn used either to reinvest in the leased enterprise or start up a new firm.

These developments radically changed the nature of the collective sector, which now included undeniably private enterprises wearing a "red hat," hybrid enterprises that combined individual entrepreneurship with varying degrees of local government involvement, and enterprises that were still subject to local government or state-sector control. The political need to label these new types of enterprises as collective enterprises resulted in a wide gap between official regulations and actual practice, and made it difficult to regulate the economy effectively. False registrations precluded the gathering of reliable statistics on which to base further policies. For entrepreneurs, meanwhile, enterprise property rights remained unclear and, because local officials wielded authority over enterprises in their area, often insecure. Thus, both the recognized private sector and the opportunities for private entrepreneurship within the collective sector developed by pushing ahead of regulation limits. This meant that both entrepreneurs and officials, aware that they were stepping over political boundaries (but unsure exactly where those boundaries lay), closely observed the winds of political change.

Despite promises to the contrary, the private sector has not been limited to a marginal role in China's reforming economy, although key elements of the state-run economy certainly have shaped the private sector. Economically, discriminatory policies designed to favor socialist ownership merely encouraged corruption, as entrepreneurs used other channels to obtain favorable economic conditions and supplies. Administratively, entrepreneurs devoted much of their time to maintaining informal agreements and personal relationships with local officials. Not surprisingly, entrepreneurs considered connections to be as important as financial capital; they even referred to connections as "capital" and calculated the worth of their relationships in business terms.

From Reform to Transition: Toward a New Economic Framework

In 1988 the central government sought to legitimize larger private enterprises and thus ostensibly to eliminate one of the major causes of administrative irregularity. Zhao Ziyang's report to the Thirteenth Party Congress laid the ideological groundwork for this move in 1987 by formalizing the theory of the initial stage of socialism. According to this theory, economic development was the primary goal of the first phase of socialism, and thus capitalistic phenomena such as large private enterprises still had a positive role to play. In April the constitution was revised to include large private enterprises (*siying qiye*) among legitimate enterprise ownership types, and in June the State Council passed a set of provisional regulations on *siying qiye*. This was followed by a drive to inspect and relicense suspected "fake" collective enterprises and reregister them as *siying qiye*.

Although these regulations offered *siying qiye* favorable tax and operating conditions compared to those of state and collective enterprises, private operators were slow to apply for *siying qiye* status. Unfortunately, an ensuing market rectification drive undermined private entrepreneurs' confidence. Moreover, in 1989 entrepreneurs were accused of widespread tax evasion and blamed for fueling corruption. Anti-capitalist rhetoric was revived, and owners of larger private enterprises reportedly were banned from joining the Communist Party. Registering as a private enterprise simply had limited appeal. Although the regulations legitimized larger private businesses, they failed to remove the bureaucratic involvement in the economy, the preferential tax-free periods offered to new collective enterprises, and the barriers that prevented private enterprises from obtaining funding, premises, and supplies of raw materials. Nor, as was demonstrated in 1989, did these regulations relieve the intrinsic insecurity of capitalist enterprise under Communist Party rule.

Nonetheless, private businesses withstood these problems. The clampdown of 1989 demonstrated how deeply the major economic reforms were entrenched. During this period, state policy attempted unsuccessfully to reassert central control over the economy; even the private sector recovered promptly after the initial attack. Indeed, some reports suggest that local officials sought to protect private enterprises. In Liaoning, for example, tax officials argued that registering and taxing *siying qiye*-type enterprises as such would drive them out of business, and in Shenyang cadres were accused of having assisted private enterprises in obtaining bogus collective registrations as a defense against the crackdown. According to some county officials, many private businesses did not close down–they merely moved out of their localities for a time.

Soon these isolated cases of local officials aiding private businesses evolved into an all-out backlash against the repression of the private sector. In order to fight the recessionary effects of the clampdown, several localities released regulations that offered more favorable conditions for private business, including tax concessions, assistance with credit and premises, and, in one case, permission for private long-distance wholesalers (actually banned under a new central regulation) to use the city's name in their business titles. Following Deng Xiaoping's tour of southern China in 1992 (during which he promoted continued market-oriented reforms), new local policies appeared encouraging private sector growth; these policies included provisions to improve private access to credit and technology, and to make private business development a part of economic plans at all levels of government. There was also renewed theoretical discussion of the role of the private sector in a socialist economy. Instead of promoting the patronizing and constrictive view of private business as a "necessary supplement," state officials now referred to the private sector as "an important economic force in

developing new productive forces" and an integral part of "socialism with Chinese characteristics."

While these measures did increase entrepreneurs' confidence in the private sector, they did not address the basic problem: China's economic administration still classified all enterprises as either state-run, collective, or private, and still operated under the assumption that a socialist government should support state and collective enterprises over private enterprises. With regard to the former, these classifications no longer matched the complex variety of ownership regimes in Chinese enterprises; with regard to the latter, this bias against private enterprises merely invited pragmatic local officials and entrepreneurs to bend the rules. At the Third Plenum of the Fourteenth Central Committee in November 1993, China's leaders attempted to address this problem by officially adopting the goal of market socialism. The policy document resulting from this plenum, quoted at the beginning of this chapter, unequivocally states the party's intention to persevere with ownership reform and abandon discrimination against the private sector. Subsequently, the party has issued a series of laws and regulations aimed at effecting real ownership reform: the new laws on companies, limited liability, shareholding, accounting procedures, and taxation apply to a variety of ownership regimes including private enterprise, and also facilitate combinations of private and public investment and control.

The leap in *siying qiye* and *getihu* registrations after 1993 reveals the impact of this new environment on the private sector (see Table 11.1), although many more entrepreneurs continue to work within collective categories or shareholding arrangements. According to Xinhua, China's official news service, China now boasts more than 3 million millionaires (in Chinese *yuan*), many of whom are private entrepreneurs. A significant new trend in urban areas is the growth of private firms in high-tech sectors such as computers and various types of consultancy services. Since 1994 these firms have benefited from tax concessions and other assistance offered to them by local governments. Significantly, their development shows increased confidence in the private sector among highly qualified professionals, who in the past tended to prefer the relative security of a state sector job.

Conclusion

The private sector in China has evolved from a limited stop-gap measure to an integral part of the Chinese economy. This transition was made possible both by economic conditions favorable to the entry of large numbers of small private businesses and by the manner in which reform policies provided strong incentives for local economic growth while simultaneously granting local officials flexibility in choosing how to develop their local economies. Meanwhile, the increased blending of property rights, the steady erosion of the traditional hierarchy of ownerships, and the increasing legitimacy of private enterprise in state policies have resulted in a growing confidence in the private sector.

However, it should be noted that reforms relating to the private sector have been achieved via a gradual process involving extensive government participation in the economy at all levels. Although China's private sector has overcome various political and institutional constraints on private business during the reform period, it has done so at considerable cost to its independence. Private businesses in China continue to rely on personal connections for their success. Furthermore, they are highly vulnerable to the whims of local government administration and sensitive to political change.

Further Reading

Bruun, Ole, *Business and Bureaucracy in a Chinese City: An Ethnography of Private Business Households in Contemporary China,* Berkeley: Institute of East Asian Studies, University of California, 1993

A detailed anthropological study of the private businesses in one street in Chengdu, based on extended fieldwork in the late 1980s. The author focuses on private business as part of each household's total strategy for survival and success, as well as on the relationships between private entrepreneurs and local administrators.

Kraus, Willy, *Private Business in China: Revival Between Ideology and Pragmatism,* translated by Erich Holz, Honolulu: University of Hawaii Press, and London: Hurst, 1991

Among the first academic studies available in English specifically about the private sector. Written by an economist, it includes many statistics on the growth and conditions of the private sector up to 1989. Although highly informative, the book is sometimes confusingly organized and is densely written. Based mainly on official sources.

Nolan, Peter, and Dong Fureng, editors, *Market Forces in China: Competition and Small Business,* London: Zed Books, 1990

A collection of translated articles by Chinese economists on the "Wenzhou model" of rural enterprise development, which relied mainly on private enterprise and thus provoked a controversy in China. The articles, very optimistic in tone, are based on detailed information and deal with issues such as rural commercialization, capital accumulation and technological improvement, vertical and horizontal integration among household businesses, small town development, and income inequalities. Additional articles by Peter Nolan and Chris Bramall provide a useful explanation of China's rural reforms and the Wenzhou model itself.

Odgaard, Ole, *Private Enterprises in Rural China: Impact on Agriculture and Social Stratification,* Aldershot, Hants.: Avebury, and Brookfield, Vermont: Ashgate, 1992

Based on extended fieldwork in Renshou county, Sichuan, this study fills an important gap by providing much information and analysis on the development of private businesses in rural China. Although not so informative on general policy developments or how local and higher levels relate, the volume has made a valuable contribution to our understanding of the relationship between local rural administrators and entrepreneurs.

Solinger, Dorothy J., *Chinese Business Under Socialism: The Politics of Domestic Commerce*

1949–1980, Berkeley: University of California Press, 1984

A well-written, comprehensive study of the politics of state-business relations since 1949, including the socialist transformation of private business in the 1950s and the revival of the private sector after 1978.

Wank, David, *Commodifying Communism: Markets, Culture, and Politics in a South China City,* Cambridge and New York: Cambridge University Press, 1998

An excellent sociological study of the strategies and networks of private entrepreneurs in Xiamen based on fieldwork in 1989–1990 and 1995. Focuses on the distinctive institutional dynamics of the relationships forged between private entrepreneurs and administrators as Xiamen's market economy developed.

Young, Susan, *Private Business and Economic Reform in China,* Armonk, New York: M.E. Sharpe, 1995

Examines the development of the private sector as a case study of the process of reform in China by combining analysis of policy development and the debates surrounding it with research on the actual implementation of policy at local levels.

Yudkin, Marcia, *Making Good: Private Business in Socialist China,* Beijing: Foreign Languages Press, 1986

A journalist's brief account of the developing private sector in the late 1970s and early 1980s, based on interviews under the auspices of the Bureau of Industry and Commerce. Many interesting and highly informative anecdotal accounts of private business dealings during the Mao and Deng eras. Mainly concerns small urban *getihu.*

Susan Young is External Lecturer in the Department of Asian Studies, Copenhagen University. She is the author of *Private Business and Economic Reform in China* (1995) and of numerous articles treating Chinese economic issues in journals and collections of essays.

Table 11.1: Registered Private Businesses (getihu and siying qiye)		
	getihu	*siying qiye*
1981	1,827,752	
1982	2,614,006	
1983	5,901,032	
1984	9,329,464	
1985	11,712,680	
1986	12,111,560	
1987	13,725,746	
1988	14,526,931	
1989	12,471,937	90,581
1990	13,281,974	98,141
1991	14,145,000	108,000
1992	15,339,200	139,600
1993	15,483,000	184,000
1995	25,285,000	655,000
Source: Statistical Yearbook of China		

Chapter Twelve

Financial Reform at the Crossroads

Paul Bowles

Because the financial system plays a central role in the functioning of any economy, developing a system capable of supporting a "socialist market economy" has received serious and sustained attention from China's policymakers. China's financial reforms appear impressive. In 1978, China still operated with a Soviet-style financial system consisting of one bank–the "monobank"–which was responsible for collecting enterprise surpluses and reallocating them in accordance with state planning priorities. But by 1996 China's economy had become monetized. China had enacted a Western-style central bank law, established the foundations for a competitive commercial banking system, had four banks ranked among the world's top 100 banks (as measured by assets at the end of 1995), including one in the top ten, had functioning stock markets in two major cities, and was participating actively in international capital markets.

Not only had the structure of China's financial system changed dramatically since 1978, but its performance in macroeconomic terms also was credible. Savings and investment rates were high, often close to 40% of Gross Domestic Product (GDP). Although inflation had surfaced periodically, it had been brought down each time (see Figure 12.1) and had been modest compared to that of other transitional economies. These factors, in the context of a rapidly expanding economy, suggest that China has met with considerable success in reforming its banking and financial systems.

This chapter provides a detailed overview of China's financial reforms, examin-ing the content and rationale of these reforms as well as the underlying political and economic debates that have accompanied them. The first section gives a brief description of the financial system as it existed in 1978, a system the reformers inherited from the previous centralized system of economic management. The second section focuses on the major reforms that have occurred since 1978, dividing this period into four sub-periods each of which marked a qualitatively different stage in the reform process. In Section 3, it is argued that despite the considerable changes that have taken place in the structure of the financial system there are still several fundamental unresolved issues. Examining how these issues may be resolved provides us with important clues as to the type of financial system toward which China is moving and, more broadly, to the type of economy into which China will evolve.

Financial Reform: An Overview

The Pre-Reform Financial System

The Chinese financial system on the eve of the reform era (that is, the period just prior to 1978) comprised the essential components of the monobank model inherited from the Soviet version of Marxist-Leninist socialism. As such, the financial system was an integral part of the centrally planned economy. The main institutions were the Ministry of Finance, which collected the surpluses of state-owned enterprises, and banking institutions that administered credit allocation. The People's Bank of China (hereafter PB) was the predominant banking institution. Organized vertically, the PB consisted of the Main Office, which was subject to control by the State Council, and branches extending down to lower administrative levels.

The PB functioned mainly to administer the planned budget allocations for working capital and to provide credit to enterprises and state bodies, operating according to the Maoist dictum of "ensuring supply and developing the economy." In other words, the PB was an instrument of the state and operated as part of the state plan. By channeling credit through the PB, the new communist regime was able to alter quickly the sectoral composition of industry and to complete the rapid socialization of industry following the 1949 revolution. Two other specialist banks also existed. The Bank of China (BoC) was responsible for foreign exchange transactions and overseas business; the People's Construction Bank of China (PCBC) was responsible for administering the fixed capital investment expenditures stipulated by the central plan. In rural areas, a network of rural credit cooperatives collected savings and channeled them into industry.

These comprised the main institutions of the pre-reform financial system (although periodic attempts also were made to establish an Agricultural Bank), which operated as an instrument of the state planning process with money playing a "passive" role; allocation decisions were made by planning agencies, and macroeconomic stability depended upon the coherence of the overall plan rather than on the performance of the banking system. By 1979, following the ascendancy to power of reformers within the Chinese Communist Party (CCP), this system was regarded, along with the rest of the economy, as inadequate. Reformers argued that the financial system was too monolithic and administrative-based, giving insufficient scope for using economic criteria in allocating credit. The financial system therefore needed to be reformed in order to meet the demands of a reforming economy that would put greater financial resources in the hands of individuals and enterprises through the decollectivization of agriculture, profit retention schemes in state-owned industry, and the opening up of China's market to the outside world.

1979–84: Financial Liberalization without Financial Markets

At first, the scope of China's financial reform was officially circumscribed, reflecting the infancy of the reform project in general. The main financial reforms focused on changing the structure and operations of the state-owned banking system. With regard to operations, the banking system was endowed with greater decision-making authority in its dealings with client state-owned enterprises, thus making the system a more active participant in the development process. Reformers viewed increasing the productivity of state-owned enterprises as a central aim of the reform process and a reformed banking system as instrumental in meeting this goal.

Thus, bank credit increased in importance relative to budgetary allocations with regard to providing working capital for enterprises. This, in turn, raised the importance of bank lending decisions. These decisions were to be based more on economic efficiency criteria, and banks were expected to become more profit-oriented institutions. To this end, banks were given greater autonomy in the setting of interest rates and in their lending decisions. The overall aim was to transform banks, which formerly had acted as the passive administrators of financial flows, into monitoring agents supervising the use of funds that they loaned.

Institutional changes accompanied these changes in operating principles. Specifically, a two-tiered banking system was introduced to replace the old monobank system. The Agricultural Bank (AB) was restored in 1979 and resumed responsibility for attracting savings and administering loans in rural areas; in the same year the China International Trust and Investment Company (CITIC) was established to facilitate foreign investment and joint ventures; and in 1983 the Industrial and Commercial Bank (ICB) was established to raise deposits and distribute credit to urban enterprises. The PB was freed now to take up its role as China's central bank, responsible for managing the government's finances, for ensuring macroeconomic stability, and for supervising the four "specialized banks," namely, the Agricultural Bank, the Bank of China, the Industrial and Commercial Bank, and the People's Construction Bank of China. This organizational change separated the operations of the lending institutions (the specialized banks) from the functions of currency issue and credit control, operations which were exercised by the PB (the central bank).

In 1981 bond issues were revived as important vehicles for channeling savings into resources for the state. Initially, treasury bonds were issued in order to provide the government with a source of revenue in the face of large budget deficits the previous two years; however, bond issues were continued thereafter as a source of permanent government revenue. Treasury bonds were the only officially sanctioned bonds during this phase of the reform process, and their issue was by mandatory allocation rather than through market processes. Enterprises were given quotas for both unit and individual bond sales and were required to ensure that these quotas were met. Central authorities determined the interest rates and maturity terms and, since these bonds were "sold" by mandatory allocation rather than by voluntary purchase, rates and terms often were unattractive.

The result of these changes was that the institutional structure of the Chinese financial system began to depart significantly from the pre-reform system. By 1984 there were strong pressures to reform the system further. Reformers within the CCP argued that the PB and the specialized banks still operated within the confines of the central plan and remained subject to administrative control. Also, reformers argued that the specialized banks each had a monopoly over particular sectors of the economy and

that inter-sectoral mobility of capital therefore was low. The banking system, it was argued, could contribute to economic development by becoming more competitive, autonomous, and profit-oriented. Reformers concluded that not only could banks act as more efficient financial intermediaries, but that other financial assets, such as bonds and shares, could play an expanded role in the direct channeling of resources from savers to borrowers. In short, reformers envisioned greater scope for making use of financial markets in raising and allocating capital.

Although treasury bonds had been reintroduced in 1981, the issue of shares had been restricted to a few experiments. The ownership of capital through shares posed fundamental challenges to socialist China, where social ownership of the means of production was considered a central feature of the economy. The proposal to expand financial reforms to include share issues led to serious debate within CCP policymaking circles. Conservative forces argued against shares in particular and cautioned against further financial reform in general on the grounds that macroeconomic instability was likely to ensue.

By 1984, however, the structure of the Chinese economy already had changed considerably. These changes were reflected by the decline in the central government's revenue as a share of GNP from 34.4% in 1978 to 26.4% in 1984. Urban and rural households and local governments now had much greater control over financial resources, and the economy had become more diversified and decentralized. Following the success of agricultural reforms, the decision was made to implement further the economic reform agenda (including more comprehensive financial reform) in the urban industrial sector.

1985–88: The Move Toward Financial Markets

The second phase of financial reform, which began after the 1984 initiatives, witnessed a qualitative change in direction.

During this period, financial reforms, in common with the reform process in general, moved into high gear in an effort by reformers to break decisively with administrative mechanisms of the past and fashion their own "great leap forward" into a market economy. Such efforts were a result of the growing confidence and optimism spawned by earlier successes in agricultural reform. These efforts coincided with the growing cosmopolitanizing of Chinese economic policy making as international financial institutions, such as the World Bank and the International Monetary Fund, became more influential. The end result was that policy-makers began to view the market as a panacea for China's economic problems.

Initially during this phase of financial reform, measures were taken to provide banks at all levels with greater autonomy from government influence, whether it be the case of the central bank gaining more autonomy from the Ministry of Finance and the State Council or of the specialized banks gaining more autonomy from local governments. Reformers hoped that these measures would enable the PB to act more independently in setting interest rates and in regulating the economy by indirect mechanisms rather than through the old system of administrative decrees and direct quantity rationing. They also expected such measures to enable the specialized banks to make their loan decisions on the basis of anticipated returns rather than at the behest of local governments pursuing local development objectives that might not be economically justified. Such changes in bank behavior were to be supported in turn by changes in the institutional environment, which would increase the degree of competition among financial institutions. Competition, it was argued, was necessary to promote the full development of a financial market. Thus, the aim was to move beyond differentiation of the state banking system—which had occurred during the first phase of financial reform—to a competitive financial system consisting of state-owned banks, non state-owned banks, non-bank financial institutions

(NBFIs), and bond and equity markets.

To spur competition in the banking system, barriers between the functions of state banks were reduced and state banks were permitted to move outside their traditional fields of operation. The interbank money market, established in 1986, expanded rapidly. Lending to the growing rural industrial sector increased as banks sought new and profitable investment opportunities. In addition, the state-owned specialized banks were joined by a variety of new financial institutions providing competition for deposits and loans. Thus, the Shanghai-based joint stock Communications Bank and a subsidiary of CITIC, the CITIC Industrial Bank, both were opened in 1987. In the open coastal regions, foreign banks and joint Chinese-foreign banks opened representative and branch offices to service foreign trade and investment. Non-bank financial institutions, especially trust and investment companies, proliferated (more than 700 were in operation by 1989), and the activities of the People's Insurance Company expanded dramatically as it sought ways to tap the burgeoning monetary assets of households. Urban credit cooperatives multiplied, supplying credit to the small-scale collective and private enterprise sectors that the specialized banks largely had neglected. This new competitive environment was evident by the fact that the specialized banks' share of total financial assets fell from 96.5% in 1985 to 86.9% in 1989.

During this period, treasury bonds were joined by bonds issued by the specialized banks and by enterprises. The annual value of bond and share issues increased nearly eightfold between 1985 and 1989. While treasury bonds continued to be allocated by administrative means, secondary trading was permitted in five experimental cities in 1986 and expanded to more than 60 cities in 1988. Bonds issued by the specialized banks and enterprises all were issued for sale at market prices and provided keen competition for treasury bonds. Enterprise bonds, from state-owned enterprises and from urban and rural collective enterprises, either were offered to local residents or to the enterprise's own workforce. Secondary trading was mostly illegal. Bonds offered to the enterprise's own workforce were often a disguised form of payment rather than a genuine instrument for channeling financial resources from savers to borrowers.

Shares, which had been the subject of debate and a few experiments in the early 1980s, were sanctioned by central authorities in late 1984. Share issues increased rapidly as a result, with embryonic and unofficial stock exchanges emerging in several major cities. However, the quantity of share issues still remained very small. The role shares could play in the development of the Chinese financial system and the economic system in general prompted considerable debate on the questions of ownership in a socialist economy and the legitimacy of income sources. To counter concerns about the latter question, shares in China were designed not to resemble the "residual claimant" shares that characterize capitalist economies but to function much more like bonds in that they offered a guaranteed rate of return (although often supplemented with an amount based on enterprise profitability) and conferred no voting rights. Secondary trading remained highly restricted.

The introduction of these reforms was accompanied by strong inflationary pressures. Inflation in China reached 8.8% in 1985 but fell slightly thereafter, only to return with a vengeance when the official price index increased by 18.5% in 1988 and 17.8% in 1989 (as shown in Figure 12.1). These figures, however, undoubtedly understate the true inflation rate. The basic problem was that financial reforms during this phase had enabled agents in the economy to pursue their claims on resources and to pressure the banking system into supplying them with more credit in an attempt to realize those claims. The proliferation of financial institutions and financial assets had enabled enterprises to obtain the financial resources necessary to expand their operations. At the same time, the state banking system was pressured by both local governments, wishing to develop their areas rapidly, and by the central government, itself

faced with a declining share of GNP, to continue financing their own favored projects. This scenario was exacerbated by the specialized banks and the People's Bank remaining under "dual leadership"; that is, the branch banks were subject not only to control from higher levels of the same bank but also from administrative bodies at the same level. Banks usually complied by expanding their lending. At the root of the inflationary process, therefore, was competition for resources between various agents in the economy but with no institutional mechanism capable of limiting the claims made to the resources available; the banking system found itself caught in the middle of this process, and inflation resulted as the banking system accommodated agents' demands. This situation could not be permitted to continue for long, and inflationary pressures were brought under control with the introduction of an austerity program in September 1988.

1988–92: Retrenchment and Reversal

The inflationary crisis of 1988 led the government to seek ways to reassert control of the economy and restore macroeconomic stability. To achieve this, central authorities returned to administrative measures such as mandatory credit ceilings and tight control over central bank lending. Central authorities also raised interest rates and the reserve requirements of the specialized banks. This combination of approaches succeeded in bringing down inflation.

The cost of this battle against inflation was an economic slowdown. The credit crunch in effect reduced the claims of some agents in the economy by controlling their access to finance. In the economic slowdown the more vulnerable rural industrial sector was severely affected: 600,000 rural enterprises went bankrupt and 3 million rural workers lost their jobs. Trust and investment companies also folded in large numbers. Although the state sector was largely protected, many state-sector investment projects were abandoned. Directed lending increased, and many NBFIs that had been brought into the credit plan were instructed to undertake directed lending. The result was that bad loans on the part of the banking sector increased during this period. The activities of the inter-bank market were curtailed sharply and those of the Shenzhen stock exchange were placed under scrutiny. Shenzhen was allowed to continue its operations, but Shanghai also was permitted to operate a stock market as a counterweight.

The reassertion of central control over the economy provided a period of economic stability at a time when political conditions were anything but stable (military suppression of the student protests at Tiananmen Square had taken place on June 4, 1989; protests in other major cities in China continued through that month). The period 1989–91 was one of economic "freezing" during which no major reforms were advanced. The credit tightening policy gradually was relaxed in 1990 as state-owned enterprises sought to ease their financial situation. State banks found it increasingly difficult to maintain credit to their clients, and state-owned enterprises complained of a liquidity squeeze that sent ripple effects through the economy. These effects were felt as nonpayment of debts rose and as the Agricultural Bank was forced to issue IOUs to grain farmers. Furthermore, the more powerful and dynamic southeastern provinces sought ways of resuming their high economic growth rates, a position supported by Deng Xiaoping's Southern Tour (a tour aimed at hastening the return of the high-growth policies of the previous decade). The period of retrenchment thus came to an end in 1992 and a new round of financial reform ensued.

1992–96: Institutional Development and Further Liberalization without Diversification

The period since 1992 has been characterized by further institutional changes and the continued, gradual move toward greater use of market mechanisms to supplant administrative control. However, the basic contours of the financial system remain unchanged, since reforms have focused on existing institutions rather than on further diversification. Lessons that the leadership seems to have taken from the previous phases of the financial reform process are to restrict the range of permitted financial assets and financial institutions and to place these institutions under the control of a more independent central bank. This, it is hoped, will curtail future inflationary pressures similar to those that arose during the 1985–88 period. In order to increase the efficiency with which resources are channeled from savers to borrowers, the government currently is seeking ways to promote greater competition and market-oriented behavior within the existing set of institutions and deepening, rather than widening, financial markets. At the same time, however, central authorities wish to maintain control over the direction of key sectors of the economy.

Furthermore, efforts to refine the roles of the People's Bank and the four specialized banks continued following the decision in November 1993 to move ahead with the overall reform process. The Central Bank Law, passed in 1995, endowed the PB with greater autonomy and a legal basis to formulate monetary policy and supervise the financial system. The law also forbids the central bank from extending lines of credit and direct loans to the central or provincial governments. At the same time that the central bank was given more power and authority to act independently with respect to the banking system, the roles and responsibilities of the specialized banks were clarified further. The specialized banks were now defined, under China's new Commercial Banking Law, as competitive banks that were to operate more as profit-maximizing enterprises. The task of meeting the central government's infrastructure and priority sector loan requirements has been shifted to the newly-formed State Development Bank and two other policy lending banks. In this way, institutional changes have sought to clarify and separate the functions of central banking, commercial lending, and policy lending. As for future plans, current government objectives include the development of a national inter-bank market for the purpose of increasing regional and sectoral mobility of resources. Government plans also call for the increased use of open market operations by the central bank as an indirect policy instrument, as well as the liberalization of interest rates, a process to be achieved gradually by the year 2000.

These new institutional changes, however, have not been accompanied by significant new developments in the variety of financial assets available or in the range of financial institutions operating in the Chinese economy. Indeed, current plans are to introduce new legislation to regulate and streamline NBFIs and to separate NBFIs from the commercial banking system in order to protect the latter from any potential financial problems (such as defaults) in the NBFI sector. The emphasis has been on making existing institutions work better and more competitively. Thus, the People's Insurance Company was restructured in June 1996 to become the People's Insurance (Property) Company, and now has a more clearly defined role as a credit agency (this illustrates the government's desire to increase competition in the banking sector, but to do so using existing rather than newly created institutions). The bond market continues to expand with the issue of treasury bonds increasing significantly in the 1990s and with other central government bonds, such as fiscal bonds and special state bonds (the latter used to finance national infrastructure projects), also being introduced during this period, as shown in Table 12.1.

Shanghai and Shenzhen have continued to develop their stock markets (although other centers have been officially discouraged) and the volume of bond and share issues remains set by the credit plan. By the end of 1994 China's bond and stock markets remained relatively small compared to those of other developing countries in the region. For example, China's stock market capitalization was 9% of GDP and the bond market was 7% of GDP, averages that are considerably lower than those for East Asian developing countries (71% and 22%, respectively).

One significant change has been that some shares, known as B shares, were made available to foreigners in 1992. By the end of 1994, 34 Chinese companies' B shares were traded on the Shanghai and Shenzhen stock exchanges. Furthermore, shares of Chinese companies were floated on the New York and Hong Kong stock exchanges as China has sought to experiment with tapping international financial markets.

Thus, the current financial system is characterized by a formal financial sector consisting of a banking system wherein the major banking institutions are state owned, by a number of NBFIs that are subject to various degrees of state control, by a bond market in which 73% of bond issues are central government bonds with the rest issued by state-owned enterprises, and by relatively small and highly speculative stock markets. Outside these formal institutions are a plethora of other mechanisms and institutions for channeling resources from savers to borrowers. These mechanisms and institutions, which assist in areas not well served by the formal banking system, emerged during the phase of financial liberalization in the mid-to-late 1980s and now have become established parts of the Chinese financial system, providing what often is termed a "competitive fringe." These mechanisms and institutions include the unauthorized sale of shares and bonds by enterprises to their workers, informal "credit clubs," leasing companies, and other financial institutions including urban and rural credit cooperatives. The magnitude of this latter sector is significant. In fact, some scholars have argued that the amount of funds flowing into fixed investment from outside the banking system is roughly equivalent to the amount of funds flowing into fixed investment through the banking system. China's financial system, therefore, is best described as dualistic, with one part heavily influenced by government policy and the other largely free of official regulations.

Assessment and Conclusion

These changes introduced since 1992 have been significant, particularly in providing the legal basis for central bank and commercial bank operations. Nonetheless, the prospects for China's current financial system—dualistic but with the formal sector moving toward greater liberalization—remain a contentious matter. For some observers, the successes of the reform period to date, inflationary problems notwithstanding, suggest that China's approach to financial reform might serve as a model for other transitional socialist economies in Europe and Asia. For others, the successes of the past cannot hide the need for further reforms.

A number of questions remain problematic for policymakers. For example, if state-owned banks are to act more like profit-oriented organizations, how would the supply of financial resources to state-owned enterprises be assured? In turn, if this supply is not assured, is the government willing to tolerate the bankruptcy of significant sections of state-owned industry and its likely social consequences? Moreover, if state-owned banks are to support state industry, how are they to compete with other financial institutions that are under no such restrictions and are free to pursue their own lending activities on the basis of expected profitability? If state-owned banks, saddled with the bad debts and losses of state industry, were exposed to full competition from non-state banks, the possibility of full-scale financial collapse is real.

These and other questions indicate that the success of financial reform depends not only on the performance of the financial sector, but also on other parts of the reform program. However, the reform program as a whole has not been clearly conceived at the theoretical level. Reforms to date have been guided by pragmatism and there remains no clear blueprint for the reformed economy. Until the end-point of the reforms has been established, financial reform will continue to contain piecemeal, incomplete, and even contradictory elements.

China's policy makers are confronted with the choice of forging a financial system in which market forces determine the allocation of financial resources, or of constructing a financial system wherein the state continues to significantly control the allocation of credit and employs the banking system to monitor the use made of such credit. Nearly 20 years into the reform process, which road China will travel is still uncertain, but analyzing the future course of financial reform is likely to reveal a great deal about the type of economy that China will become in the early part of the 21st century.

Further Reading

Bowles, Paul, and Gordon White, *The Political Economy of China's Financial Reforms: Finance in Late Development,* Boulder, Colorado: Westview Press, 1993

Assesses the theory and practice of financial reform in the light of China's specific characteristics as a large, developing country that still claims to be pursuing the goal of establishing a "socialist" market economy. Two approaches are used. First, the authors place the overall design and trajectory of financial reform since 1979 within a broad comparative framework of alternative strategies of financial reform and financial systems. Second, a political economy perspective is used to explore the complex interactions among the political and economic actors—individual, group, or institutional—that affect reform outcomes. Integrating these two approaches, the authors conclude by assessing future directions for feasible and desirable financial reform in China.

Byrd, William A., *China's Financial System: The Changing Role of Banks,* Boulder, Colorado: Westview Press, and Epping: Bowker, 1983

One of the earliest works to recognize the important changes to the financial sector occurring at the beginning of the reform period. The book provides a thorough study of the pre-reform financial system and assesses its performance. The reasons the financial system was deemed in need of reform are analyzed and the initial reforms documented.

Naughton, Barry, *Growing Out of the Plan: Chinese Economic Reform 1978–1993,* Cambridge and New York: Cambridge University Press, 1995

Provides a comprehensive study of China's economic reforms from 1978 to 1993. The book documents the gradual transformation of China's economy from a planned economy to a market economy, a transformation it achieved not by abandoning planning but by the rapid growth of the market-oriented sectors that fell outside of the government's plan. Naughton focuses specifically on industrial and macroeconomic policy and illustrates how the reforms in these as in other areas were not part of a grand design but arose through a pragmatic approach. The study maintains that a gradual transition from state planning is possible; it is useful in documenting the changing nature of the real economy and the scope of the task now facing China's policymakers as they attempt to provide macroeconomic stability in a much changed economic system.

Peebles, Gavin, *Money in the People's Republic of China: A Comparative Perspective,* Sydney: Allen and Unwin, 1991

An account of monetary developments in China since 1949. The author's approach is based on an awareness of the importance of institutions in explaining economic behavior. Peebles argues that the quantity theory of money is inapplicable to China since it ignores the Chinese institutional setting. An important part of this institutional setting is that prices are primarily set by planners, not markets. In rejecting the monetarist and New Classical explanations of inflation, therefore, Peebles focuses on an issue that is all too frequently ignored in conventional analyses, namely the behavior of the agents who actually set prices. Peebles advances his own Purchasing Power Imbalances explanation of Chinese inflationary pressures, although his analysis is applied only up to the mid-1980s.

Tam, On Kit, *Financial Reform in China,* London and New York: Routledge, 1995

This collection of papers argues that the reform of China's financial sector has lagged behind reforms in other sectors and has failed to keep pace with the changing structure of the Chinese economy. The financial system is viewed as a bottleneck on the future growth of the Chinese economy, and the need for reducing the scale and scope of government intervention is stressed. The contributors to the volume are, with the exception of the edi-

tor, all senior officials working for Chinese financial institutions or ministries. As such, they bring a good deal of institutional knowledge and understanding of the process of economic reform to their papers, which include discussion of the policy choices of the central bank, the inter-bank money market, the rural financial system, and the foreign exchange system.

Wade, Robert, *Governing the Market: Economic Theory and the Role of Government in East Asian Industrialization,* Princeton, New Jersey: Princeton University Press, 1990

A very thorough study of the role of government in East Asian industrialization. Focusing particularly on Taiwan and South Korea, Wade argues that the government has played a fundamental role in the growth of these countries. Initially regarded as a controversial argument, it has now gained increasing acceptance even within orthodox economic circles. The book is useful in providing the broad contours of East Asian financial systems.

World Bank, *China: Financial Sector Policies and Institutional Development,* Washington, D.C.: World Bank, 1990

One of the most thorough documents on the financial reforms from their inception to 1989, this report covers all the major changes to the financial system and provides statistical data for a large number of variables. Topics covered include changes to the financial sector, monetary policy, bank supervision and regulation, and the management of government debt. The report argues that further fundamental reforms are necessary to reduce the role of government in the operations of the financial system.

World Bank, *The Chinese Economy: Fighting Inflation, Deepening Reforms,* Washington, D.C.: World Bank, 1996

This volume includes a chapter that provides a detailed account of the reforms of the financial sector that have taken place since 1978 and places particular emphasis on the reforms that have occurred since the Third Plenum of the Fourteenth Party Central Committee in November 1993. The current state of the financial system is assessed and the policy options confronting policy makers are outlined together with the authors' own recommendations. A good guide to current World Bank thinking about the direction and extent of financial reforms that are still required.

Yi, Gang, *Money, Banking and Financial Markets in China,* Boulder, Colorado: Westview Press, 1994

Provides an overview of the main changes to the financial system during the reform period, presents data on Chinese monetary aggregates, and performs some econometric tests using this data. The author's main objective is to provide information on the Chinese financial and monetary system rather than to argue for a specific position. The book has chapters dealing with interest rates and their determination, the money supply process and the role of the central bank, the demand for money and the monetization of the Chinese economy, and inflation. A more narrowly economistic work than many of the others listed here.

Zysman, John, *Governments, Markets, and Growth: Financial Systems and the Politics of Industrial Change,* Ithaca, New York: Cornell University Press, 1983

Although this book is restricted to the analysis of advanced capitalist economies, it is useful in the present context because it outlines the differences in financial systems that exist in these countries and analyzes how these differences condition the ability of governments to exercise industrial policy and to influence the direction of industrial growth. Thus, the author emphasizes the strategic role of the financial system and analyzes the links between the operations of the financial system and other aspects of government policy.

Paul Bowles is Professor of Economics at University of Northern British Columbia, Canada. He is coauthor, with Gordon White, of *The Political Economy of China's Financial Reforms: Finance in Late Development* (1993); he has also contributed articles on Chinese financial structures to *Journal of Development Studies, Cambridge Journal of Economics, World Development, New Left Review,* and *Review of International Political Economy.*

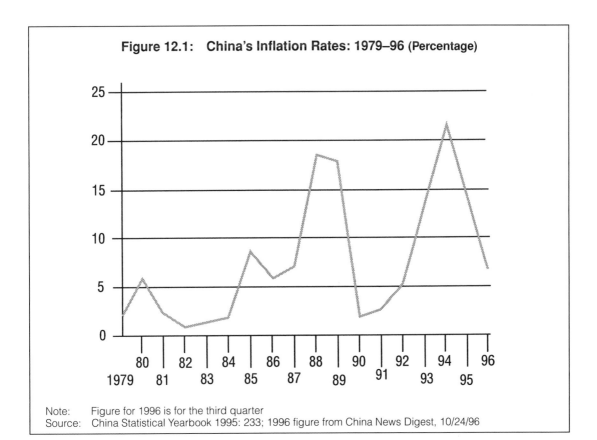

Figure 12.1: China's Inflation Rates: 1979–96 (Percentage)

Note: Figure for 1996 is for the third quarter
Source: China Statistical Yearbook 1995: 233; 1996 figure from China News Digest, 10/24/96

Table 12.1: Central Government Bond Issues, 1981–95 (billion *yuan*)

Year	Type of Bond	Issued to	Amount Issued
1981	Treasury Bonds	Enterprises	4.85
		Households	0.01
1982	Treasury Bonds	Enterprises	2.4
		Households	2.0
1983	Treasury Bonds	Enterprises	2.1
		Households	2.1
1984	Treasury Bonds	Enterprises	2.0
		Households	2.2
1985	Treasury Bonds	Enterprises	2.2
		Households	3.8
1986	Treasury Bonds	Enterprises	2.3
		Households	4.0
1987	Treasury Bonds	Enterprises	2.3
		Households	4.0
	Key Construction Bonds	Enterprises	4.9
		Households	0.5
1988	Treasury Bonds	Enterprises	3.5
		Households	5.7
	Key Construction Bonds	Households	3.1
	Fiscal Bonds	Financial Institutions	6.6
1989	Treasury Bonds	Households	5.6
	Price-Indexed Bonds	Households	12.5
	Special State Bonds	Enterprises	4.3
1990	Treasury Bonds	Households	9.3
	Special State Bonds	Enterprises	3.2
	Fiscal Bonds	Financial Institutions	7.1
	Conversion Bonds	Enterprises	9.4
1991	Treasury Bonds	Households	19.94
	Special State Bonds	Enterprises	2.0
	Fiscal Bonds	Financial Institutions	7.0
1992	Treasury Bonds	Households	39.6
1993	Treasury Bonds	Households	31.48
	Fiscal Bonds	Financial Institutions	7.0
1994	Treasury Bonds	Enterprises	2.0
		Households	106.74
1995	Treasury Bonds	Households	111.89
		Financial Institutions	36.89
	Special State Bonds	Financial Institutions	3.0

Source: Figures for 1981 derive from Paul Bowles and Gordon White, *The Political Economy of China's Finan-cial Reforms: Finance in Late Development,* Boulder, Colorado: Westview Press, 1993: 125; figures for 1982–95 are taken from World Bank, *The Chinese Economy: Fighting Inflation, Deepening Reforms,* Washington, D.C.: World Bank, 1996: 84

Chapter Thirteen

Foreign Trade Reform and Relations with International Economic Institutions

Jude Howell

For China watchers observing the turbulent and ideological years of the Cultural Revolution, the idea that China might one day court the international economic institutions would have seemed not only heretical but plainly unimaginable. Yet the changes in leadership following the death of Mao and the demise of the Gang of Four ushered in an era that departed radically in many ways from the politically loaded policies of the 1960s and 1970s. China rapidly decollectivized its agricultural system, encouraged the emergence of a private sector, and opened its doors to foreign investment. In 1980 it joined the International Monetary Fund and World Bank. Since then, it has pushed determinedly for membership in the General Agreement on Tariffs and Trade and later the World Trade Organization.

Why did China decide to join these institutions it formerly had denounced as instruments of imperialism? What were the issues that informed the process of membership? What have been the consequences for China and other member states? How long will it be before China becomes a full-fledged member of the World Trade Organization? These are some of the questions addressed in this chapter.

This chapter begins by tracing China's relationship with international economic institutions during the pre-reform period. The designation "international economic institutions" refers to those multilateral

organizations that deal with issues of international trade, the world economy, and the global monetary system. This section focuses on China's relations with the World Bank, the International Monetary Fund (IMF), and the General Agreement on Tariffs and Trade (GATT) and its successor, the World Trade Organization (WTO). Section 2 examines China's moves to join the IMF and World Bank and its ongoing efforts to become part of the WTO fold. China's gradual participation in these bodies during the reform period has reflected not only a new approach on its part toward international affairs, but also a shift in the policy of Western powers away from containment and toward engagement of this increasingly powerful economic force. Section 3 considers the implications of membership for China and other member states. The chapter concludes by speculating on the future prospects for China and the international economic institutions.

1 The Pre-Reform Period

At the end of World War II, Western leaders faced the urgent task of reconstructing the war-devastated economies of Europe, securing global peace, and revitalizing global trade. Within this context an array of multilateral institutions was established at the Bretton Woods Conference in 1944 to address issues of global monetary stability and trade. The IMF was set up to replace the gold standard, ensure the convertibility of foreign currencies, and avoid competitive devaluation, and in this capacity was able to use its resources to grant short-term loans to countries facing balance-of-payments difficulties. The International Bank of Reconstruction and Development, or World Bank, was established to support the mobilization of private investment for reconstruction of the war-torn economies in Western Europe. Because this role proved to be beyond its resource capacity (and, in any case, gradually was superseded by the Marshall Plan), the World Bank began to focus more squarely on broader development issues. Since then, the bulk of its activities have centered on the so-called developing world. In 1960 the World Bank organized the International Development Association (IDA) to provide soft loans for poorer member states, defined in terms of per capita gross national product. GATT came into operation in January 1948 with the purpose of promoting liberalization of trade through the gradual removal of protective tariffs and nontariff barriers. Contracting parties were obliged to observe the principles of reciprocity, nondiscrimination, and transparency. In January 1995, GATT was superseded by the new WTO, which not only retained all the former disciplines on international trade operating under the former GATT, but also extended its authoritative scope to include areas that had become increasingly significant in the global economy, such as trade in services, intellectual property rights, and agriculture. By April 1996, 120 of the 128 former GATT members had joined the WTO.

When the international economic institutions were founded, capitalist countries dominated membership. Although the Soviet Union participated in the Bretton Woods Conference, it decided not to join the World Bank or the IMF. After the withdrawal of Poland in 1950 and Czechoslovakia in 1954, Yugoslavia became the only centrally planned economy to belong to the IMF and World Bank (that is, until 1972 when Romania became a member). Similarly, Yugoslavia and Czechoslovakia were the only communist states to be contracting parties in GATT in the first two decades after World War II. China under the Nationalist government was a founding member of GATT, but by early 1950 Taiwan had withdrawn. It later regained observer status in GATT; however, this was annulled when the People's Republic of China became a member of the UN in 1971.

Like other centrally planned economies, the People's Republic of China (PRC) lay outside the system of international economic institutions; moreover, it shared some of the concerns of developing countries, particularly with regard to GATT. Developing countries were hesitant to join GATT, preferring instead to belong to the United Nations Conference on Trade and Development (UNCTAD). This was set up in 1964 and advocated preferential treatment for developing countries, rather than adherence to the principles of nondiscrimination and reciprocity. In 1974 the Group of 77, a key developing country lobby within the UN, called for a New International Economic Order, which would give developing countries a greater role in the decision-making processes of international economic institutions as well as preferential treatment in trade. China, the Soviet Union, and the Eastern Europe block joined in these denunciations of the international economic bodies, echoing the call for a fundamental reworking of the global economic organization.

When the Chinese Communist Party came to power in 1949, the ideological division of the world into communist and capitalist camps complicated China's membership in these international economic fora. Fearful of the communist threat, the US imposed selective trade controls on China early in 1949. Following China's entry into the Korean War in October 1950, the US embarked upon an all-out embargo on trade with China and pressured US allies to follow suit. Although the PRC sought to take up seats in the UN, only Taiwan, calling itself the Republic of China, was recognized as a legitimate representative of China. Until its own expulsion in 1954,

Czechoslovakia proposed each year that the PRC (and not Taiwan) be granted membership in the IMF and World Bank. Moreover, the issue of Chinese representation in the UN continued to be raised each year until the PRC's final accession (and Taiwan's concomitant expulsion) in 1971.

The People's Republic of China could not join any of the Bretton Woods institutions; neither did it seek membership in the Council of Mutual Economic Assistance (CMEA), which brought together communist countries for the purpose of trade and investment. Mao was wary of seeking too close an alliance with the Soviet Union for ideological and historical reasons. The ill-fated advice of the Comintern to Chinese communist forces led to the tragic slaughter in 1927 of many labor unionists in Shanghai by Kuomintang troops. Stalin's lack of confidence in the revolutionary potential of Chinese communist forces and his partiality toward the Kuomintang had taught Mao to be cautious. Aware of the need for a strategy that took into account the particular economic and cultural conditions of a largely rural China, Mao was reluctant to adopt wholesale the policies of the Soviet Union. Nevertheless, owing to the particular circumstances of the Cold War, Mao leaned toward the Soviet Union. By 1955 the Soviet Union and Eastern Europe accounted for 67% of China's total external trade; the industrialized West, Japan, and Hong Kong accounted for the remainder. Although the easing of the trade embargo on the part of Western Europe led to a significant rise in imports from 1955 to 1958, an agreement for the purchase of 125 complete plants from the Soviet Union served to bring the Soviet and East European share of Chinese external trade back to 70% in 1958. Despite the fact that China did not belong to the CMEA, it nevertheless received economic assistance from the Soviet Union in the form of loans, technical assistance, investment, and barter trade. For example, between 1950 and 1957 the Soviet Union agreed to build 211 complete plants in China. Toward the end of that decade, however, relations between the two communist giants began to worsen, leading to their eventual collapse in the early 1960s. The Soviet Union withdrew its development experts and halted its loans, and China became even more politically isolated.

Meanwhile, Taiwan was gaining international recognition as the sole legitimate representative of China. During the Korean War, US troops used Taiwan as a base from which to stage their attacks on Korea. Thereafter, Taiwan enjoyed considerable financial and political support from the US. Eager to establish international credentials, Taiwanese authorities immediately sought membership in international bodies such as the UN, the IMF, and the World Bank. In this manner Taiwan bolstered its claim to sole, legitimate representative status of China and facilitated the extension of its diplomatic ties. In turn, Taiwan's actions impeded the PRC's ability to seek membership in these international bodies. Given the dominant role of the United States in the IMF and World Bank, particularly during the late 1940s and 1950s, negotiating any change in Taiwan's position would require significant improvements in Sino-US relations.

While the Sino-Soviet split had served to isolate China further, the catastrophic effects of the Great Leap Forward necessitated and facilitated a change in economic policy in the early 1960s. This included the expansion of trade links with Europe and Japan, primarily for the import of necessary food products and fertilizers for agricultural production. By 1967, 60% of total imports came from Japan and Western Europe, while communist countries accounted for only 20% of total trade with China. However, with the launch of the Cultural Revolution in 1966 Mao and the Gang of Four led China further down the path of isolationism, sharply limiting the scope of trade and economic links with so-called imperialist nations. International economic institutions such as the World Bank and IMF were portrayed as "instruments of capitalist exploitation" that would harm the fortunes of China. Thus, hostile Sino-US relations, Taiwanese membership in international economic institutions, the UN refusal to grant China membership, and domestic political factors combined to inhibit China from making any serious effort to join these institutions.

US president Richard Nixon's historic visit to China in 1972 marked the beginning of China's gradual entry into the wider global economy and its economic institutions. The threat of a Soviet attack on China in 1969 and the US desire to curb the powers of the Soviet Union combined to forge a closer alliance between China and the US. The ascendancy of Zhou Enlai in the early 1970s also facilitated China's new approach to its capitalist foes. Aided by Deng Xiaoping, Zhou began to fashion a new national security strategy and lay plans for a different style of economic development. The emergence of a domestic leadership more favorably disposed to links with capitalist rivals, together with improved Sino-US relations, helped China regain membership in the UN in 1971. The following year Japan and China resumed full diplomatic relations. In subsequent years, numerous informal exchanges between the US and China paved the way for the eventual restoration of diplomatic ties in 1979. The volume of trade between China and the non-communist world expanded as a result of improved Sino-US relations. Between 1970 and 1973 China's trade with non-communist countries (measured in constant dollars) increased by 80%. In 1972 China agreed to import plants and equipment for the production of chemical fertilizers and artificial fibers from the US, Europe, and Japan. The following year it signed an estimated US$1.3 billion worth of contracts for the purchase of complete plants. Moreover, the use of deferred payments indicated a softening of China's approach to external borrowing.

As Sino-US relations improved, so too did the prospects of China playing a role in the World Bank and IMF. Following the death of Mao in 1976 and the subsequent downfall of the Gang of Four, a political leadership more inclined to participation in the global economy and its institutions rose to the fore. At the 11th Session of the Third Plenum in December 1978, Deng Xiaoping launched a package of reforms that sought radical

changes not only in the domestic economy but also in China's relationship to the world economy and its global institutions.

2 The Reform Period: Joining the Club

Following the introduction of economic reforms at the Third Plenum in 1978, China's economy began to undergo radical restructuring. As early as 1982 the organization of agriculture had passed almost completely from communes to households. As a consequence of China's gradual promotion of the private sector in services and manufacturing, a new class of urban and rural entrepreneurs began to emerge, providing formidable competition to the foundering state industrial sector. Keen to acquire foreign technology and up-to-date scientific knowledge, the reformers introduced a range of reforms in the foreign trade sector in order to expand China's external economic ties. Moreover, for the first time since the late 1940s China opened its doors to investment from capitalist countries, establishing in 1979 four Special Economic Zones in Guangdong and Fujian provinces for the purpose of experimentation. In 1987 Chinese officials organized a fifth Special Economic Zone in Hainan Island.

Since reforms began, China's external trade increased tenfold. In 1994 China ranked eleventh among world traders, accounting for 2.9% of exports and 2.7% of imports. By 1996 China was host to more than 250,000 foreign-invested enterprises, most of which originated from Hong Kong. In 1996 alone foreign direct investment totaled US$40 billion, compared with US$1.8 billion between 1979 and 1983. China had become the largest recipient of foreign direct investment among developing countries. Whereas in the 1960s and 1970s the emphasis on self-reliance had fostered a highly cautious attitude toward borrowing overseas, in the reform period Chinese officials adopted a more relaxed approach. China's external debt rose from US$622.9 million in 1978 to an estimated US$106.6 billion by 1995. Compared to other developing countries, China's debt service ratio was low, estimated at only 7.3 in 1995. Moreover, its foreign exchange reserves amounted to an estimated US$100 billion in 1996, the second highest in the world.

The change in political leadership and the concomitant opening up of the economy provided the political and economic context for a more concerted effort to join the global institutional fold. Membership in organizations such as the UN, IMF, and World Bank not only would enhance China's role as an international player but also provide access to much needed funds for technological renovation and infrastructure development. China's membership in the IMF and World Bank also would strengthen its position vis-à-vis Taiwan and help to consolidate its bilateral relations.

From the point of view of the international economic institutions, China's entry would enhance their claim to be truly representative of the world as well as help to dispel the notion that such institutions existed only for the expansion of capitalism. Given that nearly all member states were capitalist-oriented (with the exception of Yugoslavia), China's entry offered the economic institutions the opportunity to overcome ideological divisions in the management of the global economy and to encourage the gradual liberalization of planned economies.

For developing countries China's entry posed both a threat and an opportunity. Large developing countries such as India viewed China as a serious rival in the competition for limited resources as well as a challenge to their position in the political hierarchy. In particular, developing countries harbored concerns that granting China Special Drawing Rights (SDR) in line with its large population, GNP, and share of world trade would come at the expense of major borrowers such as Brazil, Indonesia, Bangladesh, India, and Pakistan, unless the total capital stock was increased or new borrowing rules introduced. However, developing countries hoped that China's participation in global economic institutions would strengthen the developing country lobby, even though China was not formally a member of the Group of 77 (or G77, the developing country caucus in the UN) or the Group of 24 (a similar body in the IMF and World Bank). Developing countries believed that China's alertness to matters of national sovereignty as well as its concern about protectionism could be harnessed to promote their interests. China already had proved to be a strong ally of the developing country lobby when it supported in the UN and UNCTAD in 1974 the proposal for a New International Economic Order. Moreover, China's insistence that it be granted developing country status, which the US challenged increasingly in the 1990s, further aligned China with the developing world.

Western governments and Japan also desired China's participation in global economic and political institutions because of the size of its domestic economy and its potential importance in the global economy. Indeed, by 1996 China had become a major global trader and producer. For some commodities, such as toys, cigarettes, refrigerators, and television sets, it already dominated world markets. Furthermore, Western governments and Japan recognized China's growing reliance on grain imports and wished to regulate its effects on the global grain supply. For the US government and other Western allies, a China participating in global economic institutions was preferable to an isolated China. Potential conflicts, they believed, could be managed within an international institutional setting, and China could become more acquainted with and subject to international rules.

Before China could gain membership in the international club, a range of procedural, political, and economic hurdles had to be negotiated. China was able to join the IMF and World Bank within a relatively short period; however, gaining membership in GATT and the WTO proved to be more difficult.

2.1 Becoming a Member of the IMF and World Bank

China's entry into the IMF and the World Bank in 1980 did not occur suddenly or unexpectedly. China's leaders had been preparing for membership since the early 1970s. In 1971 the PRC took its seat in the UN while Taiwan lost its claim to representative status of China. The gradual expansion of economic and commercial ties with the US, Western Europe, and Japan provided China's leaders with the opportunity to become more familiar with the global economy.

In 1973 Minister of Foreign Affairs Ji Pengfei, backed by Mao Zedong, contacted the IMF and World Bank prior to their annual meeting of governors to request the expulsion of Taiwan, implicitly seeking a seat for the PRC in these organizations. Although World Bank president Robert McNamara responded positively to an application from China to join the World Bank, the strength of the Taiwan lobby in the US Congress prevented further progress on this front. Meanwhile, Chinese officials still fretted over joining these multilateral organizations. The danger of losing control over foreign exchange and the limitations that the small size of its vote in both institutions would place on furthering foreign policy objectives were of particular concern to China's leaders. Yet when the IMF made plans in 1976 to sell back to member states some of the gold they had deposited, China quickly asserted that the gold should not find its way into Taiwanese hands. Membership in the IMF appeared on the State Council agenda in 1976; owing to political uncertainties at that time, however, no decision was reached.

The rise of a new leadership at the end of 1978 and the introduction of a market-oriented package of economic reforms set the political and economic stage for China's membership in the IMF and World Bank. In January 1979 the State Council dispatched an inter-agency delegation to Romania and Yugoslavia (which, like China, had centrally planned economies) for the purpose of learning more about the IMF and World Bank. Ministers were particularly keen to find out what kind of information they would have to provide these institutions and what kind of

loans could be accessed. Upon its return, the inter-agency delegation strongly recommended to the State Council that China seek to join these organizations. Also at that time moves were afoot in the US to court Chinese membership. An unofficial delegation of World Bank officials traveled to China in early 1979 to learn more about the country. In October of that year a Chinese official working in the UN attended the annual meetings of IMF and World Bank governors, using this opportunity to discuss Chinese membership. Unofficial contacts between China and representatives of the two institutions continued into the next year.

Having secured China's Most-Favored Nation (MFN) status with the US in 1980, the Chinese government quickened the pace of its membership drive. In the spring of 1980 both the IMF and World Bank sent missions to China. The Chinese wished to ascertain the size of their quota, their rights and obligations as Fund members, the status of Taiwan's membership, and the fate of the gold deposited by China. These matters were negotiated successfully, and two weeks after the return of the delegation the Executive Board of the IMF agreed to China's membership.

As IMF membership is a prerequisite to World Bank membership, China already had taken a major step toward joining the latter organization. In May 1980 China was granted membership in the World Bank, while Taiwan relinquished its seat. China became eligible for International Development Association funding, albeit not until the Seventh Replenishment between 1985 and 1987. Keen to influence policy, gain better access to limited resources, and secure a higher political rank than India, Chinese officials negotiated an increase in shares from 7,750 to 12,250, putting China in eighth place with 2.84% of the total; thus, China became the first nonmarket economy with representation on the board. By 1995 China accounted for 45,049 votes, or just over 3% of the total, making it a significant single-constituency member (see Table 13.1).

Similarly, China attempted to secure a prominent position in the IMF. In 1944 China had enjoyed the third largest quota in the IMF. However, because the Taiwanese government did not request an increase to China's subscription, by 1960 its quota was so low that China lost the right to elect an executive director. Upon its return to the IMF in 1980, China's quota was set at SDR 550 million, making it the seventeenth largest quota. By 1983, following the Eighth General Review, the IMF Board of Governors had increased China's quota to SDR 2.39 billion, allotting China 18,250 votes (2.82% of the total) and enabling it to elect its own executive director. In 1996 China's quota reached SDR 3.38 billion, yielding 34,102 votes (2.28% of the total) and placing China in eighth position among single-country constituencies (see Table 13.2).

Aware that inclusion of China's large economy could upset the balance of representation, both the IMF and World Bank expanded the size of their Executive Boards to accommodate China. The World Bank increased the number of its seats from 20 to 21 and the IMF from 21 to 22. This measure allayed fears that Chinese membership would come at the expense of smaller French African states, larger rivals such as India, and developing countries in general.

Next, the World Bank set up a specialist China Division headed by Caio Koch-Weser, assistant to Robert McNamara. By the mid-1980s the number of World Bank staff working on China was the third largest next to India and Brazil. A decade later the Beijing office had become the second largest World Bank office after Washington. On the Chinese side, the People's Bank of China became the key institutional partner of the IMF, and the Ministry of Finance the key institutional partner of the World Bank.

2.2 Seeking Membership in GATT

China's attempts to join GATT (and its later incarnation, the WTO) have proved more tortuous than its applications to the UN, IMF, and World Bank. China's membership in GATT would have far-reaching consequences both for China and the other contracting parties. Although China's participation in GATT would offer new opportunities for trade, it also would require China to open up its markets, divulge information hitherto classified as secret, and subject its trade regime to international scrutiny. Given the size of China's economy, its growing global economic importance, and its transitional economic character, the consequences of China not adhering to internationally agreed-upon norms and principles might have a significant impact on the realization of a global, liberalized trade regime.

China sought to join GATT for a variety of reasons. First, membership would enhance its international standing. Given China's increasingly prominent position in the global economy, it seemed only appropriate that it participate in an institution governing the rules of trade. Joining GATT also seemed a logical step to securing its place in all international economic institutions. In addition, joining GATT would reaffirm China's commitment to opening up, thus consolidating the reform process within China while demonstrating China's stability and willingness to abide by international rules to potential foreign investors.

Furthermore, China saw that multilateral agreements offered a better shield against the protectionist policies of developed countries than bilateral arrangements. The vast majority of China's trade activities involved GATT members; thus, GATT membership offered minimal tariff restraints while reducing the need for bilateral agreements. Moreover, as a member, China no longer would need to renew every year its MFN status with the US, since GATT granted unconditional MFN status to all contracting parties. Similarly, GATT membership would allow China the opportunity to acquire preferential tariff treatment under the US General System of Preferences, which granted GATT members zero tariffs for exports to the US (however, this still would be a matter of discretion for the US president, who in turn would be under pressure from businesspersons, labor groups, and human rights activists). Accession to GATT also would enable China to take part in discussions about protectionism and thus influence international economic policy.

China's accession to GATT has involved considerable bargaining over the terms under which it could join. Key axes of tension have included procedural issues, human rights, developing country status, the requisite changes to China's trade regime and economy, the degree of openness of its market, Sino-US trade relations, and the status of Taiwan. Chinese officials have argued repeatedly that the government has taken sufficient steps, particularly since the mid-1980s, toward decentralizing the trade regime, reducing tariffs and licensing requirements, liberalizing China's foreign exchange, and making its trade regime more transparent. At times, Chinese authorities have viewed requests for information (such as requests to publish China's trade plans) as interference in national affairs.

Additionally, the US, Europe, Canada, and Japan have raised a number of issues that need to be addressed before China can qualify for full privileges in GATT and the WTO. These include the lack of transparency in custom and import regulations, regional protectionism, the inconsistency in application of tariff schedules across time and place, and incomplete economic data. China's pricing system, which is not wholly determined by market forces, also ranks as a major concern to the Western powers and Japan. In particular, the US government has argued that safeguard mechanisms should be installed to protect local industry against competitive Chinese imports that are backed by hidden export subsidies.

Although GATT officials made preliminary contacts with China in 1971, the Chinese government was not adequately prepared to take action, preferring instead to observe proceedings from its UN office in Geneva. Prompted by a more favorable political climate in early 1979, Chinese officials in the permanent mission in Geneva requested to be kept informed about the Tokyo Round proceedings. As a result, a Ministry of Foreign Economic Relations and Trade official was invited to attend commercial policy courses run by GATT the following year. In April 1980 China resumed its seat on the UN's Interim Commission for the International Trade Organization, which appointed GATT's secretariat. Through this forum China indicated its desire to join GATT. In July 1981 China was granted observer status at a GATT meeting on the Multi-Fibre Arrangement (MFA), and in December 1983 it became a party to the MFA, an arrangement providing access to limited textile export quotas to the industrialized West. Also in 1983, China and the US signed an agreement on textiles.

In preparation for membership, the newly created Ministry of Foreign Economic Relations and Trade established in 1982 a special division in charge of GATT relations. Although China was granted observer status at GATT in November 1982, it still failed to join. However, aware that GATT was likely to embark upon another round of multilateral trade negotiations, China applied successfully for permanent observer status on GATT's council and other bodies in December 1984. The following year China discussed with GATT officials the implications of full participation in the multilateral forum.

Given China's centrally planned economy, GATT contracting parties were keen to ensure that China take particular steps to liberalize its trade regime and economy before granting it membership. The reduction and removal of import tariffs was far more complicated in a planned economy where imports were determined largely according to a plan, where the price mechanism administered rather than determined the rate of foreign exchange, where state trading corporations mediated the purchase of imported commodities, and where licensing abounded. Moreover, some contracting parties sought protection against the exports of nonmarket economies because the determination of the costs of production and the export price were not clear. Following a July 1986 meeting between Zhao Ziyang and Arthur Dunkel, GATT's Director General, China announced its intention to pursue membership in GATT. Because it had provided formal notification to the Council of Representatives of its desire to accede to GATT, China, unlike the Soviet Union, was permitted to participate in the Uruguay Round of multilateral trade negotiations. However, its full participation in GATT still was not granted.

In the spirit of greater openness, China submitted a memorandum to GATT in February 1987 outlining its foreign trade regime. In response, GATT officials set up a working party to consider China's entry. An initial problem centered on the question of whether China would "resume" its position in GATT or "enter" as a new contracting party. Although China wished to resume its position, this implied that China could become liable for previous contributions. Also, Australia, Japan, and the US feared that resumption would raise legal concerns about actions taken during the period of China's absence. Moreover, if China resumed its former position rather than acceded as a new member, the US could not invoke Article 35 to deny China MFN status (Article 35 gives contracting parties the option of not applying GATT tariff schedules to new members). The working party resolved to leave this issue open for further negotiation.

Since then China and GATT have been engaged in a series of negotiations over the concessions required from China, the terms of its entry, and the timing of its accession. While the traumatic events of Tiananmen in 1989 did not fundamentally disrupt relations between China and the international economic institutions, negotiations on GATT entry were delayed as human rights became a prominent issue in US Congress debates on relations with China.

The situation was complicated further by Taiwan's application in 1990 for observer status in the WTO. Timed soon after the Tiananmen debacle, this move enabled Taiwan to capitalize on international antipathy toward the PRC. Because the WTO permits any territory with autonomy in customs to enjoy separate representation, the issue of "two Chinas" was averted more easily than

was the case during negotiations for entry into the UN, IMF, and World Bank. To avert the mainland's objections, Taiwan agreed to enter as "Chinese Taipei." Although China had not opposed Taiwan's participation as a customs territory, it nevertheless argued that the PRC should be admitted first, and thus lobbied European countries to delay Taiwan's accession. As the world's 13th largest trading nation (accounting for 2% of total annual global trade), Taiwan maintained that its participation in the WTO was essential for developing a comprehensive global trading system. In September 1992 a special working party was set up to oversee Taiwan's entry. Meanwhile, Taiwan pressed ahead with bilateral negotiations. By the end of 1996 it had conducted bilateral talks with 12 of 26 contracting parties that had agreed to discuss Taiwan's accession terms, as well as seven formal working party meetings.

In October 1991 a formal working party again convened to discuss China's entry. For this occasion China submitted a report outlining its economic reforms and the development of its foreign trade since 1989. At the following meeting in February 1992, the working party requested further information on China's economic system and trade regime. Negotiations were overshadowed by a US investigation into China's market access policies. Following the resolution of this investigation, the US agreed to support actively China's entry into GATT, provided China made specified concessions and contingent upon the drafting of an acceptable protocol. Although China declared its intentions to accelerate the reforms at a working party meeting in late 1992, the US delegation expressed deep concern at China's apparent failure to implement a more uniform and transparent trade policy. In 1994 China submitted another report outlining reforms of its tax and exchange rate systems, and again the working party sought further clarification on China's tariff and nontariff measures, its price reforms and enterprise autonomy. Encouraging all sides to persist with negotiations, GATT's Director General Sutherland underlined the significance of China's participation: "I don't think any GATT member doubts the importance of China becoming a full and active participant in the multilateral trading system–the GATT as it is now, and in the future, the WTO."

By July 1994 the working party had established for the first time a set of major parameters that would provide the basis for a draft protocol. Thereafter, the pace of negotiations accelerated; by December substantive agreement had been reached on the administration of China's trade regime, special trading arrangements, price controls, taxes on imports and exports, and agricultural policies. However, strained Sino-US relations continued to impede negotiations. Chinese officials expressed dismay at the ruling that China, a founding member of GATT, could not also be a founding member of the WTO. Moreover, Chinese officials considered some of the demands for reductions in tariffs excessive, especially given China's level of economic development. Gu Yongjiang, head of the delegation to the 19th meeting of the working party on China, stated as much in December 1996: "The current reductions and concessions offered by China constitute the maximum efforts it can exert in accordance with the economic development level of a developing country." During the following year, formal and informal meetings at multilateral and bilateral levels continued apace. In July 1995 work on the draft protocol focused on key areas such as trading rights and nontrading measures and standards, although major differences persisted on issues such as safeguards.

In 1996 China continued to press for accession to the WTO, maintaining that it already had made sufficient concessions for entry. On the eve of the WTO ministerial-level meeting in Singapore in December 1996, Foreign Ministry spokesperson Shen Guofang stated that, "As far as the Chinese government is concerned, we are fully qualified to enter the WTO. At present, the biggest obstructions continue to stem from political considerations, while China has also been asked to meet excessive demands." Immediately following this conference, Minister of Foreign Trade and Economic Cooperation Wu Yi expressed his annoyance at demands to open up China's markets, stating that such demands were "unrealistic." While arguing their case, Chinese officials have emphasized the differences in economic development between contracting parties, hence the need for differential treatment. Disagreement among industrialized countries over the degree of market access in China also prolonged negotiations. The US in particular harbored doubts about China's commitment to open markets and insisted on further concessions. Moreover, continued references to China's poor human rights record served to mobilize support for a cautious approach to China's entry. Thus, by 1997 China's position in the WTO still was not resolved and negotiations appeared likely to continue into the near future.

3 Implications of Membership

What, then, has membership in the international economic institutions meant for China? First, China has had to make institutional adjustments. When China joined the UN in October 1971, the Ministry of Foreign Affairs had to recall various qualified staff from the countryside to prepare policy strategies and also to take up positions in different UN agencies. China has organized new divisions within ministries to work jointly with the IMF, World Bank, and GATT, as well as an inter-agency working group on GATT. Moreover, both the IMF and World Bank have fostered the development of institutions such as the Chinese Investment Bank, which introduced new ways of lending to enterprises, and the Shanghai Institute of International Economic Management, which launched numerous training programs. Also, the demands for information from the international economic institutions served to strengthen horizontal links and coordination between ministries such as the State Planning Commission and the Ministry of Finance.

Second, IMF and World Bank membership has granted China access to funding and development assistance. In 1981 the World Bank agreed to five development projects, including a loan of US$200 million to improve university facilities; a loan for harbor development in Shanghai, Tianjin, and Guangzhou; two agricultural loans for soil drainage in northern China and agricultural education and research; and a loan to the China Investment Bank to improve its lending of foreign exchange to small and medium enterprises. Moreover, each year the amount of new lending to China has increased. In 1983 the World Bank lent China US$600 million. By 1988 World Bank loans to China totaled US$1.7 billion. In addition, the World Bank decided to lend China more than US$2 billion annually for the following three years, becoming China's second most important source of external financing after Japan.

By 1994 the World Bank had approved a total of 82 loans to China worth US$11.76 billion, making China its fifth largest borrower and accounting for 4.7% of bank lending operations. The International Development Association (IDA) also granted China 59 credits amounting to approximately US$7.8 billion, representing 9.2% of total IDA lending. By 1995 China had become the second largest borrower of World Bank funds after Mexico, borrowing US$2.37 billion, and the second largest borrower of IDA funds after India, obtaining US$630 million. China directed these resources toward a range of projects, such as iodine deficiency disorder control, rail transportation, power transmission in Sichuan, highway development in Xinjiang, social security and enterprise housing reform, taxation reform, and economic law reform. In July 1995 the World Bank announced further loans to China totaling US$3 billion annually for a period of three years. The loans were designated for infrastructure, poverty reduction, environmental protection, and education. By mid-1995 the World Bank had committed more than US$22 billion to 157 projects in nearly all sectors of China's economy.

The IMF lent China a total of SDR 759 million in 1981 to assist with an economic stabilization program, a loan that China repaid by 1984. Subsequently, interaction between China and the IMF increased. Facing a balance of payments deficit in 1985 and 1986, Chinese officials negotiated a standby arrangement worth SDR 597.7 million over twelve months. Moreover, as inflation increased during 1988, the IMF, aware that spiraling prices could undermine the reform process, intensified its dialogue with Chinese policymakers. The tragic events of 1989 caused multilateral institutions and bilateral donors to place a temporary hold on new lending to China. However, as economic sanctions gradually were removed and foreign investment picked up in the early 1990s, the IMF continued to provide important policy advice on macroeconomic issues.

Third, greater international exposure required that China be more forthcoming with information, especially statistics. In order to participate actively in discussions on trade issues, China had to become more informed about international affairs and how international economic institutions operate. To this end, the government has supported the academic study of international trade and finance, has financed research on the IMF and GATT, and has provided opportunities for postgraduate students to study such topics overseas. Thus, China has created a cadre of intellectuals and bureaucrats familiar with the economic issues at stake, competent to engage in detailed debates, and able to advise top government leaders. Moreover, by agreeing to the IMF's Article of Agreement, China was obliged to provide statistical information on trade and its currency reserves for publication in the IMF's "International Financial Statistics." Given China's penchant for secrecy on such matters as foreign exchange reserves, overseas debts, and currency administration, this opening up to outside bodies as well as to other ministries and academic institutions reflected a serious attempt on China's part to adjust to international rules. China also benefited from new training opportunities. For example, the training that People's Bank of China officials received from the IMF enabled China to publish its first balance of payments statistics in 1985. Participation in the international institutions prepared China for its dealings with other international organizations such as the European Union.

Finally, integration into the institutional framework of the global economy also has subjected the Chinese government to greater external influence. Both the IMF and the World Bank have advised and offered support to Chinese policymakers on macroeconomic issues such as price reform, exchange rates, inflation, taxation, and promotion of the private sector, as well as sectoral matters such as social security reforms, housing, and agriculture. The 1983 World Bank Report "China: Socialist Economic Development," the 1985 Report "Long Term Development Issues and Options," as well as various sectoral reports such as the 1988 "China: External Trade and Capital" have been crucial not only in providing information to Western economists and policymakers about the Chinese economy, but also in providing policy options to Chinese policymakers. In the words of a Ministry of Finance official, "They [The World Bank and IMF] have not only helped fill capital shortfalls but also introduced into China technical know-how and management expertise that China badly needs." IMF and World Bank endorsement of China's reform process has enhanced international confidence in the Chinese government's commitment to a transition toward the market; it also has drawn China more deeply into international economic affairs. As China becomes more thoroughly intertwined with the world economy, it is likely to become more vulnerable to the vagaries of global market forces and more subject to the disciplines of international agreements.

China's membership in international economic organizations also has benefits for other member states. No longer can the international economic organizations be accused of acting as instruments of Western imperialism. Moreover, China's accession facilitated the entry of other nonmarket economies such as Hungary and Poland, and its attempts to enter GATT have encouraged other developing countries and former socialist states to follow suit. Although China proved not to be as vociferous a spokesperson for developing country interests as might have been expected (prioritizing instead its own economic goals over political matters), it nevertheless did object strongly to a US$1.1 billion IMF loan to South Africa in 1982 on the grounds of South Africa's apartheid regime. When the IMF refused to extend part of a loan to Zambia because its government would not agree to devalue, China protested by arguing that similar conditions had not been required of South Africa. While the PRC has pressed for debt rescheduling for developing countries at IMF meetings, it also has been critical of requests by Latin American countries for a moratorium on debt repayments. In chorus with other developing countries, Chinese officials have voiced their concerns about structural adjustment, yet at the same time have endorsed the IMF's call for market discipline in developing countries. China has served as mediator between the North and the South (i.e., between developed and developing regions of the world), while keeping its own economic objectives at the fore. However, China has not attempted to change the rules, norms, or principles of the global economic institutions in support of a New International Economic Order.

4 Future Prospects for International Economic Institutions in China

As the 21st century approaches, China continues to strengthen its position in the global economy. Although the death of Deng Xiaoping may intensify the struggle for power, it seems unlikely that any major reform policies will be reversed. The lines of fissure will revolve around the pace of economic reform rather than the need for reform itself. Hence, the Chinese government may be expected to consolidate its position within the World Bank and IMF. It is unlikely that it will increase its borrowing from the IMF to the extent that it would have to submit to conditionalities. For those Chinese leaders and academics anxious about China's role in the global economy and international economic institutions, the imposition of any conditions would be seen as indicative of growing dependency and an encroachment upon national sovereignty. Thus, Chinese authorities probably will continue to pursue a cautious approach to their foreign borrowing and reliance on multilateral funding.

Entry into the WTO will continue to be a top policy priority for the Chinese government. Complaints about its human rights record, pressures from exporting countries to liberalize its trade regime (particularly with regard to nontariff discriminatory practices), as well as demands on the Chinese side for the US and Europe to halt their protectionist policies will dominate negotiations. Given current US, European, and Japanese policy to integrate rather than contain China, coupled with China's own determination to join the WTO, China's full participation probably will be realized within the first decade of the next century. However, to the degree that China is persuaded to reduce barriers to imports, the pace of its own industrial development needs to be carefully monitored; many state and rural enterprises serving local markets will become increasingly vulnerable to new international competition.

Although China has maintained a low profile on North-South issues, it will continue to play the role of spokesperson for developing countries whenever its self-proclaimed aim of developing country status is challenged and Sino-US relations become fraught. Meanwhile, large developing countries such as India and Brazil will be keeping a close eye on China's use of the World Bank's and IMF funds as competition for increasingly limited resources intensifies.

How much China, or indeed any other developing country, can depend on loans from the IMF and World Bank also will be contingent on the willingness of the industrialized nations to meet their obligations. Accusations of corruption, inefficiencies, and waste in the UN system as well as concern over a growing budget deficit have served to justify the US government's reluctance to pay its dues. Since the collapse of the Soviet Union, the requests of numerous new nations for IMF and World Bank funding have put further pressure on limited resources. By 1996 Russia had become the largest user of IMF resources. Thus, whether or not China could draw more extensively on the IMF and World Bank for funds would be contingent upon the actions of the most industrialized members.

China's involvement in the international economic institutions will continue to pave the way for other transitional economies to seek entry. As China will have provided a test case for accepting a nonmarket economy into the global institutional fold, the process will be more familiar to the receiving institutions and thus procedural arrangements will be easier to manage. To the extent that formerly centrally planned economies participate in these institutions, the institutions themselves increasingly will take on a truly global character. Whether this will lead to new forms of global governance and contribute to world peace, stability, and a liberalized trade regime remains to be seen. What is certain is that China will play a key role in this process.

Further Reading

Boardman, Robert, *Post-Socialist World Orders: Russia, China, and the UN System,* London: Macmillan, and New York: St. Martin's Press, 1994

Provides a useful comparison between Russia's and China's changing relations with the UN system in the 1980s and early 1990s, assessing the effects of these on each of the countries and on the UN system.

Fairbank, John King, *China: A New History,* Cambridge, Massachusetts: Belknap Press of Harvard University Press, 1992

An excellent, comprehensive introduction to the history of China, covering the period from China's initial unification up to the era of Deng Xiaoping's reforms.

Howell, Jude, *China Opens Its Doors: The Politics of Economic Transition,* Hemel Hempstead: Harvester Wheatsheaf, and Boulder, Colorado: Lynne Rienner, 1993

This book deals specifically with the political dynamics of China's policy to open up to the global economy, with a special focus on the case of Xiamen Special Economic Zone.

Jacobson, Harold Karan, and Michel Oksenberg, *China's Participation in the IMF, the World Bank, and GATT,* Ann Arbor: University of Michigan Press, 1990

Perhaps the most in-depth coverage available of China's role in the international financial institutions, taking the reader up to 1990.

Kim, Samuel S., editor, *China and the World: Chinese Foreign Policy in the Post-Mao Era,* Boulder, Colorado: Westview Press, 1984

A useful collection of papers addressing changes in Chinese foreign policy after the death of Mao Zedong in 1976.

Riskin, Carl, *China's Political Economy: The Quest for Development Since 1949,* Oxford and New York: Oxford University Press, 1987

Although now somewhat dated, this is nevertheless an excellent introduction to China's political economy, tracing carefully the changes in development strategy under Mao and extending into the mid-1980s.

World Trade Organization, *International Trade: Trends and Statistics,* Geneva: World Trade Organization, 1995

Another very useful source of statistical information on China's external economic relations, allowing easy comparison with those of other countries.

Jude Howell is Senior Lecturer in the School of Development Studies, University of East Anglia, Norwich. In addition to numerous articles in journals, she is the author of *China Opens Its Doors: The Politics of Economic Transition* (1993) and *In Search of Civil Society: Market Reform and Social Change in Contemporary China* (with Gordon White and X.Y. Shang, 1996).

Table 13.1: Voting Power in World Bank as of 6/30/95

Country	World Bank		IDA	
	Total votes	*% of total*	*Total votes*	*% of total*
US	255,840	17.18	1,563,036	15.41
Japan	94,020	6.31	1,071,214	10.56
Germany	72,649	4.88	702,871	6.93
France	69,647	4.68	420,934	4.15
UK	69,647	4.68	518,046	5.11
Saudi Arabia	45,049	3.02	353,707	3.49
Russia	45,049	3.02	28,202	0.28
China	45,049	3.02	205,683	2.03
India, Bhutan, Sri Lanka, Bangladesh	54,945	3.69	435,434	4.29

Source: World Bank Annual Report, 1995

Table 13.2: Voting Power in IMF as of 4/30/96

Country	Votes	% of total
US	265,518	17.78
Japan	82,665	5.54
Germany	82,665	5.54
France	74,396	4.98
UK	74,396	4.98
Saudi Arabia	51,556	3.45
Russia	43,381	2.90
China	34,102	2.28
India, Bhutan, Sri Lanka, Bangladesh	38,561	2.58

Source: IMF Annual Report, 1996

Chapter Fourteen

China's Environment and Natural Resources

Vaclav Smil

All large economies consume prodigious amounts of environmental goods and depend upon the continuous provision of many environmental services, including processes that decompose organic wastes or maintain atmospheric composition. These dependencies come into especially sharp focus in China, the world's most populous nation now embarked on history's most ambitious plan for rapid socio-economic modernization.

Except for China's forests, which have been reduced to a fraction of their original extent by millennia of cutting for fuel and timber and by conversion to farmland, China's natural resource endowment is impressive in absolute terms; but divided among 1.2 billion people, these huge totals result in per capita rates in most cases below the global mean for particular resource availabilities. Of course, a richer China could supplement its domestic production by rising imports, a trend already in evidence with regard to such disparate commodities as iron ore and timber. However, this option does not address the maintenance of important ecosystemic services, natural processes that are being endangered by a combination of rapid economic growth and inadequate attention to environmental management. Furthermore, as the country moves toward incipient affluence, the quality of its water, air, and soil, and the integrity of its ecosystems, will be under even

greater pressure. Indeed, the state of China's environment almost certainly will be a major factor in determining the fate of the country's modernization efforts.

1 Natural Resources

The need to feed one-fifth of the human population from no more than one-eleventh of the world's farmland makes the availability of farmland and irrigation water the two most important natural resource concerns in China. The quest to increase the country's low forest coverage is also important: increases in forested areas would improve China's water balance, moderate its climate, and act as the only practicable long-term antidote to excessive erosion of now barren soils. While many rapidly modernizing countries have relied largely on imported energies, the magnitude of China's demand makes such a strategy impractical; thus the country must fully exploit its rich coal and water power resources.

1.1 Water Resources

China's northern provinces, comprising roughly one-third of the nation's territory with some two-fifths of total population and identical shares of agricultural and industrial output, receive just one-quarter of all precipitation. High precipitation variability and relatively long periods of aridity are common throughout the north. Moreover, the total area of farmland where crop production is reduced by at least 30% in comparison with years of normal precipitation has shown an upward trend since the mid-1980s. While neither the extent nor the intensity of recent droughts has been unprecedented when viewed in long-term perspective, rising demand for water has transformed northern water shortages from seasonal to chronic.

Furthermore, northern provinces receive less than one-tenth of total stream runoff owing to high summer evapotranspiration. In the basin of the Huang Ho (Yellow River), the region's principal stream, less than $20m^3$ of water runoff is available for each hectare of cultivated land and no more than about $600m^3$/person; comparable rates in the Yangtze basin are about eight and five times higher, respectively. By the early 1990s the Yellow River's flow into the Bohai fell to less than half of its long-term average, and since the mid-1980s the river has ceased to flow downstream from Jinan for periods of up to three months.

Consequently, north China depends on its underground water reserves, which amount to less than half of the total volume of water in southern aquifers. Excessive exploitation of underground water has led to widespread sinking of water tables and extensive surface subsidence. More than 200 of China's large cities, including the capital, have been experiencing chronic water shortages, and their total water deficit is expected to rise from roughly 10 Mt (million tonnes) a day in 1985 to as much as 100 Mt by the year 2000.

Although rapidly growing cities and industries demand a great deal of water, irrigation inflicts the greatest burden on China's water resources. In absolute terms, China has more irrigated land than any other country; in relative terms its irrigated farmland (roughly 50% of total farmland) puts it behind only Egypt (where all farmland is watered), Pakistan, and Japan (each with about 75% irrigated farmland) among nations with more than 50 million people.

Unfortunately, current Chinese practices do not reflect scarcity of irrigation water: cost of water, and hence irrigation efficiencies, remains low. The problem is most acute on the North China Plain, a region dependent upon tubewell irrigation introduced during the 1960s (the region now has more than 2 million tubewells irrigating more than 11 million hectares [Mha] of farmland). While tubewell pumping has helped to lower formerly high water tables, thus limiting soil salinization, it has led to considerable local overexploitation of aquifers during periods of prolonged drought. In order to ease these water shortages, work already has begun on a massive geoengineering project that will divert part of the Yangtze flow to the Yellow River basin. A full-scale operation of this magnitude, however, would require a great deal of energy for water pumping.

The average area disastrously affected by floods more than doubled during the 1980s, and the trend continued during the early 1990s. The chronic threat of flooding is best illustrated by the fact that about one-tenth of China's territory, housing almost two-thirds of all population and producing nearly three-quarters of all agricultural and industrial output, is below the maximum flood level of major rivers. Recent floods have caused major loss of life and extensive economic damage in the basin of the Yangtze, but potentially the most dangerous situation is found along the lower course of the Huang Ho in Henan and Shandong, where the river is confined by 1,400 kilometers of dikes that are 3 to 15 meters above the surrounding countryside. Because increased erosion now puts at least 25% more silt into the stream compared to the early 1950s (depositing annually about 400 Mt in the riverbed), the stream has risen by more than one meter per decade. Breach of the Huang Ho dikes could flood large parts of the North China Plain, affect tens of millions of people, and cut all north-south transportation.

1.2 Farmland

Chinese official figures imply substantial decline in average per capita availability of farmland, from about 0.18 hectares (ha) in 1949 to just below 0.08 hectares in 1995. If these figures are accurate, China's land availability would rate in the same class as Bangladesh, and the only other populous nations with less arable land would be Egypt, Japan, and Korea (by contrast, the European average is nearly 0.3 ha and the North American mean is almost 0.7 ha). Fortunately, official figures underestimate the actual extent of China's cropland.

China's total cropland has been estimated as high as 150 Mha (million hectares) on the basis of LANDSAT images. Detailed countrywide sample surveys compiled during the late 1980s, however, offer perhaps the most accurate indication of the extent of China's arable farmland. These studies estimated China's available farmland between 133-140 Mha (provincial differences are considerable; the poorest areas reported less than one-third of actually farmed land).

Whatever the country's actual farmland total may be, there can be no doubt that China has suffered and is continuing to suffer substantial losses of cropland. These losses stem from a combination of population growth and economic modernization (industrial, urban, and residential expansion, extension of transportation links, construction of irrigation and power generation reservoirs) and degradative processes (heavy soil erosion, desertification, salinization, alkalization) frequently initiated or accelerated by improper land management. Most studies published in China since 1978 agree that the nation suffered a staggering gross loss of almost 30 Mha of farmland between 1957 and 1977. Since 1978 farmland losses have continued to be the result of economic modernization, although it should be noted that during the initial years of reforms a substantial portion of losses resulted from the restoration of wetlands, grasslands, and slopelands that formerly had been converted into farmland during the years of mass campaigns under Mao.

Official totals published by the Land Management Bureau put the average annual farmland loss at 492,000 ha between 1980 and 1985 (losses totaled one Mha in 1985, reflecting the frenzied pace of rural house construction). Subsequently, annual losses declined, and by 1989 the Land Management Bureau believed the situation was again under control as cultivated area actually increased in six provinces. Soon after, however, an increased pace of economic expansion (which included the proliferation of rural enterprises and the establishment of special industrial and processing zones) led to renewed farmland losses. The annual mean for the first half of the 1990s was nearly 550,000 ha.

Because factors such as population growth, industrialization, and extension of transportation links show no signs of abating, long-term changes in China's rate of farmland decline seem unlikely. Moreover, losses inevitably will include some of the best yielding land. For example, during the early 1990s thousands of newly established manufacturing zones have taken more than 80% of their land from intensively cultivated fields near towns and cities.

Human dimensions of China's declining farmland area are best illustrated by translating losses into annual food production equivalents, or by comparing them with foreign farmland totals. The cumulative loss of approximately 40 Mha since the late 1950s is the equivalent of losing food production capacity sufficient to feed at least 350 million people. The mean annual loss of more than 400,000 ha during the 1980s was the equivalent of losing food production capacity sufficient to feed about 5 million people every year. In perspective, China's loss of 40 million hectares of farmland is the equivalent of all the fields in Argentina. Furthermore, even if annual losses could be held to 200,000–250,000 hectares, within a decade the cumulative loss would amount to all the arable land in Egypt. Regardless of the prevailing rate of future losses, by the year 2000 Bangladesh and Egypt will be the only two populous developing nations with less arable land per capita than China.

1.3 Forests

When China's State Statistical Bureau

resumed its regular publication of annual yearbooks in 1979, it put the country's forested area at 122 Mha, or 12.7% of all territory. This total, based on a nationwide inventory completed during the mid-1970s, referred to fully stocked productive forests (that is, areas where tree canopies cover at least 30% of the ground). A decade later the Ministry of Forestry observed that although afforestation efforts during the 1980s had increased the total forested area, wood consumption continued to surpass the growth rate. Thus it decided to remedy this imbalance by limiting timber harvests during the next five years to a maximum of 243.6 million m^3/year. During this time wood shortages forced China to prohibit many uses of wood and to become a major timber importer. Prohibitions restricted the use of wood for floors, stairs, windowsills, railway sleepers, and coffins. From the mid-1980s to the mid-1990s, China spent on average more than US$1 billion annually on timber and pulp imports in order to supplement its domestic production of timber.

Surprisingly, by 1992 the Chinese media claimed that afforestation had achieved a surplus of timber, and in December 1993 the government announced that the total annual growth had surpassed 400 million m^3 while consumption had declined further to 320 million m^3. These figures, if accurate, would indicate a fundamental reversal of deforestation trends in a single decade. Indeed, according to these figures, China's 1993 wood harvest/growth ratio would have stood at 0.8, just marginally worse than the ratios of such prodigious and heavily forested producers of wood as the US or Finland (in 1990 the wood harvest/growth ratios for the US and Finland were 0.75 and 0.73, respectively). This comparison alone should alert scholars to the fact that the Chinese figures are not wholly reliable. However, even assuming that most or even all of the 45% gain was real, the practical import of these gains must be viewed in the context of the changing composition of China's forest biomass. Because of the rising share of new plantings in the total coverage, young or middle-aged stands accounted for

82% of China's timberland in 1990. Timber reserves available for commercial harvesting declined by 2.308 billion m^3 during the 1980s (mature stands contracted by 170 million m^3 annually). The growing stock ready for harvesting in mature forests amounted to less than 1.5 billion m^3, a total which could be harvested in just seven to eight years. Reserves approaching maturity will decline from about 2.6 billion m^3 in the late 1980s to just 1.25 billion m^3 by the year 2000.

1.4 Energy Resources

China ranks among the top three countries in bituminous coal deposits. Recent figures put the total proven reserves of anthracite and bituminous coal at about 62 billion tonnes. Overall resources are greater still.

China also has the world's greatest potential for generation of hydroelectricity. China has exploited this advantage by building large multigigawatt dams, as well as thousands of small hydrostations to supply local electricity. The country's 380 gigawatts (GW) of total exploitable water power is well ahead of Russia, Brazil, and the US, but large Siberian rivers have a more even flow. Owing to large seasonal fluctuations in Chinese river flows, the potential power cannot practically be converted to hydro-generation.

Unfortunately, China has much smaller reserves of crude oil and even less natural gas. At the end of 1995 China's proved reserves of crude oil were about 3.3 billion tonnes, or less than 2.5% of the world total. Natural gas reserves amounted to 1.7 trillion m^3 in 1995, just 1.2% of the global total. Daqing oilfield, a supergiant discovered in the early 1960s, still supplies more than half of total annual extraction. Extensive exploratory drilling in the South China Sea, an area once projected to be the new Persian Gulf, has discovered only a few small scattered oilfields and one medium-sized gas reservoir. Attention now is turning to potentially promising hydrocarbon basins in Xinjiang, although any major discoveries of hydrocarbons in this remote region would take some time to bring to market.

China's annual per capita consumption of commercial energy now averages about 25 gigajoules (GJ). This consumption rate is more than twice as large as the Indian rate, but only about one-half of the global mean and—most revealingly—only one-fifth of the Japanese rate of energy consumption. Clearly, substantial increases in China's energy consumption are requisite to the country joining the ranks of developed economies.

Because coal accounts for roughly three-quarters of China's energy consumption, a share unmatched by any other large economy, a substantial increase in China's energy consumption rate could have serious environmental repercussions. China now burns 1.2 billion tonnes of the fuel every year, almost a third of the world total. In addition to generating over 70% of China's electricity, coal provides more than half of all feedstocks for chemical industries and some nine-tenths of heat for households. The air pollution that results from this combustion is discussed later in this chapter.

2 Degradation of China's Environment

When the communist regime took over in 1949, China had a number of environmental problems typical of a populous nation dependent on subsistence farming in often difficult natural circumstances: progressive deforestation, desertification, and excessive soil erosion were the most visible effects. These problems were exacerbated by China's adoption of the Stalinist model of economic development, a model that sought to compress decades of normal economic development into years, thus greatly contributing to air and water pollution. Environmental degradation during this period included astonishing waste of scarce natural resources in inefficient heavy industries, widespread agronomic malpractices in newly communized farming, and deforestation and desertification that resulted from the Great Leap Forward. Temporary muting of Stalinist-Maoist policies allowed for a much needed socio-economic recovery in the early 1960s. However, a new wave of environmental destruction ensued during the Cultural Revolution.

One lasting legacy of the Cultural Revolution derived from the Maoist policy of "taking grain as the key link." Believing grain harvests to be the answer to China's problem of feeding its large population from a limited amount of farmland, the Maoist leadership ordered farmers to cut down orchards, plow up arid grasslands, fill in lakes, and cultivate just one or two grain varieties regardless of local soil and climatic conditions. This destructive wave of the late 1960s and early 1970s created more grain fields and expanded the area of cereal cultivation to record levels, but resulting yields were mostly low, and any productive benefits were outweighed by increased soil erosion, desertification, risks of flooding, and reduced variety of typical diets.

Deng Xiaoping's reform brought welcome attention to environmental matters, including increased investment in environmental management. These advances, however, largely were negated by an historically unprecedented quest for rapid economic modernization. The official goal of quadrupling the per capita GDP for one-fifth of humanity within a single generation has led to heightened environmental degradation.

The situation has been made worse by the development of hundreds of thousands of small and medium-sized rural and township enterprises. Because these workshops and factories have become indispensable sources of employment for millions of peasants whose labor was made superfluous by farming privatization, they are subject to fewer environmental controls than other sectors of the economy.

2.1 Air Pollution

China's air pollution problems may be attributed to the country's dependence on coal. Before 1980 China ranked as the third largest producer of the fuel, behind the US and the USSR, but the post-1980 economic boom pushed China to first place. China extracted more than 1.2 billion tonnes in 1995.

China's reliance on coal is exacerbated by the poor quality of the fuel and low efficiency of its combustion. Approximately half of recent coal output has been extracted from small and medium-sized, privately and collectively-owned, mines that ship their coal uncleaned and unsorted; moreover, most of the fuel is burned in inefficient small and medium-sized commercial and industrial boilers and in tens of millions of household stoves. Consequently, emissions of total suspended particulates (TSP) and sulfur dioxide (SO_2) have been rising. Official statistics put annual TSP emissions at about 15 Mt. According to the same source, SO_2 emissions increased from some 12 Mt in 1980 to about 19 Mt in 1995, although some Chinese atmospheric scientists believe that the total may be up to 15% higher.

Concentrations of these pollutants in China's large cities frequently surpass the nation's hygienic norms. China's ambient air quality standards set the allowable annual average of SO_2 at no more than 60 micrograms/m^3 SO_2 and the highest 24-hour concentration at 150 micrograms/m^3. Despite these standards, Beijing's cleanest residential areas average between 80-100 micrograms/m^3, and mean annual levels in the most polluted northern cities are commonly twice the allowable level. By contrast, mean SO_2 levels in North American cities are commonly below 20 micrograms/m^3, and even the Tokyo megalopolis averages just 30 micrograms/m^3.

High levels of SO_2 and TSP have significant statistical correlations with higher frequency of upper respiratory infections, with increased incidence of chronic obstructive lung diseases (bronchitis, asthma), and with lung cancer. In addition, chronic obstructive pulmonary diseases now account for about a quarter of all deaths in China, a rate which is at least four times higher than the US rate. Chronic exposure to relatively high levels of urban air pollution thus has contributed to the changing patterns of morbidity and mortality (it should be noted, however, that correlating changing patterns of morbidity and mortality to outdoor air pollution is complicated by China's extraordinarily high rates of smoking and by often high levels of indoor air pollution from improperly vented stoves).

Fortunately, heavily polluted northern China has been spared one serious form of air pollution: acid deposition. Once oxidized, SO_2 emissions become the principal ingredient of acidifying deposition, but dry northern China, where most of the country's coal is burned and where most of the new coal-fired electricity-generating capacity will be located, has naturally high levels of airborne alkaline matter whose presence buffers acidifying aerosols and prevents harm to biota. By contrast, rainy southern China, where coals have higher sulfur content, does not enjoy that advantage. Several southern provinces receive rain as acid at the same levels as most countries of Western Europe (pH well below 5.0).

2.2 Water Pollution

By 1995 the total volume of China's waste water had increased to about 40 billion tonnes, or by more than 50% since 1981. By the year 2000, total volume will surpass 70 billion tonnes.

A recent survey found that 82% of China's nearly 900 major rivers were polluted to some degree, and that over 20% were polluted so heavily that it was impossible to use their water for irrigation. More than 5% had no living fish. The survey also found that some four-fifths of surface water in urban areas was contaminated. In addition, drinking water did not meet state standards in 21 of China's 27 largest cities, and underground water did not meet state standards in 23 of these cities. Contributing to urban water pollution is the practice of releasing untreated municipal wastes into rivers and lakes. Of the 8,000 tonnes of human waste generated in Shanghai, half is discharged into the Yangtze and into Hangzhou Bay.

Water pollution in the countryside may be attributed in part to the rapid growth of rural enterprises. By releasing industrial wastes into local lakes, rivers, and into dense networks of canals, rural enterprises contaminate the same waters that are used for drinking (about half of China's population draws its drinking water from surface sources), animals, and irrigation. The most common uncontrolled pollutants are phenols, heavy metals, and various organic wastes from food processing. Residues of heavy metals such as chromium, lead, and cadmium are particularly high in many staple crops because peasants use canal and river mud (where these elements accumulate) as organic fertilizer.

Another source of water pollution in rural areas is the increased use of synthetic fertilizers. In its attempts to maximize crop production, China has become the world's largest consumer of synthetic nitrogenous fertilizers. The nationwide average is close to 200 kilograms of nitrogen per hectare (kg N/ha), and in the most intensively cultivated eastern provinces, where three crops are grown per year, the average is well over 300 kg N/ha. Large leaching losses resulting from the heavy use of synthetic fertilizers lead to rising concentrations of nitrates in both surface and underground waters.

2.3 Agroecosystems

China loses more farmland soil to erosion than any other country in the world. A recent large-scale survey discovered substantial soil erosion to 31% of farmland. In northern China, where the largest area of loess (a rich but extremely erodible soil type) is found, erosion losses by wind and water average more than 200 t/ha per year.

By the late 1980s, 44% of fields in Sichuan, China's most populous province, were eroding beyond a sustainable level (marking a fourfold increase compared to the early 1950s); moreover, nearly one-third of Sichuan's total cultivated slopeland had annual erosion losses averaging 110 t/ha. The current average erosion rate in China is about 50 t/ha per year. In contrast, the US average is less than 20 t/ha annually.

Major economic costs of soil erosion include crop yield losses directly attributable to a diminishing soil base; value of lost nutrients in terms of equivalent amounts of syn-

thetic fertilizers; lost irrigation and electricity-generating capacity of reservoirs owing to silting; and damages incurred from the increased frequency and extent of flooding.

Erosion is not the only threat to China's agroecosystems. A recent national soil survey found that only 15% of China's farmland suffers no unfavorable production factors. About 5% of all agricultural soils are affected by desertification, while 9% are affected by waterlogging (insufficiently drained paddies comprise about half of the latter area). The problem of salinization, arising from inadequate drainage and improper irrigation, lowers crop yields on about 7 million hectares of farmland.

The loss of previously recycled urban waste owing to spreading sewer installations as well as pressures on privatized farming to produce higher yields of monocropped cereals have led to increased use of synthetic fertilizers and decreased use of green manures. This in turn has resulted in declining levels of organic matter in farm soil. A national soil survey conducted in about 1,400 counties revealed that 11% of China's farmland has less than 0.6% organic matter, and that the average nationwide value has dropped below 1.5% (although there is no optimal value for soil organic matter, at least 2% to 3% is considered desirable).

The most important consequence of declines in soil organic matter is the reduced numbers of soil invertebrates, especially earthworms. Earthworms are the principal soil tillers and irreplaceable agents of soil humification. Unfortunately, they can provide these ecosystemic services only in soils rich in organic wastes.

2.4 Deforestation and Afforestation

Compared to forest coverage at the beginning of the communist rule (estimated by different sources as low as 5% and no more than 8% of China's territory), the current extent of China's forests indicates a major afforestation achievement. However, as soon as Deng Xiaoping's reforms loosened the flow of previously restricted information, reports of extensive deforestation became available. Data released during the early 1980s revealed that afforestation campaigns had restored tree cover to 28–30 Mha of land during the years 1949–79. Although significant, this large area represents less than 30% of the total claimed by exaggerated official statistics released during the pre-reform era.

Although the quality of afforestation improved significantly in most of the newly permitted private fuelwood lots during the 1980s, average success rates in state-sponsored plantings remained relatively low. Even properly planted trees have had great difficulty surviving the combined impacts of prolonged droughts and pest infestation. Inadequate prevention of forest fires and poor firefighting capabilities also have contributed to low success rates. The best nationwide estimate is that about one-third of successfully established plantings eventually were damaged by fires.

Currently, many new plantings, ranging from large southern pine plantations to small, private lots of fast-growing fuelwood species, are doing well, and their growth will be reflected by the rising volume of standing stock. However, the state's efforts at replanting principal commercial logging areas has been poor, creating a major resource crisis: of the 131 state forestry bureaus in the most important timber production zones, 25 essentially exhausted their reserves by 1990 and 40 will be able to harvest only until the year 2000. At that time almost 70% of China's state forestry bureaus will have no trees to harvest.

Although growing stock may be yielding a statistical nationwide wood surplus at present, official figures for the average growing stock in forest plantings (about 20 cubic meters per hectare) make it clear that extensive new plantings offer little hope for replacing felled mature forests for many decades. The inevitable conclusion is that, even assuming that official figures are accurate, the recent quantitative growth of Chinese forests masks a major qualitative decline.

Long-term effects of deforestation on the environment include diminished water storage capacity and reduced protection of soil against both wind and water erosion (for example, the Ministry of Water Resources has reported that deforestation in the upper Yangtze basin already has inflicted more damage than soil erosion control can restore). Effects that are more difficult to quantify include changes to local and regional climate.

3 China and Global Environmental Change

Although several of China's environmental problems have captured international attention, two are of particular concern: emissions of chlorofluorocarbons (CFCs) that destroy stratospheric ozone; and generation of greenhouse gases whose rising atmospheric concentration could lead to global climatic change.

In the mid-1980s, when the world community became aware of the growing ozone hole above Antarctica, China began building a series of large CFC plants (by the end of the decade it had become the world's largest producer of domestic refrigerators). Not surprisingly, China did not join the first round of the Montreal Treaty, which called for elimination of CFCs; only after the promise of considerable financial aid to help replace the CFC plants was China persuaded to join the treaty during the second round of negotiations. Unfortunately, inadequate funding has slowed the transition, and it does not appear that the replacement of CFC plants will be accomplished according to the original schedule.

China's greenhouse gas emissions are a more serious matter. Accounting for 11% of the global total, the country is currently the world's second largest producer of greenhouse gases, just ahead of Russia but well behind the US. However, Russian emissions have declined since the post-Soviet collapse of industrial production, and US emissions are growing very slowly and, given political intent, could be stabilized at current levels or even cut. In contrast, China's emissions will increase substantially during the next generation.

Rapid economic expansion and continued reliance on coal are expected to more than double China's current carbon dioxide emissions. Large increases in other important greenhouse gases are expected as well. Methane emissions will increase as China develops its natural gas reserves. In the agricultural sector, increased rice production will amplify both methane emissions from rice paddies and nitrous oxide emissions from denitrification of synthetic fertilizers. The latter increase is noteworthy because nitrous oxide is 200 times more effective at trapping heat than carbon dioxide, and China already is responsible for more than 20% of its worldwide emissions.

Consequently, China is expected to become the world's largest emitter of greenhouse gases sometime between the years 2010 and 2025, yet official policy offers little hope for remedial action. Chinese authorities expressed their beliefs in the Beijing Declaration of 1991 that wealthy countries are responsible for the rise in greenhouse gases in terms of both current and cumulative emissions. Authorities concluded that developing countries should not be required to limit their emissions until they reach the developed world's level of current per capita and cumulative emissions.

4 Looking Ahead

China's environmental circumstances are not unique: extensive environmental degradation has been a by-product of modernization efforts around the globe. Moreover, none of the affluent nations in North America, Western Europe, or East Asia began paying significant attention to environmental problems before its per capita GDP level was three to five times the current Chinese level. From this perspective, China's growing attention to environmental problems and its slowly rising investment in environmental protection are encouraging.

Unfortunately, however, much recent Chinese planning appears to be done under the delusion that there are few limitations to the country's development. Perhaps the best example of this attitude is the official transportation strategy. Rather than develop efficient high-speed rail links between large cities (an obvious choice in a densely inhabited country), the Chinese are building six-lane highways through rice fields; this is in accordance with the government-sanctioned goal of having a car in 270 million—or 90% of all—Chinese families. Considering there are currently 600 million passenger cars worldwide, realization of this goal would increase substantially the global car fleet, and would bring heightened air pollution and land loss problems to densely inhabited eastern China.

Two recent comprehensive appraisals of the economic costs of China's environmental degradation agree that these phenomena already cost the country an equivalent of at least 10% of its GDP every year. Given the combination of continuing population growth and high developmental aspirations, it would be unrealistic to expect a reversal of any major degradative trend during the next generation. However, price reforms promoting efficient use of resources, installation of readily available control techniques, sensible urban planning, and continuous attention to afforestation and proper agronomic practices may moderate substantially further environmental degradation and contribute to modernization that combines higher disposable incomes with decent quality of life.

Further Reading

Edmonds, Richard L., *Patterns of China's Lost Harmony: A Survey of the Country's Environmental Degradation and Protection,* London and New York: Routledge, 1994

A comprehensive, well-written survey of China's environmental challenge, accompanied by an extensive bibliography.

He, Bochuan, *China on the Edge: The Crisis of Ecology and Development,* San Francisco: China Books and Periodicals, 1991

A somewhat sensationalized coverage of a wide range of China's environmental degradation.

National Conditions Investigation Group, *Survival and Development: A Study of China's Long-Term Development,* Beijing and New York: Science Press, 1992

A wide-ranging appraisal of biophysical constraints on China's modernization.

Qu, Geping, and Li Jinchang, *Population and the Environment in China,* Boulder, Colorado: Lynne Rienner, 1994

Written by the former head of China's National Environmental Protection Agency (Qu); a popular introduction to China's population and environmental problems.

Richardson, Stanley Dennis, *Forests and Forestry in China: Changing Patterns of Resource Development,* Washington, D.C.: Island Press, 1990

A detailed examination of one of China's most critical environmental challenges.

Smil, Vaclav, *China's Environmental Crisis: An Inquiry into the Limits of National Development,* Armonk, New York: M.E. Sharpe, 1993

A systematic, interdisciplinary appraisal of interactions among China's environment, population, and resources.

Smil, Vaclav, *Environmental Problems in China: Estimates of Economic Costs,* Honolulu, Hawaii: East-West Center, 1996

An attempt to estimate economic impacts of China's environmental pollution and ecosystemic degradation.

Vaclav Smil is Professor in the Department of Geography at the University of Manitoba, Winnipeg. His most recent books include *Global Ecology: Environmental Change and Social Flexibility* (1993); *China's Environmental Crisis: An Inquiry into the Limits of National Development* (1993); *Energy in World History* (1994); *Environmental Problems in China: Estimates of Economic Costs* (1996); and *Cycles of Life: Civilization and the Biosphere* (1997).

Chapter Fifteen

Law Reform and China's Emerging Market Economy

Pitman B. Potter

Since 1978, the Chinese government has attempted to coordinate its efforts at economic reform with a parallel program of reforms in the legal system. During this period China has enacted an impressive number of laws and regulations aimed at supporting the transition toward a socialist market economy. Legal relationships such as contract, property, and foreign business relations have been brought gradually within the compass of formal and increasingly detailed legislative and regulatory enactments. However, enforcement remains a serious problem; as a result the PRC law regime tends to be ineffectual in lending predictability to economic activity.

A primary reason why recent legal reforms are difficult to enforce is that economic activities in many Chinese communities traditionally have been characterized by long-term relationships based on personal empathy (*ganqing*) rather than short-term transactional approaches. Moreover, Chinese communities often have relied on family networks and clan and guild rules to set the standards for commercial behavior. Enforcement of these standards has been achieved through flexible processes that take into account the circumstances of the parties. In the context of China's formerly state-planned economy, these relational approaches have been essential, since access to raw materials, bureaucratic approvals, and business opportunities has depended mainly on political rather than economic resources.

Although many people in China welcome the legal reforms of the post-Mao period and have adjusted their activities to take them into account, old customs have been slow to fade, and relational economic activities are still dominant over transactional ties. Unfortunately, this mode of economic activity poses serious obstacles to the capacity of China's legal system to support long-term economic reform. In addition, China's leadership has sponsored law reforms only to the extent that new laws do not infringe upon the authority of the Chinese Communist Party. Furthermore, because lower-level officials interpret new laws according to the dictates of changing central policy, new law regimes have suffered from regulatory inconsistency. This chapter examines these and other obstacles to implementing China's economic law reforms.

1 Market-Oriented Law Regimes in the PRC

Since 1978, the PRC government's market-oriented reform policies have dominated the institutions and enactments of the Chinese legal system. Of particular importance are the legislative institutions and specific laws and regulations aimed at implementing economic reforms.

1.1 Legislative Institutions

During the reform era under Deng Xiaoping, the National People's Congress (NPC) has been transformed from a "rubber stamp" parliament into a vibrant institutional component of political authority. No attempt to understand the role of law in China would be complete without discussion of the NPC. Similar to legislative institutions elsewhere, the NPC functions as the center of the legislative process and plays a major institutional role in China's economic development. The NPC also has significance for the political legitimacy of the regime.

Under the PRC Constitution, the NPC's legislative duties extend to enacting basic national statutes as well as passing amendments to the constitution and reviewing decisions made by the State Council and the NPC's own Standing Committee (NPC-SC). Legislative work is coordinated by the NPC's Legislative Affairs Work Committee (*Falu gongzuo weiyuanhui*, or *fagongwei*), which oversees the work of various specialized committees responsible for the areas of finance, education and science, foreign affairs, and culture, among others. The NPC's Legislative Affairs Work Committee receives input from the State Council's Legislative Bureau (*Fa zhi ju*), which coordinates legislative proposals and drafting for various administrative offices of government.

Although the NPC theoretically is an independent body, it is influenced heavily by the Chinese Communist Party (CCP). All important NPC decisions are prepared (if not made outright) by the NPC-SC, whose membership must be approved by the CCP Politburo. Moreover, the NPC Party Members Group acts as a relatively disciplined instrument of CCP control over decision making at official NPC meetings. The legislative process often is initiated by a decision of the CCP Politburo's Politics and Law Leading Group (*Zhengfa lingdao xiaozu*), and draft laws must undergo approval in principle by the Politburo, its Standing Committee, and selected party elders. Finally, the CCP, through its network of committees and party secretaries, wields considerable authority over personnel and policy decisions at all levels.

Throughout the post-Mao reform period, the NPC has been the site of much bureaucratic wrangling over legislation aimed at effecting reform policies. The Bankruptcy Law and the State Enterprise Management Law are particularly noteworthy examples, although not unique. The Bankruptcy Law of the PRC was formally enacted by the Eighteenth Session of the NPC-SC in December 1986. The law raised sensitive issues regarding the fate of inefficient state enterprises and the disposition of their assets and employees. Because it had the potential to operate at the interstices of the planned and market economies, the law gave rise to a number of policy and ideological conflicts. These conflicts came to the fore during the course of bureaucratic infighting over the legislation, which in turn ultimately delayed its enactment and undermined its implementation.

Although the Deng Xiaoping-led reformist coalition viewed enterprise reforms and bankruptcy legislation as essential to their broader economic reform goals, significant apprehension and resistance emerged from CCP traditionalists and from government ministries responsible for state enterprises and their assets and employees. These groups found support among the leadership of the NPC and its Standing Committee, who sought to delay enactment and, ultimately, implementation of the proposed legislation. The delays in enacting the Bankruptcy Law and the State Enterprise Law reflected the extent to which bureaucratic politics affected the legislative process.

That the NPC in effect is used as a resource for elite politics may serve to elevate the stature of China's legislative apparatus over the long run. The increased prominence of the NPC-SC, and by extension the NPC itself, already has given new significance to legislative debates. In order to ensure favorable legislative outcomes, contending institutions and individuals have engaged in bargaining and the manipulation of political resources. In some respects, the use of the NPC as a tool for political struggle–and the concomitant rise of meaningful debate within its legislative chambers–signifies the NPC's growing political authority.

This dynamic raises the possibility that the NPC may serve as a source of legal authority as well.

1.2 Laws and Regulations for Implementing Economic Reform

Virtually all aspects of the Chinese legal system bear some relation to the economic reform program. Several key areas are discussed below, including laws pertaining to contracts, property, dispute resolution, finance reform, administrative reform, and foreign economic relations.

Contract Law

China has two basic contract laws, one for domestic transactions and the other for transactions involving foreigners, as well as a civil code that contains a number of general principles applicable to contract relations.

The Economic Contract Law (ECL), enacted in 1981 and revised in 1993, governs Chinese domestic contracts, including contracts between foreign invested enterprises registered in China and Chinese-owned companies. The ECL contains basic provisions for ten different types of contracts, including sales contracts, construction contracts, lease contracts, and contracts for storage of goods. Of particular importance in the original ECL were provisions recognizing the rights of parties and authorizing strict contract enforcement, while recent revisions to the ECL include replacing references to the state plan with references to state policies. The law comprised a major component of the post-Mao economic reform policies, representing a compromise between the market-oriented concept of "freedom of contract" and the policies of central planning.

The 1985 Foreign Economic Contract Law of the PRC (FECL) applies to all contracts between Chinese and foreign firms and governs nearly all foreign trade, foreign investment, and technology transfer transactions. The binding nature of the FECL is qualified by the UN Convention on Contracts for the International Sales of Goods, which China joined effective January 1988. The Convention augments, and in some instances displaces, FECL provisions when the foreign contracting party is from a signatory state.

The General Principles of Civil Law (GPCL), enacted in 1986, contains provisions for civil contract relations. Specifically, the law contains important doctrinal rules on legal capacity, contract and property relations, and the consequences of legal rights infringement. As the distinction between the FECL and the ECL suggests, the Chinese legal regime distinguishes between laws applicable domestically and laws applicable to foreign matters. The introduction of the GPCL complicated matters by further obfuscating the jurisdictional boundaries between the two main Chinese contract statutes. To rectify the situation, lawmakers currently are drafting a unified contract code.

Property Law

The General Principles of Civil Law contains a number of important provisions on property rights. The statute recognizes private ownership of personal property such as wages, dwelling place, books, animals, and inheritance. However, ownership of land and natural resources is reserved to the state and the collective; they in turn may transfer usage rights to individuals and enterprises.

The GPCL also recognizes intellectual property rights, complementing a range of laws and regulations describing the rights of inventors, writers, and designers. The PRC Trademark Law (1982, revised 1993), Patent Law (1984, revised 1993), Copyright Law (1990), and their associated Implementing Regulations purport to protect the rights of intellectual property owners in these sectors, while specialized rules offer copyright protection for computer software. A signatory to most international intellectual property conventions, including the WIPO Treaty and the Berne Convention, China's intellectual property laws and regulations are influenced heavily by the international treaty regime.

However, reception and assimilation of the norms contained in many of China's intellectual property rules have been problematic, particularly in the copyright area. For this reason, and owing to institutional weaknesses and the role of economic self-interest, enforcement has been particularly difficult. In response to complaints from the international community, notably the United States and the European Community, China is making renewed efforts to improve its enforcement regime.

Dispute Resolution

Bureaucratic compromises that had worked effectively under the state planning system to prevent and resolve commercial disputes have become less acceptable to economic actors increasingly concerned with profit and loss. As a result, China has paid increased attention to building institutions for dispute resolution. Of primary importance are the court system and the arbitral system.

Commercial litigation in China generally is handled by the People's Courts, a court system comprising specialized chambers that handle cases in criminal law, civil law, economic law, foreign business law, intellectual property law, and administrative law. The overall jurisdictional structure of the People's Courts is set forth in the Organic Law of the PRC for the People's Courts. The Supreme People's Court, which administers the court system as a whole, acts as a trial court at the national level and also as a court of last appeal. At the provincial and prefecture levels respectively, the Higher and Intermediate Level People's Courts hear appellate and trial cases. The Basic Level People's Courts hear trial cases at the county level. Unfortunately, the courts remain relatively weak in political terms; moreover, lack of funding has impeded the ability of the People's Courts to act as meaningful venues for dispute resolution.

The procedural rules for civil litigation in the People's Courts are set forth in the PRC Civil Procedure Law (1991, draft 1982). The People's Courts also are involved in carrying out foreign arbitral awards under the New York Convention on the Recognition and Enforcement of Foreign Arbitral Awards (to which China acceded effective 1987). Many problems have been encountered with this process, notably the case involving Revpower, where enforcement of a foreign arbitral award was refused in apparent violation of the New York Convention.

China has a variety of separate arbitration systems. Arbitration of disputes involving Chinese domestic enterprises may be handled by various administrative departments with jurisdiction over the subject matter. For example, labor disputes are handled by the local Labor Administration, while contract disputes fall under the authority of the State Administration for Industry and Commerce. Under China's Arbitration Law (1994), local arbitration committees are established to handle a wide array of economic disputes. Maritime disputes are subject to the China Maritime Arbitration Commission. Arbitration and conciliation between Chinese and foreign parties in economic and trade matters traditionally fell under the exclusive jurisdiction of the China International Economic and Trade Arbitration Commission (CIETAC) under the China Council for the Promotion of International Trade (CCPIT) in Beijing and its sub-councils in Shanghai and Shenzhen; now, however, the local arbitration committees authorized under the Arbitration Law are active in this field as well. Although this arrangement has the potential to expand and diversify the venues available for foreign dispute settlement, some foreign investors are wary of the effectiveness and impartiality of the new provincial arbitration bodies. CIETAC Arbitration Rules have been amended several times over the past few years to accommodate the concerns of foreign parties and to comply with the requirements of the PRC Arbitration Law. Unlike the People's Courts, CIETAC permits foreign lawyers to represent their clients directly before the arbitration tribunal.

Finance Reform: Foreign Exchange, Taxation, and Securities

China's economic reforms have included

changes in the financial system, particularly in the areas of foreign exchange, taxation, and securities regulation. Reforms in the foreign exchange area have entailed the elimination of the dual currency system and movement toward full convertibility of the Chinese *yuan* (*renminbi*). Alterations to the tax system have included changes in domestic income and turnover taxes and rationalization of the foreign tax system. New approaches to securities markets also have been introduced to add greater fluidity to the financial system.

Prior to 1980, China's currency was not convertible on the world market. A partially convertible currency was introduced in 1980, resulting in a dual currency system. The domestic currency (*renminbi,* or Rmb) was intended exclusively for use in the local economy, while the convertible currency (*waihuijuan,* or foreign exchange certificates) was intended for use in foreign transactions. The system gave central authorities an administrative mechanism for controlling China's balance of payments. Effective January 1994 foreign exchange certificates formally were abolished, although the Rmb was not yet made freely convertible. Administrative procedural restrictions and controls on the identity and number of banks authorized to engage in foreign currency transactions serve to limit full convertibility. An inter-bank market has been established for the purpose of setting the exchange rate, thereby linking China's foreign exchange reforms with changes in the state banking system aimed at increasing institutional diversity and competition. Increased foreign participation in the banking sector is also significant.

Taxation in China is subject to a wide range of laws and regulations. Particularly noteworthy are the Individual Income Tax Law (IITL) and its associated regulations; various value added tax regulations on the sale of goods, land, and services; and foreign business taxes.

The IITL (1980, revised 1993) and its Implementing Rules initially were intended to impose tax on income received by foreign expatriate personnel living and working in China. However, owing to China's rapidly expanding economy and higher living standards, the IITL was amended to bring Chinese income earners within the ambit of the law. Currently, taxpayer identification is based on domicile, and the assessed tax is based on net income from all sources, although the tax rate and the calculation of net income differ depending on the source of the income. Although each individual income earner is responsible for paying the proper amount of tax and registering with taxing authorities, the employer generally acts as the withholding agent. Thus, the IITL operates as a mechanism for social control as well as for income generation.

Prior to January 1994, China's primary domestic business tax was the Industrial and Commercial Consolidated Tax (ICCT). Effective January 1994 the ICCT was abolished and replaced by a series of new taxes, including a Value Added Tax (VAT), Consumption Tax, and Business Tax. The Value Added Tax applies to virtually all transactions in goods and services (exports, however, are not subject to VAT). The Consumption Tax applies to the production, processing, or importation of consumer goods, while the Business Tax applies to the provision of labor services and the transfer of tangible or intangible assets. In contrast to the ICCT, the new regime of transfer taxes makes clear distinctions between goods and services, and also between transfers involving added value and transfers not involving added value. Lawmakers also enacted a Land Value Added Tax to cover gains in real estate transactions.

Tax enforcement issues generally are governed by the Law of the PRC to Administer the Levying and Collection of Taxes and its Implementing Regulations. These measures replace earlier regulations on tax administration, and afford Chinese tax authorities broad discretionary authority to conduct investigations regarding tax compliance and to impose sanctions in cases of noncompliance. As a result, tax enforcement tends to involve protracted negotiations over amount of income and details of payment and enforcement.

Meanwhile, after an extended period of debate, a system of securities laws and regulations was enacted that extended economic reforms to the financial sector. Notable accomplishments in this area include the establishment of a national administrative regulatory system and the enactment of the Company Law of the PRC.

The national regulatory effort began in earnest with a series of eight separate regulations issued between June and August 1992. These regulations addressed such issues as financial management, taxation, commercial transactions, and the formation and supervision of joint stock companies. The most important enactment for the national securities regulatory structure was the Regulations on Enterprises' Shareholding System Experiment, issued jointly by the State Commission on Restructuring the Economy, the State Planning Commission, the Ministry of Finance, the People's Bank of China, and the State Council Production Office. These Shareholder System Regulations governed the use of shares as the basis for enterprise ownership.

In January and again in April 1993, the State Council announced provisional regulations on the issue and trading of stock. These regulations addressed matters such as stock issues and trading; takeovers; custody, clearance, and registration of shares; information disclosure; inspection and penalties; and dispute resolution. The regulations charged the State Council Securities Policy Committee (SCSPC) with overall administration of the national stock market, while the China Securities Regulatory Commission (CSRC) was to function as the SCSPC's executive agency. The CSRC subsequently established a special commission for examining and approving share issues. These national rules complemented local measures already enacted to govern securities exchanges in Shanghai and Shenzhen. They also paved the way for Chinese domestic stocks to be listed on foreign markets such as Hong Kong and New York. More recently, regulations have been issued governing the sale of shares in foreign investment enterprises.

Based on a draft that had been submitted the previous March after undergoing years of refinement and debate, the PRC Company Law (1994) formalizes the rules and procedures for company operations, but also refines the regulatory system's ability to address company shares. Specifically, it addresses bond issues, accounting matters, mergers, bankruptcy and liquidation, and the responsibilities of foreign company branches, among other topics.

The enactment of the Administrative Litigation Law of the PRC (ALL) signaled an effort to make administrative agencies more accountable for their actions by establishing provisions for limited judicial review. Under the ALL, individuals and enterprises may challenge in court the legality of decisions handed down by Chinese administrative organs. Although only administrative organizations may be defendants under the ALL, a cause of action may arise as a result of an individual official's act (for example, a complaint can be filed against an administrative agency as a result of an individual official's attempt to elicit graft from a business enterprise). Moreover, the ALL permits judicial review of a variety of regulatory decisions, including the imposition of fines; restrictions on property rights; interference in business operations; and denial of business licenses.

However, the ALL does not permit review of discretionary decision making, an authority lawfully conferred on administrative agencies. In light of the textual ambiguities of Chinese laws and regulations, discretionary decisions are widespread and abuses are common. Nonetheless, these decisions lie outside the scope of ALL review. In addition, ALL review does not extend to the lawfulness of administrative regulations themselves: administrative agencies can in effect legislate their own immunities to ALL review. Finally, applicants seeking judicial review first must exhaust administrative remedies within the department being challenged. Unfortunately, under the Regulations of the PRC on Administrative Reconsideration, administrative agencies virtually have unlimited power to dictate governing procedures and to limit the availability of appeal to the courts.

Reforms in China's foreign economic relations extend to nearly all aspects of the Chinese legal system. Many of the issues relevant to this area have been discussed in preceding sections. What follows is a brief survey of reforms in the foreign trade and investment sectors.

During the early years of reform, Chinese foreign trade relations were governed by a variety of disparate and often unconnected laws and regulations relating to matters such as trade licensing, commodity inspection, and the administration of tariffs. The formation in 1982 of the Ministry of Foreign Economic Relations and Trade (MOFERT), resulting from the joining of the former Ministries of Foreign Trade and Foreign Economic Relations and the State Commissions on Foreign Investment and Imports and Exports, heralded a major effort to unify the foreign trade structure under a single ministry. MOFERT's internal departments included the import and export administrations, which oversaw matters such as licensing and the approval of trade contracts. The subsequent renaming of MOFERT as the Ministry of Foreign Trade and Economic Cooperation (MOFTEC) had little to do with foreign trade issues; rather, it reflected heightened efforts to attract foreign investment.

Throughout the 1980s, China's foreign trade was conducted mainly by national foreign trade corporations (NFTCs) organized under MOFERT or under its provincial or local commissions and bureaus. Under this system, local branches of the NFTCs were subject to supervision both by local government authorities and by the main office in Beijing. In 1988, China worked to decentralize its state trading corporations by establishing the former provincial branches of the NFTCs as separate subsidiaries. Initially, the relationship between the former branches and their former central offices remained close. Gradually, however, other companies were granted authority to conduct foreign trade, and this arrangement sig-

nificantly eroded the monopoly enjoyed by the MOFERT NFTCs. Currently, an agency trading system is beginning to emerge whereby NFTCs act in exchange for service fees, while the Chinese producer or consumer bears the commercial risk of the transaction.

In May 1994 the PRC enacted a comprehensive Trade Law. The act was created in part to mollify China's trading partners on issues of regulatory transparency and market access, and to pave the way for China's entry into the General Agreement on Tariffs and Trade (GATT) and the World Trade Organization, although the law's actual effects cannot be ascertained fully as yet. While the PRC Trade Law clarifies the decentralization in China's foreign trade companies, it also affirms China's right to restrict imports and exports in pursuit of national policy goals. Furthermore, the legislation formally authorizes retaliatory measures in response to what China considers protectionist treatment by its trading partners.

The Chinese legal regime for foreign investment has evolved significantly since its inception following the Third Plenum of the Eleventh Central Committee of the Chinese Communist Party in 1978. The first foreign investment laws governing equity joint ventures were little more than broad statements of principle. Implementing regulations gradually were appended to provide much needed, albeit still incomplete, additional detail. The government approved a wider variety of foreign investment enterprises, including contractual joint ventures (also known as cooperative enterprises) and wholly foreign-owned enterprises. Generally speaking, the term "foreign investment enterprises" denotes equity and contractual joint ventures as well as wholly foreign-owned enterprises, and foreign representative offices continue to be excluded from this category. The term "foreign enterprises" indicates foreign companies, enterprises, and other economic organizations that have establishments or sites in China engaged in production or business operations, or that have no establishments or sites but derive income from sources in China. Foreign representative offices are classified as foreign enterprises.

Initially, the Chinese foreign taxation system treated equity joint ventures differently than cooperative enterprises, wholly foreign-owned enterprises, and foreign representative offices. The 1991 Income Tax Law for Enterprises with Foreign Investment and Foreign Enterprises (Unified Foreign Enterprise Tax Law, or UFETL) removed this disparity, however. The UFETL placed equity joint ventures, cooperative enterprises, and wholly foreign-owned enterprises together under the rubric of "foreign investment enterprises," while classifying other foreign business activities (such as representative offices) as "foreign enterprises." The UFETL incorporated many of the preferential tax provisions applicable under previous laws and regulations, but applied them more fairly. Foreign businesses registered in China are also subject to VAT and other taxes on vehicles, office space, and various other goods and activities.

China has concluded bilateral tax treaties with many of its trading partners to establish tax jurisdiction over foreign individuals and companies operating in China and to promote cooperation in tax enforcement. These treaties generally follow either the Organization of Economic and Cooperative Development (OECD), Model Double Taxation Convention, or the United Nations Model Convention, although the US-PRC Tax Treaty is influenced heavily by the US Treasury Department model as well, with its absence of tax-sparing provisions.

Attempting to attract more foreign investment, the government has enacted various inducement measures. These measures have included emphasizing location in Special Economic Zones, Economic and Technology Development Zones, and other specialized sites as the basis for preferences and later adding substantive operating criteria as conditions for receipt of investment incentives. Most recently, efforts have been made to remove disparities in the legal treatment (as well as unify the corporate legal status) of foreign and Chinese businesses. Similarly,

the tax system is undergoing reform to harmonize the treatment of foreigners and Chinese individuals and their business operations. In addition, China's foreign exchange system has been reformed and the dual currency system eliminated.

2 Obstacles to Enforcement and Implementation

Thus, regulation of economic activity in China has developed significantly since 1978. New laws and regulations have been enacted at a withering pace, governing essential economic relationships such as contracts, property, dispute resolution, finance, administration, and foreign business. The success of legal reform depends largely on the capacity of these relevant laws and regulations to direct economic behavior. This section focuses on a traditional Chinese approach to the role of law as well as a Chinese belief about the implementation of law which together diminish the capacity of China's legal system to support long-term economic reform.

2.1 Problems of Approach: Instrumentalism and Formalism in the Role of Law

The Chinese government's approach to law is fundamentally instrumentalist: laws and regulations are intended to act as instruments of policy enforcement. Legislative and regulatory enactments are not intended to function as expressions of general norms that apply consistently to a variety of human endeavors; neither are they constrained by such norms. Rather, laws and regulations are enacted to achieve the immediate policy objectives of the regime. Law is not a limit on state power; rather, it is a mechanism by which state power is exercised. Similarly in the economic realm, law is intended to be public and punitive, rather than aimed at empowering private persons to pursue compensatory remedies.

This approach to the role of law derives from a longstanding Chinese tradition whereby law is established, first, to achieve social control and, second, to achieve economic goals. Imperial, Republican, and Communist governments alike have emphasized law as an instrument of rule. Throughout the 1950s, law and regulation was used to transform the economy and society to achieve the revolutionary goals of the Maoist regime. The Maoist regime's instrumentalist view of law was illustrated amply when, in the late 1950s, the legal system was subjected to criticism during the "Anti-Rightist Campaign" for obstructing the policy goals of the party and state.

In the post-Mao era, legal reformers have employed the language of instrumentalism in order to enlist the support of conservative members of the regime who question the benefits of a legal system that intrudes on the CCP's authority. Although many law reformers have urged support for more universalist "rule of law" norms, notions about the public and punitive role of law are only slowly giving way to ideas about compensatory remedies and private empowerment.

Many of China's laws and regulations are ambiguous, and thus do not lend predictability or transparency to the regulatory process. Although the ambiguity of such laws allows central policymakers to modify the policy foundations for these measures and also permits local implementing officials to use broad discretion in ensuring that regulatory enforcement satisfies policy objectives, the practice of enacting vague laws makes uniform interpretation and enforcement difficult, if not impossible, to achieve.

Complementing the instrumentalist approach to the role of law in contemporary China is the formalistic approach to assessing the effects of law. According to this model, the content of law is assumed to represent reality, and little inquiry is permitted into gaps between the content and operation of law. Law is seen not only as a tool by which desired social, economic, and political goals may be attained, but also is presumed to be an *effective* tool. Where a policy is agreed upon and then expressed through law or regulation, the law or regulation serves as a conclusive indicator that the policy is being enforced.

To a large extent this formalism in assessing implementation is a predictable consequence of the instrumentalism that drives enactment. It is difficult to achieve consensus on legislative and regulatory enactments that are expressions of policy ideals; furthermore, owing to the numerous political trade-offs that accompany policy enforcement, it is nearly impossible to achieve consensus on details of implementation. As a result, policies and the laws and regulations that express them are replete with thinly veiled compromises that represent programmatic ideals rather than implementational details.

2.2 Problems of Implementation: Policy Indeterminacy and Regulatory Inconsistency in the Management of Foreign Investment

The consequences of instrumentalist and formalistic approaches to law are compounded by problems of practical implementation. The case of China's regulation of foreign investment is particularly instructive, not only because of the general importance of foreign investment to China's economic output, but also because officials and companies that are the administrators and subjects of law in the foreign business sector are more attuned to the role of formal regulation than are their counterparts in the purely domestic Chinese economy. Particularly noteworthy problems are policy indeterminacy and inconsistent regulatory performance.

Since its inception, China's open-door policy toward foreign investment has alternated between openness and restriction. During the first few years, China's opening was greeted with great enthusiasm by foreign firms, who were then disappointed by subsequent retrenchment policies and the cancellation of foreign contracts. The Chinese government's renewed interest in attracting foreign business as well as the enactment of additional regulations on joint ventures and tax matters spurred greater optimism and activity in the mid-1980s.

However, China's inadequate regulatory

regime and impenetrable bureaucracy have continued to frustrate foreign investors. The State Council's 1986 Measures for the Encouragement of Foreign Investment offered prospects for further improvements, but these appeared doomed by the Tiananmen massacre and the nationwide repression that ensued. Deng Xiaoping's 1992 visit to Shenzhen and his speeches extolling the virtues of a socialist market economy instigated yet another wave of foreign business interest.

Most recently, the concept of "macromanagement" has emerged, signaling further withdrawal of state control (based on the presumption that market-oriented policies necessitate this). The Chinese government has removed long-held barriers to foreign control over economic distribution and basic energy production. Regulations governing foreign investment in retailing enterprises will permit foreign capital to penetrate the consumer products market. Regulations permitting foreign investment in mining activity raise the possibility of foreign control over extraction and distribution of resources not merely for export (as in the case of offshore petroleum) but for use in the domestic economy. The removal of restrictions prohibiting foreign participation in infrastructure and power generation projects signals a similar trend. Although many foreign businesses have welcomed these changes, there is little basis for concluding that they have institutional permanence. Rather, they appear to be efforts to entrench reformist policies before the next conservative backlash occurs.

Long-term policy indeterminacy is likely to undermine the effectiveness of law and regulation. Officials are often unwilling to enforce current laws and regulations when they lack confidence in the permanence of the underlying policies. More importantly, in an environment where officials are granted substantial discretion to interpret regulations in order to enforce particular policies, policy uncertainty breeds regulatory uncertainty. This leads to officials interpreting and enforcing regulations based on parochial rather than national concerns. In addition to undermining official authority, this behavior obscures the meaning of laws and regulations for business operators who are required to comply with these laws. Furthermore, some officials refuse to interpret laws or, instead, arbitrarily interpret relevant laws and regulations, while business operators steadily lose confidence in the integrity of the regulatory system and seek extralegal means to accomplish their business goals. This crisis of confidence has the potential to undermine the institutional foundations for state regulation of China's foreign business relations.

One product of policy indeterminacy is inconsistent regulatory performance. Despite the continued expansion of the legal system governing foreign investment, the system's performance remains a major concern of foreign businesses. Problems include lack of consistency in interpretation of laws and regulations, bureaucratic interference in business operations, and the arbitrary imposition of levies and fees. Regulatory intervention also has been inconsistent, such that in some regions administrative agencies have been quick to impose amendments to joint venture contracts in order to resolve disagreements, while in other areas regulatory inaction has been the norm.

Inconsistent regulatory behavior is often the product of contending bureaucracies whose regulatory powers are subject to few effective limits. For example, provisions issued by the People's Bank of China prohibiting foreign bank representative offices from engaging in profit making activities were contradicted by the rules issued by tax authorities (and practiced by tax regulators) imposing foreign enterprise income taxes on such offices based on calculations of "deemed profits." Moreover, national regulations are subject to countermanding by local measures. For example, the State Council's Measures for Encouraging Foreign Investment ("22 Articles") included a specific provision granting foreign investment enterprises autonomy in hiring and firing work personnel. However, subsequent local regulations requiring labor union approval for personnel dismissals contradicted this provision. Local authorities occasionally have exceeded their authority by unlawfully dismissing joint venture managerial personnel.

A particularly useful example of inconsistencies in regulatory performance lies in the area of technology acquisition, where regulatory enactments limiting the rights of foreign technology transferors have contradicted measures expressed in various investment regulations encouraging technology development. While various investment incentives as well as China's nascent intellectual property protection system purportedly have encouraged the licensing of technology to China, regulations governing the content of technology import contracts have sought to diminish the capacity of foreign technology licensors to limit the activities of their licensees. First, these measures prevent the licensor from limiting use of the technology after expiration of the license, in effect permitting the Chinese licensee unfettered enjoyment of the technology. In addition, the contract must not oblige the Chinese recipient to accept "unreasonably restrictive" provisions, which include limits on sales of goods produced with the technology, effectively undermining the market coordination activities of foreign investors. Finally, the two sets of rules impose substantial and burdensome warranty requirements, including warranties on the quality of goods produced with the technology. These warranties effectively require the licensor to warrant the capability not merely of the technology but also of the entire production process in which it is used.

Also, the regulatory scheme for conferring investment incentives to advanced technology enterprises has the potential for counterproductive effects. In order to qualify as an advanced technology enterprise under the State Council's 22 Articles incentive scheme, a foreign investment enterprise must provide technology and engage in developing new products or the upgrading or replacement of existing products, thus increasing foreign exchange through the sale of exports or import substitution meth-

ods. In addition, the foreign enterprise needs to demonstrate to the ministry in charge that its technology satisfies certain specified criteria: the technology production processes or critical equipment used by the enterprise must be listed among those specifically encouraged or desired by the central government; must be "appropriate and advanced" in nature; and must be either in short supply, able to increase exports or import substitutes, or have the potential to develop new products. Each of these requirements effectively permits the ministry to impose escalating requirements on advanced technology enterprises as a condition for continued receipt of investment preferences.

3 Summary and Conclusions

The PRC government has devoted significant resources and political capital to the drafting of laws and regulations in response to the expressed concerns of foreign business. The legislative record is prodigious. However, the assumptions on the part of foreign businesses that, once enacted, laws and regulations would be enforced in a relatively stable and predictable manner have not proven accurate. The instrumentalist concept of law has spurred the enactment of parochial policy-driven measures, although enforcement of these measures cannot be assured in a climate of transitory policy consensus. Most often, the enactment of law is the expression of an ideal, which itself is viewed as sufficient without further effort at enforcement. Unfortunately, the mere expression of law is not sufficient for the subjects of law, namely foreign businesses seeking stability and predictability in their transactions. Thus, the PRC's instrumentalist and formalistic conceptions about the content and enforcement of law have spawned policy indeterminacy and regulatory inconsistency, resulting in a significant lack of confidence on the part of economic actors in the legal system as a whole. This pattern is readily visible in the domestic economic system as well, where economic actors who have experienced the peculiarities of PRC rule are even more ambivalent about the effectiveness of formal law and regulation.

The Chinese legal reforms carried out since late 1978 have been aimed at complementing market-oriented reforms in the economic system. However, many problems remain that inhibit the legal system's ability to support economic reform over the long term. The most fundamental problem is that laws and regulations are neither consistently nor effectively enforced. Thus, the legal and regulatory systems are unable to lend predictability and certainty to market-based economic relationships. Policy indeterminacy and regulatory inconsistency also have slowed the implementation of those laws that have been enacted. To a large extent, these are predictable phenomena in a system making the transition from a public regulatory and largely punitive institution to a system aimed at assisting autonomous and private market actors. Nonetheless, the obstacles to China's transition to a market economy are significant, and ongoing vigorous attention to the problems of concept and implementation of law is needed before the PRC's socialist legal system can serve effectively to complement China's economic reforms.

Further Reading

Alford, William P., *To Steal a Book Is an Elegant Offense: Intellectual Property Law in Chinese Civilization,* Stanford, California: Stanford University Press, 1995

An analysis of attitudes in China toward intellectual property protection, in historical perspective.

Bodde, Derk, and Clarence Morris, *Law in Imperial China,* Cambridge, Massachusetts: Harvard University Press, 1967

An excellent introduction to law during the Qing Dynasty (1644-1911). Provides useful historical context for the study of law in contemporary China. Includes text and discussion of cases from the *Da Qing Lu Li.*

Butler, William E., "The Chinese Soviet Republic in the Family of Socialist Legal Systems," in *The Legal System of the Chinese Soviet Republic* *1931–34,* edited by William E. Butler, New York: Dobbs Ferry, 1983; Epping: Bowker, 1984

Provides useful insight into Chinese communist approaches to law prior to taking power.

Chengsi, Zheng, with Michael Pendleton, *Chinese Intellectual Property and Technology Transfer Law,* London: Sweet and Maxwell, 1987

A leading treatise on the early stages of intellectual property law reform in the PRC.

China Laws for Foreign Business (looseleaf report), North Ryde, New South Wales: CCH Australia, n.d.

An invaluable source of Chinese legislation and regulations, in Chinese with English translation.

Feinerman, James V., "Economic and Legal Reform in China, 1978–91," in *Problems of Communism* (September 1991)

A useful analysis of the interplay between legal and economic reform in post-Mao China.

Gelatt, Timothy, *Criminal Justice with Chinese Characteristics: China's Criminal Process and Violations of Human Rights,* New York: Lawyers Committee for Human Rights, 1993

The leading critical review of China's criminal justice system.

Leng, Shao-chuan, and Hungdah Chiu, *Criminal Justice in Post-Mao China: Analysis and Documents,* Albany: State University of New York Press, 1985

An early overview of the post-Mao criminal law reforms.

Li, Victor H., "The Evolution and Development of the Chinese Legal System," in *China: Management of a Revolutionary Society,* edited by John M. H. Lindbeck, Seattle: University of Washington Press, and London: Allen and Unwin, 1971

A leading article on law developments in China during the 1950s.

Lubman, Stanley B., editor, *China's Legal Reforms,* Oxford and New York: Oxford University Press, 1996

A useful overview of law reform in the PRC. Includes papers from a special issue of *China Quarterly* (1995).

Moser, Michael J., and Jesse T.H. Chang, editors, *Foreign Trade, Investment and the Law in the People's Republic of China,* 2nd edition, Hong Kong and New York: Oxford University Press, 1987

A useful collection of articles on the middle stages of China's open door policy.

Potter, Pitman B., *The Economic Contract Law of China: Legitimation and Contract Autonomy in the PRC,* Seattle: University of Washington Press, 1992

An early treatise on contract law in the PRC.

Potter, Pitman B., editor, *Domestic Law Reforms in Post-Mao China,* Armonk, New York: M.E. Sharpe, 1994

Contains six articles on law reform in the domestic context. Topics include contracts, administrative law, and civil law.

Potter, Pitman B., *Foreign Business Law in China: Past Progress and Future Challenges,* San Francisco: The 1990 Institute, 1995

An analytical overview of the content, performance, and legal culture of the PRC's foreign economic law regime.

Pitman B. Potter is Professor of Law and Director of Asian Legal Studies at the University of British Columbia Law Faculty. He is the author of *The Economic Contract Law of China: Legitimation and Contract Autonomy in the PRC* (1992) and *Foreign Business Law in China: Past Progress and Future Challenges* (1995). He is also editor of *Domestic Law Reforms in Post-Mao China* (1994). He serves on the editorial boards of *China Quarterly, The Journal of Chinese Law and Practice,* and *Pacific Affairs.* A version of this essay appeared in *China's Economic Future: Challenges to U.S. Policy* (1996).

Chapter Sixteen

Political Fetters, Commercial Freedoms: Restraint and Excess in Chinese Mass Communications

Judy Polumbaum

Many stereotypes exist about mass communication in the People's Republic of China—above all, that the system functions like a well-oiled totalitarian machine. This image hardly could be further from the truth. Structurally, China's mass media are branches of the Communist Party and government; however, they have never operated monolithically or even predictably. Reasons for this are manifold, ranging from the sheer impossibility of achieving uniformity over any institution in such a vast country with such a huge population, to the intricacies of political and economic flux, to the vagaries of human nature. The post-Mao reforms have introduced new ingredients and complexities to the mix.

Mainland China's mass media have fulfilled a wide variety of functions, both intended and unintended, in the years since 1949. Used consistently as instruments for political mobilization, print and broadcast organs have served at different times to foster social cohesion, promote factional interests, air diverse voices, and regulate conflict. News media have been used to convey top-down communication and instruction, but also as a conduit for conveying complaints and problems from the bottom up. The institutions of journalism have served variously as guardians of the nation's traditions and mores, agents of development and change, human interest forums, and courts of last resort. Entertainment media, meanwhile, have worked at

times in tandem with news media to promote state programs and policies, and at other times in contradictory or subversive ways that challenge the official line.

Amid the domestic changes and global challenges of the late 20th century, Chinese newspapers, magazines, radio, television, and other communications media have increased in number, expanded in scope and ambition, and become more variegated in character and content. Telephone and facsimile services and, most recently, computerized information systems also have expanded rapidly, with advances in quality as well as increased accessibility and numbers of subscribers. Journalists, news organizations, cultural agencies, and the propaganda apparatus must answer to a broader range of demands and requirements than ever before—from the dictates of political leaders to the wants and needs of increasingly diverse and sophisticated media audiences, and from the requisites of the marketplace to the heightened influences of international media and public opinion. These developments are natural corollaries of China's economic reform strategies, of opening up to the outside world; in turn, they provide further impetus to processes of economic and social change and global interchange.

This chapter offers a status report on China's mass communication system, synthesizing a decade of Chinese and Western scholarship on contemporary PRC journalism, popular culture, and telecommunications. The first section explains the organization and operation of mainland Chinese news media. Subsequent sections describe different media sectors, including print, broadcasting, and new communications technologies; and examine emerging trends, problems, and controversies in journalism, propaganda work, and mass communications generally in the context of China's developing market economy.

Media Organization and Control

Visitors to China often are struck by the great number of news media outlets, the many levels at which they operate, and the varieties of content they offer. These are not simply features of the current media mix: specialization and local color could be found in Chinese media decades ago. However, the last two decades have brought unprecedented expansion and diversification.

The fortunes of China's mass media since the founding of the People's Republic in 1949 have always followed those of the country as a whole, with high and low tides paralleling political movements. The nadir was the Cultural Revolution decade (1966–76), when most regular publications were suspended or closed outright, while those that continued to publish or that later resumed publication were notable for their uniformity. The launching of reforms in 1978 heralded rapid growth of media outlets and activities–not only the revival of scores of pre-Cultural Revolution publications, but also the founding of hundreds more. The number of newspapers reached some 1,600 by 1988; in addition, some 4,000 limited-circulation "internal" papers were being published. The television industry, begun in 1958, came of age at this time, with the television audience growing from 34 million to 590 million between 1976 and 1987, and exceeding 900 million by the mid-1990s. Cable television reached nearly one-fourth of that audience by 1996.

With the adoption of market-oriented economic reforms from 1978 on, state subsidies to media shrank, and advertising arose as an important new sector. Audience expectations and consumer demands took on new importance. Innovations in media content designed to increase audience appeal emerged in both print and broadcasting, while greater attention was given to formerly neglected areas such as international news, service-oriented information, and human interest stories.

Restoration of the higher education system, meanwhile, led to the establishment of dozens of new journalism programs at the university level, and the Chinese press corps received an influx of younger, well-educated, critically-inclined journalists. By the end of 1992, more than 120,000 Chinese held domestic press credentials. These included some 52,000 newspaper reporters and editors, about 54,500 radio and television employees, 3,000 correspondents (*tongxunyuan*), and 12,000 working for magazines and other types of media.

Significant ideological developments accompanied the quantitative changes in journalism. Philosophical debates about the definition of news, the role of the journalist, and the relationship between journalism and politics–all topics of discussion in earlier periods–gained new life in the 1980s. Scholars and journalists spoke and wrote freely about the meaning of "freedom of the press" guaranteed in the PRC Constitution; and a loose coalition of journalists, legal researchers, and legislators sought to draft a national press law with specific provisions to safeguard press freedom. Journalists complained openly about political constraints on their work. Reporters and editors began to articulate a notion of journalistic professionalism, which drew a line between news and propaganda. To observers who had followed these discussions, journalists' participation in the demonstrations of 1989 was no surprise.

Despite these changes, however, the structure of mass communications in the PRC remained largely intact. Although elements of China's leadership promoted a more independent role for the press, media remained largely subordinate to politics.

Furthermore, in line with China's ongoing drive to develop an orderly system of laws and regulations, media management became more elaborate and, in some respects, more rigid than before.

Organizationally, news media are vertically stratified and horizontally differentiated, a setup originally modeled on the former Soviet media system. Horizontally, newspapers, radio stations, and television stations exist at descending levels of hierarchy corresponding to levels of party and government administration. Vertically, press outlets are differentiated in terms of target populations (e.g., women, youth, workers, peasants). To some degree, broadcast programming is differentiated by target audience as well.

The media network is fairly comprehensive at central and provincial levels (including provinces, autonomous regions, and the municipalities of Beijing, Shanghai, and Tianjin), and extends down to the local levels (prefectures, cities, counties, townships). National and provincial media reach virtually all localities, and, owing to the loosening of political and economic restraints on local newspapers and broadcasting stations, many new local outlets have opened since the early 1980s.

As for the control system, China's news media operate under a confusing array of what the Chinese call "mothers-in-law" *(popo)*. These include party and government organizations, quasi-official organizations such as Women's Federation or Youth League branches, and organizational or individual patrons (for instance, an influential functionary, or a factory that provides financial support). Individuals within media organizations—particularly directors, chief editors, and department heads—also may exert personal or idiosyncratic influence on newswork. Precisely who wields control in the news process, however, varies greatly from place to place and also over time.

Perhaps the greatest dilemma for Chinese journalists is how to fulfill the fundamental mission for news media dating back to the 1930s, when the Communist Party had its base in Yan'an—that is, the dual obligation to promote party and government policy and also to "serve the people." In the current era, news media are expected to serve the cause of economic reforms determined by the country's leadership, while simultaneously catering to the wishes and expressing the will of "the masses." In practice, the task of propagating official policy has dominated the balance, and Chinese officials are not reticent about this emphasis. In the mid-1990s, Chinese leaders still placed understanding of Mao Zedong Thought, Deng Xiaoping's theory of "building socialism with Chinese characteristics," and the party's basic policies foremost on the list of qualifications for journalists.

Fundamental direction for every news organization and newsworker in the country emanates from the party's Central Propaganda Department, although day-to-day control is dispersed among various agencies. Technically, each media outlet is under the leadership of party authorities at the corresponding level as well as under administrative supervision of government departments at that level. Central newspapers, for instance, are responsible to the Central Committee, while provincial party officials have authority over provincial-level papers and broadcast stations. Administratively, the State Press and Publications Administration is in charge of newspapers, journals, and book publishing, while the Ministry of Radio, Television and Film oversees radio and television stations and film studios. Authority over telecommunications is especially fragmented. In name, the Chinese Ministry of Post and Telecommunications oversees this sector, but the Ministry of Electronics Industry wields growing influence. Meanwhile, central government control is being eroded by competing state-owned and even private companies, as well as by endeavors of provincial, municipal, and lower-level entities seeking to protect local interests.

If the hierarchies of control appear complex and even tangled, how these connections are expected to work and how they actually operate in practice are more elusive questions still. Among newspapers a distinction is made between official party "organs," which explicitly speak for party organizations, and papers produced in the name of a government agency or other organization, which might be considered quasi-official. The *People's Daily*, voice of the Central Committee, and the *Anhui Daily*, official paper of the Anhui Provincial Party Committee, are examples of official organs. The *Economic Daily* is the official paper of the State Council, and the *China Women's News* is the nationally circulated paper of the All-China Women's Federation. Virtually every ministry and many national-level commissions, as well as all types of agencies and organizations at provincial and local levels, publish newspapers. With few exceptions, television and radio stations are technically organs of party and government. Recently, however, these stations have begun to branch out by dividing into sub-stations, not all of which act so explicitly as the voice of officialdom.

Complicating matters further is the existence of both openly circulated (*gongkai faxing*) and internal (*neibu*) publications. Official party newspapers operate on both tracks; stories deemed too sensitive for the public eye are printed in newsletters sent to party and government authorities. Broadcast journalists also write not-for-broadcast stories for these internal channels. Much of the best investigative reporting in China goes this route. In addition, many government departments, research institutes, and industrial enterprises publish internal newsletters or journals for use within an organization or trade. Numerous gradations of internal publications exist, distinguished by level of confidentiality. Ordinary Chinese have access to some through their work, and hear of the contents of others through the grapevine. Foreigners are not supposed to see any of them, regardless of whether the contents bear on military secrets, proprietary economic information, or translations of scholarly articles from foreign journals.

Unlike the former Soviet Union and a number of Eastern European countries before the fall of their communist parties, the PRC has not employed a formal censor-ship system. Rather, controls have tended to operate in a diffuse and often informal manner, with self-censorship playing an important role. Well into the 1980s, the likelihood of any particular news story being printed or aired, adulterated or suppressed, hinged largely on time, place, circumstance, and personality. This situation changed somewhat in the 1990s, when the administrative apparatus for supervising news and broadcasting was consolidated. The system for registration of periodicals and publishing houses was tightened up, a new system for accrediting journalists adopted, and regulations issued on many aspects of media management and control. What the government grants, however, the government can take away, and periodically it asserts this prerogative.

The regularization process enhanced the government's and party's ability to control media selectively. This ability is most commonly exercised over political coverage, which becomes obvious during times of political tension. After the crackdown in June 1989, at least three prominent publications were shut down as a result of their sympathetic coverage of the protests; the editorial leadership at several large newspapers was replaced, and a tier of mid-level editors at the *People's Daily* was reshuffled as well. Every news organization in the country was required to review three months' worth of demonstration coverage and produce a self-criticism acceptable to party authorities.

The anxiety that prevailed in newsrooms after Tiananmen dissipated within two or three years, but the party's concern for getting out its message did not. A few rules regarding political coverage have been cardinal in the 1990s. First, party newspapers as well as television and radio must give news concerning top leaders top billing. Second, ad hoc orders *not* to report on a news event should be obeyed. Yet another, more general principle is the oft-repeated admonition to emphasize "positive propaganda"; in other words, reporting on achievements is preferred over reporting on problems. Behind this instruction is a presumption that unbridled media can become a force for instability; thus, officials periodically remind journalists to refrain from "making disturbing sounds and spreading chaos."

Although violations of such guidelines are unlikely to result in imprisonment or banishment to the countryside as they might have during Mao's time, harsh sentences have been meted out to a number of reporters charged with leaking, selling, or publicizing "state secrets" related to sensitive political matters or unreleased economic information. In the spring of 1993, for instance, when Shanghai's *Liberation Daily* failed to put news about party secretary Jiang Zemin's comments on Sino-US relations on the front page, the paper's director and three editors were dismissed. Editors of at least two other papers that did run the story on page one were reprimanded merely for allowing the story to continue on an inside page.

While the practice of monitoring political coverage endures, other content areas allow greater flexibility. Provided they negotiate their way with care and intelligence, journalists and news organizations have some latitude to pursue serious coverage of important matters. Much commendable reporting on economics, environment, law, women's issues, and other subjects of social import bears this out. Conversely, media can get away with disseminating a great deal of trivial, diversionary matter in the interests of making money. The results of this latter approach to news reporting are evident in China's new media marketplace.

The Press in the 1990s

Newspapers have long been the foundation of Chinese journalism. They are the news medium with the longest tradition and the most experienced personnel, the medium most oriented toward current events and public concerns, a draw for the most idealistic young journalists, and the model for journalism generally. In the 1990s, television and radio have begun to develop distinct identities as vehicles for news and

public affairs, but newspapers remain the centerpiece.

Following the Tiananmen demonstrations, newspapers and journals were required to re-register with the government, and numbers of publications declined slightly, if only temporarily. By early 1996, 2,235 openly circulated newspapers were registered with the state, while approximately 6,000 unregistered "internal" publications also existed. By the end of 1996, the government was contemplating another review for the purpose of eliminating duplication, poor quality, and questionable management of newspapers—problems that in the past have served as convenient rationales for closing down politically pesky publications.

The State Press and Publications Administration categorizes newspapers according to main format, content, and purpose. Throughout the reform period, official organs have constituted about one-third of the total number while claiming a lion's share of total circulation. However, their predominance is waning. Circulation figures for official papers, declining since the early 1980s, plummeted in the early 1990s in spite of the fact that these papers have the advantage of a partially captive market, delivering public subsidies in the form of subscriptions from party or government offices, whereas other publications are more dependent on discretionary subscriptions or newsstand purchases by individuals.

On the rise, meanwhile, are small entertainment-oriented papers and spin-off publications, including "weekend editions" (*zhoumoban*) and specialized supplements, most in tabloid format. In Beijing alone some 50 weekly and monthly papers were competing for readers by the spring of 1993, as compared to a dozen the previous year.

This new sort of diversionary press, focusing on celebrities, lifestyle, crime, and scandal, extends the human interest tradition of the more respectable "evening newspaper" (*wanbao*), which underwent a revival after the Cultural Revolution. Evening papers, aimed at common working people, represent a partial alternative to conventional dailies, although in some respects they are merely stripped-down versions of official organs. The new tabloids and supplements of the 1990s are premised on entertainment value above all. Clearly, their main purpose is to turn a profit. Although many such papers have relatively small circulations (several hundred thousand being modest by Chinese standards), collectively they are making an impact. Managers at larger papers now view smaller operations as a source of real competition for advertising revenue.

Thus, established newspapers have joined the so-called "weekend edition craze" (*zhoumore*) and "newspaper expansion tide" (*kuobanchao*), aimed at attracting wider readership and creating more advertising space. Despite government concerns about newsprint shortages, hundreds of established papers added pages during the early 1990s. The four-page broadsheet party organ is becoming a rarity; two-thirds of provincial party papers have grown to eight pages, and some are up to 12 or 16. The *People's Daily*, the first broadsheet to go to eight pages, marked National Day (October 1) 1993 by growing to 12, with plans for an eventual 16. Other national papers increased frequency. The *China Business Times*, for example, jumped from thrice-weekly publication to a six-day paper at the start of 1994. Moreover, in a trend that began in the late 1980s and gained momentum in the early 1990s, some 300 newspapers added weekend editions. State regulators, concerned with the proliferation of "two papers under one registration" (*yihao liangbao*), issued regulations to tighten supervision over the phenomenon in the spring of 1992.

China's varied magazine marketplace adds further congestion to the crossroads of information and entertainment. In addition to standard popular magazine categories—current events, culture, sports, literature, family life—periodical offerings in China include popular science, medicine, technology, education, history, and social science magazines for general readers, as well as other specialized and scholarly journals. Economics and computers are rapidly growing segments. Some publications market themselves to particular age groups, ranging from elementary school students to college students to senior citizens. In recent years, magazines with the largest circulations have included a number of official and quasi-official journals that rely on public subsidies through organizational subscriptions, as well as others that circulate primarily through individual subscriptions and newsstand sales.

Broadcasting in the 1990s

Political, economic, and technological developments have combined to produce rapid expansion of the nation's broadcasting web. In 1949, the PRC had 49 radio stations; in 1958, there were 91, plus two television stations. By 1978 there were 93 radio stations and 32 television stations. A significant jump occurred after 1983, when a regulation banning counties from operating wireless radio and television stations was lifted; also, provincial and municipal radio stations were allowed to subdivide into subsidiary operations, creating a new brand of in-house competition. By the early 1990s, there were upwards of 900 radio stations nationwide. In addition, nearly 2,500 cities and counties had wired "broadcast stations" (*guangbozhan*), essentially local relay stations for provincial and national radio programming. By 1996 China had 980 broadcast television stations and an additional 1,000 "educational" television stations. The country also had about 1,300 licensed cable television stations, with a backlog of approximately 1,000 more awaiting licensing.

Indeed, television was *the* medium of the 1980s by virtue of its relative novelty and visual appeal. In addition to expanded entertainment programming, including dramatic and variety productions as well as imported feature films and series, news and public affairs programs flourished. Although informational programming continued to use conventional forms, ranging from newscasts to short specials and longer documentaries, the scope of topics and range of aesthetic experimentation widened.

Television now saturates the country: the State Statistics Bureau counted 89.8 television sets for every 100 households nationwide in 1995. TV audience surveys in China during the 1980s revealed that national newscasts were among the most watched programs. According to 1996 statistics, more than 300 million people watch the nightly news on China Central Television. Television films and fictional series frequently draw large audiences as well. Particularly at big-city stations, mainland TV newscasts have begun to exhibit characteristics of foreign and Hong Kong modes. Once rigidly scripted, news now makes more allowances for spontaneity. Person-in-the-street interviews are no longer a rarity. Some stations have magazine-type programs dealing with hot topics of the day. A lively example is Beijing Television's weekly *Eighteen Minutes*, inspired in part by the US weekly magazine *Sixty Minutes*.

With fewer explicit limits on content than ever before, television producers and station managers suddenly face the same quandary as their counterparts around the globe: financing. Increasingly, television programs must pay for themselves, an often insurmountable task for documentaries (as in the West, sponsors and advertisers in China seem happiest with short, simple, predictable fare). Some videomakers have gone outside the system entirely, seeking private financing and overseas outlets for their work. One result is that, in the absence of mechanisms for channeling independent creative productions to domestic outlets, talent that might help invigorate the domestic industry is increasingly oriented toward the international marketplace.

Overshadowed during the first decade of reforms, radio resurfaced in the public consciousness in the 1990s with programming genres that were new for the mainland, including talk radio. Some observers believe the innovations in radio have profound implications for the exchange of ideas and information, heralding a shift from a propaganda model of foreign exchange to a participatory model. Call-in shows on topics ranging from family life and child-rearing to legal affairs and consumer complaints became regular features of many local radio stations. Large stations, particularly those at provincial and municipal level, split into specialized subdivisions. Also, many stations sent mobile units to broadcast from department stores or other public venues.

Innovations in radio programming began in south China, where Hong Kong radio was accessible, and rapidly moved north. In 1986, Guangdong's provincial radio station established a subdivision specializing in economic matters that emphasized straightforward news, service, and immediacy. Utilizing the methods of Hong Kong radio, including live broadcasting and phone-in shows, the new Pearl River Economics Radio quickly won a loyal following. Within a few years, the provincial operation boasted six stations devoted to news, economics, culture, music, educational programming, and finance. Beijing's municipal radio station and others followed suit.

Decentralization and diversification promise to generate new forms of competition in broadcasting. In the past, although local and provincial radio stations theoretically competed for the same audiences in localities, the distinctions were minor; thus, directly competing broadcast operations simply did not exist. The launching of Shanghai's Oriental Radio, which began broadcasting from the special development zone of Pudong in the fall of 1992, marked an important change (Oriental Television, a companion television enterprise, went on the air in January 1993). The new outlets, going head-to-head with Shanghai's regular municipal television and radio, rapidly acquired audiences and advertising revenue. Like the municipal operations, Oriental Radio and Oriental Television are state owned and under the administrative supervision of the municipal broadcast bureau. Unlike the municipal operations, however, the upstarts boasted an energetic work style, greater emphasis on timeliness and live coverage, and novel modes of presentation. They relied on small but efficient staffs. The radio operation, initially comprised of 60 people who broke off from Shanghai's main municipal radio station, was the first in the nation to offer 24-hour programming. Oriental Television began with a staff of about 100, or roughly one-tenth that of its rival. To many observers, the establishment of these new stations in China's largest city marked the emergence of the first meaningful broadcasting competition in the PRC.

Cable and Satellite Television

Cable television subscriptions have increased from about 13 million nationwide in 1990 to 45 million by mid-1996, and are projected to reach 80 million by the year 2000, representing an estimated audience of 300 million individuals. This would rank China as the largest cable television market in the world.

In Beijing, where approximately half of the 3.3 million households subscribed to cable television by 1996, officials have undertaken a US$200 million project to expand the city's fiber optics network for cable capabilities over the next few years. Meanwhile, Beijing's main cable carrier plans to increase its number of channels from about 20 to 47. China's largest cable operation is located in Shanghai, with 1.8 million households signed up by late 1996. Shanghai's cable system was the first to offer a music channel and was planning a shopping channel for 1997; it also provides news, sports, drama, and general channels. The cable system produces about 20% of its own programming, buys 40% from elsewhere in China, and gets the remaining 40% from outside China (the main providers are Hong Kong and Taiwan). US fare includes cartoons and ESPN.

Additionally, although State Council regulations ban China's television broadcast and cable stations from conveying overseas satellite programs, untold numbers of Chinese are pirating satellite signals. Moreover, the manufacture of satellite dishes, including small ones that perch inconspicuously on many a balcony or rooftop, is a growth industry despite the October 1993 ban on erecting dishes for private use. Officials have found the ban difficult to enforce given the fragmentation of authority over the issue, the profits to be made from the manufacture and sale of dishes, and the steadily shrinking size of the devices.

New Communications Technologies

The burgeoning telecommunications sector has profound implications for dissemination of news and information in China. Telephone penetration remains at a low 3% nationwide but is increasing rapidly. Although half a million Chinese villages still had no phone service in the mid-1990s, fast-growing areas such as Guangzhou had achieved about 20% penetration. Fax machines have become commonplace in urban China, while access to Internet service, inaugurated in Beijing and Shanghai in 1994, is spreading quickly.

By late 1996, phone switching capacity had grown to 100 million lines, or 16 times the 1982 figure; about 10 million lines are being added per year. Phone sales amounted to approximately 30 million sets in 1996 and were expected to reach 40 million the following year. Waiting time for phone installation, formerly six months to a year, had been cut to about a month in most cities. Plans call for 140 million lines by the year 2000, representing only 10% penetration but an ambitious goal nonetheless. An optical fiber transmission network is expected to link virtually all large and most smaller Chinese cities both domestically and internationally by the end of the century. The majority of China's large cities already have direct-dial automated service for long-distance and overseas calls.

By the end of 1996, China had more than 6 million mobile phone users; that number was expected to triple by the end of the century. About 20 million Chinese owned pagers, and that figure was expected to rise 150% annually. Fax machines, which played a well-publicized informational role during the 1989 student demonstrations, were being purchased at a rate of a quarter of a million annually by the mid-1990s. A registration system introduced after the 1989 crackdown proved unworkable, and now virtually anyone with a phone jack can employ a fax.

Foreign capital has played a key role in expansion of telecom capacity. From 1978 to 1996, the mainland's telecommunications sector absorbed approximately US$656 million in foreign investment. These monies were limited to infrastructure projects, while actual provision of services remained essentially a government monopoly. However, the Ministry of Post and Telecommunications controls a diminishing proportion of the domestic market. Moreover, since the 1950s other bureaucratic agencies, including the military as well as transport and energy ministries, have had authority to construct their own telecom networks; by 1993 some 40% of China's telecom capacity belonged to these agencies. That year, much of the alternative network was incorporated into two new national services, called Liantong and Jitong. The implications and scope of these two secondary services are not yet clear, but Jitong has gained approval to supply Internet services.

Provisional regulations issued by the State Council in November 1993, which permitted collective as well as state-owned enterprises to offer telecom services under license from the Ministry of Post and Telecommunications, merely sanctioned a process that already was underway: the decentralization of telecom services. Many companies entered the cellular phone and pager markets and others began to supply on-line information. Officials have stated that the domestic telecommunications market will be opened to still more competitors in the future, including foreign companies. The first opportunities for foreign investors are likely to be in facsimile, electronic mail, and electronic data exchange. Internet projects involving foreign partners already are in progress.

Widespread use of the Internet in China is some years off. Although roughly 2.5 million personal computers were sold in the PRC in 1996 (with sales expected to rise to more than 3 million in 1997), only a fraction of these were connected to modems. As of early 1997, experts estimated that between 35,000 and 100,000 individual computers were logging onto the Internet, and the Ministry of Post and Telecommunications planned to boost Internet subscriptions by 150,000 during 1997. However, it is difficult to gauge the actual number of Internet users, because in some cases 20 to 30 people share the same account and password.

China's Internet links began with non-commercial services operated by universities and research institutes. The most ambitious, the China Education and Research Network, continues to expand and eventually will connect more than 1,000 universities. Two commercial systems developed by the Beijing Telegraph Administration–Chinapac, which currently supplies digital communications to nearly 700 cities, and the China Public Data and Digital Network, available in about 300 cities–expanded relatively slowly because of prohibitive cost. Nevertheless, these two services laid the groundwork for a national system, ChinaNet, launched by the Ministry of Post and Telecommunications in the spring of 1995. ChinaNet reported 20,000 accounts by late 1996. Another service, China Infohighway, which is 74% state owned, also was established in 1995 with nodes in eight Chinese cities. China Infohighway claimed about 10,000 customers at the end of 1996.

Meanwhile, China Internet Corporation, a Hong Kong-based company whose majority shareholder is China's official news agency, Xinhua, contracted for US$15 million worth of computers and interactive technology from Sun Microsystems to expand its China Wide Web network. CWW is an "intranet" service (indicating that it is self-contained but can be linked to the Internet proper) providing on-line financial and economic information in Chinese to domestic and international subscribers. Beginning in January 1997, users in Beijing, Shanghai, Guangzhou, and Shenyang could access the service. Plans called for connecting a total of 20 cities by the end of the year and 50 by the turn of the century.

In another joint venture, Rupert Murdoch's News Corporation and the New York-based publishing company Ziff-Davis have collaborated with the national Communist Party newspaper *People's Daily* on a Chinese-language web service, ChinaByte. The service began in January 1997. The *People's Daily* went on-line the same month, following at least four other newspapers and two magazines.

These developments illustrate China's willingness to enter the modern information age, but not without ambivalence and some degree of cyber-censorship. The Chinese government blocks access to politically sensitive or sexually explicit Internet sites, and for several months in 1996 kept users off Web sites of several Western news agencies, including CNN and the *Washington Post*. The government's desire to monitor computer networks is evident in the establishment at the end of 1996 of a special group to "manage and coordinate" network services in China: the Information Technology Development Leading Group under the State Council. However, the diffuse new technologies of communication are inherently difficult for government to control, and efforts to inhibit Internet communications may prove futile. For example, anyone can bypass Beijing or Shanghai servers with a simple telephone call to Taiwan or Hong Kong.

Media Commercialism

In the past, China's news organizations directly and indirectly were financed by the state. On the one hand, Communist Party and government departments covered capital and operating costs as well as employees' salaries, housing, and other benefits. On the other hand, party and government departments were the primary patrons of newspapers and magazines through organizational subscriptions. Publications also benefited from government monopolies, which kept costs of services such as rail transport and postal delivery artificially low. Now that media are caught

between reduction of state subsidies and rising production and distribution expenses, advertising revenue is becoming the primary source of media income. After an initial period of caution, press and broadcast media are making the most of opportunities to sell space and time. The growing dependence on advertising revenue has problematic byproducts, and questions about the relationship between news and advertising have yet to be sorted out. However, the mere fact that news operations no longer rely entirely on state financing is viewed widely as a positive change.

The notion of advertising, forbidden for two decades, has been accepted in the PRC only since the late 1970s; nevertheless, many newspapers and television and radio stations entered the 1990s with more advertising than they could handle, a reflection of the country's economic boon over the subsequent decade. At big-city dailies, it is not uncommon for advertising to be lined up half a year in advance. Assured advertising revenue does not necessarily sustain large media organizations, however. Staffs ballooned in size after the Cultural Revolution, employees' expectations regarding income and benefits have risen steadily, and costs of producing publications and programs have soared, all while audience demands have intensified. Market forces could increase pressures on the larger and most entrenched news outlets; meanwhile, smaller, innovative operations are likely to benefit.

The development of supplements and weekend editions as well as the proliferation of small papers, combined with increases in advertising rates, likely will intensify competition for advertisers. As advertising space expands and costs for certain forums rise, advertisers may become more discriminating. Eventually they are likely to tie their advertising purchases more directly to audience characteristics, which in turn should link commercial value more tightly with audience appeal, and thus with media content. Those media will suffer that are unable to demonstrate to advertisers their ability to deliver content sought by readers, listeners, or viewers.

Currently, however, the clamor for advertising space and time appears boundless enough to fill any available niche, and, with demand outrunning supply, advertising rates have risen steadily. The government sets general standards for advertising charges as well as limits on proportions of space or time that may be allotted to advertisements, although these guidelines appeared to be applied loosely. In January 1993, print and broadcast advertising rates were hiked some 30%. Among newspapers, the national standard for a full-page advertisement became 26,000 *yuan* for domestic advertisers and 36,000 *yuan* for international advertisers, with rates at nationally circulated publications and popular local papers ranging considerably higher. Advertisements in weekend editions, color advertisements, and advertising bought by foreign companies or joint ventures command surcharges. In the same period, China Central Television's domestic rates for a 15-second advertisement ranged from 2,000 *yuan* during weekday daytime hours to as high as 21,000 *yuan* during prime time hours on Saturdays and Sundays. The comparable range for 15 seconds on Beijing television was 500 to 3,850 *yuan*, and 5,500 for foreign companies.

Advertising revenues naturally reflect differential economic conditions in different areas, and local newspapers in prospering cities can command more than even the most prominent national papers. Total newspaper advertising revenue in China, reported as 7 million *yuan* for the year 1983, mounted steadily through the 1990s, rising from about 9.6 billion *yuan* in 1991 to 45 billion in 1994. Five newspapers in cities with fast-growing economies (three in Guangzhou, two in Shanghai) had exceeded the 2 billion *yuan* mark in annual advertising revenue by 1994; the same papers were earning as much as 2 to 3 billion *yuan* per quarter in 1996. During the first three quarters of 1996, only one national paper, the Beijing-based *Economic Daily*, reached a top ten ranking for advertising revenue.

One of the decade's more astonishing developments in Chinese press commercialism was the complete displacement of front-page news by advertising. Shanghai's *Wenhui News* claimed the distinction of being first in 1993, selling the entire front page of its January 25 issue to an air-conditioning manufacturer for 900,000 *yuan*. Some days later, Shanghai's *Liberation Daily* ran a similarly placed advertisement. No controversy arose over whether advertisements properly belong in the prime news spot; much to the contrary, the phenomenon was touted as a great breakthrough in journalism's adaptation to the market economy.

In addition to advertising, news organizations seek other ways to supplement income. Government strictures bar them from pursuing revenue-making activities unrelated to their central line of work, but permissible methods apparently include accepting contributions from enterprises or other units willing to sponsor special columns, programs, or activities; organizing contests, conferences, concerts, or other events designed to raise money through fees or ticket sales; and setting up money-making enterprises that deploy existing facilities and resources.

The quintessential model of the entrepreneurial media organization is China's official news agency, Xinhua. Based in Beijing and comprised of numerous bureaus in China and around the world, Xinhua retained its status as the definitive voice on Chinese governmental matters and foreign affairs while evolving into a multi-tentacled conglomerate during the 1980s and 1990s. Most of its money-making ventures were natural extensions of its news operations, e.g., photo, translation and information services, and printing and publication ventures.

This approach has been followed to a more modest degree by smaller news organizations. In January 1996, the central government put a stamp of approval on such diversification with formal recognition of the first "newspaper industry group" *(baoye jituan)*, an enterprise centered on the *Guangzhou Daily*. Such recognition gave an official name to a development that was already underway.

Political and Social Implications of China's Media

China's economic reforms place the news media in a peculiar position. On the one hand, news organizations and journalists are entrusted with ideological responsibilities to promote the reform efforts; on the other hand, the media are supposed to participate actively in their own economic reform by becoming self-supporting enterprises in a competitive marketplace. Thus, the news and information system must respond to many new economic pressures while remaining beholden to politics.

Many PRC media scholars and journalists believe the ongoing transformations of the economic basis of newswork are bound to alter the media's social and political roles. Indeed, economic forces already are a major dynamic in news industries, affecting organizational priorities, daily work, and media content. Although perceptions and opinions of these changes vary considerably, the assertion that change is inevitable seems beyond dispute.

Two decades since news media began to be weaned off state subsidies, many older outlets are still struggling, while new ventures must address the question of financing before virtually all other considerations. Newspaper and broadcast station officials and editors seem increasingly preoccupied with financial issues. Moreover, Chinese work units are organized as self-contained communities; their concerns go far beyond meeting payroll obligations and maintaining routine news operations. In this age of economic expansion, rising expectations, and rapid technological change, managers and editors must contemplate major capital improvements such as new office buildings and equipment, while also considering the needs of their employees, such as housing, medical care, and other benefits. Not surprisingly, the focus on becoming self-supporting has drawn attention away from editorial work.

The quest for new money-making formulas has led media organizations to create all sorts of new publications, often piggy-backed on existing ones. In addition, many government departments are developing papers as strictly for-profit ventures. Apart from officially registered publications, unauthorized publications appear irregularly. Although some are fly-by-night operations, many are produced under respectable auspices. By 1993 press authorities began to complain that party and government agencies, mass organizations, and businesses were putting out any number of newspapers in the name of "trial issues" (*shiban*), or publishing periodicals without authorization, sometimes using fake registration numbers to gain permission to publish.

Indeed, the rise of the commercial ethos turned press registration numbers into lucrative commodities. In May 1994, four newspapers and 41 magazines had their registrations revoked for having resold their licenses to publish to other organizations (in the same month, four successful financial newspapers in Shanghai that had not even bothered to register also were shut down). A year earlier, state press authorities publicized the case of a newspaper in Anhui province which, in the guise of changing its focus and contracting out management tasks, in fact had sold its registration permit for a "management fee" of 10,000 *yuan* to an organization in Wuhan that wished to publish a money-making tabloid. The resulting publication featured sensational stories of murder and incest that attracted the attention of investigators.

Given the new communication opportunities opened up by the decentralization of economic authority, many journalists and other intellectuals are willing to overlook the preponderance of what they consider trivial content on today's newsstands and bookstalls. Although few journalists would deny that use of scandal and sensation to attract readers falls short of high journalistic ideals, they are likely to view problems and contradictions as unavoidable. Officials who oversee the media, on the other hand, vacillate in their willingness to tolerate unsavory byproducts of the reforms. Those who perceive media to have transgressed political, moral, or other boundaries–boundaries that are largely undefined and constantly shifting–are liable to seek remedies through additional press regulations or stricter enforcement of existing regulations.

An example of official reaction to the rise of press sensationalism was the response to a spate of books about the private lives of prominent revolutionaries, including Mao Zedong and Zhou Enlai. Propaganda officials condemned the books, reminding the biographers of directives requiring that reports about the lives of leaders be cleared by appropriate party and government departments, or by the subjects themselves.

Regulators also worried that the proliferation of supplements and weekend editions had gotten out of hand, introducing undesirable content into the marketplace. Owing to this and other concerns, in 1992 the State Press and Publications Administration promulgated half a dozen new regulations on such matters as unification of the registration system, management of newspaper bureaus and weekend editions, and control of "unhealthy tendencies" in press work.

Legal and Ethical Problems

Corruption is the biggest fissure in the new market-oriented edifice. By 1993, enough questionable practices had emerged in newswork to make journalism ethics a focus of consternation. Suddenly, editors were reiterating much-ignored proscriptions on journalists soliciting advertisements or accepting bribes, news organizations were attempting to clarify how journalists should behave in gray areas (such as moonlighting or accepting gifts and favors), and officials were making frequent references to journalism's moral lapses.

Journalism ethics is not an entirely new issue in China. Concerns about the appearance of advertising in the guise of news led the All-China Journalists Federation to introduce a code of ethics in early 1991. In addition to an obligatory preface requiring the press to follow Communist Party leadership, the document also contained provisions about truth, accuracy, and separation of news and advertisements that Western journalists would find commendable. Essentially the same document was recirculated in mid-1994, prompting critics to observe that the guidelines had been ignored and that simply reiterating them was unlikely to make them take hold.

Two news stories that broke in the spring of 1993 lent a sense of urgency to the discussion of ethics: the case of Daqiuzhuang, lauded since the late 1980s as an exemplar of village industrialization, which turned out to be a tightly held local fiefdom; and the fate of the Great Wall Company, touted for nearly two years as a highly successful electronics firm and desirable investment opportunity, but actually an enormous scam. Both cases represented sensational downfalls of individuals and ventures that largely were creations of media build-up. Both cases illustrated the dangers of propagating "models," a perennial topic of complaint among mainland journalism circles which nevertheless persists as a prevalent mode of reporting. Furthermore, both cases reinforced public beliefs about the corruptibility of the press corps. The kingpins in both cases were said to have used unsavory means, including bribery, to ingratiate themselves with journalists. Ultimately, two journalists were imprisoned for having reported favorably on the Great Wall Company in exchange for money.

As some journalists had hoped and others feared, the 1990s brought a succession of formal efforts to regulate media behavior. In July 1993, party and press authorities issued a ban on "news for compensation" (*youchang xinwen*). In April 1994, following the convictions of at least two reporters on corruption charges, the Propaganda Department issued another, more emphatic, circular against paid news. In January 1997, party and government agencies along with the All-China Journalists Federation promulgated a set of regulations for newswork. The rules prohibit journalists from accepting any form of payment for interviews or for editing and publishing news stories; from accepting money, gifts, gratuities, or favors from sources or subjects; and from taking advantage of their work privileges for personal benefit. They also advise strict separation of editorial matter from advertising in media content, as well as separation of news departments from business operations in media organizations.

Enforcement of the latest set of rules is left to individual news organizations, although the document warns that fines, penalties, "criticism," "discipline," administrative measures, and even criminal charges may result from neglect or violation of the regulations. However, reporters and editors believe that additional directives and stricter enforcement of rules from above are unlikely to remedy the situation. Ultimately, press ethics in China must rest on occupational beliefs and practices that are internalized rather than externally imposed. The current flux and confusion in society at large and the media system in particular do not constitute a hospitable climate for ethical journalism, and thus a cohesive occupational ethos for the new era has yet to emerge.

Interestingly, discussion of press ethics in China has mounted during the 1990s, while once-heated controversies over press legislation are quiescent. Similar to ethical concerns, concern for law in Chinese journalism has risen and fallen as corollaries to larger political trends, and also in reaction to discrete problems of the moment as perceived by journalists, regulators, and politicians. For the most part, discussions of ethics and discussions of law have proceeded along separate tracks, in contrast with the close linking of law and ethics in Anglo-American journalism tradition.

Public and professional pressure to ensure legal safeguards for press freedom, part of the movement for political reform that gained momentum through the 1980s, did not return to earlier levels after the 1989 Tiananmen demonstrations, despite the resurgence of economic reform efforts from 1991 on. However, one facet of media law gained new prominence: the phenomenon of media-related lawsuits. A surge in law-

suits alleging press errors, defamation, and invasion of privacy had provoked dismay among both journalists and officials during the late 1980s. After a hiatus, such lawsuits appeared to be on the rise again, together with economic lawsuits against media alleging appropriation or copyright infringement. Reasons for the burgeoning of litigation may include the comeback, albeit modest, of "criticism reports" (*piping baodao*); the popularity of human interest reporting with its inevitable focus on personal matters; the increasing economic stakes involved in artistic, literary, and journalistic production; the passage of copyright protections, an administrative law with provision for citizens to sue government agencies or functionaries, and other new tools for legal challenges; and, presumably, a growing awareness of the law's potential by those wishing to redress grievances, declare outrage, or merely express frustration.

New Tensions and Trajectories

In the context of China's changing economic climate, it is only logical that the Communist Party and government have become more selective in efforts to manage propaganda and cultural works. Administrative control over areas of news and information that are overtly political in content (e.g., diplomatic and governmental affairs, political and ideological commentary, questions of national security or sovereignty) has not abated, and in some respects has intensified. New bureaucratic agencies and formal rules and regulations for press control have supplanted what used to be a fairly amorphous system. This regularization process should not be interpreted as part of the backlash to the Tiananmen demonstrations of 1989, because the process has been evident at least since the spring of 1987.

Official statements on newswork continue to emphasize the importance of adhering to party policy, and insist that no incompatibility exists between party requirements and audience preferences. Newsworkers are exhorted to carry out the ideological tasks of propaganda on behalf of reform, openness, and socialist modernization; they also are expected to perform the practical tasks of supplying the public with reliable news and useful knowledge. News media are admonished to strengthen their role in political guidance and simultaneously increase their public appeal. One result of this forced coexistence is a kind of bifurcation in media content, with one mode of coverage adhering to political strictures and another straying as far from politics as possible. Another result, however, is the appearance of serious journalistic coverage and commentary at the margins, and the gradual expansion of some marginal areas into territories of considerable vitality.

China has a large, and largely untapped, market for political coverage and commentary, but as long as the party and government continue to monitor political news and information more closely than anything else, this remains the riskiest sector in the new media marketplace. Fortunately, the Chinese populace also has a vast appetite for straightforward coverage of everything from economic development to education, from agronomy to finance, from environmental affairs to child psychology. Although such issues cannot be divorced from political considerations, journalists who are adept at relegating politics to a subtle or tangential position may go far in satisfying the public's informational demands. Reporting strategies that skirt the edges of political sensitivities while avoiding direct confrontation with party and government authorities are particularly suitable for certain specialized areas of news coverage, such as economics, environment, law, and women's issues.

The geographic dispersion of media offers other unexpected channels for dissemination of information and ideas that may not suit current orthodoxy. Intellectuals whose views are considered daring and whose articles are not welcomed by national party or government publications find outlets in the provinces, particularly in the growing economics-oriented press. Unusual or controversial articles often are picked up, distilled, and disseminated further by another growing genre, the "digest" press.

In addition, the rise of new technologies has thrown unpredictable factors into the media mix. Accelerating advances in telecommunications and the integration of phone, fax, and computers into domestic and international communications networks are opening up new channels of information beyond the confines of conventional state controls. In combination with new social forces, the new technologies have expanded possibilities for sending and receiving messages across organizational and bureaucratic boundaries within China, as well as to and from overseas locations. Although China has yet to experience unbridled freedom of information and expression, these developments certainly put pressure on the floodgates.

Further Reading

Barmé, Geremie, and John Minford, editors, *Seeds of Fire: Chinese Voices of Conscience,* New York: Noonday Press, and Newcastle upon Tyne: Bloodaxe, 1989

Barmé, Geremie, and Linda Jaivin, editors, *New Ghosts, Old Dreams: Chinese Rebel Voices,* New York: Times Books, 1992

These two anthologies introduce a wide range of iconoclastic literary and journalistic works from the post-Mao period.

Chu, Godwin C., *Radical Change Through Communication in Mao's China,* Honolulu: University Press of Hawaii, 1977

Good background on mass communications in the PRC up to the reform period.

Chu, Godwin C., editor, *Popular Media in China: Shaping New Cultural Patterns,* Honolulu: University Press of Hawaii, 1978

Examines popular media formats in their cultural contexts.

Goldman, Merle, *Sowing the Seeds of Democracy in China: Political Reform in the Deng Xiaoping Era,* Cambridge, Massachusetts: Harvard University Press, 1994

Examines freedom of speech and the press and changing views of civil liberties in the decade leading up to the 1989 student movement.

Journal of Communication 44, no. 3 (Summer 1994)

Special issue focusing on "Communication in China," providing a literature review of work on PRC media and discussions of relevant debates in China, as well as original studies of broadcasting and cable.

Lee, Chin-Chuan, editor, *Voices of China: The Interplay of Politics and Journalism,* New York: Guilford Press, 1990

Lee, Chin-Chuan, editor, *China's Media, Media's China,* Boulder, Colorado: Westview Press, 1994

These two volumes focusing on mainland China's media since Mao represent some of the best contemporary scholarship on this subject.

Li, H.C., "Chinese Electric Shadows: A Selected Bibliography of Materials in English," in *Modern Chinese Literature* 7, no. 2 (Fall 1993)

A guide to the large body of film studies devoted to the Chinese cinema.

Liu, Alan P.L., *Communications and National Integration in Communist China,* Berkeley: University of California Press, 1971

Good background on mass communications in the PRC up to the reform period.

Lull, James, *China Turned On: Television, Reform, and Resistance,* London and New York: Routledge, 1991

Provides insight into the impact of popular media in China.

McClelland, Stephen, "China: Toward the World's Largest Market," in *Telecommunications* (International Edition) 30, no. 10 (October 1996)

An overview of recent telecom developments.

Nathan, Andrew J., *Chinese Democracy,* Berkeley: University of California Press, 1985

Provides good background on Chinese political philosophy and traditions regarding expression.

Saich, Tony, editor, *The Chinese People's Movement: Perspectives on Spring 1989,* Armonk, New York: M.E. Sharpe, 1990

A useful collection on the 1989 movement that includes an essay by Seth Faison entitled "The Changing Role of the Chinese Media."

Stranahan, Patricia, *Molding the Medium: The Chinese Communist Party and the Liberation Daily,* Armonk, New York: M.E. Sharpe, 1990

Provides background on pre-1949 roots of Chinese Communist Party journalism policies and practices.

Womack, Brantly, editor, *Media and the Chinese Public: A Survey of the Beijing Media Audience,* Armonk, New York: M.E. Sharpe, 1986

Presents one of the first audience surveys conducted by Chinese scholars during the early 1980s; with an excellent introduction by the editor.

Zha, Jianying, *China Pop: How Soap Operas, Tabloids, and Bestsellers Are Transforming a Culture,* New York: New Press, 1995

Offers a delightful discussion of the inroads and implications of media commercialism.

Judy Polumbaum is Associate Professor in the School of Journalism and Mass Communication, University of Iowa. She has been a consultant and writer for many periodical publications, including *China Daily,* Beijing, and the Xinhua News Agency, Beijing. Among her numerous articles on Chinese affairs are "Developments in PRC Journalism in the Context of Market Reforms" (*China Exchange News,* 1994), "Chinese Journalism Since the Tragedy of Tiananmen" (*China Briefing 1991,* 1992), and "Dateline China: The People's Malaise" (*Foreign Policy,* 1990–91).

Society and Human Dimensions of Development

Chapter Seventeen

Population Policy

Penny Kane

"Many difficulties China has encountered in its economic and social development are directly related to the problem of population"–so declared China's State Council in 1995. Although the statement referred to the circumstances of China's development during the reform era (1978 to the present), it could as easily have been made about the Maoist era. In fact, the basic elements of China's population policy have remained unchanged since 1970, when targets for reduced population growth were included in the Fourth Five-Year Plan. Only the strategies for implementing policy have been altered over time, owing to coincidental political and structural developments. This stable policy environment contrasts markedly with most other areas of Chinese experience over the past quarter-century, as earlier chapters have shown.

The Development of Population Policy

China's immense population and the constraints it places on China's natural and economic resources have been a major concern for China's policymakers. China ranks as the world's largest country, accounting for 21% of total world population. Unfortunately, although China has a landmass similar to that of the US, more than half is arid or semi-arid and largely unsuitable for agriculture; thus, it is easy to see why Imperial and Republican governments alike have made food procurement a top national priority. With half the arable land of the US, five times the number of people, and a backward economy, China's efforts to ensure grain supplies remains a major national preoccupation. Despite general improvements in living standards over the past decade, in 1996 some 65 million Chinese were still unable to grow or purchase sufficient food for themselves, and thus relied upon government grain allocations and other welfare subsidies.

Not only is China's population large, but it has grown rapidly since 1949. The introduction of widespread primary health care measures, together with land redistribution and greater internal stability, resulted in high birthrates and a rapid decline in infant mortality rates during the 1950s. Population growth, however, did slow during the years 1959–1961, when famine spread across China. Largely a consequence of the policies of the Great Leap Forward, the famine claimed the lives of between 14 million and 26 million Chinese, while reducing the expected number of births (63 million to 85 million over the three-year period) by approximately one-third. Nevertheless, the famine imposed only a temporary constraint upon China's population growth. By 1970, the population had risen to 830 million and was expanding at a rate of 2.8% annually. This growth rate, if maintained, would have doubled the population in 25 years. Concern over the implications of these figures for development aspirations seems to have impelled leaders at that time to include growth reduction targets in the Five-Year Plan.

The uneven nature of China's population growth also has posed serious challenges to

China's leaders. Although the 1950s "baby boom" was terminated by the famine, a second emerged after 1963 to create another set of pressures on schools, health care services, and—in due course—on the employment sector. Moreover, fulfilling the needs of different birth cohorts was made more complex by differences in the sizes of each successive baby boom; worse still was the "echo effect": larger baby boom cohorts would in turn produce larger cohorts of babies, so that population instability was liable to continue well into the future.

In the 1970s, the dynamics of collective planning, including allocation of the collective's resources, began to change. Formerly, collective units known as "brigades" coordinated the allocation of community funds for education, medical care, and other communal needs. Brigade members, acutely aware of the implications that childbearing had for the collective as a whole, often exerted pressure on other member families not to have a second or third child. Although these local efforts served to curtail population growth to a degree, they were not sufficiently widespread or comprehensive to stem the tide.

Exacerbating the problem was the Maoist leadership's inattentiveness to population indicators. After the "hundred flowers" campaign (a campaign whose casualties included Ma Yinchu, China's best-known demographer), the study of most social sciences, including population, was frowned upon by the government. Population statistics, although collected and collated, were seldom analyzed. Not until 1975 were the first demography departments established in universities, and the economists, statisticians, and other academics drafted to teach in these departments initially struggled to stay a step ahead of their students.

Once reestablished, demographers quickly recognized the magnitude of the problem. Owing to successive baby booms, approximately half of China's population was below the age of 21 by the early 1980s. Furthermore, these young people would be starting their own families throughout the rest of the century. Demographers calculated that, even if these young people had fewer children than their parents, China's population would continue to expand.

In addition, it seemed unlikely that the initial success in reducing China's birth rate from around 33.5 per 1,000 population in 1970 to approximately 19 per 1,000 by the end of the decade could be maintained. Efforts to disseminate family planning information and services and the provision of early abortion facilities by the late 1970s presumably had eliminated much unwanted fertility. However, third or subsequent children still comprised 30% of all births; thus, it was clear that parents—especially among peasant farmers—continued to want comparatively large families. Their rationale was understandable: daughters traditionally left their natal homes and families upon marriage; sons alone could carry on the family lineage and provide a guarantee of support for their elderly or infirm parents. Moreover, recognizing that rural mortality rates among children were high, few peasants were prepared to stake their future on a single son.

Even if it had been possible to persuade rural families to stop producing after two children, China's immense population of young people implied that it would be many years before the total population stabilized. In order to reach the target population growth rate of zero by the year 2000, more drastic steps were required. Thus, in 1978, China's leadership initiated the policy of one child per family. Government officials did not intend the policy to be strictly and universally implemented. Rather, the idea was to increase, through various incentive programs, the proportion of couples agreeing to have only a single child. The one-child family policy was, therefore, less a new policy than an incentive-based strategy for achieving the existing government objective of zero population growth.

In 1980, a group of scientists built the first Chinese population models, incorporating data on economic development, food and water supplies, and ecological balance. They concluded from their projections that China would need to reduce its population from 1 billion to 650–700 million over the next 100 years in order to meets its modernization goals. This measure, the scientists suggested, might be achieved by enforcing universal single-child families until the year 2000 and gradually relaxing the policy thereafter. Owing to the potential effects of this policy on the population age-structure as well as the magnitude of the undertaking, these proposals soon were discredited.

As a consequence of this heightened attention to population matters, the idea that one or two generations would have to make sacrifices for the future of their children and of China was further established. The notion of sacrifice introduced a tense question into population policymaking: how far could the government go in asking for compliance? Initially, lawmakers sought to codify the one-child strategy in a national law. The government, encouraged by the success of one-child trial campaigns in several provinces, introduced a draft law as early as 1979, but this failed to receive support. Subsequent efforts to introduce national legislation on family size also have failed to gain approval among the public and the National People's Congress (although the duty of couples to practice family planning was incorporated into the 1982 Constitution).

In place of a national law, several provinces developed their own regulations setting out various incentives for single-child families, disincentives for larger families, and conditions under which such disincentives would be waived. Although specific packages varied from province to province depending upon local circumstances, most contained similar ingredients: incentives frequently included promises of priority access to health care services and schooling, small monthly cash payments, old-age pension insurance, or (for farmers) an additional allocation of land.

In practice, however, these incentive schemes were of doubtful value. Promises of priority access to services may have been valid where single-child families accounted for a minority of the population (for example, in rural areas) but clearly were of little value in some cities where 70% or more of couples had only one child. Meanwhile,

cash payments and pensions offered under provincial regulations applied only to government officials or to workers in the rapidly declining state sector.

Unable to provide incentives for the self-employed, the unemployed, and farmers, provincial authorities recommended that village and township authorities offer inducements to their constituents. Not surprisingly, then, these inducements were determined at the local level in the context of local conditions; thus, the poorer the village or township, the less it was able to promise. Nor have local authorities always delivered on their promises. During the mid-1990s, Chinese couples often complained to those investigating the family planning program that they had not received the incentives to which they were entitled.

Disincentives for those couples with more than the allowed number of children also are included in provincial regulations. Arguing that large families burden the communities in which they live, some localities assess a "social obligation fee" or fine on those couples who choose to have additional children. In addition, government officials and workers in the state sector may be refused promotion for a specified time, while those in rural areas may be forbidden to change their status (e.g., to become recognized city-dwellers) for an extended period of time.

Both penalty implementation and its impact vary. The social obligation fee differs from place to place, and frequently is not collected when the couple involved is very poor. Wealthier farmers reason that the fee is a small price to pay for the benefit of having a large family. To combat this line of reasoning, some officials argue that the social stigma should be as much a deterrent as the amount of the fine. However, this argument is based upon the overall level of compliance (or noncompliance) that the policy elicits from the local community; in many instances, the social stigma is negligible.

In any case, it is apparent that the impact of both incentives and disincentives on family size has been limited. By 1994, reports estimated that one in five women of child-bearing age had volunteered to have only one child. Most of these women lived in the cities, where the overall fertility rate in 1990 (that is, the average number of children a woman would have in her lifetime if current rates continued) was 1.26. In the country-side where some three-quarters of all Chinese live, the overall fertility rate was 2.8—remarkably low for a rural sector that remains poor and unevenly developed. Nevertheless, this rate is well above replacement level and reveals that the one-child strategy has not been effectively implemented throughout China.

The impact of incentives and penalties on couples employed in the private sector remains unclear. Many of these workers earn above-average wages and thus are able to pay monetary penalties without much difficulty. The Guangdong provincial regulations (revised in 1992), for example, do not mention private sector workers. Moreover, many private sector workers belong to the "floating population," a term used by the Chinese to describe the migrant labor force that emerged with the economic reforms of the 1980s. This growing rural labor surplus resulted from the increases in rural population, the introduction of family contracts in agriculture, and increased rural mechanization. As restrictions on individual movement were lifted or became difficult to enforce, more and more of these workers drifted into the eastern—particularly south-eastern—cities where rapid economic expansion offered employment opportunities. Currently, at least 100 million people, heavily concentrated in the peak childbearing age, are estimated to have joined the floating population. Owing to the immense size of this labor group and to the short-term nature of the work it performs, enforcement of temporary registration regulations is almost impossible; thus, these laborers often are able to avoid penalties.

Additionally, members of the floating population are given no inducements—such as grain rations, which used to be allotted to all recognized permanent city residents—to register. The growth of urban shantytowns as well as a private housing market for those migrants who do well has eliminated the major barrier preventing earlier generations from migrating to cities and towns. Meanwhile, there are many advantages to remaining anonymous, including the potential for tax evasion as well as for escaping other government restrictions.

Population Data and Their Limitations

The increasing ease with which migrant workers have avoided registration has not only created problems in implementing population policy; it has made it difficult for government planners to gauge the extent of population-related problems. Until the 1980s, reporting of births, marriages, and deaths in China was remarkably comprehensive. Local officials were effective at compiling family planning statistics, and reporting was generally reliable. Since then, however, pressures on local officials to meet family planning targets have resulted in much false reporting, while economic reforms have given many Chinese the means to avoid the registration system. Moreover, owing to the government's confidence in the reliability of population data (based on past experience), much time elapsed before officials realized how badly the system had deteriorated.

Hence, from the early 1990s, Chinese demographers have been reviewing both routine statistics and the results of sample surveys and censuses to determine the extent of underreporting. One study found that national family planning statistics between 1982 and 1989 had underreported births by 31.4%; another study estimated the percentage of underreported births in 1991–92 at between 25% and 28% (Zeng Yi, "Is Fertility in China in 1991–92 Far Below Replacement Level?" in *Population Studies* 50 [1996]: 27–34). From these analyses it appears that in the first half of the 1990s Chinese fertility hovered around replacement level, far above what would have resulted from widespread compliance with the one-child policy. In early 1995 China's population reached 1.2 billion, a figure that Chinese officials had hoped not to surpass until the year 2000.

Data unreliability also has added to the much-publicized controversy over "missing females." Across the world, approximately 103–106 males are born for every 100 females. However, some Asian countries, including South Korea and India, show markedly higher sex ratios, especially since the 1970s. After 1980, the reported Chinese ratio at birth rose steadily, reaching 113.8 in 1989. The causes of this imbalance are still not entirely clear, but perhaps the most exhaustive study (Zeng Yi et al, "Causes and Implications of the Increase in China's Reported Sex Ratio at Birth," in *Population and Development Review* 19, no. 2 [1993]: 283–302) concludes that underreporting accounts for between 43% and 75% of the missing females. This underreporting is significant because unregistered female children may receive lesser-quality childcare, medical care, and education. Sex-selective abortion most likely accounts for most of the remainder of missing females (prenatal sex determination–except for medical reasons–is illegal in China, but remains widespread).

Policies and Programs in the 1990s

In 1993, Mme Peng Peiyun, Minister of the State Family Planning Commission, announced a renewed commitment to three key guidelines of the family planning program, which had been developed a decade earlier. These guidelines stressed:

- use of publicity and education as strategic tools rather than coercion
- promotion of contraception over abortion
- constant availability of services rather than irregular intensive campaigns

Although coercion is forbidden in the official program, officials under pressure to meet their targets have not always abided by the rules. Peng Peiyun's solution to this problem was to offer a supervisory role to the China Family Planning Association

(CFPA). Founded in 1980, CFPA was one of the first nongovernmental organizations (NGOs) to be established as part of the "opening up" of China. Its initial roles included recruiting and organizing volunteers to support the government family planning program and working with other NGOs internationally. In 1995 the CFPA's monitoring and supervisory function was formalized in a set of regulations. Mme Peng contributed a firmly stated preface to these regulations to ensure that the CFPA's role was accepted at all levels of the Family Planning Commission. Family Planning Associations at every level of administration currently are being trained to assess public opinion systematically (through surveys and other techniques) and to report abuses of policy implementation.

In addition, the FPAs mobilized their vast numbers of volunteers (totaling 80 million across the country) to instruct rural women on reproductive health. Declines in the numbers of "barefoot doctors" and the increased costs of medicine and medical care had left many rural families with little access to health services. The retired doctors in the FPAs offered annual and biannual health examinations and immunizations for rural women and children and made referrals where necessary. They also explained and promoted the use of various contraceptives.

Although coercion played a role in many late-term abortions, most abortions in the 1980s were the result of the poor quality and limited selection of contraceptives. In many rural areas, the steel ring interuterine device, which had a high failure rate, was the sole alternative to sterilization. With support from the United Nations Population Fund and other international organizations, China in the 1980s began to produce copper-T IUDs; by 1994 steel rings no longer were manufactured. Factories were set up to produce better quality condoms, and while a basic range of contraceptives continued to be available free of charge, a more comprehensive selection of brands became available in cities and in an increasing number of towns.

Further policy developments of the 1990s

were summed up in a campaign called "three integrations." These called for the integration of family planning with:

• economic development
• the current emphasis on working hard to become wealthy
• the development of "happy and civilized" families

This integrated approach had a dual function. Proponents of the campaign believed that, on the one hand, economic development would lead to couples wanting smaller families, as would rising consumption. On the other hand, proponents believed that family planning workers would achieve greater credibility with rural Chinese by demonstrating concern for their general welfare. Toward this end, FPA volunteers were encouraged to promote a variety of income-generating schemes primarily aimed at women.

Although the Chinese government since 1949 has emphasized policies and programs to increase the status of women, the impact of these policies and programs has been limited. Fundamental cultural attitudes—which are not unique to China—remain deeply entrenched, and are reinforced by practical concerns such as the need to have sons for old-age security. Moreover, other economic reform policies have had some unintended negative consequences for women. For example, the introduction of educational fees (formerly, primary education had been free) decreases the likelihood of a young girl receiving even secondary education. Other consequences are more ambiguous; for example, women are increasingly left to run the farm while men from their families and communities work elsewhere.

Thus, the FPAs identified experts in various branches of farming, fisheries, and forestry to assist local farm women in improving their skills and in marketing their products. FPAs also made available small loans for seeds or other investments. FPA members offered classes during the off-seasons to develop literacy and other talents, whether for song and dance or

embroidery and weaving. Rural Chinese now recognize the benefits of improved technological inputs and education. Village women seek, where possible, more education for themselves, but are even more enthusiastic about educating their children. They frequently earmark income from handicrafts or other off-farm activities for their daughters' schooling. Chinese officials and foreign observers alike consider this recognition on the part of rural Chinese to be an important factor in changing their attitudes concerning the family (Susan Greenhalgh et al, "Restraining Population Growth in Three Chinese Villages," in *Population and Development Review* 20, no. 2 [June 1994]).

In support of these efforts to alter rural ideas about family building, state insurance companies, various banks, and the Chinese government have assisted in developing local pension schemes in rural areas. These pensions may include insurance against a child's ill-health as well as measures to ensure old-age security. The latter do not always require cash savings: a "green bank" alternative encourages villages to invest in communal planting of trees whose produce will provide funds for the aged in future years.

Prospects for the 21st Century

Examining the data from the 1988 Two Per Thousand Fertility Survey, Wang Fang and Yang Quanhe ("Changes in Sexual Behavior among Chinese Couples," in *Population and Development Review* 22, no. 2 [1996]: 299–320) found that intervals between marriage and first birth have been reduced over time; the mean length of the first birth interval declined from 34 months in the 1950s to less than 18 months in the early 1980s. While this reduction is partially owing to a rise in the average age at marriage, it also reflects changes in sexual behavior. The authors calculated that at least five out of every 100 pregnancies were conceived before marriage, compared with fewer than two in the 1950s. Moreover, in Shanghai the proportion of induced abortions among single women increased from 14% in 1982 to 25% in 1988. Increases in premarital sexual activity probably are owing to the decline in arranged marriages; in addition, greater opportunities exist for young people to meet each other as more women participate in the workforce outside their homes. As members of the floating population, young men and women may work many hundreds of miles from their places of origin, where they are no longer subject to traditional community constraints.

It remains to be seen whether the increasing frequency of premarital sexual activity leads to an increased use of premarital contraception and—as has happened in many Western countries—to eventual increases in the average age at first marriage. Under the marriage law, women are not to marry below age 20 and men below age 22; however, earlier marriages can still be found, especially in poor rural areas. Throughout the 1980s the typical age of first marriage for women was between ages 20 and 23 (Zeng Yi et al, "Marriage and Fertility in China 1950–89," in *Genus* 2, no. 3–4 [1993]).

Extramarital sex and prostitution also have increased in recent years, accompanied by an increased incidence of sexually transmitted diseases (STDs) and HIV/AIDS (the latter also is linked to a rise in drug use, especially in the southwest). The relaxing of "traditional values" and a lack of experience with STDs have contributed to delays in recognizing the dangers of potential STD epidemics, especially among the floating population. This rural surplus labor is expected to double by the end of the century, further exacerbating the problem.

Another challenge to policymakers will be the increased number and proportion of the elderly in the population as the baby boom generations of the 1950s and 1960s mature. Life expectancy in 1990 averaged 66.8 years for Chinese men and 70.5 years for women. Although declines in the proportion of the younger population indicate a reduction in the overall dependency burden, the particular needs of the aged call for considerable investment.

In the case of health care, for example, the diseases of old age—cancers, strokes, and heart attacks—cost considerably more to treat than the largely communicable diseases of childhood; treating them also necessitates major changes in the types of health services that are provided. Government attempts to eliminate the "iron rice bowl" of lifelong employment and social security in the state sector were owing in part to the anticipated size of the elderly population. One study (Lin Jiang, "Changing Kinship Structure and Its Implications for Old-Age Support in Rural and Urban Areas," in *Population Studies* 49 [1995]: 127–46) suggests that the combination of declining family size and increasing life expectancy implies that the burden of supporting the elderly will quadruple in urban areas and more than double in rural areas over the next 40 years, and that families alone will not be able to meet the needs of the elderly. It remains to be seen whether the growth of the private sector and of pension schemes are sufficient to prevent the aged from becoming China's new poor.

It has taken China longer to reach replacement fertility than originally was hoped, and the age-structure of the population suggests that the population will continue to grow for several decades; in recent years, the net annual increase has averaged approximately 14 million people. However, a higher standard of living together with increased efforts on the part of family planners have spurred a fundamental change in Chinese attitudes about family size. Even in the countryside small families of two or three children are not merely the outcome of government policy, but are viewed by rural dwellers as advantageous in their own right.

Increasingly, Chinese demographers have called for a cautious relaxation of the one-child policy and a move toward a "two-child plus spacing" policy promoting late marriage, a delay in first birth and appropriate spacing between first and second births, and rewards for those who choose to have only one child. Even if the one-child policy is not officially dropped, experiments with innovative policies like the "two-child plus spacing" policy are likely to become increasingly widespread.

Further Reading

Banister, Judith, *China's Changing Population,* Stanford, California: Stanford University Press, 1987

The fullest overview of population changes in health and mortality, and population distribution from 1849 to the 1980s. This is a scrupulous statistical study, marred by exaggerated attacks on the Chinese population policy.

Croll, Elisabeth V., *The Politics of Marriage in Contemporary China,* Cambridge and New York: Cambridge University Press, 1981

Croll's identification of various gradations of marriage types ranging from arranged to free choice remains helpful, as does the portrayal of attitudes concerning marriage, family, and family formation.

Croll, Elisabeth V., Delia Davin, and Penny Kane, editors, *China's One-Child Family Policy,* London: Macmillan, 1985

This collection of essays remains the sole book to consider the potential implications of the one-child policy. Economic reforms and other changes have overtaken some of the discussion but the sociological data remains useful.

Kane, Penny, *The Second Billion: Population and Family Planning in China,* Ringwood, Victoria, and New York: Penguin, 1987

Sets the Chinese fertility transition in the context of social and political change and in changes in China's perception of its place in the world. Limited demographic data.

Peng Xizhe, *Demographic Transition in China: Fertility Trends Since the 1950s,* Oxford: Clarendon Press, and New York: Oxford University Press, 1991

The most authoritative account of fertility change in China, this book covers population policy, trends in childbearing and marriage, and determinants of China's fertility transition over three decades. It looks in detail at each province and examines the large variations in behavior among them.

Wang Jiye, and Terence H. Hull, editors, *Population and Development Planning in China,* Sydney: Allen and Unwin, 1991

A collaborative project between the Chinese State Planning Commission, UN Population Fund, and the Australian National University, the contributions are uneven in quality, and many of the specific points have been dated by economic and social developments. The Chinese contributions provide insight into the PRC planning process.

Penny Kane is Senior Associate at the Key Centre for Women's Health in Society, University of Melbourne, Australia. She is the author of *The Second Billion: People and Population in China* (1987) and *Famine in China 1959–61: Demographic and Social Implications* (1988); she is also coeditor, with Delia Davin and Elisabeth Croll, of *China's One-Child Family Policy* (1985).

Chapter Eighteen

Chinese Labor in the Reform Era: Changing Fragmentation and New Politics

Ching Kwan Lee

That the Chinese socialist state, like social-ist states elsewhere, proclaims itself a "work-ers' state" and a dictatorship of the proletariat speaks volumes about labor's role in post-1949 Chinese society and poli-tics. Seminal works by China scholars con-sistently show that such statements cannot easily be dismissed as mere ideological rhet-oric. Political scientist Elizabeth Perry, for instance, argues that labor politics shaped the course of the Chinese revolution and communist state formation. The legacy of labor politics also found its way into succes-sive political upheavals even after 1949, including the Cultural Revolution and the 1989 Tiananmen protests. Likewise, sociolo-gist Andrew Walder (1986) writes that studying the working class provides "a win-dow on political relationships" that are char-acteristic of communism.

Given labor's pivotal role both as an agent of change and pillar of support for the socialist regime, the pathway and outcome of socialist reforms must be understood in the context of the changing fortunes and politics of Chinese labor. This chapter pro-vides an overview of the Chinese labor con-ditions in the reform years and examines how a set of state-initiated labor policies, in combination with market forces, led to a recomposition of the working class and trig-gered diverse forms of labor politics.

1 Workers, Work Units, and the State

The Chinese working class always has com-prised a fragmented social group. In the first decade after the Communist Revolution in China (1949–59), the Chinese socialist state pursued such a rapid process of industrial-ization that it "literally created, almost from scratch, a new tradition of labor relations" (Walder, 1986: 34). A hierarchy of industrial labor was formed with four major categories of workers, each of which had its own "pub-licly defined rights to income, job tenure, social security, labor insurance, housing and ... a distinctive style of life" (40). At the bot-tom of this hierarchy were rural workers in collective town and village enterprises oper-ated by brigades, communes, and towns. Employment in these small rural enterprises was often temporary or seasonal and gener-ated little cash income. These workers usu-ally worked in agriculture for at least part of the year, especially during peak harvest sea-sons. A second group in the hierarchy com-prised temporary workers (both urban and rural residents) in urban enterprises. The employment conditions experienced by these temporary laborers varied greatly because these jobs largely lay outside of state regulation and planning; thus, job ten-ure was not guaranteed and workers were not entitled to full state insurance and benefits. A third group of laborers worked in urban collective enterprises operated by towns, counties, and cities. Over the decades, as collective enterprises developed from independent accounting units that functioned outside the state budget into permanent, subsidized appendages of state enterprises, their workers' employment was relatively stable, well-paid, and offered more benefits than the two aforementioned groups. However, the fourth group, the permanent workers of state enterprises, comprised the aristocracy of the working class. They were the most numerous (totaling 32 million, or 42% of industrial workers in 1981) and the highest paid among the labor force. In 1981, their average wage was 40% higher than that of urban collective workers and twice as much as the other two groups. Enjoying virtual lifetime tenure, state workers also were provided with subsidized meals, housing, medical care, and benefits for their dependents. None of these benefits was available to the other groups of workers.

While research on non-state workers has been relatively scarce, urban workers in state enterprises form the focus of Walder's 1986 study on industrial authority in China. Walder demonstrates how the Chinese state established effective control over the working class through state work units (*danwei*) that monopolized the distribution of scarce consumer resources. The Communist Party maintained ties both with management and with a minority of activist workers who exchanged political loyalties for preferential access to resources and careers. Under the *danwei* system, the working class was divided vertically between party activists and non-activists, while individual workers were compelled to develop informal ties with factory cadres in order to gain access to scarce goods and services. This multifaceted web of dependence, carefully cultivated by the state, represented a paternalistic approach to power, one that mixed "firm and consistent demands for obedience and an emphasis on loyalty . . . with elaborate displays of concern for workers' material

life" (239). This approach resulted in "a stable pattern of tacit acceptance and active cooperation for the regime that no amount of political terror, coercion, or indoctrination [could] even begin to provide" (249). Even as workers' dependence on their enterprises diminished during the first stage of reform in the mid-1980s, Walder maintains the trend was still toward paternalism as a control strategy. Although critics have pointed to Walder's false homogenization across employment sectors, historical periods, and communist regimes, his study provides a benchmark for broaching the changes brought about by reforms.

2 Reforms From Above: From Entitlement to Contract

Since the mid-1980s, the Chinese government has implemented a panoply of labor reforms in state-run factories in an effort to boost these enterprises' efficiency and market adaptability. These reforms have transformed the employment relationship between workers and their enterprises so that workers are no longer guaranteed lifetime employment, and managers enjoy greater flexibility with which to pursue efficient production. Meanwhile, most state workers find themselves in a double jeopardy: their enterprises are retreating from socialist welfarism while simultaneously engaging market disciplines that threaten worker livelihood. Several state policies have been most consequential to labor reforms, including the labor contract system, wage reform, and social security reform. Because the government intends to universalize these policies across enterprises of all ownership types, these policies also set the institutional framework for non-state workers in the years to come.

2.1 Labor Contract System

In the past, state workers not only enjoyed lifelong tenure but could also, upon their retirement, pass on as property privileged employment status to their children. This job inheritance practice (*dingti*) combined with guaranteed job tenure has constrained the power of managers to discipline workers on the grounds of performance or dismiss workers in the interest of production efficiency. To alleviate these constraints the Chinese government promulgated the Temporary Regulations on the Use of Labor Contracts in State-Run Enterprises in 1986 (the state had experimented with these reform measures in Shanghai and in Special Economic Zones in the early 1980s). Owing to workers' opposition, the labor contract system initially exempted incumbent permanent workers, applying only to new recruits; however, state efforts at universalizing the system to incorporate incumbent workers persist. The total number of workers under the new contract system rose from 160,000 in 1982 to more than 10 million by the end of 1988. By 1993, 55 million workers, or 31% of all workers in all types of enterprises had signed contracts with their employing enterprise. The length of contract varies across localities and enterprises, ranging from one to eight years, and renewal is based on mutual consent.

A related reform is the "labor reoptimization" policy, first launched on a trial basis during the late 1980s. According to this policy, managers can dismiss a national total of 20 million surplus workers, or 10% to 15% of workers in large and medium enterprises throughout China. As a result, in 1989, 423,000 permanent and contract state workers (0.5% of the total) were laid off, quit, or did not have their contracts renewed. As the number of unemployed workers climbed toward a new high of 10 million (or 2.9% of urban state workers) in 1996, the central government emphasized the need to keep unemployment at a 3% level, and admonished local governments and enterprises to prevent strikes and public protests by the unemployed.

As a variant of the labor reoptimization policy, enterprises may declare some workers "off-duty" (*xiagang*). These workers are paid reduced wages or just the minimum level of living allowance prescribed by the local government. Significantly, union surveys reveal that nationwide some 60% of all unemployed and "off-duty" workers are women, despite the fact that women comprise only 37% of employees in state-owned industrial enterprises. These unemployed persons now constitute a new group of urban poor—the impoverished workers.

2.2 Wage Reform

Prior to the 1980s, China's wage policy sought to control inflation, spur economic growth, and lessen income differentials among social groups; the use of wages to control workers' effort was given less priority. Instead, wage policy relied on moral and political incentives to assure worker productivity. Since the early 1980s, however, the government has promoted the principle of "pay according to work" (*an lao fenpei*), using wages to spur higher productivity among workers. In 1986 the government initiated wage reforms by abandoning the central wage fixing system, known as the "eight-grade occupation wage system" (a system wherein the state determined the quota for promotion and periodic pay rises). The aim was to strengthen the link between performance and income. Enterprises now are able to determine wage distribution as long as they conform to limits on the total wage bills (which are linked to profitability). Workers' wage packets now are comprised of basic wages, seniority and task-specific supplements, incentives, and bonuses. Data show that, as a component of total wages, bonuses grew from 9.1% in 1980 to 17.6% in 1989. Piece-rate wages (wages calculated on a worker's total output), which accounted for 3.2% of total wages in 1980, rose to 9.2%, while time-rate wages (basic wages plus responsibility wages that are based on the technical and skill level of a worker's position) declined from 85% to only 47.4% over the same period.

These changes have brought in tow new and pronounced inequality across regions and enterprises, as well as among co-workers. In order to maintain social stability and equality, a minimum wage policy was included as part of the 1995 Labor Law.

According to this policy, minimum wage levels are fixed by provincial governments and apply to all workers and enterprises of all ownership types. Guangdong province boasted the highest minimum wage level in 1995 (320 *yuan* in some localities). Other minimum wage levels ranged from 125 *yuan* in poorer provinces to 210 *yuan* in Beijing and Tianjin and 220 *yuan* in Shanghai.

2.3 Social Security Reform

To establish a "modern" enterprise system, central officials have taken steps to relieve enterprises of their social welfare functions. Under the pre-reform system, as Walder explains, the state enterprise had functioned as "the central point of distribution for housing" and would "ration coupons for major consumer durables, and daily necessities (such as cloth and coal); subsidized food and staple goods; and the delivery of major social services and medical care." State enterprises also provided state labor insurance as well as other services and subsidies, and would even make loans (Walder, 60). These compensations amounted to some 82% of the state worker's average wage in 1978. Furthermore, social services under the pre-reform system overwhelmingly favored urban residents, especially the proletariat in the state sector. In the 1980s reformers sought to dismantle this system by fundamentally altering the long-standing dependence of state workers on their enterprises.

Toward this end, the State Council in 1991 formalized its Decision on the Reform of the Old-Age Pension System for Enterprise Employees, a document based on the 1986 provisional measures applied to contract workers in state enterprises. This reform aims to replace the enterprise insurance system with a social insurance system, thus shifting the burden of social security from the state and the enterprises to the workers. The government has approached this task with some urgency, reiterating that the state lacks the capacity to bear the increasing load of retirement benefits (China's retirees totaled 27.5 million in 1993, while the ratio of retirees to working staff in many old enterprises reached 1:1.5 and even 1:1). Meanwhile, this heavy burden has crippled many state enterprises as they seek to compete in an increasingly marketized economy.

Under the new system, which will be universalized across all types of enterprises, work units contribute a certain percentage of their total wage bill to provincial or county pension and insurance funds under the unified management of local labor insurance departments; and workers pay premiums equivalent to 2% to 3% of their salaries. Retirees draw their pensions from banks or social insurance institutions rather than from work units. State sources claimed that 49% of urban employees were participating in the new system by the end of 1993, and that retirees in 1,406 cities and counties nationwide drew their pensions from social security institutions. In many areas enterprises also contribute 0.6% of their total wage bill to unemployment funds, which pay for relief allowances and re-employment training fees for redundant and "waiting-for-employment" workers. By the end of 1994, the unemployment insurance program covered 95 million employees. Meanwhile, reformers gradually are introducing socialized management of insurance funds in the areas of medical care, industrial injury, and child-rearing.

In short, these labor reform policies reflect attempts on the part of reformers to break with China's socialist model of employment. These reforms targeted state enterprises in their initial stages; gradually, however, they have been applied to all enterprises, albeit with varying degrees of success. In the long run, these state-initiated reforms likely will result in a homogenized institutional environment wherein employment relations are based on terms of contract rather than on life-long job tenure endowed by the state. Currently, however, the uneven enforcement of labor reforms, combined with the increased role of the market in China's economy, has crafted new segmentation within the working class.

3 Recomposition and New Segmentation of the Chinese Working Class

Not only have economic reforms in general and labor reforms in particular redefined the employment relationship between workers and their enterprises, they also have brought about new groups of workers: employees of privately-owned and foreign-invested (*sanzi*) enterprises. Table 18.1 indicates the distribution of workers among enterprises of different ownership types. The following discussion further explains the internal diversity among and within major groups of Chinese labor.

3.1 Workers in State Enterprises

Although 33 million workers or 61% of industrial labor still belong to the state sector, state workers are no longer considered the aristocracy of Chinese labor. Labor reforms have removed most exclusive privileges of employment in the state sector, including high income, life-long tenure, and free and full medical, pension, and labor insurance coverage. Surveys administered in the 1990s by the All-China Federation of Trade Unions consistently have found that state workers' average wage levels lag behind those in foreign-invested and urban and rural collectives. For instance, in 1991 state workers earned an average yearly income of 2,935 *yuan*, while those in the foreign-owned sector and the collective sector earned 5,624 *yuan* and 3,477 *yuan*, respectively. In terms of welfare provision, many state employees are required to contribute to different insurance funds out of their own wage packets. Additionally, many state enterprises have commodified their enterprise welfare services, charging their employees for child care, meals, housing, and clinic services at close to market rates.

In theory, labor contract reform has allowed state workers to leave their enterprises for better employment at the end of a contract term. In practice, however, only the younger workers in their mid-20s and early 30s secure high-paying jobs in foreign enterprises, while veteran workers in their 40s and 50s are forced to moonlight as street vendors, cab drivers, and part-time repairmen to supplement their shrinking paychecks. By 1989, observers estimated that, in regions where the market economy and private sectors were more developed (Guangdong province, for example), some 30% of state enterprise workers had second jobs. A 1991 survey of a large state enterprise in Guangzhou city found that 89.6% of the 1,923 workers interviewed had second jobs; 94.1% of these moonlighters reported that their second income amounted to 30% to 40% of their regular wage.

Meanwhile, wage reform (which affords managers new leverage to extract more effort from workers) and the new emphasis on state enterprise efficiency has intensified the labor process inside state enterprises to an unprecedented degree. A study of three textile mills revealed that "scientific management" consisted of accelerating the production line, raising production quotas, lengthening work hours even on national holidays, and imposing harsher monetary penalties for absenteeism and faulty work.

However, state workers do not form a homogeneous group. Even during the pre-reform period, workers' labor conditions depended upon the size and budgetary rank of their enterprises. Currently, larger firms and those occupying higher ranks in the state's fiscal hierarchy still are better able to retain their profits owing to greater state dependence on these enterprises for tax revenues. In turn, these enterprises are able to provide more benefits for their workers.

Another variable accounting for inequalities among workers of different state enterprises has been the introduction of market competition. Researchers have found that the average wage of workers in large and medium profit-making enterprises and those in strategic or monopolistic sectors (such as infrastructure and public utilities) is three times higher than the average wage of state workers on the whole. Yet many state workers find themselves in dire poverty as the proportion of loss-making state enterprises continues to expand (currently, more than 40% of all state enterprises belong in this category). A 1992–93 survey compiled by the All-China Federation of Trade Unions classified more than 7 million state workers as "poor"; these workers' average monthly income was only 62.2 *yuan*. In 1994, a survey of 13 provinces concluded that approximately 10% of workers in five of the provinces suffered dire economic circumstances while 5% to 10% of workers in six other provinces suffered similar difficulties. State workers have become the most disgruntled segment of the working class under reform, and their deep-seated discontent has found expression in protests and strikes.

3.2 Workers in Foreign-Invested and Joint Venture Enterprises

The so-called "three types of investment enterprises" (*sanzi qiye*) refer to Sino-foreign joint investments, Sino-foreign cooperative projects, and wholly-owned foreign investments. In 1993, 21,200 foreign-invested industrial enterprises employed more than 3.5 million workers (or about 4% of industrial labor). Workers in foreign-invested industrial enterprises earned an average income of 6,096 *yuan* in 1993, or 130% that of state enterprise workers in the same locality. The majority of these workers served one- to five-year contracts.

Urban high school graduates, former employees of state and collective enterprises, and migrant workers from rural areas constitute the majority of workers in foreign firms. As a group, these workers are younger and higher-paid, but also are subjected to intensified labor conditions and despotic management. Because foreign enterprises are allowed a high degree of autonomy in labor management, workers' conditions in these firms manifest more local variations than those of state workers. Data on Guangdong province, where 60% of China's foreign-invested enterprises are located, provide a glimpse into this sector. Both the Chinese press and academic researchers have reported the "pitiful" conditions to which workers in these enterprises

are subjected. For instance, Beijing's *Fazhi ribao* (*Legal Daily*) reported that working hours in these enterprises totaled 9.3 hours per day on average, while some work days lasted 12–24 hours. Some enterprises required employees to work on Sundays and allowed workers only two days off every month. In another report, a labor bureau official claimed that many workers in the foreign enterprise sector are forced to work overtime shifts and are not always paid on time; some even encounter physical abuse like beating, body-searches, and sexual harassment, or are compelled to pay heavy monetary penalties. In particular, South Korean and Taiwanese enterprises have gained notoriety for their military style of factory management. Workers in foreign-invested enterprises that are better monitored by the local labor bureau may not experience physical attacks or sexual harassment; nonetheless, they usually are subject to conditions not found in typical state enterprises.

3.3 Workers in Rural and Urban Collectives

About 7.4 million industrial township and village enterprises (TVEs) employed 28.6 million workers and accounted for 26.6% of China's GNP in 1991 (the sector registered an average growth rate of 25.3% from 1979–91). TVEs widely are hailed as the driving force behind Chinese economic reforms, and researchers have suggested that knowledge of the TVEs' institutional dynamics is key to understanding the success of China's reform program.

Workers in TVEs, or "peasant workers," retain their official residential registration (*hukou*) as peasants but return to the field in the busy harvest seasons or after completing their factory shifts. In some communities, TVE employees account for some 80% of the local surplus agricultural labor. Wages vary greatly across regions and within enterprises, depending on local labor market conditions and the degree of communal government intervention. One study found that some 65% to 75% of workers' wages derives from piece rate wages, while bonuses and other supplementary wages comprise the remaining income. Wages also vary according to a worker's place of residence. TVE workers who reside outside an enterprise's locality often are docked 20% to 30% of their wages as deposits and are repaid only at the end of their contracted term of employment; thus, these migrant workers effectively are held hostage by their employers.

Workers in urban collectives form the lowest earning group among Chinese workers. Historically, urban collectives were small street workshops run by neighborhood cooperatives that produced low-priced household goods. Since the early 1980s, urban collectives and their workers have encountered economic hardship as a result of competition from private and foreign-invested enterprises, and employment in this sector is now considered the least desirable of all types of employment. It should be noted, however, that many urban collectives are actually newly-emerged private enterprises that wish to access the preferential tax treatment given to collectives, and their workers are classified more aptly as private employees.

3.4 Workers in Private Enterprises

Currently, 125,000 private industrial enterprises employ 2.02 million workers nationwide, or 80% of all employees in all types of private enterprises. Geographically, two-thirds of these workers reside in the coastal cities, towns, and villages of southeastern China. The average private enterprise employs 14 persons, and workers are either recruited openly from the local labor market or through the kinship networks of private employers. Workers in this sector earn more than those in state and collective enterprises but less than workers in foreign-invested firms. However, similar to their counterparts in the collective and foreign enterprise sectors, these workers enjoy little labor insurance protection or welfare provisions. Only 57.7% of private entrepreneurs provide some kind of medical insurance for their employees, while 24.9% provide old-age pensions and 29.1% provide housing. Private employ-

ers enjoy wide discretion in stipulating contract terms to their advantages, and some even knowingly violate labor laws. Research suggests that up to two-thirds of private contracts do not specify the length of employment or the responsibilities of employers in case of industrial accidents.

According to a recent study, workers in a private knitting factory in Guangzhou are allowed only one day off each month, and often work from 7 A.M. to 9 P.M. when production demands require. These workers' monthly wage ranged from 400 *yuan* for less experienced workers to 800 *yuan* for veteran employees. The piece rate system employed by owners is designed to prevent workers from withholding labor: workers are informed of the piece rates they work for only at the end of the month when they receive their paychecks. Furthermore, workers do not receive medical insurance or pensions, although employers are keen to cover the medical costs of technical and supervisory level employees.

4 Labor Politics: Action and Consciousness

Two groups of workers have become the most volatile and politically active during the past decade: state enterprise workers and those employed in the foreign and private sectors. Toiling in different worlds of labor, they also engage in divergent politics owing to their different traditions and institutional surroundings. For veteran workers, or the generation of state-designated vanguard proletariat, the socialist state unilaterally has broken the long-standing political alliance between state workers and the state. A sense of state betrayal prevails among these workers, and many protest in defense of their past status and privilege. By contrast, the nascent proletariat, which includes mostly young migrants from the countryside, aim their protests at the capitalists–foreign or national–who exploit them.

4.1 The Veteran Vanguard

In recent years, both Chinese and foreign

presses have reported on the rising discontent among state workers. The most dramatic incident involved the massive worker turnout at the 1989 protests; numerous state workers took to the streets in Beijing and other big cities to decry double-digit inflation, rampant bureaucratic corruption, and social inequalities, and independent trade unions were among the protest organizers. Following the events at Tiananmen, state worker protests continued unabated into the first half of the 1990s. According to official union statistics, 1,620 incidents of arbitrated labor disputes involving some 37,450 workers were filed in 1990. Incidents of collective sit-ins (10 workers or more), slowdowns, strikes, protests, and filing of complaints increased 87% from 1990 to 1991, and a similar rate of increase in collective actions was registered between 1992 to 1993. In mid-1994, incidents of labor unrest were claimed to have occurred once or twice a week in the provinces of Hubei, Hunan, Heilongjiang, and Liaoning. Reports of laid-off workers physically assaulting their managers also circulated.

State workers' grievances have focused on issues of unemployment, workers' low standard of living, income inequalities, and welfare distribution among workers and cadres. While workers seek to improve their economic standing in China's increasingly market environment, their sense of injustice also harkens back to a moral economy peculiar to this segment of the Chinese working class. Some Chinese scholars point out that many state workers feel deprived of the "capital interest" they have invested in their own enterprises through many years of low-wage labor. This sentiment derives from the official ideology of the Maoist period, which proclaimed workers as the masters of their "publicly-owned" enterprises. For instance, researchers find that workers calculate their contribution to the capital accumulation of their enterprise. Workers oppose housing reform—which requires workers to purchase enterprise apartments rather than "rent" them free of charge—on the same grounds: as owners and investors in enterprise wealth (according to

Maoist ideology) workers should not be asked to pay for what is rightfully their own.

The plight of state workers is compounded by institutional changes within the state enterprise. Previously, the communist regime organized the state factory so that the party secretary stood at the apex of a tripartite power structure composed of the party branch, the factory management, and the enterprise union. However, since reformers initiated the factory director responsibility system in the mid-1980s, the factory director and managerial leadership have enjoyed far greater authority than either the party branch or the enterprise union, which have been relegated to consultative roles. The demise of the enterprise union has served to alienate workers from their designated union representatives; as a result, unions are no longer able to articulate workers' interests, and workers seek to voice their grievances outside the boundaries of their enterprises. Specifically, workers choose to air their complaints in public forums rather than before the local labor bureau, and their demands have targeted the state and its central leadership for failing to revitalize state enterprises. For example, workers at a Beijing state enterprise recently changed their demonstration slogan: rather than demanding rice and food they called on the government to pursue policies to improve the efficiency of state enterprises.

4.2 A New Generation of Workers

The immense migrant workforce laboring in foreign and private enterprises also engages in labor politics, although these workers confront different problems in a different institutional context. These young workers' experience of Chinese socialism has largely been confined to the countryside and peasantry, and thus their main concerns lie elsewhere: namely, in resisting foreign or capitalist exploitation.

Many reports suggest increased militancy among workers in foreign-owned enterprises. In Shanghai, arbitrated labor disputes involving foreign investors increased threefold between 1991 and 1995. During the first half of 1996, 80% of all labor disputes involved foreign firms. In Guangdong province, where the majority of China's foreign-invested enterprises are concentrated, reports of spontaneous strikes and slow-downs abound. In Shenzhen, labor disputes in foreign firms totaled 853 incidents in 1991, or 68.6% of the city's total. Moreover, instances of more serious labor conflicts are on the rise: while only 21 work stoppages occurred in Shenzhen in 1986–87, the number rose to 69 in 1989–90 and 255 in 1992. Most of these incidents were triggered by arbitrary deduction of wages, delay of wage payment, harsh disciplines, and other maltreatment of workers. Lasting only a few days, these events usually ended with employers dismissing troublesome employees or angry workers quitting their jobs for employment in other factories (for some details of these labor actions, see the publication of The Asia Monitor Resource Center, 1996). Finally, although no official data is available on labor disputes involving privately-owned enterprises, workers are widely reported to resist unwelcome labor conditions by destroying production equipment or imposing slow-downs in these small factories. However, discontented workers most often respond by securing alternative employment in other factories, which continue to mushroom in provinces like Guandgong and Fujian.

Weak unionism in the foreign-invested and private sectors partly accounts for the short-lived and sporadic nature of these workers' outbursts. Only about 10% of foreign enterprises and 8% of private enterprises have unions. Government and party authorities have resisted unions out of fear that organized labor would scare off investors. Although workers reportedly have organized their own independent unions in foreign-funded enterprises, the Chinese government has set about stalling these unofficial mobilizations.

Instead of unionism, China's new working class seems to have embraced an even older labor tradition in battling for a political space. Perry observes that "familiar cleavages within the working class continue to structure styles of protest on contemporary China. As in the pre-communist period, divisions along lines of native-place origin serve as powerful catalyst for labor militance." She cites press reports as evidence: "workers from the outside have formed 'regional gangs' which often create disturbances and could become a factor of social instability in the long run. For instance, 15 strikes took place in Longgang Town in Shenzhen, with eight of them instigated by Sichuan workers, three by Guangxi workers, two by workers from the south of the Chang Jiang, and two by Hunan workers." Another report notes that secret societies in Guizhou have gained a foothold in factories, where they "agitate workers to go slow or go on strike and make unreasonable demands on the government" (Elizabeth Perry, in Davis, 1995: 323–24).

The role of localistic networks in labor activism in the foreign and private sectors is linked to the key role played by localism in organizing the labor market of the migrant workforce and their production politics within the enterprise. Migrant workers are extremely dependent on localistic networks for survival in the urban labor market; they rely on these networks to find jobs and initial lodging, to obtain forged identity documents necessary to gain financial assistance, and for protection and promotion within the firm or job-change recommendations. Not surprisingly, strong localistic solidarities rooted in these mundane struggles for livelihood can be invoked in times of collective activism.

Concluding Remarks

Compared to peasants, cadres, and entrepreneurs, the Chinese working class as a group have become losers in the process of market socialist reform. This chapter has delineated the contours of reform policies that have fundamentally redefined the economic and political relations between the socialist state and Chinese labor, especially those in the state sector. Instead of the pre-reform neo-traditional regime wherein the state could demobilize the working class by granting them entitlement to a set of material and ideological privileges, Chinese labor in the reform era enters into contractual relations with the employing enterprises; discontent over workers' downward mobility has given rise to different forms of political activism.

Yet this does not mean that the working class has turned unambiguously from a pillar of support to an opposing force against the state. Surveys and in-depth studies have pointed toward labor's ambivalence and contradictory consciousness. Many respondents pledge their support for the leadership's market reforms, which have raised their living standards and created new economic opportunities. Yet, as we have seen, increasing numbers of workers confront dire poverty and extreme exploitation in both the state and the private and foreign sectors, and their protests no doubt articulate labor's collective critique of Chinese market socialism. The state, on the other hand, has taken these labor agitations seriously and has become cautious in the pace of reform lest it exceed workers' capacity to cope. Hence, the government has initiated the new labor law providing for minimum wages and unemployment allowances, more stringent monitoring of enterprise bankruptcy application, etc. The future of Chinese labor, therefore, will most poignantly be shaped by the dynamic between an internally fractured yet politically active working class and a Chinese socialist state still negotiating for a right mix of market and plan to provide a material base for its rule.

Further Reading

Bian, Yanjie, *Work and Inequality in Urban China*, Albany: State University of New York Press, 1994

Examines the impact of work organization on the social stratification of socialist workers in Chinese cities. Using survey data, personal interviews, and official statistics, the author explains how interpersonal connections, political virtue, status inheritance, and educational achievement influence a worker's polit-

ical and economic life chances.

Chan, Anita, and Robert A. Senser, "China's Troubled Workers," in *Foreign Affairs* 76, no. 2 (1997)

A recent look at the plight of China's workers.

Davis, Deborah S., Richard Kraus, Barry Naughton, and Elizabeth J. Perry, editors, *Urban Spaces in Contemporary China: The Potential for Autonomy and Community in Post-Mao China*, Washington, D.C.: Woodrow Wilson Center Press, and Cambridge: Cambridge University Press, 1995

A collection of essays exploring different community formation in urban China during the reform period. Several chapters focus specifically on labor's politics and associations, their leisure patterns, and the social organization of migrant labor or the "floating population." Chapters on other aspects of Chinese cities provide an updated background for understanding labor in the reform era.

Lee, Ching Kwan, *Unraveling the South China Miracle: Two Worlds of Factory Women*, Berkeley: University of California Press, 1998

A comparative ethnographic study of women workers in global factories in Shenzhen and Hong Kong, this book depicts and explains the formation and organization of two different factory regimes found in South China's export-oriented industrialism.

Solinger, Dorothy J., "The Chinese Work Unit and Transient Labor in the Transition from Socialism," in *Modern China* 21, no. 2 (April 1995)

A comparison of labor conditions of transient migrant workers in both state and private factories.

Walder, Andrew, *Communist Neo-Traditionalism: Work and Authority in Chinese Industry*, Berkeley: University of California Press, 1986

A seminal work on the relation between Chinese labor and the communist regime from 1949 to the early 1980s. Based on in-depth interviews with Chinese workers and secondary materials on factory life in China, Walder builds an influential theoretical model of neo-traditionalism to understand state-society relations in communist systems. He traces the intricate networks of clientelism institutionalized with the state factory through which the state vertically divides the working class and creates consent to its rule.

Walder, Andrew, "Workers, Managers, and the State: The Reform Era and the Political Crisis of 1989," in *The China Quarterly* 127 (September 1991)

A review of state workers' grievances and labor conditions brought about by reforms since the mid-1980s and which led to workers' participation in the 1989 pro-democracy movement.

Wilson, Jeanne L., "Labor Policy in China: Reform and Retrogression," in *Problems of Communism* 39, no. 5 (September 1990)

An informative review of employment and union policies from the 1980s to 1990.

Zhao, Minghua, and Theo Nichols, "Management Control of Labour in State-Owned Enterprises: Cases from the Textile Industry," in *The China Journal* 36 (July 1996)

Details of changing labor control mechanisms within state textile factories, based on interviews in three factories.

Ching Kwan Lee is Assistant Professor in the Department of Sociology, Chinese University of Hong Kong. She is the author of *Unraveling the South China Miracle: Two Worlds of Factory Women* (1998) and of articles on gender and labor in China published in *American Sociological Review, China Review,* and *Gender and Society.* The present chapter draws on data from research funded by the South China Program of the Hong Kong Institute of Asia-Pacific Studies, the Chinese University of Hong Kong.

Table 18.1: Employment Structure of Chinese Labor Force, 1978–90

	Total (million)	Employees in state, collective, and private sectors						Rural Workers and Peasants (million)
		State Units (million)	% of Total Employees	Urban Collective Units (million)	% of Total Employees	Joint Ventures and Private Firms	% of Total Employees	
1978	94.99	74.51	78.4	20.48	21.6	-	-	306.38
1979	99.67	76.93	77.2	22.74	22.8	-	-	310.25
1980	104.44	80.19	76.8	24.25	23.2	-	-	318.36
1981	109.40	83.72	76.5	26.51	23.5	-	-	326.72
1982	112.81	86.30	76.5	26.51	23.5	-	-	338.67
1983	115.15	87.71	76.2	27.44	23.8	-	-	346.90
1984	118.90	86.37	72.6	32.16	27.0	370,000	0.3	359.68
1985	123.58	89.90	72.7	33.24	26.9	440,000	0.4	370.65
1986	128.09	93.33	72.9	34.21	26.7	550,000	0.4	379.90
1987	132.14	96.54	73.1	33.88	26.4	720,000	0.5	390.00
1988	136.08	99.84	73.4	35.27	25.9	970,000	0.7	400.67
1989	137.42	101.08	73.6	35.02	25.5	1,320,000	1.0	409.39
1990	140.59	103.46	73.6	35.49	25.2	1,640,000	1.2	420.10

Sources: 1990 China Statistical Yearbook and 1991 China Statistical Extract

Table 18.2: Employment Structure of Chinese Labor Force 1991–95

| | Total (million) | Employees in state, collective, and private sectors | | | | | | Rural Workers and Peasants (million) |
		State Units (million)	% of Total Employees	Urban Collective Units (million)	% of Total Employees	Joint Ventures and Private Firms*	% of Total Employees	
1991	152.60	106.64	69.9	36.28	23.8	2,820,000	1.8	430.93
1992	156.30	108.89	69.7	36.21	23.1	3,750,000	2.3	438.02
1993	159.64	109.20	68.4	33.93	31.1	7,040,000	4.4	442.56
1994	168.16	112.14	66.7	32.85	29.3	10,820,000	6.4	446.54
1995	173.46	112.61	64.9	31.47	27.9	13,680,000	7.9	450.42

* Joint ventures and private firms include joint-owned units, share holding units, foreign-funded units, private enterprises, and units funded by overseas Chinese in Hong Kong, Macau, and Taiwan.

Source: 1996 China Statistical Yearbook

Chapter Nineteen

Education and Economic Reform

Stanley Rosen

China's gradual adoption of market-oriented reforms over the past two decades has transformed the Chinese educational system in a manner that could not have been anticipated at the start of the reform period. This transformation has not been limited to purely educational issues, although major changes have taken place in areas such as curriculum, student recruitment, and job assignment. Of equal significance, economic reform has had substantial impact on larger societal processes, compelling schools, work units, families, and individuals to rethink their strategies for success as they continue to adjust and readjust to an ever-changing competitive marketplace. This chapter examines how China's ongoing reform process has shaped the educational system as well as attitudes and behavior about education.

Overview of Chinese Education Today and Goals for the Future

In a long internal report delivered to the Higher Party School of the Chinese Communist Party (CCP) in November 1995, Zhu Kaixuan, Director of the State Education Commission, offered the government's assessment of the state of Chinese education, while also anticipating potential difficulties in the future. Not surprisingly, Zhu noted that "investment in education is gravely insufficient," pointing out that "the average per student amount of public funds for education of all grades and categories

has actually diminished year by year over the past few years." Indeed, as the State Education Commission reported in October 1996, total government spending on education fell to 2.46% of GNP in 1995 from 2.52% the previous year. While total state spending rose 26% that year, education outlays increased only 16%. Total government spending for education is slated to reach 4% of GNP by the year 2000 according to the Ninth Five-Year Plan (1996–2000), but current government investment trends suggest this estimate is overly optimistic. While the world average totaled 5.1% of GNP in the early 1990s, Zhu himself notes that, except for 1991, China's state budgetary outlay for education hovered below 3% throughout the Eighth Five-Year Plan.

In his report, Zhu emphasized China's struggle to achieve two basic goals. At the bottom of the system, the state has sought to universalize compulsory education and wipe out illiteracy (the "two basics"). At the top of the system, it has promoted "Project 211," which seeks to bring about substantial improvements in approximately 100 institutions of higher education and in selected disciplines. Improvements at the basic level, Zhu argued, are "primarily a local enterprise" and "should rely, in the main, on the leadership of local governments at all levels and on the support of society as a whole." In contrast, the top level of the system will be heavily funded by higher-level state organs and external sources. Project 211, for example, will receive 10 billion *yuan* (about US$1.2 billion) over five years to support its targeted universities. Zhu recognized the dangers in this two-tiered system, remarking that the state "should resist [the tendency to] reduce investment in basic education because of impatience to set up Project 211 institutions," while further warning that "it is not advisable to grasp only the key projects and sacrifice the basic interests of other institutions of higher learning. This line of thinking in our work is bound to be unpopular."

Director Zhu's comments define the central characteristics and contradictions of the Chinese educational system. The reform period "rationalized" Chinese education in accord with Deng Xiaoping's views on the role of education in economic development. Deng's educational agenda largely downgraded the political and social functions of education in favor of an educational strategy that would accelerate China's march toward modernization. It explicitly sanctioned the creation of a bifurcated system, wherein a small "elite" sector trains the first-class scientists and engineers (who in turn will assist the government in meeting the ambitious targets of the "four modernizations" program) and a large "mass" sector provides the basic educational skills, and possibly additional vocational training, for the majority. Over time, as Project 211 suggests, the elite sector will become more and more hierarchically structured, while the mass sector will remain more "open" and diverse. For Chinese youth, this bifurcated, hierarchical system offers differential rewards. For those who reach the elite sector, benefits may include the opportunity to study abroad; those who fall short often receive education only through junior high. This competitive system has spurred students and their parents to calculate optimal strategies for educational success in their localities.

In 1985 China enacted the Nine-Year Compulsory Education Law, which required the most developed areas of the country (encompassing about 25% of the population) to offer nine years of compulsory schooling by 1990. Those areas of "medium-level development" (about 50% of the population) were required to meet this goal by 1995, while economically backward areas (the remaining 25%) were simply told to do their best (for a discussion of the various problems of popularizing education, see Suzanne Ogden, *China's Unresolved Issues: Politics, Development and Culture*, 3rd edition, Englewood Cliffs, New Jersey: Prentice Hall, 1995: 311–48). National-level aggregate data, if taken at face value, suggest that localities have responded well to this policy. According to 1995 figures, 98.52% of primary school age students entered the classroom at the beginning of the year, and the retention rate was 88.5%. Indeed, in areas inhabited by 91% of China's population, primary education appears to have been universalized. The promotion rate of primary school graduates to junior high was 90.8%. This surpassed China's previous high of 90.6%, accomplished during the latter stages of the Cultural Revolution in 1975, when students were required to remain in schools where the quality of education often was poor. In addition, about 75% of the relevant age cohort attended junior high school, and nearly 50% reached the senior high level. University education, however, lagged behind. In 1995 a total of 1,080 colleges and universities (not including nonformal educational institutes) instructed 2.8 million undergraduates and 130,000 graduate students. Thus, based on 1995 figures, 67.1% of China's student population were enrolled at the primary level, 31.5% at the secondary level, and only 1.5% at the tertiary level. Moreover, only 3% of the relevant age cohort were enrolled in colleges or universities. One study noted that, based on this enrollment ratio, China ranked 100 among the 118 countries investigated. However, the current plan calls for this ratio to increase to 8% by the year 2000.

Based on aggregate data, the Chinese educational system would appear to be functioning comparatively well. However, educators in China who have conducted their own field surveys remain skeptical regarding official statistics, noting that data often are self-reported by localities and have not been confirmed by independent investigation. Data on illiteracy provide a good example of how official statistics may be inaccurate. Although Zhu Kaixuan's 1995 report claimed that 22 million illiterates achieved literacy over the course of the Eighth Five-Year Plan (1991–95), a member of a production brigade in backward Ningxia province reported in the *People's Daily* in March 1985 that the county had offered brigades 10 *yuan* for each individual who became literate. This may have led to widespread false reporting of literacy gains.

Indeed, many popular books and articles published in China report a "crisis" in education, particularly at the primary and secondary levels (for example, see Gerard A. Postiglione, editor, "Heavy Laden Wings: Sad Contemplations on China's Education, I and II," in *Chinese Education and Society* 28, no. 1 [January-February 1995] and 28, no. 2 [March-April 1995]). Observers point to the high number of dropouts. A 1991 newspaper report noted that during the 1980s an average of approximately 4 million middle and primary school children did not attend school each year. The State Statistical Bureau reported dropout rates in lower middle school at 5.8% and in primary school at 2.2%, yielding a figure in excess of 5 million pupils. While the latest data show some improvement in these figures, it is important to note that official figures do not take into account the number of "invisible dropouts"–those students who do not attend classes yet have not officially withdrawn. Thus, evidence of improvement may be misleading.

Many studies, particularly in rural areas, have attempted to determine the reasons for leaving school. Researchers consistently have found that economic reforms play a major role in school dropouts. The increased cost of education, including both school fees and student expenses, have made schooling unaffordable for many families. Rising tuition costs are the result of increasing fees imposed on schools. A study of five provinces conducted by the State Education Commission found that on average each school was assessed 10,000 *yuan* in

fees to support a variety of projects and activities, ranging from local militia training to construction of the Three Gorges Dam; the schools could only survive by passing the costs on to students. Meanwhile, a trade union study of 200 parents with children attending 108 primary and middle schools in Chongqing, one of China's largest cities, found that the average cost of miscellaneous fees for primary students beginning in the fall term of 1994 totaled 95.93 *yuan*; for junior high students, 155.5 *yuan*; and for senior high students, 257.3 *yuan*. Student expenses such as textbooks and school supplies also have risen sharply, making it difficult for peasant families to afford to keep a child in school.

While fees and expenditures for education clearly are the leading reason that dropout rates have increased, other factors related to economic reform either directly or indirectly play a role. First, the new policy of charging tuition (see below) at the university level has begun to have an impact, particularly on rural households. Already compelled to pay close to 1,000 *yuan* to send a child to high school, families dependent on agriculture recognize early on that they cannot afford the minimum 1,000 *yuan* of yearly college tuition. Second, the reform of the state's personnel system, under which college and specialized secondary school graduates are no longer guaranteed job allocations, has served to lessen the attraction of higher education for peasant families. Previously, the main attraction of schooling for rural families was the possibility that their children would be able to "leap over the village gate" and leave farming altogether. Now that graduates are expected to find their own jobs, parents fear that even if their children pass the matriculation examination, enter a college, and pay the required tuition fees, poor employment prospects may lurk at the end of the process. For many families the risk is unacceptable given a cost-benefit analysis and the other options available to them. Many students choose instead to "jump into the sea" (i.e., engage in business). Examples of dropouts who have succeeded in business are legion and, unlike the past when entrepreneurs were suspected of "capitalist tendencies," such people today elicit awe and admiration.

Economic Reform and the Increase in Differentiation and Disparity

Current trends in education suggest increasing differentiation and disparities among schools at every level, as well as between regions. This in turn has increased the influence of money to ensure quality education. Indeed, since 1992 private schools have proliferated, ranging from extraordinarily expensive elite schools in the booming province of Guangdong to rural primary schools that charge less than state schools. Not surprisingly, press reports have focused on the most outrageously expensive schools. However, except at the kindergarten and primary school levels, where private schools offer individual care, service, and boarding facilities during the week, these have provided little competition to the state school system.

At the tertiary level, differentiation has developed both among schools (owing to increased competition) and among students (owing to new financial considerations). Regarding the former, China's leading universities have discovered their reputations are no longer sufficient to attract students. Many Chinese young people are choosing instead to enroll in upstart entrepreneurial colleges that offer training in nontraditional specializations and that are market-savvy. Meanwhile, the current five-year plan (1996–2000) calls for the implementation of Project 211, which seeks to enhance via state financial assistance the educational capacity of China's top 100 universities. As a State Education Commission official in charge of higher education stated, the chosen universities "are expected to grow into 'mega-versities' that can help China compete on the world stage." Not surprisingly, universities have competed intensely to be chosen for Project 211.

Author Wei Feng recently examined how the market has begun to alter traditional conceptions of educational success and to shake up Chinese higher education. Wei notes that by 1992 Beijing University, long considered China's foremost seat of learning, had begun to encounter some difficulty hiring instructors to teach in some of its most famous departments, such as literature, history, and philosophy. The same was true of other leading universities in China. In stark contrast, colleges of economics and trade schools, also recruiting in the more developed regions, enjoyed high enrollment despite relatively low rankings in the hierarchy of institutions. Educators soon realized that the problem stemmed from the impracticability and obsolescence of certain disciplines and specializations. One high-achieving student attending a school of finance offered his assessment of the situation: "From the time I was in primary school, I revered Beijing University as a holy place. In these times, however, the specialization is more important than the school. You lose more than you gain if you go to a first-rate university by making first-rate test points, but end up five years later with a third-rate job" (Wei Feng, "The Great Tremors in China's Intellectual Circles: An Overview of Intellectuals Floundering in the Sea of Commercialism," in *Chinese Education and Society* 29, no. 6 [November-December 1996]:16. The following paragraph also is drawn from Wei Feng's discussion).

Wei further notes that China's most elite comprehensive institutions, including Beijing University and Fudan University, have encountered difficulties updating curricula, eliminating redundant specializations, and establishing new ones. The most favored courses are those that lead to high-paying jobs, particularly those in joint venture or foreign-invested companies. This naturally has drawn students to specializations such as foreign languages, economics, and law. Since the appearance of Wei's book in 1993, many traditional institutions (including the aforementioned universities) have established elite schools in areas such as business management or finance, often using funding from Taiwan, Hong Kong, or overseas Chinese to do so.

The Chinese press often reports on how the market economy has affected student attitudes regarding education and employment. The officially promoted ideal had been for the graduating student to accept the job assignment of the state, working where he or she was most needed. In recent years, however, students generally did not even give lip service to this ideal, openly admitting that they wanted high-paying jobs in large, coastal cities (many students listed joint venture companies as their first preference). One study looked at the employment choices of the entire university graduating class of 1995. While 48.6% of graduates originally had come from small cities, towns, or the countryside, only 0.6% chose to go to such locations. Another 31.6% of students had come from prefectural or county-level cities, but 42% of those graduating opted to seek employment in these locations. Finally, only 18.6% of the students hailed from China's major cities, but fully 57.2% of graduates chose to seek jobs there (Tang Zijing, "The Tremors Stemming from the Influence of the Market Economy on the Job Choices of University Students and the Measures We Should Adopt to Cope With This," in *Youth Research* [January 1996]: 1–4).

The importance of money at the tertiary level has developed gradually in recent years (the following discussion draws from Huiping Wu and Ruth Hayhoe, "Fee-Paying Public Universities and Private Institutions," in *China News Analysis* 1534 [May 1, 1995]). Fee-paying in public higher education originated in the early 1980s when national institutions set up branch campuses in major cities. In 1985, the state began encouraging "commissioned training," under which enterprises paid the full cost for students they planned to hire upon graduation. By 1993, 40% of the total students enrolled were commissioned training students. In 1986, universities were permitted for the first time to enroll a limited number of self-paying students. Similar to the commissioned training students, these students were not required to meet the same national unified entrance examination standards as the

regularly admitted students. The enrollment of self-paying students climbed from 3% in 1986 to 25% in 1993.

When universities were given the right to determine their own fee structure in 1992, some immediately raised fees for popular subjects such as business and finance. In 1993 the state issued a major policy document stating that higher education should move gradually from a system under which the government guaranteed education and employment to a system in which students were held responsible for both. As a result, fewer students who qualified under the plan were admitted, while qualified students who were unable to pay high fees were excluded. In response to this growing problem, the State Education Commission introduced a trial policy in April 1994 that set unified admissions standards and standard fees for the 37 universities under its direct administration (in the end, 40 universities participated); by 2000 all universities were to be subject to a similar plan. According to the 1994 policy, fees are not uniform but vary depending on the university and the demand for the specialization. While Beijing University's standard fee is 1,500 *yuan* per year, at Fudan University in Shanghai fees range from 900 to 2,300 *yuan.* The most expensive schools are located in Guangzhou city and Guangdong province, where fees at the Guangdong Foreign Language and Foreign Trade University are set at 3,500–4,000 *yuan* and those at Shenzhen University at 4,000–4,500 *yuan.* Foreign languages and international trade programs tend to be the most expensive, since these fields offer bright prospects after graduation.

As Huiping Wu and Ruth Hayhoe point out in their account of these changes, the new policy of charging tuition will further disadvantage students from rural areas as well as poor families more generally. The cost of maintaining a student at a university has climbed to about 3,400 *yuan* annually, counting tuition and living expenses. While many urban families can afford this (given the one child policy and the greater likelihood of two incomes), rural families cannot. Thus, rural students often pursue other avenues of education. Many apply to specialized institutions that offer unfashionable majors and have difficulty recruiting qualified students; such majors include agriculture, forestry, mining, and teachers' training. The government still fully subsidizes these courses. Universities have opened another avenue by redistributing a liberal percentage of the fees they receive in the form of scholarships. The press, however, already has reported on the problems rural students have experienced under the new system.

Strategies for Success Through the Educational System: Three Case Studies

Under China's meritocratic system, everyone theoretically has an opportunity to enter the elite sector. In every province and municipality, "key" schools are given priority funding and are allowed to recruit the best students. Below the provincial and municipal levels, counties and districts operate their own key schools, a cut below those at the higher level, but still better than ordinary academic secondary schools. In addition to these academic schools that offer the standard coursework and prepare students to take the university entrance examination, a variety of technical and vocational schools are also available, and graduates of these schools immediately enter the job market. For the brightest and most ambitious students, the standard route to success usually includes entering a key school, moving on to a key university, and then receiving a state sector job allocation in a major city, a so-called "iron rice bowl." In recent years, however, largely because of the differential effects of economic reforms on different localities, there is no longer a "standard route" up the educational ladder. A comparative analysis of the parent/student strategies in different localities will serve to illustrate the diversity of the educational process in China. The following discussion examines how this process occurs in Guangzhou (an economically advanced region); in the Qinhuangdao area of Hebei province

(in the hinterland); and in Beijing.

The reform program, as one slogan puts it, allows those who work hard and who enjoy better circumstances to get rich first. In the coastal cities, where foreign investment is concentrated and the local economy is booming, student perceptions about schooling have reflected the new prosperity. As early as the mid-1980s, survey data showed that students in Guangzhou, in contrast to their counterparts in China's interior cities, saw university entrance as only one of several options For example, 73.5% of graduating high school seniors in Xian said they would retake the university entrance examination if they did not succeed the first time, while only 33.6% of Guangzhou seniors planned to do so. Moreover, 26.2% of Guangzhou seniors but only 8.4% of Xian seniors expressed confidence about finding a job if they did not get into a university. In addition, more than twice as many Guangzhou seniors were prepared to study part-time and about three times as many wanted to study abroad. For Guangzhou's junior high graduating class of 1986, spaces in secondary technical schools (which do not lead to university entrance) were even scarcer than those at provincial and municipal key senior high schools, although the quality of students applying to the latter schools was higher. In fact, only one of three junior high graduates chose a regular academic senior high as his or her first preference, and about half of these chose neither a provincial, municipal, nor district key school. Recent reports from Shenzhen, the special economic zone bordering Hong Kong, suggest that students still prefer technical schools, in part because of the ease with which graduates find jobs, but also because entrance to a technical school no longer precludes university entrance. In affluent areas like Guangzhou and Shenzhen some students are able to gain admittance to universities by having their firms choose them as commissioned training students (the author is grateful to Gerard Postiglione for bringing this finding from Sam To's interviews in Shenzhen to his attention).

Indeed, job market options in Guangzhou continue to outpace those in other areas.

In the Qinhuangdao area of Hebei province, technical schools are also more popular than key schools; however, the competition to enter these schools is far more intense than in Guangzhou (this section is based on a report in the internally circulated *Neibu wengao,* published by *Qiushi,* the leading Communist Party theoretical journal. See Yang Shiyi, "The Current Situation of the Recruitment of Students in Key Middle Schools Is Cause for Worry," in *Chinese Education and Society* 26, no. 2 [March-April 1993]: 83–92). For example, among those who took part in the junior high graduation examination in Changli county, 2,420 students–including the best in the county–applied to the technical school as their first preference, but only 243 were accepted. Meanwhile, the county's key middle school admitted 400 out of the 659 who applied. Other counties have reported even more extreme figures.

The reasons for this situation are essentially economic, based on simple cost-benefit calculations. First, it is far more expensive for students in the countryside to attend a key senior high than a technical school. Key senior highs are located in county seats, compelling students to reside in dormitories; the estimated cost of three years of senior high in Qinhuangdao city is 2,000–3,000 *yuan.* Technical schools, by contrast, are inexpensive to attend and even provide a monthly stipend. Moreover, university graduates and technical school graduates earn similar wages. Even ignoring the new tuition costs at universities–which will only exacerbate this situation–at current wage levels a university graduate would have to work 30 to 40 years to make up the income lost by not attending a local technical school. Since assessments of job qualifications, housing distribution, and wage increases are based primarily on job seniority, students are well advised to join the workforce early.

In addition, adult education programs have grown in popularity. College-level credentials can be obtained through a "five-year self-education" program. This saves expensive tuition costs, allowing the technical school graduate to receive wages and build seniority while working toward a degree. Graduates of this program earn wages and other benefits on par with graduates from regular colleges. Moreover, in many areas hiring units already have a surplus of cadres and administrative personnel, and thus college graduates often encounter more difficulty than technical school graduates in finding employment.

Perhaps the most important reason for choosing technical schools derives from the continuing gap between the city and the countryside. As noted in an earlier section, students with rural backgrounds place a high priority on escaping the countryside. Given this mentality, choosing to attend a technical high school becomes the "single leap" that carries the student over the village gate. Attending a key senior high, on the other hand, is merely a preparatory stage for the college entrance examination. When students take the examination three years later, the degree of difficulty is far greater than the matriculation exam for technical schools, and most are skeptical about their chances for success. Choosing a technical school thus offers quick results and short-term benefits.

The constraints are even greater in lesser-developed areas of the country. In those areas that lack an expanding job market, studies have shown that students often are compelled to retake matriculation exams several times in an attempt to squeeze into local technical schools or teacher training schools, since these are the only way to ensure a job assignment. Meanwhile, because opportunities for higher education are minimal, ordinary academic senior highs have trouble attracting students, while vocational schools often are considered the worst option. Local labor bureaus, aware of the poor quality of these schools, simply recruit their workers and cadres elsewhere.

The situation in Beijing is markedly different. Although students in Beijing, like their counterparts elsewhere, generally would prefer to find high-paying jobs in foreign-invested enterprises, China's capital remains the center for scholars and government officials. The family culture, at least among intellectuals, still regards a university education as essential. Technical schools, while undoubtedly becoming more popular, still are considered by intellectuals as non-academic training centers. Interviewees like to point out the differences between Beijing and other major cities, noting that people go to Guangzhou to make money, to Shanghai to become a professional, and to Beijing to become a scholar or government official. The traditional concepts of honor and rank (*gongming*) are still important in the north. Indeed, one survey found that 43.4% of parents in Beijing plan to have their children complete regular college courses and 17.2% want them to go on to graduate school (Zheng Li, "A Preliminary Exploration into the Phenomenon of 'Memo Students, Connections Students, and Banknote Students' among Middle and Primary School Enrolees in the Capital City," in *Neibu wengao* 12 [1996]: 26–29. This source is used for some of the additional data in this section).

Because of the continuing attraction of university education, students compete to climb the educational ladder as early as primary school. Over the years it has been particularly important to parents that their children pass the unified municipal examination given upon graduation from primary school and test into one of the city's excellent key junior highs, which until recently recruited throughout Beijing. Since the establishment of the Nine Year Compulsory Education Law, educational authorities have sought to reduce the negative side effects resulting from this competitive system, including the ranking of schools solely on the basis of their promotion rates; the pressure to maintain high rates year after year; the excessive burdens on young children who spend most of their time on homework, test-taking, and tutorial classes after school; and the relatively long commute the students make in order to attend the school of their parents' choice. In 1993, authorities abolished the examination for junior high entrance and mandated that primary school graduates, save for an exceptional few, attend their neighborhood junior highs. The real competition thus was delayed until senior high, at which level the municipality's key schools still were allowed to recruit citywide.

Almost immediately parents in Beijing (and in other large cities with strong academic traditions like Tianjin and Shanghai, which had adopted similar guidelines) protested that "the alley in which they lived determined their [child's] whole life" (*hutong ding zhongshen*). The complaints grew so loud that the State Education Commission felt it necessary to alleviate concerns by explaining the rationale of the new policy in the nationally-circulated education newspaper. Although Beijing's educational authorities made some minor concessions in response to the protests, a brief examination of how families and schools have adapted to the new system reveals a great deal about the complexities of educational policy under the current market economy.

Put simply, families and schools have been able to gain mutual advantage from a loophole in government policy. In order to solve special problems some students may encounter in transferring from one school to another, schools for some time have selected a few students outside the government target after they have fulfilled their enrollment plan. The number of additional students generally had been limited to five per class. Since 1993, however, there has been a large increase in the number of such students, who are now called "school-selecting students," or more colloquially, "three types of students," referring to "memo students," "connections students," and "banknote students," since they attend their schools by virtue of power, connections, or money. In key middle schools in Beijing "school-selecting" students often account for more than 50% of enrollment. This phenomenon has spread to "Category II" schools, just below the key schools in quality. Although the State Education Commission has issued many directives against this practice, the number of school-selecting students has increased each year.

Meanwhile, tuition costs–which vary considerably depending on a student's marks, the quality of the school, the connections the parents have to the school, and so forth–range from about 10,000–60,000 *yuan* per year for a top school. For schools, tuition income is crucial given the urgent need to retain qualified teachers who often choose to leave the teaching profession for higher-paying jobs. Indeed, secondary schools have been trying to avoid what has become an increasingly serious problem at the university level. A 1993 study of 121 universities and colleges in 22 provinces revealed a 16.4% decline in the total number of faculty that year; two-thirds of those leaving were young or middle-aged. At Beijing Normal University the proportion of departing faculty with master's and doctoral degrees jumped to 53.3% in 1992 from 13.5% in 1987. A private consulting firm in Beijing estimated that more than half of all professors have jobs on the side. Married teaching couples routinely arrange for one person to maintain an academic job (thus guaranteeing subsidized housing entitlement) while the other takes a job in the private sector. To combat this problem, school authorities have sought to ensure that a reasonable amount of school funds are passed on to teachers and other staff members in the form of benefits. Many university professors now lament that they receive less remuneration and benefits than their lower-level counterparts.

The government is torn between competing values as well, despite its public criticism of the "backdoor" entrance to the quality schools. On the one hand the government is pushing for equity and opposing privilege. Conversely, it recognizes that schools cannot survive solely on the limited budget allocations they receive from the state. Moreover, as noted above, the government is committed to the establishment of a hierarchical system. At the university level this commitment takes the form of Project 211; at the primary and secondary level, the government favors the continuation of a small number of elite schools in Beijing that "play an exemplary role in the country as a whole

and serve as windows to the outside" (Zheng Li, 1996). Regarding the latter, the government policy is to keep the number of elite schools to a minimum and, if possible, to reduce the differences that exist among the various schools in the city. Yet the government also recognizes its own limitations to effect a solution. The vice-director of the research office of Beijing Municipality noted in an internal report that while the government did not approve of the "three types" of students, it was unable to end the practice. He suggested that the only option was to require a certain minimum score for backdoor admissions. His solution is notable because it reveals the power of the market and the relative weakness of the state in combating market forces:

> Use the evening papers to announce to society as a whole which schools are available for selection by school-selecting students; make public the number of school-selecting students enrolled by each school outside of [enrollment] planning; make public the minimum points threshold for enrolling school-selecting students; and make public each school's maximum fee level (Zheng Li, 1996).

A comparison of the three localities discussed above reflects the nature of China's uneven development. Qinhuangdao and Beijing have highly competitive school systems, albeit the competition is manifested differently. For hinterland areas, the underlying goal has been the establishment and consolidation of compulsory education through junior high. China has made admirable progress toward achieving that goal. It is at the high end of the system, where the goal is to enter a technical school and find a good job, that the competition is most acute.

In Beijing the government has sought, through public policy, to reduce the competitive fires at the lower end of the system, so that competition between schools over promotion rates and between students over school choice is delayed until students apply to senior high. Ironically, gaining admittance to college in Beijing has never been easier. Since the university entrance examinations were restored in 1977, the admission ratio (the total number of applicants to the number of applicants admitted) in Beijing has grown more favorable each year, increasing from more than 16:1 in 1977 to 1.3:1 in 1994. However, competition has increased among the "hot" specializations, including foreign economics, foreign trade, tourism, medicine, electronics, computer science, and biochemistry. While the new policies may prove successful in the long term, in the short term they have spurred schools and families not yet reconciled to a less competitive system to work around policy constraints.

Education in Guangzhou, where an expanding commercial economy offers many options after graduation from junior high, appears to be less overtly competitive than either Qinhuangdao or Beijing. While many Chinese argue that this reflects the differences between northern and southern culture, between the pursuit of "honor and rank" and the pursuit of wealth, the level of economic and commercial development clearly plays a major role.

Conclusion

The purpose of Zhu Kaixuan's internal speech on education to the Higher Party School was to introduce and explain the sections on education in the Proposal of the Chinese Communist Party Central Committee Concerning the Formulation of the Ninth Five-Year Plan for National Economic and Social Development and the Long-Term Targets for the Year 2010, which had been passed at the recently concluded Fifth Plenum of the Fourteenth Party Congress. After summarizing the six main aspects of the proposal, Zhu forcefully concluded that educational work now has one key characteristic:

Education is no longer dissociated from the economy and disposed of by setting up a separate item for it. Education is closely linked with the economy, and has become an organic component and key

content of the plans for economic and social development; elements of education permeate the main clauses concerning the economy, including its guiding policies, construction tasks, strategic deployment, and foci of investment.

Zhu's assessment differs markedly from the standard view of education often held by Chinese officials and Chinese economists, who believe that education is a form of consumption and not production, and that investment in education will bring a less effective return than investment in some alternative "productive" enterprise, such as a factory. Indeed, this mentality has contributed significantly to China's low level of investment in education, even during the reform period. However, if Zhu's views now prevail among the higher reaches of the CCP, investment patterns for Chinese education are likely to change. Zhu's comments regarding educational funding in the Ninth Five-Year Plan reflect this optimism.

Further Reading

Chinese Education and Society: A Journal of Translations, Armonk, New York: M. E. Sharpe, bimonthly

This journal offers English translations of material that originally appeared in Chinese. Each issue covers a different aspect of Chinese education, or the relationship of education and society. The journal began publishing in 1968 as a quarterly under the title *Chinese Education,* and became a bimonthly under its new name in 1993.

Educational Statistics Yearbook of China, Beijing: People's Education Press, annually

An extremely useful compendium of statistical data on various aspects of Chinese education. In recent years the volume has included a table of contents in English and English translations of the relevant Chinese terminology in the different sections.

Epstein, Irving, editor, *Chinese Education: Problems, Policies, and Prospects,* New York: Garland, 1991

A compendium of 17 papers and over 500 pages on a wide variety of topics, this volume offers a formidable amount of information, centered primarily on the urban school system. In addition to the more standard topics covered, the book features a number of subjects less frequently discussed, including chapters on education in the special economic zones, military education in the PLA's officer corps, advanced legal education, and medical schooling.

Hayhoe, Ruth, editor, *Education and Modernization: The Chinese Experience,* New York and Oxford: Pergamon Press, 1992

This collection of essays is divided into three parts, with the first part (4 chapters) focusing on historical perspectives, the second part (2 chapters) discussing formal and nonformal systems of education, and the bulk of the book—part three (7 chapters)—addressing more specific issues and groups involved in Chinese education. The historical perspective is broad enough to include material ranging from Confucius and traditional education to an analysis of the Great Leap Forward and the Great Proletarian Cultural Revolution. The seven chapters in part three cover women, management training, teaching, moral-political education, foreign-language education, special education, and the education of national minorities.

Hayhoe, Ruth, *China's Universities, 1895–1995: A Century of Cultural Conflict,* New York: Garland, 1996

The latest of a number of books Ruth Hayhoe has written or edited on Chinese higher education, the current volume is notable for its use of a comparative education framework to examine the history of Chinese universities. Equally important is her reliance on oral history, in effect treating Chinese campuses as communities that persist over the course of several generations. While tracing the chronological development of these universities, Hayhoe is able to explore such important subjects as modern curriculum, gender issues, the role of teachers, educational expansion, and the politics of education, and to do so in each of the major historical periods of 20th-century China: republican, socialist, and reform.

Lewin, Keith M., Xu Hui, Angela W. Little, and Zhang Jiwei, *Educational Innovation in China:*

Tracing the Impact of the 1985 Reforms, London: Longman, 1995

This volume, a collaboration between two Chinese and two British specialists on comparative education, offers a fairly comprehensive analysis of the effects of the much-touted educational reform of 1985. With up-to-date data from Chinese-language sources, the book is not so strong, however, in offering a political analysis of educational developments in China. For example, while problems in education are duly noted—e.g., the lack of resources allocated by the state, a variety of previous policy mistakes, and so forth—criticism and analysis of current policy is generally avoided, presumably because of caution on the part of the Chinese coauthors.

Pepper, Suzanne, *China's Education Reform in the 1980s: Policies, Issues, and Historical Perspectives,* Berkeley: Institute of East Asian Studies, University of California, 1990

A precursor to the larger book listed below, this monograph is an expansion of two conference papers presented in the 1980s in which the educational reforms of the 1980s are placed in the broader context of China's educational reform tradition. The book is divided into two parts, with the first part covering the origins and development of the "two-line struggle" in Chinese education and the second part offering four chapters on developments in the 1980s when one line prevailed. The monograph is particularly valuable in showing how Mao's political decisions guaranteed that his educational reforms would be totally repudiated, and how Deng Xiaoping as well fell victim to the logic of the two-line struggle, since he made no real distinction between the radical political agenda that deposed him and the more positive educational reforms of that period. Because Pepper is a political scientist her work focuses much more squarely on the politics of education than others writing on educational matters.

Pepper, Suzanne, *Radicalism and Education Reform in 20th-Century China: The Search for an Ideal Development Model,* Cambridge and New York: Cambridge University Press, 1996

Pepper sets out to explain why the Chinese "education revolution," which had been hailed by foreign observers in 1976 as an inspiration for all low-income countries, had, by 1980, been repudiated by the Chinese themselves. Indeed, it was now seen as having no redeeming virtues. Her search for answers leads her to an analysis of educational developments in China from the turn of the century up through 1979. In the course of her analysis, she shows how educational innovations under the communists had clear pre-1949 antecedents, as well as the continuing contention over the application of foreign models in a non-Western context. This is the best place to begin a study of Chinese education.

Postiglione, Gerard A., and Wing On Lee, editors, *Social Change and Educational Development: Mainland China, Taiwan and Hong Kong*, Hong Kong: Centre of Asian Studies, The University of Hong Kong, 1995

Most of the 21 chapters in this book were presented at a conference at Hong Kong University in June 1992. Although most articles cover mainland China, there are useful chapters on Hong Kong and Taiwan as well, which help to put mainland education into a broader context. Separate sections consider theoretical approaches to educational development and social change, documentary and policy studies, empirical studies, historical studies, and "comments and discussions." Contributors include leading scholars from the mainland, Hong Kong, Taiwan, and the West.

Stanley Rosen is Associate Professor of Political Science at the University of Southern California. He has written extensively on social and political change in China, including *Red Guard Factionalism and the Cultural Revolution in Guangzhou* (1982) and *Survey Research in the People's Republic of China* (with David S.K. Chu, 1987). He is also coeditor, with Anita Chan and Jonathan Unger, of *On Socialist Democracy and the Chinese Legal System: The Li Yizhe Debates* (1985) and, with John P. Burns, of *Policy Conflicts in Post-Mao China: A Documentary Survey with Analysis* (1986).

Chapter Twenty

China's Social Welfare Reforms for a Market Economy: Problems and Prospects

Jane Duckett

China's social welfare system currently is undergoing enormous change. The welfare system created by the Chinese Communist Party (CCP) after 1949 is inappropriate to the market economy that has emerged during the post-Mao reform period (1979–). The institutions formerly providing social welfare are no longer able to carry out this function: the communes have been dissolved and many urban state enterprises are being closed or cannot afford to provide pensions and health care for their employees. In any case, growing numbers of people now work outside the state sector and so fall outside the scope of the old welfare system. Concurrently, market reform has produced new and serious social inequalities. This chapter examines the reforms that have been introduced to address some of these problems and assesses the extent to which they are providing for the needs of Chinese society.

Introduction: Economic Reform, Social Change, and Welfare in China

During the Maoist period (1949–78), welfare provision was founded on the principle of full employment. Urban workers were allocated jobs for life in the "iron rice bowl," a system that provided a high level of economic security in comparison with most developing countries. On this basis, most welfare was provided to urban dwellers via their work units (*danwei*), including state enterprises, large collective enterprises, and other state institutions such as hospitals, schools and government offices. These work places provided a range of welfare for their employees, from cheap housing, health clinics, and nurseries to cash and material subsidies. The Labor Insurance Regulations issued in 1951 stipulated that state and collective enterprises should provide for employees in case of sickness, pregnancy, work injury, disability, death, and also in old-age. Other state institutions provided similar coverage, and the system was more or less comprehensive by the 1960s (by then, almost all private business had been eliminated). However, the range and quality of provision was uneven and dependent on the size and resources of the work place. Large state industrial enterprises, for example, typically offered better provisions to their work forces than did small collectives. Quality of coverage often was dependent on locality, type of work, sex, and whether employees were white collar, blue collar, skilled or unskilled (women, blue collar, and unskilled workers received lower-quality provisions).

To supplement the work unit-based system, residual welfare provisions existed for people with no work unit (and therefore no source of income) or family, primarily disabled and elderly people and orphans. Additionally, a system of basic financial assistance was available for the most destitute, usually a small number of households in a given locality. Army veterans, retired soldiers, and the families of revolutionary martyrs and servicemen received regular compensation. However, the government emphasized self-reliance and discouraged dependence on state financial assistance.

Rural dwellers did not receive such generous provisions. Although rural communes (the basic form of organization in the countryside from the late 1950s until the early 1980s) provided some security, commune members did not enjoy the same range of welfare and social security benefits as most urban residents. Some provisions were financed through commune funds, but these were confined primarily to health and collective welfare projects. The most impoverished households and individuals limited financial relief. Otherwise, rural dwellers relied on their families (and primarily their sons) for support and care in old age.

Although reform era rural decollectivization and industrialization has created a need for a new welfare system, welfare reform in rural areas has been limited. Social security schemes to cover natural disasters, health care, and old age have been introduced in some areas, but are not comprehensive. Welfare reform has been promoted more vigorously in the cities because the old urban welfare system has grown too costly for the state and its public enterprises (state-owned enterprises, or SOEs), which bore all the costs of housing construction, pensions, welfare homes, as well as maternity, work injury and medical expenses.

The government is promoting welfare reforms to improve SOE efficiency and assist market reform by shifting some welfare costs from enterprises onto employees. SOE reform has invested public enterprise managers with greater authority to dismiss workers, and the "iron rice bowl" has been abandoned. As a result, unemployment has risen and growing numbers of workers are employed on temporary contracts. In 1984, 2.09 million urban workers were employed on temporary contracts (or 1.8% of all workers); by 1995 the number had risen to nearly 61 million (just over 40% of all workers). In this context, unemployment insurance has been introduced to promote labor mobility and also to provide for those who lose their jobs. This new system of benefits is also desirable to China's leadership; without the system, a disgruntled urban population could create instability and threaten the CCP-dominated regime.

Other socio-economic changes have made reform of the welfare system imperative. First, the growth of private businesses has meant that increasing numbers of employees fall outside the state sector welfare system. In 1978, urban private and individual (*getihu*) enterprises employed 150,000 people; by the end of 1995, the number had risen to 20.45 million people. A more comprehensive labor insurance system covering all kinds of enterprises is therefore needed. Second, China's rapidly expanding elderly population, soaring divorce rates, and one-child policy are weakening family support structures. This has spurred the central government to focus on reforming the pensions system and improving other provisions for the elderly.

Generally, welfare reforms have sought new forms of welfare finance and have begun to shift some welfare costs onto urban dwellers, while also dividing the burden of welfare costs among enterprises. Welfare reforms also have sought to bring in private or voluntary services, increase provision by the lowest levels of government, and promote mutual help among neighbors. The following sections discuss in greater detail the current provision of housing, pensions, unemployment insurance, maternity and work injury coverage, health care, social relief, community services, and welfare homes.

Housing

During the Maoist period, housing provision in the cities was nationalized, especially from 1958; by the late 1970s only about 20% of housing was owned. Public housing was provided either directly by city governments or indirectly by state work units, particularly state enterprises. The ratio of housing provided by the state and that provided through work units varied from city to city, but on average work unit housing accounted for 46% of total public housing in 1978; this figure increased to 59% by the mid-1980s.

Urban residents enjoyed a low national average monthly rent of 0.13 *yuan* per square meter, or as little as 1% of the average basic wage by the mid-1980s. However, revenue for the maintenance of housing stocks derived solely from rents; with rents so low, income was insufficient for even basic repairs, let alone for reinvestment in construction. As a result, housing deteriorated and population growth created an acute housing shortage. The average per capita living space in the cities decreased to $3.6m^2$ by the late 1970s.

Unlike their urban counterparts, rural Chinese have never received housing from the state. Rural housing often lacked amenities such as running water and electricity, although rural houses were usually larger than urban homes and housing space per capita levels were far higher. In 1978 the average per capita living space in rural areas was $8.1m^2$. Although average rural per capita living space increased to more than $21m^2$ by 1995, this was not owing to increased state spending, but probably reflected the growing wealth of some rural residents.

Since 1978, policymakers have sought to reform the public housing system and increase the quality and quantity of housing stock. Housing reform has gradually developed in several strands. At first, both central and local government increased their public investment in housing construction. These efforts resulted in some cities replacing their oldest slum housing. However, policymakers soon argued that public finance was insufficient to meet housing needs, and non-state sources were sought to supplement state sources. Specifically, the government promoted home ownership as a strategy to generate revenue for more housing construction. Believing that many urban dwellers had disposable income that could be channeled from the purchase of consumer durables into housing, the government encouraged urban residents to purchase old public housing and newly built apartments. However, urban Chinese have been unable or reluctant to buy. Because public housing rents were low and housing purchase prices relatively high in proportion to earnings, there was little incentive to buy.

Thus, the government initiated rent reform in the mid-1980s. Planners sought to increase incentives for home buying as well as to generate revenue for public housing maintenance and construction by raising rents to reflect the actual costs of inputs and maintenance. Rent reform policy was formulated during experiments in the mid-1980s in Yantai, Bengbu, and Tangshan. In 1988 the state issued the National Program for the Step by Step Implementation of Housing Reform in Cities and Towns, extending rent reform to other cities. However, city governments have been reluctant to raise rents owing to fears that this might lead to urban unrest. In addition, city officials feared that some residents would be unable to afford increased rents. Rent increases in many cities were accompanied by subsidies to workers. According to a measure known as "raising rents and subsidies" (*tizu butie*), workers residing in public housing were compensated for rent increases with a subsidy calculated at 2% of their wages. Despite these subsidies, city governments were reluctant to raise rents significantly, especially following the widespread urban protests in 1989.

While rent increases and home ownership schemes remained on the reform agenda, a third strategy was adopted to raise revenue for housing construction and renovation. The government promoted "cooperative funds" to pool state, local government, enterprise, and individual assets for housing investment. These funds usually consisted of contributions from workers and employers, and sometimes from local governments. In Guangzhou, for example, each party (worker, employer, and local government) contributed the equivalent of 5% of a worker's wages. However, similar to public housing sales, cooperative housing funds have been slow to take off.

Meanwhile, housing problems continue to plague policymakers. Although official statistics indicate that urban average per capita living space rose from 3.6m^2 in 1978 to 8.1m^2 in 1995, housing is still in short supply. Despite central government attempts to push reform over the past 15 years, rents for public housing remain low, and home ownership is limited. The trend is toward the privatization of housing provision, although the state continues to invest in and exercise control over the housing system. Although individuals purchased 143 million m^2 of commercial housing between 1986 and 1995, this comprised only a third of total commercial housing purchases. Work units still build and purchase a high proportion of housing, and most urban dwellers either cannot afford to purchase housing or are unwilling to do so because rents remain low.

The prospects are for slow change in the housing provision system. Because rapid rent increases are politically unattractive, incremental rent hikes and gradual increases in home ownership are expected. As the population continues to grow, the state will have difficulty improving housing unless it invests much more. Furthermore, current reform strategies are based partly on the assumption that urban residents' purchasing power will continue to grow; declines in urban income may render reforms ineffectual. In any case, the housing conditions of the urban poor are unlikely to improve dramatically.

Pensions and Old-Age Insurance

Under the pensions system established in the 1950s, state enterprises and other state work units provided retirement pensions to urban workers, and each work place was responsible for funding its own pension expenditures. Individuals did not make pensions contributions, and after they retired received pensions calculated at between 75% and 100% of their last wage. Additionally, pensioners were allowed to remain in their state or work unit housing, and were eligible for health coverage from their former work unit. However, rural dwellers–the vast majority of the Chinese population–were not covered by a pensions scheme, and were forced to rely on their families in old age.

Owing to the reform period emphasis on enterprise efficiency, together with rising demands on the state, the government has argued the need to relieve the pensions burden on work places. Changing population demographics also concern government officials: the ratio of pensioners to workers decreased from 1:30 in 1978 to 1:6 in 1990, with the trend expected to continue. Moreover, owing to the one-child policy, the current generation of children each will have four grandparents to support. The government is aware that a non-family-based support system for the elderly is imperative, and for this reason a new pensions system is being introduced both in cities and in the countryside.

Initiated in 1986, urban pension reform was designed to divide the burden of pension costs among employees and various kinds of enterprises. Significantly, the reform obligated urban dwellers for the first time to contribute directly to pension funds run by local governments. It also aimed to pool pensions among enterprises of different kinds in state-run pension funds. This arrangement was designed to distribute the burden more evenly among old enterprises that have many retirees and new enterprises that have fewer. Employees pensions were to be paid from the fund, rather than by the enterprise itself.

At present, the system usually works as follows: first, the local government sets up a social insurance company to administer pension funds. Enterprises contribute to the fund, calculating their contributions as a percentage of their total wage bill. Initially, this was fixed at between 12% and 15%, although it has risen to 20% in some localities. An individual account is also set up for each employee, who contributes a percentage (now usually 4%, although the rate may vary) of her or his wage to that account.

Government "contributions" are made via tax breaks on employee pension contributions and via financial support to state enterprises unable to fulfill their pension fund obligations. The amount of pension payments to retirees depends on the contributions they have made, and often there is no set payment. Uncertain of the future value of pensions, some local governments only guarantee that retirees will receive enough to maintain a basic standard of living.

At first, the new pension scheme was extended to state enterprise workers hired after 1986. Since then the scheme has been extended to workers in collectives. By early 1997, approximately 25% of urban employees still had not joined. Of these 25%, most are workers in private or overseas-funded enterprises, rural laborers working in the cities, and the self-employed. Some of these enterprises take out commercial pension insurance for their employees rather than contribute to state-run funds, but many employees are not covered at all. Although local regulations sometimes stipulate that the reformed pension system should include those workers not covered by their work places, local government officials claim they cannot enforce these regulations in non-state enterprises. There are also plans to include employees in government departments and other public institutions in the new pensions system. This is considered less urgent, however, because public institutions are not subject to enterprise reform, and the state is the main direct contributor regardless of whether payment is made by the work place or via state social insurance companies.

Owing to increases in the elderly population in the countryside, pensions also are being introduced in rural areas. Implementation has been patchy and slow. Not surprisingly, although provincial governments have attempted to set up pension schemes in the poor regions of Guangxi and Yunnan in the southwest, a pensions system has yet to take root in the many areas where incomes are still low. In 1995 rural old-age pensions schemes covered only 6% of China's 800 million farmers. Targets are markedly lower than for urban pension reform; planners hope to cover 50% of the rural population by 2020.

Currently, state officials face numerous difficulties in implementing pensions reforms. First, while poor enterprises often are willing to join the pooling system, wealthier enterprises choose to abide by the old system, take out commercial insurance for their employees, or provide no pensions at all. This limits the capacity of state insurance funds to relieve the pension burden on old enterprises. Second, because pensions schemes are controlled at the local level and individuals cannot transfer their pensions between localities, labor mobility is limited. The central government aims to have a unified system in place by 1997 and, on that basis, to pool funds at the provincial level by the year 2000. Ultimately, the goal is to create a national system; however, because this would require redistribution between regions, a national system remains a rather distant objective.

In addition, effecting pension reform is complicated by rising unemployment. One mechanism for increasing finances available for pensions would be to raise the retirement age, which now is relatively low (at 55 for women and 60 for men). However, owing to unemployment the government prefers to retire older workers to open up jobs for the young. Thus, the government's limited options include raising the levels of worker contributions. In early 1996 officials announced their goal of raising individual pension contributions to at least 4% of workers' salaries in 1997, and by one percentage point every two years after 1998 until contributions reach 8%.

The high profitability of the pensions business (currently, pension contributors exceed retirees, creating a fund surplus) has had both positive and negative effects on the development of the pension system. By late 1995, urban pension funds had accumulated 300 billion *yuan* nationwide. These funds are expected to remain profitable until at least 2010, when the number of workers retiring and drawing pensions from the funds begins to increase significantly.

Meanwhile, rural pensions insurance funds had reached 6.4 billion *yuan* by early 1997, increasing the likelihood that local governments will continue to extend coverage in the short to medium term. Their success will be dependent on the extent of and increase in rural wealth.

Not surprisingly, misuses of pensions funds are common. Local governments and their social insurance companies reportedly have used pensions funds for a range of illegitimate ends, such as buying stock market shares or investing in capital construction. In response, the central government has sought to tighten controls over the use of pension funds, urging local governments to establish supervisory institutions.

Despite efforts to expand pensions coverage, a significant number of workers still are not included under the new schemes. In 1995 most workers and state institution employees and officials were still receiving their pensions under the old system, indicating that these workers were receiving pension payments from their work units and that their pension payments were calculated as a percentage of their last pre-retirement wage. By the end of 1995, official sources reported that 71.4% of urban employees' pensions were calculated in this way. However, by early 1997 officials sources claimed that over 87 million people (or 76% of all urban employees) and more than 22 million retirees (94.7% of the total) had joined the pensions insurance program. This sudden increase in the number of participants may reflect the expansion of the schemes over those two years, but more likely it reflects crude statistical calculations.

Unemployment Insurance

Because of the Maoist leadership's commitment to full employment, no unemployment insurance system existed prior to the mid-1980s. Since then, unemployment insurance has been introduced primarily to promote labor mobility and facilitate enterprise reform by providing safety nets for workers made redundant or on short-term contracts.

The new unemployment insurance system, like the new pensions system, aims to pool contributions from different enterprises, usually within cities or rural counties. The schemes initially were limited to state-owned enterprises (SOEs), then extended to collective enterprises, and in some areas have now been extended to foreign-funded and private enterprises. Under the new system, enterprises pay 1% of their total wage bill to a fund, and employees who lose their jobs are paid 60% to 80% of the "lowest wage standard" for up to a maximum of 24 months. This is more generous than similar schemes in Canada, Germany, and the US.

So far, the new unemployment insurance schemes have been introduced in 22 provinces and provincial level cities. According to official sources, 100 million employees were participating in unemployment schemes by 1995. However, many fall through this safety net, especially rural migrants and others not registered as unemployed. Officially, there are now approximately 7 million people registered as unemployed in China, or 3.5% of the total urban population. The definition of "unemployed," however, is narrow; falling outside this category are the "unofficial" unemployed, mainly persons who have been suspended from their work because their enterprises have no work for them or cannot afford to pay full employee wages. The official number of people in this category is 15 million, although the actual figure is probably higher. These workers do not qualify for unemployment relief because they are considered to be only temporarily laid off. Although their enterprises are supposed to continue paying a percentage of their wage, some enterprises are unable to do so, and many people are now forced to survive by other means. In some places, people have to pay a fee to be registered as unemployed, and thus are discouraged from doing so. As a result, unemployment insurance schemes have failed to provide comprehensive safety nets. Moreover, if the number of long-term unemployed continues to grow, officials will need to extend the current system and combine unemployment payments with retraining measures.

Other problems lie in the management of unemployment insurance funds. By the end of 1996, these funds had accumulated 500 million *yuan*, and, similar to pensions funds, had amassed large surpluses. Consequently, greater supervision is needed to prevent mismanagement of these funds.

Work Injury Insurance

Work injury insurance was stipulated in the 1951 Labor Insurance Regulations, and like other forms of labor insurance has been under threat. Public enterprises struggling to compete on open markets often are unable to fulfill their insurance obligations. In order to overhaul the work injury insurance system, reforms are being introduced with the aim of pooling contributions and setting up individual accounts. In 1996, official sources claimed that 30 million people were participating in trial work injury insurance systems, or about 5% of the working population. In August 1996, the Ministry of Labor issued the Measures on Trials of Enterprise Employees Work Injury Insurance in an attempt to systematize the new local schemes. These measures are now being extended and are slated to be more heavily promoted in 1997. Official sources claim that work injury insurance will be available in 2,000 cities and counties to 70% of employees nationwide by the end of 1997. These targets may be overly optimistic, however. In practice, local governments are encountering problems in introducing this new insurance owing to difficulties in anticipating costs and in reconciling different work injury risks and rates across different industries.

Maternity Insurance

Until the late 1980s, women in SOEs and collectives were entitled to 56 days paid maternity leave. In September 1988, new regulations extended that leave to 90 days. Although these regulations were intended to improve women's rights (the costs of both

paid maternity leave and hospital treatment are paid by employers), they effectively have reduced employers' willingness to hire women. In these efficiency-sensitive times, female workers are viewed as less cost-effective than male workers, and are the first to be made redundant.

Maternity insurance provisions are now being reformed. In 1995 the Ministry of Labor's Provisional Measures for Enterprise Employee Maternity Insurance took effect. Under these rules, all urban enterprises are required to make payments to maternity insurance funds, while individuals do not make contributions. Local governments estimate the maternity costs in the locality and set the rate of enterprise contributions accordingly, although payments are not to exceed 1% of the total wage bill. Women on maternity leave are paid the equivalent of the average wage in that enterprise from the insurance fund that is managed by the local state social insurance company. Because all enterprises are required to participate, officials believe that implementation of these provisions will reduce the perception that individual female employees impose a financial burden on their employers. In practice, officials have promoted this reform with much less enthusiasm than other labor insurance measures. In 1995, 11 million employees were participating in maternity insurance fund pooling systems, or less than 2% of the working population. By 1996, trials were being carried out in 740 counties and cities, and the official target is to make maternity insurance available in 1,000 cities and counties by the end of 1997; however, progress likely will be slow.

Health Care and Medical Insurance

Health standards in China have improved considerably since 1949. Through programs aimed at improving public hygiene and preventative health care, many contagious and endemic diseases were eradicated. Life expectancy in China rose from 32 years for both women and men in 1950 to 71 years for women and 68 years for men in 1985. However, a widening gap in health provision existed between rural China, which enjoyed only basic preventative care, and urban China, which enjoyed curative hospital care (additionally, many urban dwellers received health care free of charge).

In rural China under Mao, health coverage was provided via the commune, which organized collective funding of preventative care and public hygiene. Under this system, rural dwellers paid into funds set up to provide medicines, immunization, and to pay barefoot doctors and some hospital costs. However, decollectivization and the introduction of the household responsibility system during the reform period have diminished the power of the collectives and their ability to raise funds for health programs. Whereas collective health schemes covered nearly 85% of rural dwellers in 1975, that number had dropped to a startling 5% by 1989. Currently, many rural dwellers now rely on their own resources to cover medical costs, even for primary health needs. Although the central government has promised to intervene, declines in rural health care coverage are not likely to be significantly reversed in the near future.

Prior to the reform period, many urban workers were the beneficiaries of a health care system that placed the burden of payment on the state and its enterprises. Under this system, government and state enterprise employees and their dependants received comprehensive health care coverage, including sickness benefits and benefits for employees that became disabled. Because enterprises paid for these benefits out of their own operating funds, those with a higher proportion of older, disabled, and chronically sick and retired workers were at a clear disadvantage when forced to enter the competitive market system in the 1980s. Escalating worker medical costs exacerbated the problem, rising from a total of 2.7 billion *yuan* in 1978 to 55.8 billion *yuan* in 1994.

Changes in urban demographics during the reform period have led to increases in the number of urban dwellers who fall outside this health care scheme. Owing to the growing number of unemployed urban workers, rural migrants, and workers in the private sector, the government has sought to reform the urban medical insurance system. Trial reforms have focused on pooling enterprise contributions and creating individual employee accounts. In the city of Zhenjiang, for example, enterprises pay the equivalent of 10% of an employee's gross wage to a fund, of which 50% goes into an individual account in the worker's name, according to different ratios for workers of different ages. Workers contribute 1% of their total annual pay to their individual accounts. Workers' medical expenses are first paid from the individual accounts and then by the individuals themselves. However, after self-paid expenses exceed 5% of annual wage income, they are paid from the social fund (workers still pay a percentage, which decreases as expenses rise).

These reforms have proceeded slowly. Similar to pensions schemes, newer, wealthier enterprises, including large private and foreign-invested enterprises, often are unwilling to participate. Despite this, officials announced in April 1996 that trials would be extended to 57 cities. Soon after, plans were announced to extend the reform further to cover 15 million people in 28 provinces by the end of 1997. Meanwhile, medical insurance coverage varies according to region and employment status. Professionals, managers, and skilled workers more often are provided for than unskilled or migrant workers.

Other reforms have damaged health care. Attempting to contain its health care spending, the government has reduced subsidies to health providers (such as hospitals) and has tried to increase health providers' financial accountability and incentives to operate more efficiently. Hospital fees have been made to reflect the cost of treatment; as a result, medical treatment is now more expensive. Higher medical fees have reduced the number of patients in hospitals, and so hospital managers often seek alternatives to state funding to raise revenue. These alternatives may include establishing factories or other businesses. Meanwhile, making hospitals more self-reliant has created several other problems. For example, hospitals increasingly focus on providing costly, revenue-generating treatment and services, rather than on providing much needed basic care. In this commercialized atmosphere, instances of bribing doctors has increased. Overall, the numbers of health care practitioners has risen, as have health care costs for urban dwellers.

Currently, China spends 3.2% of its GDP on health care, below the World Health Organization's recommended 5%. Moreover, a larger proportion of this spending is aimed at hospitals and curative care, while spending on preventative care has declined. Patient fees are now a higher percentage of health expenditures, and budgetary spending is down. Because many SOEs are unable to reimburse employee medical costs, more Chinese than ever before are forced to pay for their own health care treatment. Overall, the system remains inefficient; for example, hospital treatment for relatively affluent urban dwellers drains resources from the rural poor. Less than 20% of the population are estimated to consume almost 60% of the total health care budget.

Provisions for Disabled People

Official estimates put the number of disabled people in China at around 50 million, or more than 5% of the population, although the number could be even higher. During the pre-reform period, the state provided jobs (often in so-called "welfare enterprises") for those disabled persons who were able to work. Otherwise, the disabled were dependent on their families, and for those that had no family, the state provided minimal support.

During the reform period, Deng Pufang, the disabled son of Deng Xiaoping, has promoted disabilities awareness as well as the rights of disabled persons. His efforts have resulted in more positive portrayals of disabled people, the creation of the National Federation for the Disabled (which has local branch associations

throughout the country), and, in 1991, the Law of the Protection of the Disabled, which prohibits discrimination against disabled people.

However, government support for disabled people still focuses on encouraging self-reliance by enabling them to work, and the number of welfare enterprises has expanded during the reform period.

Welfare enterprises are run by municipal and district governments, and sometimes by neighborhood offices. In addition to state welfare enterprises, the number of non-state, semi-private welfare enterprises has increased, partly because such enterprises are given tax breaks by the state. In 1995, 950,000 disabled people were employed in these enterprises. The older state-run welfare enterprises often have difficulty surviving in the competitive market economy because their technology is outdated and they lack sufficient funds for capital investment. However, some of the newer welfare enterprises, including those in the countryside, can be highly profitable.

Disabled people who cannot work are cared for primarily by their families. "Community-based" support services for families (provided by local government and residents) are sometimes available but vary in quality and offer only minimal care. Although some local authorities have set up clinics and other facilities such as gymnasiums, therapy centers, special schools, and hospitals for mentally disabled children, these are not widely available. Some local authorities provide services to help the disabled set themselves up in business. These services mainly consist of advice and support, but not capital investment. In addition, some local governments occasionally provide modified housing for disabled residents.

Social Welfare, Social Relief, and Community Services

In pre-reform China "social welfare" (defined here as financial assistance for the impoverished) and "social relief" (including provision of welfare homes and other minor social services) covered those who fell outside the work-place based social security system. However, where possible, families were expected to provide support for the disabled and elderly. The primary recipients of non-work-place based state welfare were orphans and the disabled or elderly who had no family.

Social Relief

Prior to the reform period, rural relief work was targeted mainly at "five guarantee households" (*wubaohu*). This meant that food, clothing, education, housing, medical care, and burial were guaranteed to orphans and disabled and elderly persons who had no other means of support. In 1978 only 2.7 million persons received this relief. Although aid also was made available to families experiencing particular hardship, the decline of rural collectivity since 1983 has jeopardized community welfare funding, and villages have not always been able to provide the five guarantees to the poorest households.

In the cities, social welfare and relief programs were targeted at people who had no work unit and no family, and therefore no means of support. Aid was also available for "households with special difficulties" (*tekun-nan hu*), although this aid was usually short-term and provided only to a small number of families. Army veterans and the families of servicemen who died while in service also received some form of assistance. The urban funding for social welfare was greater than in rural areas, but still a low priority in overall government spending. From 1950–78 the spending of "civil affairs" departments that deliver social relief averaged approximately 1.6% of public spending. These departments allocated about one-third of their budgets for urban relief and related administration, and even less on rural relief.

Since 1978 unemployment and inflation have created greater income inequalities and a new urban poor. Officially the urban poor now number 20 million, although the actual figure is probably higher. Migration

has weakened and fragmented family support structures, and those eligible for social relief has doubled in many cities. In response to these developments, the government is broadening the scope of social welfare and relief provision. Since 1993, 31 cities have adopted the "basic living guarantee" system. According to this system, each municipal government sets a minimum income line and supplements (sometimes together with work units) the incomes of those who fall beneath the line. Minimum income lines vary from city to city, since living costs depend on local prices and levels of economic development. Current minimum income lines range from 230 *yuan* per month in the wealthy southern city of Foshan to 100 *yuan* per month in poorer areas. Although official sources claim that relief expenditures are not burdensome to city governments, some cities have delayed setting the basic living guarantee line because they cannot afford the increase in spending. Nevertheless, officials plan to have this system operating in every Chinese city by the year 2000.

Even families receiving social relief struggle to feed and clothe themselves. In cities that have not adopted the new relief system, inflation has devalued relief payments, which remain at a low average of 40 *yuan*. Regular fixed support for urban elderly and disabled persons without families is only 50 *yuan* on average, while relief for families of revolutionary martyrs and ex-servicemen is also inadequate and in need of reform. Instead of raising relief levels, local governments usually try to solve problems by non-financial means. The Women's Federation, individual work units, and "neighborhood offices" (the lowest level of state administration in the cities) are charged with assisting unemployed or temporarily laid-off workers, usually by finding them alternative work. Social relief is often not available to unemployed or temporarily laid-off workers unless a minimum living standard has been set.

In rural areas, the family still provides basic support for the elderly. Poverty relief is available only for meeting emergency needs such as food and clothing. Rural relief payments average only 12 *yuan*, and rural relief expenditures have risen more slowly than urban relief spending (in 1994 rural relief accounted for just over one-tenth of total relief spending). However relief is also available for rural victims of natural disasters; central disaster relief in 1995 alone totaled 1.9 billion *yuan*. In addition, loans have been issued to help the poor start economic projects, although these monies often are diverted from disaster relief funds. Overall, very little state spending is allocated for social relief.

Community Services

In 1986 the Ministry of Civil Affairs launched a "community services" initiative aimed at increasing the range of welfare facilities provided to urban dwellers by the lowest levels of the "civil affairs" administration and by local residents and other volunteers. In fact, the initiative formalized many practices that already were in place, often uniting them under the roof of a single local "community services center." It also has led to an expanded range of amenities provided by neighborhood offices and residents' committees such as nursing homes for the elderly, nurseries, clinics, and organized recreational activities and household help. By 1992 a total of 112,000 such community service facilities had been established. The 4,300 urban community centers in operation by the end of 1995 offered a range of recreational activities, including exercise classes, health lectures, and other educational services. Owing to changes in population demographics resulting from the one-child policy, community services are targeted less for children and more for the elderly. Unfortunately, the centers are poorly resourced, and thus largely dependent on charging fees or conducting business activities to stay afloat financially. Some centers are also financed by "welfare lotteries." Although gambling is forbidden in China, civil affairs departments can stage lotteries to raise funds for welfare projects such as community service work.

The community services initiative also encourages local citizens to visit the elderly and sick or assist others with household repairs. The task of organizing these activities has fallen to the residents' committees who already provide some basic social welfare services in the cities. Significantly, although they are staffed by volunteers, residents' committees are formal institutions created by the state. Thus, local governments provide organization but little investment for most welfare activities. Instead of increasing the funding of residents' committees, the government has allowed them to set up income-generating businesses or to charge small fees for their services. This arrangement has led to a wide range of facilities (both in quality and types) provided under the rubric of "community services."

Welfare homes include homes for the elderly and for orphans as well as psychiatric institutions. Previously, these mostly were administered by local governments; however, in the reform era the number of homes run by neighborhood offices and funded by non-state sources has grown. Some are run jointly by neighborhood offices and other units, including hospitals with reciprocal agreements, and do not receive state subsidies. Construction and operating costs for urban welfare homes administered by higher levels of local government are increasingly set up with contributions from enterprises and individuals. Often, although the state may provide the salaries of several staff members, these homes are otherwise self-financing. Many homes now charge fees for their services, and on this basis provide some beds free of charge to those elderly people with no family or income.

Overall, the number of welfare homes has risen from approximately 8,000 in 1979 to over 40,000 in 1991. Currently, most are run by neighborhood offices or other collectives. Despite this increase, welfare homes are still in short supply. In 1995, the 980,000 beds available in welfare homes across urban and rural China (or 8.2 beds for every 100,000 people) fell short of the central government's goal by 20,000 beds. Although homes for the elderly have increased, orphanages and psychiatric homes have suffered even greater investment shortages.

Conclusion and Prospects

In rural China, the dismantling of the communes and the decollectivization of agriculture has spurred the state and welfare providers to search for new sources of welfare finance. This often proves difficult (especially in poor localities) and produces significant variation in the quality of welfare provision across rural China. Welfare reforms are further developed in urban China, where the former system heavily burdened the state and thus created a much greater imperative for change. However, rural localities gradually have introduced pensions schemes. According to official accounts, 33% of townships and towns had begun to set up social security networks by the end of 1995.

Overall, the current welfare system is marked by a trend toward transferring welfare costs to the population. Some observers refer to this trend as the "privatization" of the system (Wong 1994). In all spheres of welfare provision, including housing, pensions, unemployment, injury, maternity, and health insurance, welfare planners have sought to increase individual contributions while reducing the state's share of the welfare burden. However, there has been no consultation or public debate over the content, form, or pace of the welfare system reforms. Because China does not have independent trade unions, these changes have not been negotiated, despite the fact that many of the reforms entail substantial changes to the terms and conditions of work for urban state employees.

Spending on social welfare and relief is also low. Although civil affairs departments spending rose from 1.4 billion *yuan* in 1978 to 10.3 billion *yuan* in 1995, the average annual percentage of public expenditure increased only slightly from 1.6% to 1.64%. While the state still provides some measure of social relief, community services and welfare institutions now rely on non-state sources of investment and funding. Welfare providers often generate income by charging fees for services, by conducting business activities, and by holding welfare lotteries. Also, providers rely increasingly on charitable contributions and activities. However, the state has maintained its role in setting policy and organizing and supervising welfare provision.

Although reformers gradually have extended the scope of the new labor insurance systems, coverage is still limited. Old-age insurance reform, which has sought to created a unified system by pooling insurance funds at provincial and then national levels, have been implemented with some success. However, implementation of unemployment, work injury, maternity, and medical insurance reforms has been fraught with difficulties. Thus, many workers still rely on their work units, especially for housing and medical coverage. This places undue burden on state-owned enterprises, undermining their ability to compete in an increasingly market-oriented economy. Meanwhile, many Chinese who are not employed by state enterprises fall through the safety nets.

At present the social welfare system is fragmented; several state organs each administer separate strands of welfare provision. Labor departments administer labor insurance, including urban pensions; civil affairs departments oversee residual welfare, social relief, community services, and rural pensions; health departments administer health care and insurance; and personnel departments handle the pensions of public employees outside the enterprise sector. Although officials have discussed the creation of a single Social Security Ministry to improve the efficiency of welfare provision, none has been implemented. Some cities have managed to unify social security in a single municipal bureau (including Shanghai and Guangzhou), but in other areas officials note that differing rates of reform implementation among welfare-sponsoring state agencies have undermined their attempts to standardize the system. In addition, state agencies are unwilling to surrender control of their insurance funds.

Currently, the lack of strict supervision and control poses the biggest problem for welfare provision and the welfare reform program. While welfare policies and the regulations for their implementation provide for generous coverage, regulations are often ignored or not fully implemented, and many migrants and workers in loss-making SOEs do not receive the insurance coverage due to them.

The central government's inability to enforce the implementation of laws and regulations governing official behavior has allowed for mismanagement of social insurance funds by local governments and social insurance companies. Although some officials admit that they are not competent to manage the funds, lacking the knowledge to invest safely and properly, others misappropriate the funds knowingly. In response, the central government announced in early 1997 its intention to tighten control over these funds. Indeed, a key task facing central government leaders is to ensure the effective implementation of new laws, regulations, and reforms.

As the urban work place-based system of welfare provision in China has crumbled under market reforms, many workers have been left unprovided for. Some no long receive their full wages or pensions; for others without health coverage, sickness can plunge them into poverty. In both rural and urban areas, safety nets are needed to cushion the impact of growing inequalities and thereby promote more balanced development. While some of the welfare reform measures have sought to create social safety nets, the lack of consultation and negotiation over their form and the pace of their introduction, together with problems of implementation, means that some of the groups hardest hit by market reform do not receive adequate social relief. A large number of people remain disadvantaged and excluded from the benefits of the country's economic growth.

Further Reading

There are very few books on social welfare in China, and those that do exist are rapidly becoming outdated as China reforms its system of welfare provision. The best available books and articles are the following:

Chan, Cecelia L.W., *More Welfare After Economic Reform? Welfare Development in the People's Republic of China,* Hong Kong: Department of Social Work and Social Administration, University of Hong Kong, 1992

A slim volume that deals more comprehensively than most with the Mao era welfare system. It also deals with the post-1979 period, with the focus largely on the work by civil affairs administration. It also deals with the philosophy that underpins both old and new welfare systems.

Chan, Cecelia L.W., "New Challenges to the Forms of Welfare Provision in China After a Decade of Economic Reform," in *International Social Work* 35 (1992)

Brief coverage of occupational welfare, social relief, and community services.

Chan, Cecelia L.W., *The Myth of Neighbourhood Mutual Help: The Contemporary Community-based Welfare System in Guangzhou,* Hong Kong: Hong Kong University Press, 1993

Concentrates on the Community Services initiative, with analysis from the point of view of social policy.

Hussain, Athar, *Reform of the Chinese Social Security System,* London: LSE Research Programme on the Chinese Economy, 1993

A pamphlet in the STICERD working paper series. Though short, it is well informed on the welfare reforms up to the very early 1990s. Covers health, pensions, and unemployment insurance reforms, and provides some comparative analysis.

Leung, Joe C.B., "Dismantling the 'Iron Rice Bowl': Welfare Reforms in the People's Republic of China," in *Journal of Social Policy* 23, part 3 (July 1994)

Examines occupational welfare, rural social security, and community services, with a consideration of future development trends.

Leung, Joe C.B., and Richard C. Nann, *Authority and Benevolence: Social Welfare in China,* New York: St. Martin's Press, and Hong Kong: Chinese University of Hong Kong Press, 1995

Discusses the "iron rice bowl" but concentrates largely on neighborhood-based welfare and the work of civil affairs departments; considers the extent to which the welfare system is "Confucian."

Wong, Linda J., "Privatization of Social Welfare in Post-Mao China," in *Asian Survey* 34, no. 4 (April 1994)

Discusses community services and welfare institutions and trends in privatization.

Wong, Linda J., and Stewart MacPherson, editors, *Social Change and Social Policy in Contemporary China,* Aldershot, Hampshire, and Brookfield, Vermont: Avebury, 1995

This is probably the best single volume on welfare in China, with good, reasonably up to date contributions on various aspects of the welfare system. See especially Nelson Chow on labor insurance issues, Veronica Pearson on health, Linda Wong on social relief, and Peter Nan-shong Lee on housing.

Jane Duckett is Lecturer in the Department of Government, University of Manchester, England. She is the author of *Guidance Note on Ethnicity: Indigenous Peoples and Ethnic Minorities* (with others, 1996).

Chapter Twenty-One

China's Nationalities and Nationality Areas

Katherine Palmer

When Deng Xiaoping announced in December 1978 the beginning of a "profound and extensive revolution to socialist modernization," the Chinese government also proclaimed the start of a "new era" in minority affairs. The Chinese Communist Party (CCP) declared that during its first 30 years in power it had established minorities' *political* equality with the majority Han population; now it promised that it would promote *economic* equality among the nationalities as well. No longer would minorities wallow in the throes of poverty as their Han neighbors enjoyed nearly twice their income, attended the best schools, and dominated the most prestigious public offices. Under the "new era" of socialist modernization, the party promised, inequality and prejudice would be eradicated completely and mutual prosperity established throughout the country.

However, despite official pledges to reduce economic inequality and provide equal opportunities for all nationalities, reforms since 1979 have exacerbated the economic disparity between the minorities and the Han. Although the nationalities comprise only 8% of China's total population, more than 50% of all counties below the abject poverty line in 1985 were minority areas. By 1988, 74.5% of the poorest counties were occupied by minorities, and the discrepancies continue to grow. Productivity rates in minority areas are scarcely half those in Han areas, and have fallen steadily in relative terms since the mid-1980s.

The CCP appears to recognize the potential dangers of continued inequality among the nationalities. In 1989 President Jiang Zemin declared that improving the minorities' standard of living had become one of the most pressing problems facing the regime. "Eliminating poverty in minority areas is not just a question of economics," he reminded his audience. "It is essential to ensure stability . . . and protect the fatherland." The government's alarm soared as open rioting erupted throughout many of the autonomous areas in the late 1980s. The party declared martial law in Tibet in 1989 to quell a series of bloody clashes between Tibetan monks and Han police, and reportedly more than 500 ethnic activists died during a failed independence movement in northwestern Xinjiang Autonomous Region. Ethnic Mongolians in the Inner Mongolian Autonomous Region established at least two organizations—The Self-Governing Committee of Inner Mongolia and The Asian Mongolian Freedom Front—to agitate for full independence from China and union with Outer Mongolia. Clashes between Mongolian activists and the government reportedly left 200 dead in May 1990. Even minorities such as the Zhuang, traditionally hailed as no different than the majority Han, began calling for their members to "wake up" and "take charge of their own leadership."

More than 72 million people make up the 55 officially recognized minority nationalities in China. While great social disruption would occur if even 1% of these people decided to challenge government rule, the minorities' political power far outweighs their mere numbers. Although minorities account for only 8% of the country's population, minority communities are spread across roughly 65% of China's total landmass, 18% of the nation's arable land, 94% of the grassland plains, and 38% of the national forests; moreover, territories with minority communities contain 40% of the coal deposits, more than 50% of the water resources, and possess a large percentage of the country's mineral resources. Assuring the nationalities' loyalty and participation in the Chinese nation-state is particularly important to the Chinese government given that 90% of China's international borders fall in minority territory. These borders arbitrarily divide more than 30 Chinese nationalities from their counterparts in neighboring states. For example, Kazaks, Tajiks, Uzbeks, Uigurs, and Kirghiz are found along both sides of the Sino-Soviet border, and Zhuang live in southwest China as well as in Burma, Laos, Thailand, and Vietnam.

China has boasted the world's fastest growing large economy since 1978, yet minority groups have become increasingly embittered over their relative drop in economic status. Many nationality activists have accused the government of neglecting minority needs, and, more incendiary still, a number of groups openly have charged the Han with exploiting minorities and stripping them of their land's natural resources. What explains the rise in minority activism over the past two decades, and how is the government responding to increasingly vocal challenges to its control?

The surge in ethnic demands for preferential economic policies is not solely a result of the increasing gap in wealth between the minority and Han areas. Early CCP minority policy, developed in the 1920s and implemented throughout the Maoist era, radically increased minority consciousness and led minorities to believe they had unique claim to autonomous rights and preferential government treatment. Since 1978, the central government's promise to eradicate ethnic inequality has galled ethnic groups as they have become impoverished in relation to their Han counterparts. This chapter first briefly examines how early CCP policy inadvertently contributed to a rise in ethnic consciousness. The chapter then examines the sources of increasing disparity since 1978 and the minority response to their relative impoverishment.

Early CCP Policy

The minorities in China are extremely diverse, speaking more than 60 separate languages that belong to at least five separate language families. Different minority groups adhere to all of the world's major religions, and many practice religions unique to their nationality. Some groups historically have cooperated with the Han and gradually adopted many of their customs, while others have long traditions of open conflict and warfare with the ruling Han majority.

Prior to this century, no Chinese government had succeeded in integrating the minorities. The history of Imperial China is riddled with incidents of minority raids on the Han mainland and bloody repression campaigns against the nationalities. In exchange for peace, the Imperial administration allowed minorities to govern themselves and to offer only nominal tutelage to the Emperor. On the eve of the communist takeover, nearly all of the minorities lived in isolated, self-sufficient communities and had little contact with their Han neighbors. Few could speak Mandarin Chinese, and most treated all outsiders with suspicion.

Upon its rise to power, the CCP wanted to change the existing administrative system. Its minority policy was designed to integrate the hundreds of ethnic groups living in scattered isolation throughout Chinese territory into a unified communist state. When the communists first entered minority territory in the 1930s, they encountered fierce resistance from the nationalities. In order to gain their support, the CCP promoted itself as the protector of minority interests and promised the minorities self-rule. In keeping with Marxist theory, the party believed that nationality was a reflection of class relations and would fade as communism took root. It therefore saw little threat in promising minorities full autonomy. Ultimately, however, the party's policy inadvertently increased minority consciousness and later ethnic mobilization in three primary ways.

First, the CCP officially recognized numerous nationalities that had not been considered separate ethnic groups by earlier governments, and acknowledged that each had its own unique culture and traditions. Until the 20th century, the Chinese government labeled nearly all non-Han "barbarians" and did not consider them separate peoples. Although the Kuomintang officially recognized five nationalities (Han, Manchu, Mongolian, Tibetans, and Muslim Turks), it generally pursued a policy of forced assimilation. Republican leader Sun Yat-sen declared in 1921 that the government should "facilitate the dying out of all names of individual peoples inhabiting China." By contrast, in an effort to distinguish themselves from the rival Nationalist party and to encourage pride among the nationalities, the CCP unleashed a flood of propaganda against pre-communist "oppression" of the minorities. By stressing minority recognition and promoting the minorities' right to preserve their unique cultures and languages, the CCP heightened the nationalities' awareness of minority issues.

Second, and perhaps more important, the party implemented a policy of regional autonomy, granting areas with dense concentrations of minorities the right to govern themselves. Dividing administrative regions on the basis of nationality provided the minorities with political legitimacy and an incentive to voice their interests and concerns.

Finally, the party granted the minorities a number of special economic, political, and social privileges to ensure minority autonomy and compensate them for centuries of Han exploitation. Among the economic benefits minorities received

were greater control over local budgets than non-minority areas, preferential tax terms, special scholarships and loans, and extra investment funds. Politically, the party guaranteed the minorities proportional representation on legislative bodies, established special schools to train minority cadres, and allowed nationalities to alter central government laws to "suit local minority traditions." On the social front, minorities officially were encouraged to develop their cultural traditions, use their own language, and practice their own religions.

Although many of the special privileges afforded the minorities were suspended during the Cultural Revolution, the policies designed and implemented during the Maoist period on the whole encouraged the minorities to conceive of themselves as unique nationalities with rights to preferential government treatment. Once these rights and privileges began to be challenged by the post-Mao reforms, the minorities began to resist central directives. Before recounting the ethnic response to the reforms, it is necessary first to examine the major sources of minority impoverishment under the reforms.

The Sources of Inequality

Poverty is not a new phenomenon to the minorities of China. Four key factors have limited development in minority regions since the CCP took control in 1949: geography, a weak infrastructure, low educational levels, and poorly developed trade and light industry. The economic reforms initiated by the government since 1978 have accentuated the negative influence of each of these factors rather than provided the means for overcoming them. The five primary tenets of the Dengist reforms brought rapid growth to the coastal areas, where most of the Han population lives, but contributed to a comparative disadvantage for the minority regions. These policies, which this chapter examines in turn, are incomplete price reforms, fiscal decentralization, the shift of government emphasis from regional equality to economic efficiency, increased reliance on new technology, and the easing of restrictions on foreign trade.

Geography

The impoverishment of China's minorities began nearly 2,000 years ago. The people who today call themselves Han originally lived in the center of present-day China. As they migrated out of the central plains beginning in the Han Dynasty (206 BC) they pushed their way into minority regions in the southwest, north, and northwest, often encountering prolonged resistance from the indigenous populations. As the Han consolidated their own position in the border regions, they grouped together in enclaves on the best land available, forcing the minority peoples into harsh, generally mountainous or desert terrain.

Most of the Xinjiang Uighur Autonomous Region in the northwest, for example, is covered by the formidable Gobi Desert. The region is cut off from its neighbors by great mountain ranges on three sides, and by the vast desert on the fourth. To the south, the very name "Tibet" conjures up images of an isolated mountain kingdom, occupied by rugged nomads who have learned to endure the region's harsh and inhospitable terrain. Within each of the autonomous regions, the best lands tend to be occupied by the Han settlers, while the minorities live in the more remote mountainous areas. In Guangxi, for example, more than 90% of the Zhuang, China's largest nationality, live in the western mountains of the province. Nearly 70% of Western Guangxi is comprised of minorities, while less than 10% of the eastern, more fertile flatlands, is non-Han.

Weak Infrastructure

The harsh terrain of the border regions has hindered the development of transportation and communication infrastructure in minority areas. Although significant infrastructure improvements have been made in the minority regions since 1949, these areas remain far less developed than the national average. For example, the number of roads in Tibet has more than quadrupled since 1949, yet the density and quality of these roads remain far below the national average. Nearly 64% of Tibet's roads are unpaved while 90% of all roads across the remainder of China are paved. Moreover, less than 34% of paved roads in China are classified as "low grade" while nearly 90% of paved roads in Tibet receive this rating. The Guangxi government often notes that more than 17,900 kilometers of road have been laid in its minority regions since 1949. Many of these roads, however, are barely traversable. Visitors to the region often hear of a "brand new, good road" between two county capitals, only to find that buses average only about 20 kilometers per hour owing to poor road conditions. Roads throughout the minority regions often are destroyed completely by floods, landslides, and poor maintenance. Beyond road quality, the sheer density of roads in the minority areas is only 42.8% of the national average. Likewise, the length of railroad lines in minority areas has more than doubled since 1949 in minority areas, yet the density of railroads remains only 37.53% of the national mean.

Low Educational Levels

Low educational levels also have contributed to the relative underdevelopment of minority areas. The minority areas have few means to fund their education system, and minority children are further disadvantaged because most textbooks are written in the Han language. Many minority children often encounter their first words of Mandarin Chinese in the primary school classroom.

The State Education Commission reported that the gross enrollment rate of school age minority children is about 20 percentage points lower than the national mean, with female enrollment rates even lower. The dropout rate for minority students also far exceeds the national average. Whereas across China the average citizen has 8.36 years of schooling, the figures for Inner Mongolia, Guangxi, Tibet, Ningxia, and Xinjiang were 6.5, 5.94, 1.92, 5.4, and 6.2, respectively. In the countryside (where most of the minorities live) the discrepancies between educational levels are even more striking. Nationally, 20.7% of non-urban workers are illiterate or semi-illiterate. These figures are much higher for minorities, including above 36% illiteracy rates in Ningxia and nearly 74% in Tibet.

The educational level of minority cadres falls far below the national average as well. The percentage of nationality cadres with a college level education in Inner Mongolia, Ningxia, Guangxi, Xinjiang, and Yunnan is 15.4%, 10.52%, 10.13%, 8.65%, and 7.97%, respectively, as compared to the national average of 19%.

Low Levels of Trade and Light Industry

Trade and light industry are particularly underdeveloped in minority regions. In 1949, although 60% of China's land was occupied by minorities, only 3.8% of the country's total industrial output was produced in minority regions. Subsequently, the government made a significant effort to develop industry in the minority regions, channeling large investments into several key industrial projects. Of the 650 large scale industrial projects established in minority regions through 1993, 72% were in heavy rather than light industry. These types of projects require large government support to build and operate, and, since the government has withdrawn its direct funding of major industrial plants as part of the greater reform initiative, the minorities have been left to watch as their primary source of revenue shrinks correspondingly.

Although the initiation of the Agricultural Responsibility System in the early years of the reform era led to significant growth in agricultural output throughout China, the bulk of the nation's growth rate has come from the development of its light industry and from the rise in foreign trade and investment. Fewer than 10% of China's minorities are involved in the non-agricul-

tural sector, and they have been increasingly left behind as light industry and trade have taken off in the eastern Han regions.

Economic Reforms Since 1978

Five key components of the economic reforms since 1978 have impacted the minorities' relative economic position. First, the reforms have moved China's former command economy toward a more liberal market economy, a transition that has been achieved in part through a multi-stage pricing reform. Second, in its effort to dismantle China's command economy, the central government has decentralized the country's fiscal system. Third, the CCP has abandoned the Maoist focus on regional equality in favor of economic efficiency. Under Mao, the government poured investments into some of the country's poorest areas in an effort to achieve regional equality. By contrast, the Dengist reforms not only allow greater inequalities but inadvertently exacerbate them. Fourth, China has opened its doors to the outside world in an effort to attract and develop new technologies. Finally, China has eased its restrictions on foreign trade. Each of these policies has contributed to the increasing gap in wealth between the Han and non-Han populations.

Incomplete Price Reform

After the Chinese Communist Party seized power in 1949, it instituted a state-fixed pricing structure designed to spur heavy industrial growth. Under this system, both the prices and the tax rates for raw materials and agricultural products were set at a relatively low rate, while high taxes and high prices were fixed for manufactured consumer goods. The government relied on the tax revenue from manufactured goods and had a vested interest in assuring that the manufacturing industries received all input factors necessary for production. The government thus purchased raw materials at a low cost and allocated them to the manufacturing industries. Once the government collected its revenue, it redistributed funds as it saw fit, often in the form of investment funds to the economically backward minority regions. However, the central government has lost much of its redistributive power owing to the fiscal decentralization reforms discussed below. Moreover, the pricing reforms have placed the minorities at a clear disadvantage. As noted above, the vast majority of industry in minority areas is heavy extractive industry. Because price reforms generally require producers of raw materials to sell a quota amount of goods to the state at low prices, the minority areas effectively are forced to provide important natural resource inputs to the manufacturing mills of the eastern, Han areas—regions that already enjoy greater central investment and benefits—at little profit to the minority communities.

Fiscal Decentralization

Another key component of the Dengist reforms has been fiscal decentralization. Although the government experimented with several different fiscal allocation systems between 1949 and 1979, generally the central government monopolized the control and allocation of fiscal resources until the early 1980s. Localities collected the taxes and turned them over to the central government, who in turn utilized the taxes extracted from coastal regions to aid the minority areas. The Dengist reforms allow localities to keep a greater percentage of tax revenues and to make more independent investment decisions. This policy, known as "eating from separate kitchens," disadvantages the minority areas in relation to the Han in two primary ways. First, since all localities now are allowed to keep a larger percentage of their local revenue, the wealthier Han areas end up with more funds in absolute terms. Second, the central government is less able to subsidize poorer regions because its share of total revenue has fallen.

From Regional Equality to Economic Efficiency

Prior to 1980, the Chinese government invested more heavily in the underdevel-

oped minority regions than in the Han regions because it hoped to achieve regional and ethnic equality. By 1986, however, the government decided that investment funds could not be utilized as efficiently in minority areas as in the Han regions, where infrastructure was better developed. The government announced that the Seventh Five-Year Plan (1986–90) would divide the country into three economic zones—eastern, central, and western—with the bulk of investment allocated to the eastern coastal provinces. Although the policy did not directly target minority regions for reduced investments, given the geographic distribution of nationalities, the policy effectively redirected funds away from minorities to the Han.

Within the first few years of implementing the coastal-oriented development strategy, the government recognized that the gap between Han and minority wealth was becoming increasingly wide. The government announced that the Ninth Five-Year Plan (1996–2000) would reverse earlier investment policies favoring the coastal areas and focus instead on developing the western and central regions. Although presumably this will limit any further negative impact of the coastal investment policy on the minorities, the results of the shift are not immediately apparent.

New Technology

While much of China's early development was based on increased factor input and extensive development policies, the reforms of the past two decades have been based largely on improving intensive growth, that is, on technological improvements. Low levels of education among the minorities have further disadvantaged them vis-à-vis their better trained Han counterparts.

To combat this problem, the government has launched a massive propaganda campaign to encourage minority children to attend school. Giant billboards are painted throughout minority areas urging the minority population to "become cultured (edu-

cated) to improve the nationalities' position."
Ironically, just as increasing numbers of
minorities recognize the value of education,
school access is declining owing to increased
burdens on the local minority governments
to fund their own educational systems.

Easing Restrictions on Foreign Trade

Recognizing that its economy could not
keep pace with its Asian neighbors if it continued its policy of banning all foreign
investment, China began to open its doors
to investment and trade. Moreover, because
the "four modernizations" (the declared aim
of the Dengist reforms; see the glossary
appendix) depended on utilizing foreign
technology and expertise, the party initiated
measures to attract foreign investment and
technological transfers immediately after
Deng Xiaoping came to power.

From a local perspective, foreign investment can create hundreds of new jobs and
increase tax revenue for infrastructure
development and education, among other
areas. Unfortunately, the minority regions
clearly have not been competitive with their
coastal Han neighbors in attracting foreign
firms. Between 1979 and 1987 more than
90% of foreign investment projects were
concentrated in the coastal provinces.
Although utilization of foreign funds
increased by 11.39% nationwide between
1994 and 1995, it fell significantly in the
minority areas. Only Inner Mongolia
increased its use of foreign capital, while
Guangxi reported a drop of nearly 17% and
Ningxia of 32.8%.

Through the 1990s, the minorities' share
of the country's foreign export earnings
failed to reach even 1%. The combined outlay for foreign imports of all five autonomous
regions did not reach 2% of China's total.
Moreover, within each of the autonomous
regions, foreign investment tended to be concentrated in the Han-populated areas.

The Ethnic Response

The reforms launched in the late 1970s have
liberalized both the command economy
and the absolute political control of the
communist party-state. Increased focus on
economic equality for all minorities during
the reforms and the gradual relaxation of
political dogmatism have allowed minority
organizations greater independence; these
developments also have provided concrete
issues around which to rally ethnic opposition and strengthen each nationality's internal solidarity. In turn, as ethnic groups have
mobilized against key aspects of the
reforms, their demands have expanded to
include greater political and social rights in
addition to economic equality. Minority ire
has been particularly strong against the
skewed pricing system, the center's explicit
favoring of eastern areas, and reductions in
preferential policies for minorities. Minority
activists have seized upon economic issues
to argue for greater cultural and religious
freedom, language reforms, and greater
minority representation in the government.
For example, two Zhuang authors argue
that "without economic equality we cannot
have political or cultural equality. We cannot become the true masters of our own
homes as long as economic inequality exists
in practice."

Price reforms over the past decade have
made the minorities increasingly aware that
they have not received the full benefits of
their rich natural resources. Qin Naichang,
director of the Guangxi Nationalities
Research Institute and former member of
the Guangxi Zhuang Nationalities Affairs
Commission, has become a leading spokesperson for greater minority economic and
political rights. In 1990 he attacked the government's practices:

> Not only has the central government *not*
> taken the interests of the nationalities into
> account when developing our natural
> resources, but it has forced them to make
> such huge sacrifices that their self-gover-
> nance and self-strengthening capabilities
> have been all but destroyed. If the poli-
> cies continue as they are, strengthening
> the national autonomous areas' economy
> and their ability to stand on their own
> will be nothing more than empty words.

Significantly, the skewed pricing system has spurred some ethnic nationalists to express their broader resentment of the Han. These activists note that the natural resource development strategies of state-owned enterprises regarding taxation, hiring, and division of revenue are implemented at the expense of the minority communities.

Limitations on Further Mobilization

A record number of large states have crumbled into smaller units as a result of ethnic agitation during the 1990s. The Soviet Union, Yugoslavia, and Czechoslovakia are but a few examples of this global trend. Given the apparent rise in minority discontent in China, the question arises whether China will fragment along the same ethnic lines. The answer is that China is not likely to follow the same course as its former communist neighbors to the west, despite the ominous signs of growing ethnic political mobilization. Even if minorities were so inclined, a number of factors limit their chances of seceding from the PRC. First, the demographic distribution of the minorities as well as the administrative boundaries within China weaken the minorities' ability to mobilize. Second, internal conflicts continue to divide the nationalities. More importantly, however, the minorities recognize the benefits of incorporation in China. What most of the minorities seek (with the exception of many Tibetans and some of the Xinjiang Muslim groups) is more, not less, government involvement in their development efforts. Moreover, the divisive effect of increased disparities among the minorities and Han has been mitigated by the economic strength of the central government, and by a number of policies explicitly designed to integrate the minority areas with the Han neighbors. By first examining the limitations to further ethnic mobilization, then briefly discussing two government policies designed to ease ethnic economic division, this chapter concludes that the minorities likely will continue to press the government for special benefits but are unlikely to defy the government openly or violently. The future of minority politics in China is more likely to resemble minority relations in the United States than those of the former Soviet Union.

Demographics

The demographic distribution of the Chinese minorities greatly influences their reluctance to mobilize against the state. First, the minorities make up a relatively small percentage of China's total population. By way of comparison, the Soviet Union's minority population comprised 48% of its total population, whereas the Chinese minorities account for only 8% of China's population. The contrast is equally marked within each of the autonomous zones. Within the Soviet Union, the total population represented by the titular group within each of the 14 non-Russian union republics was nearly 70%. In China, with the sole exception of Tibet, the nationalities are a minority even within their own autonomous areas. Less than 18% of the Inner Mongolian Autonomous Region's population is Mongolian, and the Zhuang account for less than 34% of the Guangxi Zhuang Autonomous Region. Second, the minorities are scattered throughout China's border regions and often have little contact with ethnic compatriots outside of their immediate villages. Poorly developed communication and transportation channels render the distances between villages greater still.

Another key characteristic of minority demographics in China is the weak congruence of ethnic and regional divisions. Many minority groups are scattered throughout several provinces in the southwest. Just over 60% of the minority population actually lives within its own autonomous region, as compared to 84% in the former Soviet Union.

Internal Divisions

In addition to geographic distribution, further minority mobilization is likely to be hindered by internal divisions within the minority groups. Two divisions are paramount within most ethnic groups. First, the rural-urban divide impedes ethnic solidarity. Many nationality members who flee the side for the city adopt Han lifestyles. Moreover, rural minorities are much poorer than their urban counterparts and generally are less educated. Urban minorities often are unwilling to acknowledge their ethnic heritage and have little understanding of the economic difficulties facing their rural members.

Second, localism continues to override nationalism. Villagers tend to have a stronger sense of loyalty to their locality than to their ethnic group. When surveyed, villagers in the Guangxi Zhuang Autonomous Region almost unanimously expressed their willingness to elect to office a Han leader from their own village over another Zhuang from outside their local area. Numerous factors contribute to the strength of localism among China's minorities. First, poor communication channels and the predominantly self-sufficient agricultural economy of many of the minority regions limit the amount of contact, and corresponding sense of inclusion, with ethnic compatriots in neighboring areas. Second, until very recently, internal migration within China was regulated strictly by the government, and persons rarely left their birthplace. Third, localism is reinforced by Chinese religious and ethical traditions. Sons, for example, are considered unfilial if they "abandon" their paternal homeland. Such teachings are common among many of the minority groups as well as among the Han.

Conclusion

The growing discrepancy in wealth between the Han and non-Han since 1978 has increased ethnic ire, inciting many groups to mobilize for more equitable growth policies. Nonetheless, the minorities' economic status has risen significantly both in relation to their position in 1949, when the communists came to power, and to their position in 1978, at the outset of the reform era. After ten years of reform, the net per capita

income for minority farmers was 436 *yuan*, nearly triple the 1978 figure (adjusting for inflation). Per capita urban wages doubled during the same decade. Total savings increased eightfold in the five autonomous regions between 1980 and 1988, from 3.83 million to 35.06 million *yuan*.

Despite economic inequalities, the vast majority of nationalities in China show no interest in seceding from the Chinese state. Instead, most of the minorities, with the exception of many Tibetans and some Muslim groups in the northwest, are demanding *more* central government involvement in minority areas. Two government policies in particular have increased the minorities' dependence on the central government and exchange with the Han areas. First, in 1979 the central government began promoting "horizontal linkages" between minority areas and the more advanced eastern areas. By 1983 Tibet already had contracted 43 joint projects with outside provinces. By 1988, more than 100 economic associations crossed either provincial or industry lines. Despite the minorities' reservations, economic contacts have increased the interdependence of the minorities and the Han. Second, the government's decision in 1990 to reverse earlier investment policies favoring the coastal areas, and to focus instead on developing the western and central regions, has begun to slow the growth in economic disparities between the Han and the nationalities. It is hoped that this trend will continue and thus diminish ethnic tensions in China.

Further Reading

Brown, Melissa J., editor, *Negotiating Ethnicities in China and Taiwan,* Berkeley: Institute of East Asian Studies, University of California, 1996

A collection of ten essays by nine anthropologists and a social historian, this volume examines the complexity and porous nature of ethnic identity formation. The volume uses a variety of methodological approaches and effectively illustrates that identities in China are "negotiated" over time by an intricate network of ethnic elites, government officials, scholars, and foreign viewers.

Dreyer, June Teufel, *China's Forty Millions: Minority Nationalities and National Integration in the People's Republic of China,* Cambridge, Massachusetts: Harvard University Press, 1976

Rich in historical detail, this was one of the first major studies on nationality policy. Dreyer offers a balanced and nuanced assessment of the CCP's minority policy, examining how the policy was developed and implemented throughout the country.

Gladney, Dru C., *Muslim Chinese: Ethnic Nationalism in the People's Republic,* 2nd edition, Cambridge, Massachusetts: Council on East Asian Studies, Harvard University, 1996

As an anthropologist, Gladney examines the meaning of the term "Hui," or Muslim, in China. He notes that the term holds different connotations in different Muslim communities throughout the country, and examines which factors influence these various forms of identity.

Heberer, Thomas, *China and Its National Minorities: Autonomy or Assimilation?* Armonk, New York: M.E. Sharpe, 1989

A short introduction to minority policy, this book focuses primarily on southwestern China.

MacKerras, Colin, *China's Minorities: Integration and Modernization in the Twentieth Century,* Hong Kong and New York: Oxford University Press, 1994

An excellent update to June Dreyer's 1976 political study, MacKerras examines Chinese government policy toward the minorities and assesses the degree to which minorities have been integrated into the Chinese state. The book offers an overview of minority policy from the turn of the century to the present. Based on extended field research, the book is clearly organized and captivating. Contains separate chapters on the impact of foreign influence on minority policy and of the policy's influence on minority population and gender issues.

MacKerras, Colin, *China's Minority Cultures: Identities and Integration Since 1912,* New York: St. Martin's Press, and Melbourne: Longman, 1995

Whereas MacKerras' earlier work focuses on government minority policy and its impact on the nationalities, this second book concentrates more on the relationship between minority identities and their integration into China. Examines the tension between tradition and change in the minority cultures. Divided into separate chapters on religion, education, marriage and divorce, gender issues, and literature and the performing arts.

Katherine Palmer is a Ph.D. candidate in the Woodrow Wilson Department of Government and Foreign Affairs, University of Virginia. Her dissertation is entitled "Ethnonationalism Ascendant: National Identity and Interest Articulation among the Zhuang of Southwest China." She is also the author of "Mao Zedong and the Sinification of China's Minority Policy" (1995).

Appendices

Stephen B. Herschler

Appendix 1

Chronology

1949	October 1	The People's Republic of China is formally established.
1950	February	The Sino-Soviet Treaty of Friendship, Alliance and Mutual Assistance is signed in Moscow.
	October	Chinese troops publicly enter the Korean War in support of North Korea.
1955	July	The NPC adopts the First Five-Year Plan for the Development of the National Economy (1953–57).
1956	May	Mao initiates a politically and socially more liberal period with the slogan "let a hundred flowers bloom, and a hundred schools of thought contend."
1957	June	Start of the Anti-Rightist Campaign.
1958	May	The Second Session of the Eighth Congress of the CCP endorses the Great Leap Forward.
	August	By approving plans to expand the people's communes, the Beidaihe Conference induces the rapid creation of 26,000 communes.
1959	March	In Tibet, an armed rebellion against the Chinese government is suppressed and the Dalai Lama flees to India.
	April	Liu Shaoqi is appointed president of the PRC, replacing Mao Zedong.
	July-August	Extreme drought exacerbates famine conditions prompted by the Great Leap Forward.
1960		The Soviet Union notifies China of its plans to withdraw Soviet experts from China.
1962	October	Clashes occur on the Sino-Indian border, with the Chinese launching a major offensive later in the month. In November China declares a unilateral cease-fire.
1964	October	China conducts its first nuclear test.
1965	September	The Tibetan Autonomous Region is established.
1966	May	The Politburo announces its decision to set up the Cultural Revolution group.
	June	Peng Zhen comes under attack as a revisionist and is removed as first secretary of the Beijing Municipal CCP Committee.

1967	**June**	China explodes its first hydrogen bomb.
1968	**July**	Mao Zedong criticizes Red Guard leaders for engaging in armed struggle, marking the end of the Cultural Revolution's most radical period.
	October	The Twelfth Plenum of the Eighth CCPCC announces that Liu Shaoqi has been dismissed from his posts and expelled from the party.
1969	**December**	The United States partially lifts its trade embargo against China.
1971	**September**	Lin Biao's assassination attempt against Mao Zedong fails. Lin allegedly dies in an airplane crash attempting to flee the country.
	October	The PRC is admitted to the United Nations.
1972	**February**	US president Richard Nixon visits China; a joint communiqué is issued in which the US declares there is only one China, of which Taiwan is a part.
	June	French president Georges Pompidou visits China, meeting with Mao Zedong.
	September	China and Japan formally reestablish diplomatic relations.
	October	China and the German Democratic Republic formally reestablish diplomatic relations.
1975	**January**	Deng Xiaoping is elected deputy chairman of the CCPCC at the Second Plenum of the Tenth CCPCC.
	June	Philippine president Ferdinand Marcos visits China, leading to the establishment of diplomatic relations.
	June-July	Thai prime minister Kukrit Pramoj visits China, leading to the establishment of diplomatic relations.
	Sept-Oct	The First National Conference on Learning from Dazhai in Agriculture is held.
1976	**January**	Premier Zhou Enlai dies of cancer. Hua Guofeng subsequently is appointed acting premier.
	April	Violence breaks out in Tiananmen Square between the police and people mourning for Zhou Enlai. Similar incidents occur across China.
		Hua Guofeng is appointed first deputy chairman of the CCPCC and premier of the State Council; Deng Xiaoping is dismissed from all party posts, but not from the party.
	September	Chairman Mao Zedong dies September 9.
	October	The "Gang of Four" is arrested, along with 30 other radical high-ranking party members.
		Hua Guofeng is appointed chairman of the CCPCC and its Military Affairs Committee while retaining his position as premier.

1977	**April**	National Conference on Learning from Daqing in Industry is held.
	July	Third Plenum of the Tenth CCPCC restores Deng Xiaoping to deputy chairmanship of the CCPCC and other posts. "Gang of Four" members are expelled from the party.
	August	Eleventh National Congress of the CCP adopts a Party Constitution preserving Marxism-Leninism-Mao Zedong Thought as the ideological foundation of the CCP.
	October	University entrance examinations are reinstated; graduate schools reopen in February 1978.
1978	**July**	Chinese government ceases providing economic and technical aid to Vietnam.
	August	Chinese and Vietnamese forces clash at Friendship Pass on their border
	November	First batch of posters appear on Democracy Wall in Beijing.
	December	China and the US issue a joint communiqué stating their intention to establish diplomatic relations starting January 1, 1979.
		The Third Plenum of the Eleventh Party Congress meets; socialist modernization with an emphasis on agricultural reform replaces class struggle as the guiding ideological principle of the CCP. Chen Yun joins the Politburo.
1979	**January**	China promulgates its first law on joint venture enterprises.
	Jan-Feb	Deng Xiaoping visits the United States, meeting with President Jimmy Carter.
	February	Chinese troops launch attacks into Vietnamese territory. Hostilities end on March 5, with China formally withdrawing from Vietnam on March 16.
		Deng Xiaoping gives a speech stating the "four cardinal principles" must be adhered to in order to achieve socialist modernization.
	March	The State Council decides to raise the purchase price for farm and sideline products by an average of 25%.
	July	The Second Session of the Fifth NPC adopts China's first Criminal Law and the Organic Law of the Local People's Congresses and Local People's Governments, as well as five documents expanding enterprise autonomy.
		The National People's Congress approves a policy of economic readjustment, which involves scaling down some aspects of the "four modernizations."
		Special Economic Zones (SEZs) are established in Guangdong's Shenzhen, Zhuhai, and Shantou, and also in Fujian's Xiamen.
	October	The China International Trust and Investment Corporation (CITIC) is established.
	December	The Democracy Wall movement ends with the general banning of big and small character posters.

1980	January	The Xinhua News Agency announces that economic transactions in China must be transacted with foreign exchange certificates issued by the Bank of China; the use of foreign currency is prohibited.
	April	The International Monetary Fund (IMF) admits China as a member.
		The State Statistical Bureau announces the results of the first comprehensive census: 970,920,000 (excluding Taiwan).
	May	The World Bank admits China to representation in the World Bank Group.
	August	The central government grants greater responsibility to regional governments for the planning and implementation of economic policy.
	September	The NPC approves the Income Tax Law Concerning Joint Ventures with Chinese and Foreign Investment of the PRC and the Individual Income Tax Law of the PRC. The one-child policy goes into effect for all of China except minority areas.
		The government announces an experimental profit-retention policy for enterprises to be universally implemented starting in 1981.
	December	Deng Xiaoping and Li Xiannian issue an emergency document calling for the immediate cessation of investment in ill-conceived industrial projects.
1981	January	Special court trying the "Gang of Four" condemns Jiang Qing and Zhang Chunqiao to death (later reduced to life imprisonment), Wang Hongwen to life imprisonment, and the others to long prison terms.
	June	Communiqué of the Sixth Plenum of the Eleventh CCPCC adopts the "Resolution on Certain Questions of Party History Since 1949." It condemns the Cultural Revolution as an unmitigated disaster and criticizes Mao Zedong's role in the campaign, determining that 70% of Mao's acts were good while 30% were bad. Deng's victory is consolidated as he replaces Hua Guofeng as chairman of the Military Commission and Hu Yaobang replaces Hua as party chairman.
	September	Ye Jianying calls for negotiations with the Kuomintang over Taiwan, proposing that after reunification Taiwan could retain a high degree of autonomy and its own armed forces.
	Nov-Dec	The Fourth Session of the Fifth NPC decides to continue rural reform while placing greater emphasis on opening China's economy to the outside world.
	December	A conference of Chinese and Japanese officials concludes with the announcement that Japan will disburse US$1.37 billion in financial aid to Chinese industry.
		At a Central Committee meeting, Chen Yun voices opposition to expansion of Special Economic Zones (SEZs), asserting that the state should retain its primary role in the economy.
1982	January	China reduces customs duties on imports of such items as energy, raw materials, and machinery for light industry and textile production.
	February	The China National Offshore Oil Corporation is officially set up to take charge of the

exploitation of offshore petroleum resources in cooperation with foreign enterprises.

May-June Zhao Ziyang visits Japan, meeting with the emperor.

August The US and China sign a joint communiqué in which the US promises gradually to reduce the quantity of arms sold to Taiwan.

September The Twelfth National Congress of the CCP sets the objective of quadrupling China's gross annual industrial and agricultural production by the year 2000. Hu Yaobang is named general secretary (the position of chairman being abolished), while Deng Xiaoping is named chairman of the newly created Military Commission and chairman of the Central Advisory Commission.

British prime minister Margaret Thatcher visits China to begin discussion on the future of Hong Kong.

December The NPC ratifies a new constitution that defines the NPC as the highest organ of state power, replaces communes with townships, and stipulates top officials can hold no more than two consecutive terms (ten years).

1983 April China and India agree to renew diplomatic ties.

May French president François Mitterand visits China.

June The State Council announces that state-owned enterprises will be made to pay taxes and that the state will no longer bear sole responsibility for enterprise losses.

July The People's Press publishes the *Selected Works of Deng Xiaoping.*

September The State Council promulgates Regulations for the Implementation of the Laws of the PRC on Joint Ventures Using Chinese and Foreign Investment.

October A decision adopted by the Second Plenum of the Twelfth CCPCC signals the beginning of a campaign against "spiritual pollution."

1984 January China becomes a member of the International Atomic Energy Agency.

Deng tours the SEZs to drum up support for them and other foreign investment programs.

February The Central Committee implements a second stage of land reform, allowing farmers to keep their land for 15 years.

March China opens 14 coastal cities to foreign investment.

April United States president Ronald Reagan pays an official visit to China.

May The Second Session of the Sixth NPC adopts the Law on Regional Autonomy for Minority Nationalities of the PRC.

The State Council issues provisional regulations granting state-owned enterprises greater decision-making power in economic affairs.

June Deng Xiaoping tells Hong Kong business leaders that the colony will be able to maintain its current socio-economic system after reunification in 1997, formulating the "one country, two systems" policy.

September   China's first nuclear reactor is reported to be operational.

The government announces that the structure of foreign trade will be decentralized through the use of more local-level trade agencies.

October   The Third Plenum of the Twelfth CCPCC adopts its Decision on Reform of the Economic Structure, shifting the focus of reform to urban centers and calling for the creation of a "planned socialist commodity economy."

December   British prime minister Margaret Thatcher and Zhao Ziyang sign the Sino-British Joint Declaration on Hong Kong, returning sovereignty over the colony to the PRC on July 1, 1997.

1985 January   New policy allows above-quota industrial goods to be priced at market and managers' discretion. The price of many food products is no longer fixed by the state, although the state continues to provide subsidies for urban residents.

February   China's first trade center in Western Europe is opened in Hamburg.

The Standing Committee of the Sixth NPC adopts the Foreign Economic Contract Law of the PRC.

At the Third Session of the Sixth NPC, Zhao Ziyang emphasizes that the two major tasks in reforming the economic structure will be wage and price system reforms.

June   Deng Xiaoping announces China's intention to reduce the size of its army by 1 million troops over the following two years.

A document issued by the Ministry of Civil Affairs declares the end of commune restructuring and the replacement of communes with towns and township governments.

September   The Fourth Plenum of the Twelfth CCPCC approves the resignations of 64 of its members on grounds of old age, including ten Politburo members.

1986 March   China becomes a member of the Asian Development Bank.

Zhao Ziyang announces that China has ceased atmospheric nuclear tests and will not undertake them in the future.

April   Hong Kong joins GATT.

The NPC adopts the Law on Enterprises Operated Exclusively with Foreign Capital.

The NPC adopts the Law of the PRC on Compulsory Education, which stipulates nine years of compulsory education in most areas by the end of the century.

August   The Shenyang Explosion-Prevention Equipment Factory is declared bankrupt, the first bankruptcy case in the PRC's history.

September   The CCPCC and State Council issue regulations on the implementation of a factory director responsibility system in publicly-owned industrial enterprises.

The Shanghai stock market reopens.

The Sixth Plenum of the Twelfth CCPCC adopts a resolution "on the guiding principles for building a socialist society with an advanced culture and ideology"; this resolution serves to launch a campaign against "bourgeois liberalization."

October   Labor contracts are introduced for state-owned enterprise workers.

State Council provisions encouraging foreign investment come into effect, offering foreign firms financial incentives and greater autonomy.

December   The NPC Standing Committee approves trial implementation of the Bankruptcy Law for state-owned enterprises.

Student demonstrations begin in Shanghai, spreading to other major cities across China.

1987   January   Hu Yaobang is dismissed as general secretary of the CCP. Writer Wang Ruofang, reporter Liu Binyan, and physicist Fang Lizhi are expelled from the CCP for "bourgeois liberalization" and opposition to the "four cardinal principles."

April   Portuguese prime minister Anabal Cavaco Silva and Zhao Ziyang sign the Joint Declaration on the Question of Macau, transferring sovereignty over Macau to the PRC on December 20, 1999.

October   The Foreign Ministry closes Tibet to foreign tourists and correspondents after clashes between monks and Chinese authorities result in fatalities.

At the Thirteenth Congress of the CCP, Zhao Ziyang states that China is now in the "primary stage of socialism," which will continue for another century.

November   The NPC Standing Committee adopts the Organic Law of the Village Committees of the PRC.

Zhao Ziyang is elected general secretary of the CCP by the First Plenum of the Thirteenth Party Congress, replacing Hu Yaobang. Deng Xiaoping resigns from the Central Committee and Li Peng is approved as acting premier.

China and Laos agree to renew diplomatic relations.

December   Beijing authorities reintroduce rationing of pork and sugar; other major cities follow suit.

1988   January   Taiwan's president Chiang Ching-kuo dies. The CCPCC sends condolences to the Kuomintang Central Committee.

April   Hainan Island is upgraded to the status of province and Special Economic Zone concurrently.

The NPC elects Yang Shangkun as president of the PRC and Wang Zhen as vice-president; Wan Li is elected chairman of the Standing Committee of the NPC; Deng Xiaoping is re-elected chairman of the Central Military Commission.

July   Li Peng signs regulations designed to encourage Taiwanese investment.

The State Council publishes the first set of regulations for private enterprises in China, facilitating the establishment of larger private enterprises.

Prices for luxury items are allowed to be set by market forces.

August   The Politburo decides to allow prices for most commodities to be regulated by the market, resulting in accelerated inflation fueled by panic buying.

The State Council issues an urgent directive to control serious inflation.

September   At the Third Plenum of the Twelfth CCPCC, conservatives impose an economic austerity program.

December   Rajiv Gandhi pays the first visit to China by an Indian prime minister in 34 years, meeting with Deng Xiaoping.

1989   January   The State Council and Central Committee approves policies that will transfer tax revenues from the coastal regions to fund projects in the interior.

February   Eduard Shevardnadze visits China, the first Soviet foreign minister to do so since 1959.

March   Violent anti-Chinese demonstrations occur in Lhasa. The State Council declares martial law on March 7.

At the Second Session of the Seventh NPC, Premier Li Peng criticizes government policies sparking inflation and excessive price hikes.

April   Hu Yaobang dies of a heart attack in Beijing, sparking a series of demonstrations during that month by students in Tiananmen Square who demand his posthumous rehabilitation as well as democratic reform. Similar demonstrations spread to other major cities across China.

May   Mikhail Gorbachev makes the first visit of a Soviet leader to China since 1959, during which diplomatic relations are formally reestablished.

Li Peng declares martial law in Beijing.

June   Deng Xiaoping orders military troops into Beijing. The military takes action in cities across China, resulting in the deaths of many citizens.

The Fourth Plenum of the Thirteenth Central Committee removes Zhao Ziyang as general secretary. Zhao is stripped of his other positions within the party and government but not expelled from the party. Jiang Zemin is named the new general secretary.

The World Bank suspends consideration of Chinese loan applications

November   The CCP Central Military Commission accepts Deng Xiaoping's resignation as its chairman, naming Jiang Zemin to replace him.

| 1990 | January | Martial law is lifted in Beijing. |

The British government grants full British citizenship to 50,000 select Hong Kong residents, giving them the right to emigrate to Britain.

Lee Tung-hui is reelected by the National Assembly to a six-year term as president of Taiwan.

April   The NPC closes session after passing the Basic Law for Hong Kong and amending a PRC law on joint ventures.

China closes Kashgar to foreigners following reports of ethnic unrest.

A Chinese carrier rocket launches Asia's first regional communications satellite, American-made Asiasat 1.

President Yang Shangkun promulgates the Basic Law for Hong Kong, to take effect as of July 1, 1997.

Li Peng pays the first official visit to the Soviet Union by a top Chinese leader in 26 years.

May   Martial law is lifted in Lhasa, Tibet.

August   China and Indonesia reestablish diplomatic relations after 23 years.

October   The Administrative Procedure Law goes into effect, giving Chinese citizens the power to sue government officials.

China and Singapore reestablish diplomatic relations.

China and South Korea agree to establish trade offices with consular functions in Seoul and Beijing, respectively.

European Community foreign ministers decide to ease sanctions on China.

The Agriculture Ministry announces a plan to raise state-controlled grain prices for the first time in 40 years.

State Statistical Bureau announces a population census figure of 1.13 billion as of July 1, 1990.

November   China abstains in a UN resolution authorizing the use of force in the Persian Gulf.

Officials at the ADB reactivate review of Chinese loan applications.

December   The World Bank ends its freeze on loans to China.

The Securities Exchange opens in Shanghai.

1991   **March**   At a national meeting on economic reform, Prime Minister Li Peng endorses reforms to decentralize the economy further.

At the Fourth Session of the Seventh National People's Congress, Li Peng promotes the lifting of price controls and expanding the role of market forces.

April   Li Peng presents a new tax law to NPC aimed at attracting foreign investment.

The People's Bank of China announces a cut in deposit and loan interest rates to spur reform.

May   Grain and cooking oil prices are raised for the first time in 25 years.

June   Three reformist leaders removed after the 1989 Tiananmen demonstrations (Hu Qili, Yan Mingfu, and Rui Xingwen) are given vice-ministerial positions.

New China News Agency reports the suicide in prison of Jiang Qing, Mao Zedong's widow and member of the Gang of Four.

July   Britain and China reach an agreement on the building of a new Hong Kong airport on the condition that China gain more influence in Hong Kong affairs.

August   Japanese prime minister Toshiki Kaifu begins a three-day visit to China to normalize ties after Tiananmen.

The Chinese government issues a statement supporting the anti-Gorbachev Soviet coup.

Chinese Red Cross officials are the first PRC representatives to visit Taiwan since 1949.

China rejects a UN resolution expressing concern over human rights violations in Tibet.

October   The Democratic Progressive Party in Taiwan approves a resolution renouncing claims to sovereignty over China.

November   China and Vietnam normalize diplomatic relations.

A CCP plenum issues a communiqué stressing rural development, strengthening party building, and socialist education in rural areas.

December   China's first nuclear power plant begins trial operation in Zhejiang province.

In the first full elections for seats in Taiwan's National Assembly, the Kuomintang wins 71% and the Democratic Progressive Party receives 24% of the popular vote.

China recognizes Russia and the other republics of the new Commonwealth of Independent States. China subsequently normalizes relations with Belarus and the Baltic States.

1992   **January**   The US and China reach an agreement on protection of US copyrights and patents, narrowly averting US imposition of tariffs in retaliation.

Deng Xiaoping begins his "Southern Tour," visiting Shenzhen, Zhuhai, Shanghai, and Wuchang to drum up support for market reform.

February	China allows foreigners to participate in the Shanghai stock market.
March	China and Vietnam agree on direct rail, air, postal, and shipping links.
	China formally agrees to comply with the Nuclear Nonproliferation Treaty.
	A CCP Politburo meeting endorses aggressive liberalization of the economy and calls for 100 years of market-oriented reforms.
	The Chinese media launch a campaign praising Deng Xiaoping's call for faster economic reform.
April	Government subsidies for urban grain prices end.
	The NPC approves construction of the Three Gorges-Yangtze River dam.
May	Taiwan allows student exchanges with China.
June	China publishes a law banning all but officially authorized public demonstrations.
	A US oil company announces a contract with China to explore for oil in the disputed South China Sea.
July	Three areas in Xinjiang province are allowed to experiment with free-market prices.
	Chris Patten becomes Hong Kong's 28th colonial governor.
	China resumes border trade with India after 30 years.
	Taiwan's parliament approves the Statute for Relations across the Taiwan Strait, lifting bans on a wide range of contacts with China.
August	Riots break out in Shenzhen as people flood the city hoping to buy new shares on its stock exchange.
	A State Council circular offers amnesty to Chinese students who took part in anti-government actions while studying overseas.
	China and South Korea announce the establishment of diplomatic ties.
September	President Roh Tae Woo of South Korea arrives in Beijing for the first Sino-South Korean summit.
	The State Price Administration lifts price controls on 593 items and materials, reducing the number of commodities directly priced by the central government to only 89.
October	Hong Kong governor Chris Patten presents plans to expand the voting rights of Hong Kong citizens prior to 1997.
	The Fourteenth Party Congress calls for the adoption of a "socialist market economy," supporting Deng Xiaoping's economic reform program.

Hong Kong governor Chris Patten pays his first official visit to Beijing.

The Central Discipline Inspection Commission purges 874,000 CCP members for violating party rules.

Emperor Akihito pays the first Japanese imperial visit to China.

November   The Standing Committee of the NPC declares China will not abide by Patten's democratic reforms in Hong Kong after 1997.

China removes price controls on grain in Sichuan province.

China declares that contracts signed by Hong Kong but not approved by Beijing will be invalid in 1997.

December   Beijing announces price increases for meat, eggs, and vegetables.

Russian president Boris Yeltsin signs agreements on trade and nuclear plant cooperation in Beijing.

The first fully democratic elections are held in Taiwan; the ruling KMT party retains control of the parliament.

1993   **February**   Tiananmen student leader Wang Dan is released from prison.

March   The Eighth NPC adopts the Basic Law of the Macau Special Administrative Region of the PRC, to take effect when China resumes sovereignty over Macau on December 20, 1999.

Finance minister Liu Zhongli announces a 15% increase in the military budget.

The NPC announces that General Secretary Jiang Zemin is to become PRC president. Li Peng is reelected to another five-year term as premier.

April   The State Council issues its first regulations on securities.

May   World Bank statistics reveal that China has the world's fastest-growing economy, estimated at 12% to 13% per year.

Thousands of peasants riot over taxes and other fees in Renshou County, Sichuan province.

June   The State Council cancels 37 kinds of fees and taxes on peasants to mitigate rural unrest.

August   Taiwan president Lee Tung-hui is reelected as leader of the KMT in the party's first-ever secret ballot vote.

September   China and India sign an accord pledging to reduce troops and respect cease-fire lines along the Himalayan border.

Dissident Wei Jingsheng is freed after serving more than 14 years in prison.

October   New rules requiring licenses for telecommunications firms are published in the *Economic Daily.*

November Volume 3 of *The Selected Works of Deng Xiaoping* (1982–92) is released, signaling a major campaign to preserve and reignite Deng's reform agenda.

The Third Plenum of the Fourteenth Central Committee adopts the Decision on Some Issues Concerning the Establishment of a Socialist Market Economy, providing a blueprint for a new round of reform measures.

December The National Tax Administration reveals a new plan to simplify collection and boost revenues for the central government.

Hong Kong governor Chris Patten formally introduces his political reform bill to the Hong Kong legislature.

1994 January In a major step towards currency convertibility, the government ends its dual-rate foreign exchange system and stops issuing foreign exchange certificates (FEC).

The DDP wins a number of important seats against the KMT in Taiwanese local elections.

February Over Beijing's protests, the Hong Kong legislature passes the first stage of democratic reforms.

May The Daya Bay nuclear power plant in southern Guangdong province becomes operational.

An editorial appears in the *People's Daily* criticizing aspects of Deng Xiaoping's reforms.

US president Bill Clinton states that consideration of human rights will be de-linked from considerations of renewing China's Most Favored Nation status.

July The NPC passes a series of laws, including the PRC's first labor law, first real estate law, and a revision of the State Security Law that strengthens the state's ability to crack down on dissidents and foreigners' political activities.

The Securities Regulatory Commission cancels any new listings on China's two stock exchanges for the rest of the year, while also suspending share issues delayed from the previous year.

August The Ministry of Labor releases projections that unemployment will reach 268 million by the year 2000, of which 200 million will be in the countryside.

September China issues a regulation announcing its intent to disband Hong Kong's democratically elected legislature after the take-over in 1997.

PRC president Jiang Zemin and Russian president Boris Yeltsin sign agreements in Moscow to reduce military tensions and increase trade between the two countries.

In a major shift in US policy toward Taiwan, the Clinton administration announces its intent to increase ties with Taiwan.

Hong Kong holds its first-ever democratic election, with democratic parties winning 5 of 18 districts.

October   Beijing again breaks the international moratorium on nuclear tests, exploding a device at Lop Nor.

Premier Li Peng visits South Korea.

November   Hong Kong and China reach agreement on the construction of the new US$20 billion airport.

December   In the first democratic elections for higher-level government positions in Taiwan, the KMT retains the governorship but loses the Taipei mayoral race to DDP candidate Ch'en Shui-pien.

Construction officially begins on the Three Gorges dam.

1995 **January**   In an effort to fight inflation, food coupons are reintroduced in major urban centers.

February   Narrowly avoiding a trade war with the US, China agrees to strengthen efforts to curb infringement of international intellectual property rights.

March   China passes its first central bank law.

April   Beijing vice-mayor Wang Baosen, under investigation for corruption, commits suicide. Beijing mayor Chen Xitong, who is later implicated, resigns from his post and is stripped of his party positions later in the year.

Chen Yun dies at age 90.

Land contracts to farmers are extended for another 30 years.

May   New regulations on a 5-day, 40-hour work week go into effect.

The US government allows Taiwan president Lee Tung-hui to visit Cornell University, his alma mater, to present a commencement speech as a private citizen, prompting strong protest from Beijing.

July   China is granted observer status in the new World Trade Organization.

Chinese-American human rights activist Harry Wu is arrested at a frontier inspection post in China. He subsequently is tried, sentenced to 15 years in prison, and then expelled from the country.

November   Dissident activist Wei Jingsheng is arrested and charged with trying to overthrow the government. At his trial the following month, Wei is sentenced to another 14 years in prison.

December   Vietnam and China agree to restore rail links and increase trade and investment between the two countries.

The NPC Standing Committee approves a bill outlining procedures for declaring and implementing martial law.

In a blow to Hong Kong's democratic reforms, China appoints a 150-person preparatory committee to oversee Hong Kong's return to Chinese sovereignty.

1996	**February**	China issues a new set of rules limiting use of the internet.
	March	Just prior to Taiwan holding its first-ever direct presidential elections, China conducts military maneuvers near Taiwan's shores, firing some missiles and causing panic in Taiwanese financial markets.
		In the Taiwanese elections, KMT candidate Lee Tung-hui wins 54 % of the vote while DDP candidate Peng Min-min receives 21%.
	April	Russian president Boris Yeltsin visits Beijing, signing trade and diplomatic agreements to improve relations between the two countries.
		Having succeeded in lowering inflation, the Central Bank of China cuts interest rates for the first time since 1993.
	June	Foreign law firms are permitted to open offices in China.
		China agrees to more stringent supervision of intellectual property rights, at the last minute avoiding a trade war with the US.
	July	China permits the free buying and selling of foreign currency by foreign companies at specially designated banks.
	August	For the first time, China surpasses Japan as the largest source of the US trade deficit.
	October	Wang Dan, a leader of the 1989 Tiananmen student movement, is charged with trying to subvert the government and sentenced to 11 years in prison.
	November	Dai Xianglong, governor of the Bank of China, announces that China has achieved low inflation and a high growth rate.
	December	Beijing picks Pro-China Hong Kong businessman Tung Chee-hwa to be chief executive of Hong Kong after July 1, 1997.
		A selection committee created by China meets in Shenzhen to choose the 60 members who will replace Hong Kong's currently democratically elected legislature when China resumes sovereignty.
1997	**February**	Deng Xiaoping dies on February 19 at age 92.
	July	Hong Kong reverts to Chinese sovereignty on July 1, after 155 years as a British colony.

Appendix 2

Glossary

ADB: See Asian Development Bank

Agricultural Responsibility System: See Household Responsibility System.

Anti-Spiritual Pollution Campaign: A political campaign launched by factions in the CCP leadership who feared the spread of Western liberal ideas brought about by the "open policy." The campaign lasted from October 1983 to February 1984, attacking such social problems as crime, corruption, and pornography.

Asia-Pacific Economic Cooperation (APEC): Headquartered in Singapore, this organization was formed in 1989 and as of 1997 was composed of 18 member governments from the Asia-Pacific region (including the United States and Canada). It serves as a forum for discussing regional trade questions, economic cooperation, and means by which to foster cooperation between developed and developing countries through trade. The annual ministerial-level meetings have served as occasions for high level talks between officials.

Asian Development Bank (ADB): Founded in 1966, this multilateral financial institution based in Manila seeks to promote economic growth, reduce poverty, improve women's status, develop human resources and natural resources, and also promotes environmental protection. The ADB extends loans to member countries and also promotes public and private investment in the region for development purposes. Members of the ADB include 40 countries and territories in Asia as well as 16 countries in North America and Europe.

Bourgeois Liberalization: First initiated in 1981 in response to the Solidarity movement in Poland, this political campaign sought to restrict reform efforts by associating the increase in political and social problems with economic liberalization. This campaign would be revived by conservative leaders after the student unrest of 1986.

Cadre: A ubiquitous term in the PRC, cadre (*ganbu*) originally denoted party and administrative officials holding government positions. In recent years, the meaning of the term has expanded to include white collar workers in managerial positions as well as business leaders more generally. The creation of a civil service in the 1990s may help to narrow the definition of the term over time as functionaries in the bureaucracy are now officially designated as "civil servants."

Central Advisory Commission (CAC): Established in 1982 to serve as a consulting body to the Central Committee of the CCP, the CAC was created to encourage party elders to retire from active duty by providing them with positions of prestige and benefits but little power. Membership was restricted to those serving at least 40 years in the party. In fact the CAC became far more influential than ever anticipated or desired, often serving as a conservative counterweight to pro-market factions. For this reason the CAC was abolished at the Fourteenth CCP Congress in 1993.

Central Committee: This committee of about 300 members ostensibly directs party affairs when the National Party Congress is not in session. Because of its large size and infrequent meetings, however, real power over day-to-day management of party affairs resides in smaller organizations such as the Politburo. Generally, although central committee meetings (called plenums) may discuss new policy measures, they play little part in actually drafting them.

Central Military Commission (CMC): One of two commissions charged with exercising authority over the People's Liberation Army, which includes the armed forces, army, and navy. Both the party commission and the state commission have essentially the same personnel and function. Although the constitution says that the state CMC commands the armed forces under the delegated authority of the NPC, in fact the CCP controls it. Chairmanship of the CMC is thought to be an important means for paramount leaders to consolidate and preserve power.

China International Trust and Investment Corporation (CITIC): This corporation was established by the government in 1979 to help the PRC's modernization efforts by promoting the utilization of foreign capital, technology, and machinery. This business conglomerate is directly accountable to the State Council.

Chinese Communist Party (CCP): The ruling party of the People's Republic of China since its establishment in 1949. The CCP was founded in 1921 and spent much of the 20 years prior to 1949 engaged in a civil war against the ruling Kuomintang. As of 1997 the party had about 50 million members.

Chinese People's Political Consultative Congress (CPPCC): Established in 1949, the CPPCC was created to provide an institutional forum for interactions between the CCP and other political parties and mass organizations. It usually meets at the same time as the NPC. Official propaganda presents the CPPCC as evidence of the cooperation and unity of all societal and political organizations but in actuality its meetings primarily serve to communicate CCP policies and agendas to non-party groups and organizations.

Communes: See People's Communes

Contract Responsibility System: See Factory Manager Responsibility System

Cultural Revolution: A decade of political and social turmoil extending from 1966 to the arrest of the Gang of Four after Mao Zedong's death in 1976. The first three years were marked by intense urban conflict led by Red Guard units comprised largely of students. Fearing damage to the national economy and government structures themselves, many of these youths were then sent to the countryside in a campaign to help rural areas. The second phase of the Cultural Revolution consisted largely of factional struggles between the top leadership, Mao Zedong using his preeminent authority to shift the balance of power back and forth between the economic pragmatists Deng Xiaoping and Zhou Enlai on one side, and the radically leftist Gang of Four on the other. Seeking to prevent another Cultural Revolution, the post-Mao leadership worked to demystify Mao as well as to depoliticize society more generally. The "Historical Resolution on Some Problems of Party History" (1981) declared the Cultural Revolution an unmitigated disaster.

Democracy Wall: In 1978, on a wall near Beijing University, a number of posters appeared criticizing the Cultural Revolution and calling for reform. This flourishing of popular expression lasted until 1979 when posters critical of the leadership began appearing. Wei Jingshen's appeal for democracy as a "fifth modernization" and accusation of Deng as an autocrat resulted in Wei being sentenced to a fifteen-year prison term.

Democratic Progressive Party (DPP): The leading opposition party in Taiwan.

Deng's Southern Tour (Trip to the South): In February 1992, after several years of conservative fiscal policy introduced after the Tiananmen student movement of 1989, Deng Xiaoping toured the SEZs in a campaign to promote renewed economic liberalization and fast-paced development. Several months after this trip, a massive propaganda and mobilization campaign broadcast his call for a new round of reforms around the country, initiating a period of rapid economic development and economic liberalization. This new period received official sanction in the Fourteenth Party Congress' adoption of a new platform calling for the creation of a "socialist market economy." Deng's speeches on this trip are the ideological foundation for Chinese economic policy in the 1990s.

Dual-Track Price System: See Two-Track Price System

Factory Manager Responsibility System: First proposed by Deng Xiaoping in 1980 but not really implemented until the mid-1980s, this reform reduced party involvement in production decisions within factories. Formerly, party secretaries were very powerful within factories because they controlled information and decisions about personnel. After this reform, party secretaries were increasingly restricted to ensuring the general ideological correctness of actions and their accordance with general policies rather than the details of production. Managers were granted a substantial increase in power but with it came greater responsibility for enterprise profit and loss.

Five Guarantee Households: As stipulated in the Chinese Constitution, the state promises to provide food, clothing, housing, and medical care to those individuals or households with no capacity to work, no family to help them, and no means of support. The state also promises to provide proper arrangements upon death (or in the case of children, with education).

Floating Population: With the disbanding of the communes in the late 1970s, peasants were allowed greater mobility. Because of the high level of excess labor in the countryside and the attraction of higher salaries in the cities, many peasants migrated to urban centers to work in unskilled jobs, remitting wages back to families still in the countryside. Because these workers do not have urban resident permits, they are denied many of the welfare and social privileges the government accords legal urban residents. 1997 estimates place this "floating population" at upwards of 50 million people.

Four Cardinal Principles: Initially set forth by Deng Xiaoping in 1979 and subsequently included in the PRC Constitution, these four principles are: to keep to the socialist road, to uphold the people's democratic dictatorship, leadership by the Communist Party, and Marxism-Leninism-Mao Zedong Thought. These four principles define the parameters of permissible dissent in the PRC. Opposition to any one of these principles meets with swift and strong suppression.

Four Modernizations: This refers to the modernization of agriculture, industry, national defense, and science and technology. First advocated by Zhou Enlai, these were subsequently championed by Deng Xiaoping and adopted as the official party line at the Third Plenum of the Eleventh Central Committee Party Congress in 1978.

Gang of Four: The ultra-left faction promoting political struggle and ideological purity during the Cultural Revolution. The four were Jiang Qing (Mao Zedong's widow), Wang Hongwen, Zhang Chunqiao, and Yao Wenyuan. They were in constant struggle with Deng Xiaoping and others who believed the national priority lay with economic growth and modernization. The Gang of Four was arrested and purged after Mao's death in 1976. In 1981 all four were sentenced to long prison terms. Jiang Qing reportedly committed suicide in prison in May 1991. Deng and other reform-oriented leaders have repeatedly held up the example of the Gang of Four as an instance of the dangers of extreme leftist ideology in China.

General Agreement on Tariffs and Trade (GATT): Headquartered in Geneva, Switzerland, GATT was drawn up in 1947 to help promote nondiscriminatory trade practices. In 1993 it underwent significant expansion following negotiations with 117 industrialized and developing countries. GATT provided a forum for international trade negotiations, and also helped to administer and implement multilateral trade agreements. In 1995 the World Trade Organization (WTO) replaced GATT, increasing the scope of its authority to include trade in services, international property rights, and agriculture. China is not a member of WTO (nor was it a member of GATT) and has been hampered in its efforts to join by criticism of its protectionist policies, uneven application of trade regulations, and secretive trade practices.

***Getihu*/Individual Economy**: Although never really abolished, the individual economy only began to flourish after Deng legitimated its existence in the late 1970s as a necessary supplement to the planned economy, allowing farmers to engage in sideline operations. Officially, *getihu* were limited to private businesses employing seven or less people, all family members. With the increase in size and complexity of these urban and rural enterprises, however, the government officially created another category of enterprise in 1988. *Siying Qiye,* or private enterprises, refers to enterprises that employ over seven workers and which are owned by individuals, partnerships, or up to 30 shareholders. These enterprises are concentrated in the southern and coastal regions. This kind of entrepreneurial activity tends to be in manufacturing, construction, and transportation.

Great Leap Forward: This utopian campaign started in 1958 and sought to make China an advanced industrial country in the span of several decades by employing mass collectivization and mass political mobilization. The campaign resulted in economic disaster and a devastating famine. By the time the GLF was abandoned in 1960, tens of millions had died of starvation. Mao lost significant authority as a consequence of the GLF and would never again attempt to control economic policy, but his distrust of those who helped repair the economy after the GLF (Liu Shaoqi and Deng Xiaoping, among others) would culminate in their purges during the Cultural Revolution.

Hong Kong Basic Law: Passed by the NPC in 1990 after five years of consultation with the British government, this law provides the blueprint for PRC governance of Hong Kong when China resumes control of the territory in 1997. The Basic Law outlines how Hong Kong will preserve much of its institutions, social practices, and capitalist system as a Special Administrative Region. When Hong Kong Governor Chris Patten began implementing democratic reforms in the early 1990s, China cried foul, pointing out that under the provisions of the Basic Law democratic elections were slated to begin only after 1997.

Hong Kong Legislative Council (Legco): An advisory body in the Hong Kong political system whose main functions are to enact laws, control public expenditure, and review government policy and actions. The Council consists of 60 members. Of the 39 elected members, 21 are chosen by functional constituencies and 18 are chosen by direct elections in geographical constituencies. After Tiananmen in 1989, the British authorities asked the PRC government to allow officials elected to the council prior to 1997 to be allowed to serve out their terms after China regained sovereignty. The PRC government adamantly refused to accept the legitimacy of those chosen by direct election, creating and convening a "shadow legislature" composed of hand-picked candidates in late 1996.

Household Responsibility System: A contracting system that revolutionized agriculture in the early Deng period. Rather than contracting to large agricultural collectives, some local leaders began dividing up the land among work units or families and then sub-contracting production quotas to these smaller units. One particularly popular method was called "contracting everything to the family," wherein families had to sell a set amount of produced goods to state officials at stipulated prices, but anything produced above these quotas could be sold at higher prices to other buyers.

International Bank of Reconstruction and Development: See World Bank

International Monetary Fund (IMF): Established in 1944, the IMF complements the development and investment role of its sister institution, the World Bank, by overseeing the monetary and exchange rate policies of its member governments. China became a member in 1980. To foster its agenda of promoting exchange stability and removing exchange restrictions, the IMF can issue temporary loans, such as it did for China in the early 1980s to aid in an economic stabilization program. Since then, the IMF has played an important advisory role for a number of complex reform processes including price reform, inflation, taxation, promotion of the private sector, and other areas. Membership is a prerequisite to joining the World Bank.

Iron Rice Bowl: An expression referring to the traditional employment status of workers in state-owned enterprises, which included life-time tenure and comprehensive benefits irrespective of the worker's job performance. In the reform era, the government has sought to break the "iron rice bowl" without causing massive labor unrest.

Kuomintang (Guomindang, Nationalist Party, KMT): The governing party in Taiwan. The KMT was initially organized by Sun Yat-sen in 1912 and became the major political party in Republican China. In 1928 Chiang Kai-shek became chairman of the KMT and head of the ROC government. In 1949, with the communist victory on the mainland, Chiang retreated to Taiwan where he established the ROC government, which claimed it was the true government of China. The KMT ruled Taiwan with dictatorial control until the late 1980s but in recent years democratic competitive elections have been held. Lee Tung-hui, a native of Taiwan, is the leader of the KMT and president of the ROC.

Legco: See Hong Kong Legislative Council

Missile Crisis of 1996: In March 1996, Taiwan held its first-ever direct presidential elections. The PRC government was worried by the implicit challenge this posed to its non-democratic government and feared that pro-Taiwanese independence groups would seek separation from the mainland. The PRC government responded by conducting military maneuvers off the coast of Taiwan, during which several anti-ballistic missiles were fired. The crisis caused significant capital flight from Taiwan, but soon thereafter economic investment in Taiwan as well as that between the ROC and PRC returned to normal.

Most-Favored Nation (MFN): A trade status arrangement between two countries, the phrase refers to the idea that each country will extend to the other the same trading terms that it would extend to other countries with which it is on good terms, imposing no special tariffs or restrictions. The United States extended MFN status to China in 1980, which had the effect of greatly reducing the tariffs imposed on Chinese goods exported to the US. After the suppression of the Tiananmen student movement in 1989, the US president and congress were locked in annual battles over whether to extend MFN to China. Presidents Bush and Clinton have succeeded in preserving China's MFN status. In September 1996 the US Senate voted to revise the term "most-favored nation" to the more accurate phrase "normal trade relations," in part to mitigate such battles.

National Party Congress: See National People's Congress

National People's Congress (NPC): The supreme state legislative body in the PRC, consisting of 2,700 delegates elected to five-year terms by local people's congresses. Its duties include amending the constitution, passing laws, and approving the national economic plan and budget. The NPC also is officially responsible for electing the president and vice-president of the PRC, membership to the State Council, Central Military Commission, and the Supreme People's Court. For much of its history the NPC has been a largely passive body, convened to approve party policy and decisions. In recent years there is some evidence of the NPC playing a more active role in drafting policy as well as thwarting pet projects of individual party leaders.

One-Child Policy: Introduced in 1978, this policy seeks to reduce the population of the PRC over time. The original idea was to use a combination of incentives and penalties to induce every family to have only one child. Initially, national minorities were exempt from the policy, but as their birth rates have increased these exceptions have been revoked. The policy's limited success has been restricted primarily to urban centers. In the rural areas, underreporting of birth rates is rampant. The policy also has contributed to a sex ratio imbalance within the PRC as a preference for male progeny has resulted in greater infanticide or abortion of females.

One Country, Two Systems: The PRC's proposed method for reunifying Hong Kong, Macau, and Taiwan with the mainland. This method involves creating Special Administrative Regions of each territory and, in the case of Hong Kong's reunification in 1997, allowing the preservation of pre-1997 government and economic systems under the administration of Beijing.

Organization of Economic and Cooperative Development (OECD): Established in Paris in 1961, the OECD consists of 26 member countries primarily from North America and Europe, but including Japan, Australia, and New Zealand as well. Its aims are to promote economic growth and higher standards of living in member countries, contribute to the expansion of world trade, and stimulate and harmonize members' efforts in favor of developing countries.

Open Policy (also known as the "Open Door Policy"): Adopted in 1978 by the Chinese government, this development strategy marked a direct reversal of the economic isolationism practiced during much of the Maoist era. With this policy China's leaders sought to accelerate economic growth via foreign direct investment and technology transfers. In addition, China sought to be more active in international institutions and promoted study and training abroad.

People's Communes: Initially created in 1958 to institute a more egalitarian mode of production as part of the Great Leap Forward, on average communes comprised about 5,000 households. All property was jointly owned and income was distributed according to a work-point system that undervalued individual contribution. Communes possessed governmental, political, and economic functions. Beneath communes in the organizational hierarchy were productions brigades and production teams. During the Cultural Revolution, communes were introduced into the urban centers as well. With the agricultural reforms of the early 1980s the commune system was slowly disbanded, replaced by townships in most areas by 1985.

People's Liberation Army (PLA): The armed forces of the People's Republic of China, including the army, navy, and air force. The size of the PLA is estimated to be close to 3 million active troops.

People's Republic of China (PRC): Established by the CCP under the leadership of Mao Zedong on October 1, 1949, following the communist victory over the Kuomintang in the Chinese civil war.

Politburo (or Political Bureau): Elected by the Central Committee, membership in the Politburo varies between 14 and 25 people. The politburo oversees the daily affairs of the CCP and makes major decisions for the party. Although members are powerful political leaders, the greatest power resides in the Politburo's Standing Committee.

Privately-Owned and Foreign-Invested (*Sanzi*) Enterprises; "Three Types of Investment Enterprises": A category of business enterprise distinct from both the state-owned and collective enterprises. The latter expression refers to Sino-foreign joint investments, Sino-foreign cooperative projects, and wholly-owned foreign investments. These firms do not generally provide the comprehensive social packages that state-owned enterprises offer, but wages are usually higher and labor is performed on a contractual basis. These firms do not experience government monitoring, which means that exploitation of workers is more common.

Renminbi (Rmb): The standard monetary unit in the PRC. Also called *yuan*. Until recently, its exchange rate was determined by the government rather than by market forces. Prior to 1994, foreign exchange certificates (FEC), a parallel currency, was reserved for use by foreigners or for purchases from stores carrying imported goods as a means of increasing foreign currency reserves and keeping imports down. In early 1994 the government abolished FEC and increased the renminbi exchange rate from about 5.8 to about 8.7 per US dollar as part of a process to make Rmb convertible on international currency exchanges.

Republic of China (ROC): Established by Sun Yat-sen in 1912 after the overthrow of the Qing Dynasty, the ROC government and its ruling party (the KMT) governed China from the late 1920s until the KMT's defeat by the communists in 1949, whereupon it retreated to the island of Taiwan which it has governed ever since. The US government recognized the ROC on Taiwan as the only legitimate government of China until 1979, when it recognized the PRC.

Rural Enterprises: See Township and Village Enterprises

Sino-British Joint Declaration on the Future of Hong Kong: Signed by the two countries in December 1984, the declaration restores sovereignty to the PRC on July 1, 1997. According to the provisions, Hong Kong will become a Special Administrative Region (SAR) under the direct authority of the central government in Beijing. The SAR will be vested with executive, legislative, and independent judicial power. According to the agreement, pre-1997 social and economic systems will remain unchanged, as will lifestyles. In addition, the SAR will have independent finances and will be able to maintain and develop economic and cultural relations and conclude agreements with states, regions, and relevant international organizations.

Siying Qiye/**Private Enterprises:** See *Getihu*

Socialist Market Economy: At the Fourteenth Party Congress in 1993, the Chinese leadership took the major ideological and political step of redefining the goal of political and economic reform to include the construction of a socialist market economy, thereby granting full legitimacy to marketization in China. The Constitution was subsequently revised to reflect this new goal. Previously, the official characterization of the Chinese system was that of a "planned socialist commodity economy." Coined in the Decision on the Reform of the Economic Structure adopted by the CCP in 1984, this expression suggested a compromise between factions favoring state planning and those seeking market reforms.

Special Administrative Regions (SARs): Areas allowed to maintain their own government and economic systems under the administration of the PRC. SARs were proposed as a means of reincorporating Hong Kong, Macau, and Taiwan into the PRC.

Special Economic Zones (SEZs): Created in the Southern China cities of Shenzhen, Zhuhai, Shantou and Xiamen in 1979, SEZs were designed to attract foreign direct investment to the PRC by providing special economic incentives, including lower tariffs and tax rates, superior infrastructure and facilities, flexible labor policies, and more enterprise autonomy. They also became a testing site for market-oriented economic policies. "Open development zones" are SEZs on a smaller scale and with less autonomy.

Standing Committee of the Politburo: A committee within the Politburo composed of four to six members, all among the most powerful leaders in the PRC. Generally meetings are held weekly.

State Council: The highest organ of the PRC state administration, the State Council consists of the prime minister and the heads of numerous ministries, commissions, and subordinate organizations. Its duties include developing the economic plan and budget for NPC deliberation, drafting legislative bills, and issuing administrative measures. The State Council meets about once a month, but most power is concentrated in its Standing Committee, a smaller group that convenes twice weekly and serves essentially as a government cabinet.

State-Owned Enterprises (SOEs): Large industrial enterprises exclusively owned and operated by the government, state-owned enterprises exist at all levels of the administrative hierarchy. Only the largest are under the direct management of national ministries; most are operated by sub-national government units including the provincial, city, county, or town level. As opposed to workers in private and collective enterprises, workers at SOEs enjoyed virtual life-time tenure as well as many benefits, including subsidized meals and housing, free medical care, and benefits for their dependents. Once the backbone of Chinese industry, the proportion of SOEs relative to TVEs and TVCEs has been declining over the course of the reform era. Burdened with the comprehensive care of their workforce, outdated technology, and slow response to market trends, many SOEs are losing money, which places a significant strain on national and local budgets. A key concern of reform is how to reduce the burden SOEs pose without sparking labor unrest among the numerous workers still employed in this type of industry.

Third Plenum of the Eleventh Party Central Committee: At this meeting in December 1978, Deng

Xiaoping effectively consolidated his power. "Class struggle" was repudiated, ideology downplayed, and the new national agenda switched to "socialist modernization" and a focus on economic reform, beginning with the countryside. Hua Guofeng retained some central leadership positions, but became a minor actor in national politics. Many of Deng's supporters were rehabilitated and gained positions of power and prominence at this meeting.

Tiananmen: The "Gate of Heavenly Peace," which is part of the "Forbidden City" that was home to China's emperors prior to the end of the imperial system in 1911, now generally refers to what is the largest public square in the world, located just to the south of the gate. Tiananmen is the symbolic epicenter of the PRC. At Tiananmen Mao Zedong declared from a rostrum the founding of the PRC on October 1, 1949. During the Cultural Revolution, millions of Red Guards gathered on the square to be greeted by Chairman Mao. In 1976 Tiananmen was the site of mass protests against the Gang of Four. In the spring of 1989, the square was the focal point of pro-democracy demonstrations that culminated in the bloody repression of June 4.

Township and Village Collective Enterprises (TVCEs): These enterprises are much like TVEs except that their ownership is based on place of residence. Local governments play a strong role in their creation and operation. As opposed to TVEs, they tend to be larger-scale factories that employ a greater number of workers. TVCEs are also more capital intensive, making them more vulnerable to credit crunches such as occurred in the mid-1990s.

Township and Village Enterprises (TVEs): A blanket term covering a variety of economic entities but generally referring to nonagricultural businesses owned and run at the township and village levels. These firms tend to be relatively small in size, labor intensive, and utilize rather simple machinery. TVEs are not part of the central planning system and therefore are free to operate largely according to market forces. TVEs do not provide comprehensive benefits for workers as SOEs do, but rather employ a workforce composed largely of rural laborers and farmers who continue to live at home and work the fields in the harvest season or after work hours. TVEs have played a significant role in fueling economic growth in the reform era, helping to industrialize the countryside while creating employment for excess rural labor.

Two-Track Price System: A pricing mechanism by which the Chinese government combined elements of both a planned and a market economy. To promote higher production but safeguard prices preferential to the state, some goods were allowed to have two prices. For such agricultural and industrial goods, a set amount had to be sold by farmers or enterprises for a pre-set price. Anything produced above that quota, however, could be sold at market prices. This provided a great impetus for farmers and enterprises to increase production, which in turn helped to alleviate shortages and bottlenecks. Now that China intends to create a market economy, the aim is to phase out this pricing system over time.

Work Unit (*Danwei*): Until recently most urban residents lived in relatively autonomous societies created by the institution with which they were affiliated (factory, school, etc.). These work units provided housing, schooling, health care, food ration coupons, and other basic goods and services. Citizens lived in the work unit for most of their lives as movement between units was rare. The work unit system in China served to connect the bureaucracy with the common citizen. It also served a political purpose by giving the state bureaucracy greater ability to monitor and isolate groups and also by facilitating party efforts to conduct political campaigns and indoctrination. Reform has greatly weakened the prevalence of the work unit as more people live and work outside of the work unit system and employment has become far more flexible. However, the work unit still plays a significant role in state-owned enterprises.

World Bank (International Bank for Reconstruction and Development, IBRD): Established in 1946, the organization seeks to reduce poverty and promote the economic development of member countries by providing loans and technical assistance for matters relating to economic development. Viewed by Mao Zedong as an "instrument of capitalist exploitation," under the post-Mao leadership the World Bank has been an important source of loans funding China's development projects. China became a member of the World Bank in 1980. The world bank has extended billions of dollars in loans to China since then, making China the bank's fifth largest borrower. Governments must first be a member of the IMF to apply for IBRD membership.

Yuan: See Renminbi

Appendix 3

Personalities

Chairman of the Central Committee

NOTE: the position of chairman was abolished in 1982.

Mao Zedong	1949–76
Hua Guofeng	1976–81
Hu Yaobang	1981–82

President of the PRC

Li Xiannian	1983–88
Yang Shangkun	1988–93
Jiang Zemin	1993–

Chairman, Central Committee Military Affairs Commission

Mao Zedong	to October 1976
Hua Guofeng	1976–81
Deng Xiaoping	1981–89
Jiang Zemin	1989–

Premier

Zhou Enlai	1949–76
Hua Guofeng	1976–80
Zhao Ziyang	1980–87
Li Peng	1988–

Chairman, Standing Committee of the National People's Congress (NPC)

Zhu De	1965–78
Ye Jianying	1978–83
Peng Zhen	1983–88
Wan Li	1988–93
Qiao Shi	1993–

NOTE: Some of the individuals filling these positions may change after the Fifteenth Party Congress in the Fall of 1997.

CHEN Yun (1905–95); One of the preeminent political leaders of the 1980s, along with Deng Xiaoping. Chen participated in the Long March and joined the Politburo in 1945, ascending to party vice-chairman in 1956. Chen helped rehabilitate the economy after the disastrous Great Leap Forward, but was branded a revisionist by Mao and remained politically inactive from 1962 until Mao's death. After the Third Plenum of the Eleventh Party Congress in 1978, Chen rejoined the Politburo, becoming vice-premier in 1979 and chairman of the State Finance and Economic Commission. Chen promoted a greater role for state planning than Deng, and often opposed him over the pace and degree of economic liberalization. In 1992, however, Chen supported Deng's drive for a new wave of economic reform.

CHIANG Ching-kuo (1910–88); Son of Chiang Kai-shek. Chiang succeeded his father in the leadership of the Republic of China, becoming premier in 1976 and then president in 1978. In his later years, Chiang initiated many reforms that facilitated Taiwan's eventual transition from martial law to democratic rule.

DENG Xiaoping (1904–97); Paramount leader of China in the post-Mao era. In the early 1920s, Deng spent time working and studying in France and Moscow. Upon his return to China, he became active in CCP military affairs, rising to the rank of political commissar during the civil war. He joined the Politburo in 1955 and was named the secretary general of its Standing Committee in 1956. He worked with Liu Shaoqi and Chen Yun to repair the damages caused by the Great Leap Forward, but was purged during the Cultural Revolution. Although reinstated briefly (1973–75) with Zhou Enlai's support, Deng was purged again for criticizing the Cultural Revolution. He quickly rose to power after Mao's death, gaining firm control by the early 1980s. Deng favored policies promoting economic liberalization while maintaining strict political control. Inflation and student unrest in 1986 and 1989 challenged his power temporarily. He played a key role in coordinating the military response to the student movement in 1989. Deng resigned from his last official government post (Chairman of the Military Commission) in 1989, but his "Southern Tour" of Special Economic Zones in 1992 helped reignite and legitimize economic liberalization. During the last few years of his life, Deng, in poor health, played a minimal role in political affairs.

FANG Lizhi (1936–); Scientist and dissident. Fang, an astrophysicist at Hefei University of Science and Technology, became a member of the Academy of Sciences in 1985. In the aftermath of student demonstrations at Hefei University in 1987, Fang, who had called for greater democratization in China, was expelled from the Communist Party and dismissed as vice-president of the university for "bourgeois liberalization." He spoke out again during the student movement of 1989, seeking asylum in the US embassy after the June 4 crackdown. He was allowed to leave for England in 1990.

HU Jintao (1942–); Member of the central committee of the CCP since 1985. Hu's education was in hydraulic engineering. In 1988 he was appointed party secretary of Tibet, where his suppression of demonstrations earned him praise from central officials. He joined the politburo standing committee in 1992.

HU Qili (1929–); Hu rose through the ranks of the Communist Youth League and Students' Federation in the 1950s and 1960s, but was purged during the Cultural Revolution as a supporter of Liu Shaoqi's revisionism. In 1977 he returned to Beijing, serving as vice-president of Qinghua University and mayor of Tianjin, among other activities. Hu joined the Politburo in 1985. Like Hu Yaobang, his patron, Hu was a strong proponent of reform and of reducing the party's role in economic affairs. He was removed from office along with Zhao Ziyang for showing sympathy for student demonstrators during the 1989 demonstrations, but was subsequently appointed to the Central Committee of the CCP in 1992.

HU Qiaomu (1912–92); A leading theoretician for the Communist Party. Hu served as Mao's secretary in the 1940s. After 1949, he worked in the party secretariat, serving under Deng Xiaoping, and played a key role in drafting important documents. Hu was purged during the Cultural Revolution, but was brought back by Deng, becoming president of the Chinese Academy of Social

Sciences in 1977. He oversaw drafting of the "Resolution on Party History" (1981), which sought to reconcile the legitimacy of the regime with its mistakes and to judge Mao's contributions and errors. Hu became a Politburo member in 1982 and a member of the Standing Committee of the Central Advisory Commission in 1987.

HU Yaobang (1915–89); General Secretary of the PRC (1981–87) and staunch supporter of reform. Hu joined the CCP in 1933 and participated in the Long March. He was elected to the Central Committee in 1956 but underwent "reeducation" during the Cultural Revolution for supporting Liu Shaoqi, along with Deng Xiaoping. Hu was one of Deng's protégés, joining the Politburo in 1978. Party elders appreciated his efforts to redress the errors and injustices of the Cultural Revolution, but his economic liberalism often put him at odds with more conservative leaders. As a result of high inflation and student unrest, Hu was removed from office in 1987. Considered a liberal reformer, he was a catalyst in the 1989 demonstrations when what began as students mourning his death in April eventually snowballed into the Tiananmen student movement.

HUA Guofeng (1920–); Chairman of the PRC in the Mao-Deng interregnum (1976–81). Hua originally achieved prominence for his energetic support of Mao's policies in Hunan during agricultural collectivization campaigns of the 1950s, rising through the ranks during the Cultural Revolution. Hua was called to Beijing to help Zhou Enlai after Lin Biao's failed coup. He joined the Politburo in 1973. After the death of Zhou and Deng's second purge (1976), Hua became acting premier and chairman of the CCP. Following Mao's death he quickly moved to arrest the "Gang of Four." Criticized by Deng for favoring continued collectivization (the Dazhai model), promoting massive industrial projects, and for upholding the "two whatevers," Hua was replaced as premier by Zhao Ziyang in 1980 and as party chairman by Hu Yaobang in 1981. He preserved his position on the Central Committee, but has served in relative political obscurity.

JIANG Qing (1914–91); Wife of Mao Zedong and radical leftist leader in the Cultural Revolution. Jiang was a stage and screen actress before she joined the CCP in 1933. She married Mao Zedong in Yan'an. Jiang was not active politically until the Cultural Revolution, when she promoted the most extreme cultural and institutional criticism. Arrested as one of the "Gang of Four" immediately after Mao's death, Jiang was tried and sentenced to death (later commuted to life imprisonment). She committed suicide in prison in 1991.

JIANG Zemin (1926–); General secretary of the CCP (1989–) and president of the PRC (1993–). Jiang began his political career in Shanghai. In the early 1980s he worked in import-export affairs and the State Foreign Investment Commission, becoming a member of the Central Committee in 1982. In 1985 Jiang returned to Shanghai to serve as mayor and party secretary, where he proved to be liberal on economic reform but stern in political affairs. Deng Xiaoping brought Jiang in to replace Zhao Ziyang as general secretary when the latter resigned in 1989, and Jiang was subsequently named chairman of the Central Military Commission and president (1993). As of 1997 Jiang was nominally the most powerful figure in China, but the depth and strength of his support was uncertain after the death of Deng Xiaoping.

LEE Tung-hui (1923–); President of the Republic of China, succeeding Chiang Ching-kuo in 1988. Lee is the first native Taiwanese to hold such a high political position. Educated in agricultural economics and receiving a Ph.D. from Cornell University, Lee returned to Taiwan where he championed agricultural reform. Lee served as mayor of Taipei (1978–81), governor of Taiwan (1981–84), and vice-president from 1984 until Chiang's death. In March 1996, Lee became the first president of the Republic of China chosen by direct democratic elections.

LI Peng (1928–); Premier (1988–). Li was adopted by Zhou Enlai at the age of 11 after his father was martyred in the communist cause. He received part of his engineering education in the Soviet Union. Li became a member of the Central Committee in 1982, vice-premier from 1983–88, and joined the Politburo Standing Committee in 1987. He pushed for economic retrenchment in 1988 and took a hard-line stance against student demonstrators in 1989. Li is a strong proponent of the Three Gorges dam project and is considered to be more conservative in economic matters than Zhao Ziyang, whom he replaced.

LI Ruihuan (1934–); Chairman of the CPPCC (1993–). Li started his career as a worker in the Tianjin region, eventually rising to the level of mayor in 1982. He was elected to the Central Committee in 1982, joining the Politburo in 1987 and its Standing Committee in June 1989. He is perceived as moderate on economic matters but hard on political affairs.

LI Xiannian (1907–92); President (1983–88) and conservative counterweight to Deng Xiaoping for much of the 1980s. A veteran of the Long March and a commander in the Red Army, Li joined the Politburo in 1956, becoming minister of finance. He survived the Cultural Revolution unscathed and was named vice-chairman in 1977. In 1978 he drafted the ten-year plan that was subsequently criticized for overemphasizing heavy industry. In subsequent years, Li was suspicious of Deng's reforms. Some believe he played a role in the ouster of Hu Yaobang and Zhao Ziyang. As president he visited the US in 1985. In 1988, he was named to head the Chinese People's Political Consultative Conference.

LIN Biao (1907–71); High military commander charged with a coup attempt against Mao Zedong during the Cultural Revolution. Lin was a key military leader in the CCP's Red Army during the civil war. In 1959, he was named defense minister. He supported Mao's launching of the Cultural Revolution and was written into the 1969 constitution to succeed Mao. However, Mao and Lin increasingly clashed on a number of issues, including détente with the US. In September 1971, Lin allegedly died in an airplane crash after a failed coup attempt against Mao.

MAO Zedong (1893–1976); Paramount leader of the CCP for more than three decades. Mao led the CCP to victory against the Kuomintang. In addition to the position of chairman, which he held until his death, Mao served as president of the PRC from 1949 to 1959. Mao was instrumental in launching the Cultural Revolution; he did so presumably to bolster his power, which had suffered as a result of the Great Leap Forward. After his death, the "Resolution on Party History" declared that while Mao remained a great leader, he had made many mistakes late in life, most notably the Cultural Revolution.

PENG Zhen (1902–97); Politburo member who focused on legal work. Peng became a member of the Politburo in 1945 and mayor of Beijing in 1951. He was the first Politburo member to fall victim to the Cultural Revolution, being charged with criticizing Mao. Peng was rehabilitated in 1979 and made a vice-chairman of the NPC's Standing Committee, subsequently rejoining the Politburo. Peng worked to create a legal structure in post-Mao China. He retired from his posts in 1987 but reappeared after the 1989 demonstrations as an outspoken supporter of the government's military response.

QIAN Qichen (1928–); Career diplomat instrumental in foreign affairs during the reform era. Qian began diplomatic work while a student in Moscow in the 1950s. During the Cultural Revolution, he was sent away for "reeducation" but reappeared in 1972. He was appointed vice-minister of foreign affairs in 1984, ascending to foreign minister in 1988. Appointed to the State Council in 1991 and joining the Politburo in 1992, Qian played an important role in handling the difficult diplomatic situation after 1989. He has also been involved in negotiating Hong Kong's return to Chinese sovereignty in 1997.

QIAO Shi (1925–); A leader in the Communist Youth League in the 1950s and 1960s who then joined the International Liaison Department, Qiao was purged during the Cultural Revolution, returning to the Liaison office in 1978. In the 1980s, he worked on legal reforms to promote economic reforms as well as anti-corruption campaigns. He became a Politburo member in 1985 and vice-premier of the State Council in 1986. Qiao was named chair of the NPC in 1993.

WEI Jingsheng (1950–); A prominent dissident from the working class. Wei first challenged the state during the Democracy Wall movement of 1978, calling for democratization as the "fifth modernization" to supplement the four proposed by Deng. Arrested and charged with attempting to overthrow the government, Wei was sentenced to 15 years in prison. He served more than 14 years before being released just prior to the Olympic Committee's decision on the 2000 Olympics. Wei was rearrested in November 1995 and sentenced to another 14 years in prison.

YANG Shangkun (1907–); A reformist-minded second generation leader with strong ties to the military. Yang participated in the Long March and was secretary general of the Eighth Route Army, stationed at its headquarters in Yan'an for much of the civil war. He joined the Central Committee in 1956 and the NPC Standing Committee in 1964, but was purged during the Cultural Revolution. He reappeared as vice-governor of Guangdong in 1979 and also served in provincial military offices. In 1981 he became secretary general of the Military Commission of the Central Committee. From 1988–93 Yang served as president of the PRC and also vice-chairman of the Central Military Commission. Yang helped to stage the military response to the 1989 demonstrations, but allegedly lost political clout when he failed to rehabilitate Zhao Ziyang. Yang was stripped of his political posts and his brother (Yang Baibing) was purged. Yang still exerts some political influence, however.

YE Jianying (1897–1987); A major conservative force in early reform-era China. Ye studied with Zhou Enlai in Moscow and participated in the Long March. After 1949, Ye was appointed mayor of Beijing and later Guangzhou. In 1954 he was named the Army's delegate to the NPC. He survived the Cultural Revolution, joining the Politburo in 1966. After Lin Biao's fall, Ye was appointed minister of defense. He supported Hua Guofeng and helped in arresting the "Gang of Four." Although he continued to hold various positions including his Politburo and Central Committee seats, Ye's influence declined after Hua's fall from power.

ZHAO Ziyang (1919–); Premier (1980–87). Zhao served as party secretary of Guangdong in the mid-1960s but was purged during the Cultural Revolution. Beginning in 1971, he served as a high party official in Mongolia, Guangdong, and then Sichuan, where his successful experimentation with reform promoting economic incentives and efficiency caught the attention of Deng Xiaoping. He joined the Politburo in 1979, its Standing Committee in 1980, and held various high party and government positions through the 1980s, including Minister for Restructuring the Economic System (1982–88) and CCP Secretary General, replacing his dismissed colleague Hu Yaobang in 1987. An active promoter of economic reforms, Zhao was stripped of all his government and party positions in 1989 for being too lenient toward student demonstrators. He has remained in enforced retirement ever since.

ZHOU Enlai (1898–1976); Premier of the PRC until his death. A top leader who sought to moderate extreme policies, Zhou was a consummate diplomat both domestically and internationally. During the Cultural Revolution, he struggled to minimize the Gang of Four's influence and supported Deng Xiaoping. Zhou helped to formulate the concept of the "four modernizations" that Deng later championed.

ZHU Rongji (1929–); Often referred to as China's economics "czar" of the 1990s. Zhu worked in the State Planning Commission in the 1950s. For his involvement in the "hundred flowers" campaign, he was denounced as a rightist and spent part of the Cultural Revolution in the countryside. From 1979 to 1988, he worked at the State Economic Commission, rising to the position of vice-minister. In 1988 Zhu was named mayor of Shanghai, where he proved to be liberal in economic affairs and conservative on political matters. His tough response to the 1989 demonstrations in Shanghai coupled with his economic successes helped pave the way for his being named to the Politburo in 1991. In 1992, Zhu became the head of the new Economic and Trade Office as well as the Securities Commission. He served as governor of the People's Bank of China from 1993 to 1995.

Appendix 4

Government Structures

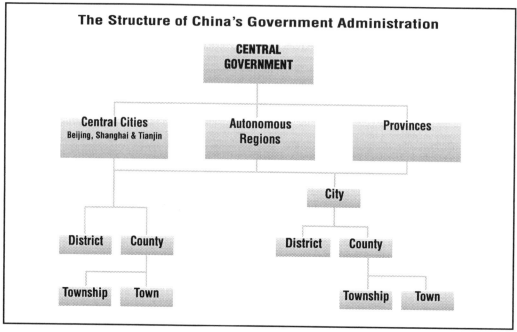

The Structure of China's Government Administration

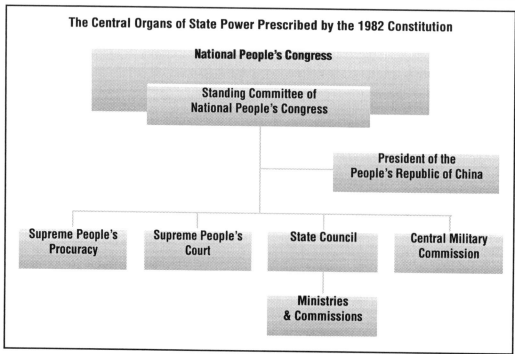

The Central Organs of State Power Prescribed by the 1982 Constitution

Appendix 5

Bibliography

China is the subject of a vast and ever-increasing body of literature. The texts listed below do not pretend to be comprehensive but are intended to indicate the variety of subjects and available approaches. The sections in this bibliography attempt to categorize texts according to their dominant analytic and substantive concerns. In reform-era China, however, politics and economics permeate not only each other but practically every facet of society. Almost all books must address the power of the Communist Party as well as the impact of economic reforms.

The emphasis is on recent book-length publications. Many fine studies published prior to the 1990s have been left out as have journal articles unless part of an issue is devoted to a particular topic. The general categories presented below are: reference, general texts, politics and institutions, economics and development, foreign relations, society, and culture. Citations are organized alphabetically according to the author or editor's name and occasionally according to the title of the journal or name of the publishing body.

Reference

China Review, Hong Kong: Chinese University of Hong Kong Press

An annual edited volume with a wide range of timely articles on the social, political, economic, and cultural events of the preceding year. Includes a statistical summary and a chronology.

FBIS Daily Report: China, Washington, D.C.: Foreign Broadcast Information Service (FBIS)

Issued daily (Monday through Friday), this invaluable service provided by the US government offers English translations of articles, speeches, and documents appearing in newspapers and journals of the PRC, Hong Kong, Taiwan, and Macau. Translations are divided according to topic area or region of origin. Note: as of August 1, 1996, FBIS is no longer available in paper form but only with an electronic subscription.

Hong Kong 1996: A Review of 1995 and a Pictoral Review of the Past Fifty Years, Hong Kong: Government Information Services Department, 1996

Part of a series of annual reports published by the Hong Kong government. This volume provides a comprehensive survey of the colony's development and is a convenient source for official statistics.

Joseph, William A., editor, *China Briefing, 1995–1996: The Contradictions of Change*, Armonk, New York: M.E. Sharpe, 1997

The most recent volume of a series produced in cooperation with the Asia Society, *China Briefing* is published every year or two. Each volume contains a series of insightful articles by scholars analyzing the major events and trends of the previous year in politics, culture, economics, and society (both in the PRC and Greater China), as well as a chronology.

MacKerras, Colin, and Amanda Yorke, *The Cambridge Handbook of Contemporary China*, Cambridge and New York: Cambridge University Press, 1991

Although somewhat dated, this still provides a highly useful general reference source for the persons, events, and trends shaping the PRC's first 40 years. The book provides a thumbnail sketch of the country's social, economic, political, and cultural affairs, with a chronology from 1900, a bibliography of English publications, and brief biographical information on the key figures of the 20th century.

People's Republic of China Year Book, Beijing and Hong Kong: PRC Year Book

The official yearbook of the PRC. Each volume reviews events of the previous year. A comprehensive review of the political and economic system, laws and regulations, social and cultural affairs, as well as some statistics and a chronicle of major events. Because this is produced by the PRC government, the contents present a strongly pro-PRC image.

Republic of China Yearbook, Taipei: Government Information Office

Published annually, this official Republic of China yearbook presents an overview of events and trends in social, political, economic, cultural, and environmental affairs, supplemented with a historical chronology extending from 1911 to the present and brief biographical data on Taiwan's elite.

Statistical Yearbook of China, Beijing: China Statistical Publishing House

Compiled annually by the State Statistical Bureau, these volumes provide statistical charts and figures for the previous year on a broad range of social and political subjects including population, investment, energy, trade, industry, and social welfare, among other subjects. Most are statistics for the year although some charts present changes over time. Captions are in Chinese and English.

General Texts

Banister, Judith, *China's Changing Population*, Stanford, California: Stanford University Press, 1987

A long-term view of demographic changes from 1849 to the 1980s, the volume focuses on such issues as health, mortality, fertility, and birth planning. While the general tone of the book is highly critical of China's one-child family policy, the statistical analysis is meticulous.

Deng Xiaoping, *Selected Works of Deng Xiaoping, Volume III (1982–1992)*, Beijing: Foreign Languages Press, 1994

A collection of statements and speeches made by the late paramount leader of post-Mao China. It includes Deng's thoughts and policy on such issues as political and economic reform, international relations, culture and ideology, as well as Deng's celebrated speeches given during his Southern Tour of the Special Economic Zones in 1992. A must-read for those seeking to understand official government policy in the Dengist and even post-Deng era.

Eastman, Lloyd E., *Family, Fields and Ancestors: Constancy and Change in China's Social and Economic History, 1550-1949*, Oxford and New York: Oxford University Press, 1988

A comparatively concise review of social and political trends prior to the establishment of the PRC. The author divides his review by topic area rather than strict chronology, tracing changes in such areas as the family, religion, commerce and manufacturing, agriculture, and society. A synthetic work that seeks to collect information rather than present a particular argument.

Evans, Richard, *Deng Xiaoping and the Making of Modern China*, London: Penguin, 1995

A biography of the late patriarch of the reform era. The author carefully traces Deng's life from his childhood in Sichuan to his experience abroad and later to his long eventful career in the Chinese Communist Party, including his eventual rise to preeminence. Presented in a very readable narrative form.

Fairbank, John King, *China: A New History*, Cambridge, Massachusetts: Belknap Press of Harvard University Press, 1992

A comprehensive history of China from its earliest history up to the late 1980s. This volume comprises an impressive historical review written by a man who was long the doyen of Chinese studies in the United States. Includes a list of suggested readings.

Kristof, Nicholas D., and Sheryl WuDunn, *China Wakes: The Struggle for the Soul of a Rising Power*, New York: Vintage, 1995

Combines anecdotes and research written by

two *New York Times* correspondents about their experiences while stationed in China, 1988–93. The text is broken down thematically, with each author writing every other chapter. A text that is both critical and empathetic.

Nathan, Andrew J., *Chinese Democracy*, Berkeley: University of California Press, 1986

A classic exploration of a subject that has become even more topical after the events of spring 1989. The author explores Chinese conceptions of democracy prior to and after the establishment of the PRC, concluding that political and cultural factors pose serious impediments to the establishment of democracy in the near future.

Putterman, Louis G., *Continuity and Change in China's Rural Development: Collective and Reform Eras in Perspective*, New York: Oxford University Press, 1993

This text presents an overview of rural development, focusing on the late-Maoist and Dengist eras. In the process it examines such issues as changing efficiency, growth, and incentive structures in the collective and reform eras. The analysis employs micro-analysis of processes in Dahe Township in Hebei province, using aggregate data to place these findings in a broader national context.

Riskin, Carl, *China's Political Economy: The Quest for Development Since 1949*, Oxford and New York: Oxford University Press, 1987

Written in a style both analytic and narrative, this text traces the evolution of the national economy up to 1985. Much of the volume focuses on the Maoist approach, arguing that its failure lay in the lack of national economic integration. It also examines post-Mao reforms and their impact on development performance.

Schurmann, Franz, *Ideology and Organization in Communist China*, 2nd edition, Berkeley: University of California Press, 1971

An encyclopedic, in-depth analysis of how communist ideology and organization restructured society and politics in the PRC in the 1950s and 1960s. The author combines rich historical description with a detailed analysis of the inter-linking of ideology, organization, and society.

Shue, Vivienne, *The Reach of the State: Sketches of the Chinese Body Politic*, Stanford, California: Stanford University Press, 1988

Four essays presenting different ways by which to view the changing nature of state control over and relations with local government and society. Focusing predominantly on the Maoist era but also considering early Dengist reforms, the essays seek to interweave state and society, structure and culture, and fine detail with grand design.

Sun Yat-sen, *Prescriptions for Saving China: Selected Writings of Sun Yat-sen*, edited by Julie Lee Wei, Ramon Hawley Myers, and Donald G. Gillin, Stanford, California: Hoover Institution Press, 1994

The father of the Republic of China, Sun Yat-sen is revered not only in Taiwan but also in the PRC, where he is esteemed as an early revolutionary. His thoughts have had a profound impact on Chinese political ideology in the 20th century. This volume contains translations of selections of his writing from 1894 to 1924.

Womack, Brantly, editor, *Contemporary Chinese Politics in Historical Perspective*, Cambridge and New York: Cambridge University Press, 1992

A collection of essays using 20th-century Chinese history to place contemporary PRC politics in perspective. Major concerns informing the book are the events of Tiananmen in 1989 and the possibility of a less authoritarian system.

Yang, Dali L., *Calamity and Reform in China: State, Rural Society and Institutional Change Since the Great Leap Famine*, Stanford, California: Stanford University Press, 1996

An in-depth look at the policies and practices of the Great Leap Forward. The author traces its consequences for subsequent policy, arguing that the pattern of decollectivization in the countryside can be traced back to localities' experiences at that time.

Politics and Institutions

Baum, Richard, *Burying Mao: Chinese Politics in the Age of Deng Xiaoping*, Princeton, New Jersey: Princeton University Press, 1994

Drawing upon extensive research as well as personal experience, the author explores Chinese reforms from 1976 to 1993. The analysis focuses on elite politics, tracing the changing power relations of conservative and reform-oriented leaders and the fluidity of factional politics in ideological, political, and economic affairs.

Blecher, Marc, and Vivienne Shue, *The Tethered Deer: Government and Economy in a Chinese County*, Stanford, California: Stanford University Press, 1996

An in-depth examination of Shulu county in Hebei province over the years 1970 to 1990, based on numerous fieldwork trips. A rich description of changing governance at an administrative level bridging the central and local governments. The authors argue that local government's developmental orientation remains constant over both periods but that the means available to it change significantly.

Chan, Anita, Richard Madsen, and Jonathan Unger, *Chen Village Under Mao and Deng*, Berkeley: University of California Press, 1992

An updated version of the 1984 classic *Chen Village*, this book extends study of the village into the Dengist era. Drawing from subsequent fieldwork and interviews in the community, this edition provides fascinating insight into changing rural social and political practices wrought by trade, migration, and commercialization in the Hong Kong hinterlands.

Fewsmith, Joseph, *Dilemmas of Reform in China: Political Conflict and Economic Debate*, Armonk, New York: M.E. Sharpe, 1994

Examines debates over reform policy in the 1980s, presenting the conflicting agendas of prominent policy advocates and the political battles surrounding their proposals. A rich analysis that seeks to explain how previously agreed upon procedural rules broke down at Tiananmen. It also indicates that China's economic reform was fraught with debate and tensions.

Goodman, David S.G., and Gerald Segal, editors, *China Deconstructs: Politics, Trade, and Regionalism*, London and New York: Routledge, 1994

This collection of articles is united by a common theme: that reforms have not led to a critical weakening of the central government. Rather, the central government continues to play an important role in creating the institutional and political frameworks facilitating trade. The articles include analysis of central-local relations as well as relations between domestic regions with the central government and foreign countries and territories.

Hamrin, Carol Lee, and Suisheng Zhao, editors, *Decision-Making in Deng's China: Perspectives from Insiders*, Armonk, New York: M.E. Sharpe, 1995

A collection of articles written by intellectuals and officials formerly involved in creating and implementing reforms in post-Mao China. The book provides an interesting and useful "inside" look at political and organizational processes often underspecified in more general texts. Topics include central leadership and executive systems, bureaucratic structure and politics, and experiments in system reform.

Howell, Jude, *China Opens Its Doors: The Politics of Economic Transition*, Boulder, Colorado: Lynne Rienner, and Hemel Hempstead: Harvester Wheatsheaf, 1993

This book focuses on the Open Policy, its impact on foreign trade and investment, and the politics between central and local interests. The author argues for a "spiral model" of reform in which tendencies toward decentralization and recentralization constantly trade off. The residue of former reforms, however, precludes any real backtracking. The book includes a case study of the Xiamen Special Economic Zone and in-depth analysis of labor policies for foreign firms.

Lieberthal, Kenneth, and Michel Oksenberg, *Policy Making in China: Leaders, Structures, and Processes*, Princeton, New Jersey: Princeton University Press, 1988

Written by two preeminent experts with impressive access to inside information, this volume was one of the first books providing in-depth analysis of bureaucratic politics in the reform era. In tracing policy creation and implementation in three case studies on petroleum, the Three Gorges Dam, and energy, the authors convey the complex negotiations and inconsistencies of bureaucratic politics. The text also includes extended discussion of leadership structures and their interrelations with ministries and commissions.

Lieberthal, Kenneth, *Governing China: From Revolution Through Reform*, New York: Norton, 1995

This text presents a detailed description of the Chinese administrative system in the Maoist and Dengist periods. The author emphasizes the continuity between the two eras, characterizing China as having a fragmented authoritarian system that is at its apex lawless and riddled with contention. Includes a detailed and lucid presentation of current intra-governmental structure and practices.

Oi, Jean Chun, *State and Peasant in Contemporary China: The Political Economy of Village Government*, Berkeley: University of California Press, 1989

Starting from the simple question of "how shall the harvest be divided," this book crafts an in-depth and influential analysis of institutional structures and clientelist politics at the local level. The volume focuses on the production team and the importance of informal ties between state cadres and their clients, arguing that even with market reforms local cadres have preserved their power.

Perry, Elizabeth J., and Christine Wong, editors, *The Political Economy of Reform in Post-Mao China*, Cambridge, Massachusetts: Council on East Asian Studies, Harvard University, 1985

An excellent collection of articles on the process and consequences of reform in the early post-Maoist era. As agricultural reform was the focus of reform efforts at this time, many of the articles explore the impact of reform on areas such as production, income, and power relations in the rural areas, although some articles examine industrial reform.

Shirk, Susan L., *The Political Logic of Economic Reform in China*, Berkeley: University of California Press, 1993

Working from an institutionalist rational choice approach with an explicitly comparativist theoretical framework, this book examines the reform process in state-owned enterprises in the 1980s and the bargaining between central and local state actors. Shirk argues that central officials needed to "play to the provinces" in order to gain the upper hand in inter-bureaucratic factional politics against conservatives.

Walder, Andrew, editor, *China's Transitional Economy*, Oxford and New York: Oxford University Press, 1996

This collection of articles by prominent scholars looks at the interaction and interrelationship of politics and economics, examining such issues as the importance of institutions and history, incentives in business and government alike, and suggesting the relevance of the Chinese case for other transitional economies. Many of the articles in this volume originally appeared in the *China Quarterly* (December 1995).

White, Gordon, *Riding the Tiger: The Politics of Economic Reform in Post-Mao China*, London: Macmillan, and Stanford, California: Stanford University Press, 1993

This book explores the impact of the creation of markets on Chinese communist government control. Analyzing reforms up to the early 1990s, the author focuses on the political battles and changing power relations prompted by market reforms, both within government as well as between the government and society, arguing that markets have weakened the central government's ideological authority and institutional power. The book concludes with a consideration of the long-term impact of reform on central control and the prospects for democratization.

Economics and Development

Byrd, William A., and Qingsong Lin, editors, *China's Rural Industry: Structure, Development, and Reform*, Oxford and New York: Oxford University Press, 1990

A foundational work on township and village enterprises resulting from the cooperative research of scholars at the World Bank and Chinese institutions in the mid-1980s. Drawing from intensive research and interviews in four counties displaying different industrial and economic characteristics, the articles discuss such topics as temporal and geographical variations in structural characteristics, ownership, enterprise performance, labor conditions, and the role of local government.

Chen, Derong, *Chinese Firms Between Hierarchy and Market: The Contract Management Responsibility System in China*, London: Macmillan, and New York: St. Martin's Press, 1995

As a significant feature of enterprise reform, the Contract Management Responsibility System sought to weaken party power in enterprises so that experts could have greater control over production decisions. This book explores the consequences of this reform. Informed by four case studies of enterprises in Beijing, the author finds that actual changes are not as great as are generally assumed.

Feinberg, Richard E., John Echeverri-Gent, and Friedemann Müller, editors, *Economic Reform in Three Giants: US Foreign Policy and the USSR, China, and India,* New Brunswick, New Jersey: Transaction Books, 1990

Part of the Overseas Development Council's US-Third World Policy Perspective series, this collection of articles compares the strategy and outcomes of economic development in China, India, and the USSR. Three of the articles focus on specific countries' policies and experiences, while the other three are explicitly comparative. While somewhat dated, the book provides a good overview of processes in the 1980s. Includes a statistical appendix.

Findlay, Christopher C., Andrew Watson, and Harry X. Wu, editors, *Rural Enterprises in China,* London: Macmillan, and New York: St. Martin's Press, 1994

Rural enterprises have played a critical role in fueling economic growth in China. This collection of articles focuses on the impact and significance of the growth of rural enterprises up to the early 1990s. Issues covered include variations between regions and their political consequences, efficiency and productivity performance, capital markets, national policy, the changing workforce, and how rural enterprises differ from other types of ownership in the countryside.

Harrold, Peter, E.C. Hwa, and Lou Jiwei, editors, *Macroeconomic Management in China: Proceedings of a Conference in Dalian, June 1993,* Washington, D.C.: World Bank, 1993

Resulting from a conference attended by both Chinese reform economists and World Bank staff, this book presents an interesting conjunction of Chinese and non-Chinese perspectives of the problems and goals of economic reform in the mid-1990s, the period during which the PRC implemented a new round of economic reforms. The book consists of a series of presentations by high

Chinese government officials on such topics as macroeconomic control, tax reform, and industrial policy in a market economy, each followed by a commentary by their World Bank counterparts. At times the discussion is quite specialized but rarely unintelligible to the layperson.

Jacobson, Harold Karan, and Michel Oksenberg, *China's Participation in the IMF, the World Bank, and GATT: Toward a Global Economic Order,* Ann Arbor: University of Michigan Press, 1990

This is one of the few texts devoted to examining China's changing relations with international economic organizations. Drawing on interviews with officials in Chinese and international organizations as well as documentary sources, the chapters trace the negotiation processes with the respective institutions and posit conditions and consequences of China's membership in these bodies.

Lardy, Nicholas R., *China in the World Economy,* Washington, D.C.: Institute for International Economics, 1994

This book is packed with useful information on trends in the Chinese economy and their impact on China's role in the international arena. General topics include trade trends and balances, foreign investment and loans, and issues in US-China trade relations. The text includes a prognosis of China's future role in the international economy, policy recommendations, and a chronology of China and GATT through 1994.

Naughton, Barry, *Growing Out of the Plan: Chinese Economic Reform, 1978–1993,* Cambridge and New York: Cambridge University Press, 1995

This volume presents an insightful review of economic reforms from the early state sector reforms to the post-Tiananmen policies implementing a socialist market economy. The author takes a generally positive view of the reform process but stresses it was fraught with contention and uncertainty. He counters the conventional wisdom by arguing the feasibility of command economies becoming market economies and by stressing the positive role state enterprises played in the reform process.

Wong, John, Rong Ma, and Mu Yang, editors, *China's Rural Entrepreneurs: Ten Case Studies,* Singapore: Times Academic Press, 1995

This collaborative effort by Singapore and Chinese academics presents survey reports of ten township and village enterprises in southern Jiangsu and Shandong provinces. These cases serve to introduce the reader to some of the details of TVE structures and practices, providing a useful supplement to more theoretically informed analyses.

World Bank, *China: Macroeconomic Stability in a Decentralized Economy*, Washington, D.C.: World Bank, 1995

A more technical examination of economic reform and monetary policy in contemporary China that focuses on the causes and solutions to inflation, based on research conducted in 1993 and 1994. The analysis argues the need for greater local economic autonomy but not an abandonment of the central government's role in coordinating macroeconomic policy. Half the volume contains annexes summarizing components of the PRC's fiscal system and focused policy analysis.

Young, Susan, *Private Business and Economic Reform in China*, Armonk, New York: M.E. Sharpe, 1995

This book undertakes a thematic exploration of private business, focusing on the 1980s. The analysis explores the tensions between central policy, local officials, and the profit motive driving the individual economy. Private business has gained substantial autonomy but remains dependent on the goodwill of local administration.

Foreign Relations

Chan, Ming K., and Gerard A. Postiglione, *The Hong Kong Reader: Passage to Chinese Sovereignty*, Armonk, New York: M.E. Sharpe, 1996

A collection of articles on the process of Hong Kong's return to Chinese sovereignty that looks at both past events and future prognoses, including topics such as the judiciary, education, democratic reform, and economic relations. The book concludes with an essay outlining possible alternative scenarios for post-1997 Hong Kong. The volume is part of a series started in 1991 on "Hong Kong Becoming China: The Transition to 1997."

Cheng, Tun-jen, Chi Huang, and Samuel S.G. Wu, editors, *Inherited Rivalry: Conflict Across the Taiwan Straits*, Boulder, Colorado: Lynne Rienner, 1995

Bringing together scholars from the US, Taiwan, and the PRC, this volume explores the domestic and international influences on PRC-ROC relations. An underlying concern is identifying Taiwan's best strategy for dealing with the mainland. Many of the articles employ rational choice theory. Includes a chronicle of the major events of the cross-straits rivalry.

China Quarterly 136 (December 1993), special issue on Greater China

This special volume is dedicated to exploring China's relations with Taiwan, Hong Kong, and Macau. The articles address a variety of issues including political and social change as well as foreign and economic relations. The introduction argues against excessive fears of a power bloc forming.

Dittmer, Lowell, and Samuel S. Kim, editors, *China's Quest for National Identity*, Ithaca, New York: Cornell University Press, 1993

A collection of essays addressing issues of national identity in both dynastic and reform-era China. Articles on the more recent period examine such issues as regional identities within China, intellectuals and the state, as well as China's changing identity both regionally and internationally.

Leng, Tse-Kang, *The Taiwan-China Connection: Democracy and Development Across the Taiwan Straits*, Boulder, Colorado: Westview Press, 1996

The focus of this book is the changing role of the Taiwanese state in policy-making during the period of political and economic transition as well as the increased influence of social groups, particularly business. The Taiwanese business community's powerful desire to exploit economic opportunities in China served as a lever to move a state initially unwilling to foster relations between the two governments.

Overholt, William H., *The Rise of China: How Economic Reform Is Creating a New Superpower*, New York: Norton, 1994

Reviewing China's spectacular growth from 1979 to 1992, this book traces the politics and contents of reform and the reasons behind

China's success. The book also addresses the interdependence of the regional economies as well as the international consequences of a stronger China.

Roberti, Mark, *The Fall of Hong Kong: China's Triumph and Britain's Betrayal*, New York: Wiley, 1994

Written by a journalist working in Hong Kong from 1984 to 1993, this book presents a journalistic account of the Sino-British negotiations on ending British sovereignty over the territory and the drafting of the Basic Law. The material comes largely from interviews conducted with 142 people. As the title indicates, the analysis is extremely critical of British actions.

Shambaugh, David L., *Beautiful Imperialist: China Perceives America, 1972–1990*, Princeton, New Jersey: Princeton University Press, 1991

Based on seven years of interviews with many of the most influential "America watchers," this book, both amusing and sobering, indicates the deep misunderstanding even Chinese specialists have of the United States. Examining Marxist and non-Marxist camps, the author finds that both groups tend to believe that business controls American politics but are less critical of US society.

Wachman, Alan, *Taiwan: National Identity and Democratization*, Armonk, New York: M.E. Sharpe, 1994

Taiwan reminds us that democracy and Asian societies are not necessarily incompatible. This book examines the history and process of democratization in Taiwan from the perspective of the national identity problem. Working from interviews and empirical research, the author traces the growth of civil society and its ability to make demands upon the state. The book concludes with a discussion of what the Taiwan case can contribute to theories of democratization and nationalism.

Zhao, Quansheng, *Interpreting Chinese Foreign Policy: The Micro-Macro Linkage Approach*, Hong Kong and New York: Oxford University Press, 1996

This book reviews the changes in Chinese foreign policy during the Maoist and Dengist eras by means of a theoretical framework that links transformations in macro-symbolic, institutional, and regime structures with their impact on the micro-policies of foreign policy. The text posits that China will continue toward greater cultural and economic exchanges as well as cooperation with the international community.

Society

Alford, William P., *To Steal a Book Is an Elegant Offense: Intellectual Property Law in Chinese Civilization*, Stanford, California: Stanford University Press, 1995

A well-written and learned volume tracing the historical roots of China's lack of regard for intellectual property rights. The book draws upon Chinese legal history as well as the history of Chinese philosophy and literature. The analysis extends to current times in which leaders' distrust of a free marketplace of ideas and general disregard for the individual contribute to current problems in adhering to international protocols. Includes extensive endnotes and bibliography.

Davis, Deborah S., Richard Kraus, Barry Naughton, and Elizabeth J. Perry, editors, *Urban Spaces in Contemporary China: The Potential for Autonomy and Community in Post-Mao China*, Cambridge: Cambridge University Press, and Washington, D.C.: Woodrow Wilson Center Press, 1995

Using a variety of disciplinary perspectives, this collection of articles drawn from a 1992 Woodrow Wilson Center conference explores changes to China's urban landscape caused by reforms. The articles examine issues of identity, local autonomy, culture, and urban structure. The volume focuses on the impact of increased commercialization and reduced state power in associations, economics, government, and creative activity in urban areas.

Kelliher, Daniel, *Peasant Power in China: The Era of Rural Reform, 1979–1989*, New Haven, Connecticut: Yale University Press, 1992

This critical examination of state relations with peasants argues that peasants played an active role in pushing forward reforms while trying to fend off state attempts at control and extraction. The author illustrates his argument with three case studies examining the creation of family farms, the politics of buying and selling rural harvests, and privatization.

Kent, Ann, *Between Freedom and Subsistence: China*

and Human Rights, Hong Kong and New York: Oxford University Press, 1993

This analysis of a highly contentious topic differs from most by taking a more economic perspective on human rights issues. In doing so, it often parallels the Chinese government's characterizations of the reasons for China's lack of political rights. An interesting, if not totally satisfying, counterweight to the moral standpoint usually shaping foreign discussions of human rights in China.

Link, Perry, *Evening Chats in Beijing: Probing China's Predicament,* New York: Norton, 1992

Focusing on the years prior to Tiananmen, this insightful examination of China's current environment draws from interviews and extended interactions with leading intellectuals. The lively writing style allows these figures to speak for themselves, expressing their aspirations and anxieties as they negotiate patriotism and integrity in a political system that constrains independent voices.

Lubman, Stanley B., editor, *China's Legal Reforms,* Oxford and New York: Oxford University Press, 1996

A timely collection of essays on legal reform in the 1980s and 1990s written by leading American and English scholars. Topics include criminal law, foreign investment law, family law, the law-making process in China, and China's place in the international legal order. While some improvement has been made in all these areas, the authors note that China must take further steps in implementing the rule of law.

Miller, H. Lyman, *Science and Dissent in Post-Mao China: The Politics of Knowledge,* Seattle: University of Washington Press, 1996

This text explores the politicization of the scientific community and the challenge this posed to the PRC government in the 1980s. The author shows that beyond the political activities of dissident scientists, the scientific endeavor itself threatens the ideological authority of the central government.

Peng Xizhe, *Demographic Transition in China: Fertility Trends Since the 1950s,* Oxford: Clarendon Press, and New York: Oxford University Press, 1991

This book traces the demographic changes from the founding of the PRC to the early 1990s, with an emphasis on fertility issues. Looking at both national and provincial-level processes, the author argues that lower birth rates can be explained by the government's population control policy and not the rising standard of living.

Pepper, Suzanne, *China's Education Reform in the 1980s: Policies, Issues, and Historical Perspectives,* Berkeley: Institute of East Asian Studies, University of California, 1990

This study undertakes an historical examination of education in the PRC. The book explores how current education practices and policy debates in China are rooted in pre-1949 Chinese ideologies about education. Most of the analysis is dedicated to tracing how the political debates about education in the 1980s played out in elementary, secondary, and higher education.

Perry, Elizabeth J., editor, *Putting Class in Its Place: Worker Identities in East Asia,* Berkeley: Institute of East Asian Studies, University of California, 1996

Presenting both historical and contemporary research by scholars well versed in their subject matter, this collection of articles explores the impact of rapid industrialization in East Asia on workers' identities and agendas. Most of the articles focus on China and Taiwan. While workers' identities display significant differences across space and time, the authors concur that a politics of "place" (social and economic status) rather than a politics of "class" characterizes workers' ambitions.

Qu, Geping, and Li Jinchang, *Population and the Environment in China,* Boulder, Colorado: Lynne Rienner, 1994

Written by two people who worked at China's National Environmental Protection agency, this book provides an overview of the problems China's enormous population pose to the limited natural resources of the PRC. The final chapter presents some general policy suggestions.

Smil, Vaclav, *China's Environmental Crisis: An Inquiry into the Limits of National Development,* Armonk, New York: M.E. Sharpe, 1993

An award-winning book combining in-depth analysis with a readable style, the chapters explore the environmental degradation caused by China's large population. Among the topics examined are land and water use, the burdens of feeding and providing energy for the Chinese population, as well as the tensions between modernization, improving the quality of life, and preserving the environment.

Walder, Andrew, *Communist Neo-Traditionalism: Work and Authority in Chinese Industry*, Berkeley: University of California Press, 1988

A seminal work on the relation between Chinese labor and the communist regime from 1949 to the early 1980s. Based on in-depth interviews with Chinese workers and secondary materials on factory life in China, Walder builds an influential theoretical model of neo-traditionalism to understand state-society relations in communist systems. He traces the intricate networks of clientelism institutionalized in the state factory through which the state vertically divides the working class and creates consent to its rule.

Wong, Linda J., and Stewart MacPherson, *Social Change and Social Policy in Contemporary China*, Aldershot, Hampshire, and Brookfield, Vermont: Avebury, 1995

This timely volume contains a collection of articles written by Hong Kong academics presenting a balanced examination of social policy reforms that have transfigured social and economic values, management structures, and national social welfare responsibility. Chapters are devoted to health care, social security, education, privatization, migration, and gender issues.

Zhou, Kate Xiao, *How the Farmers Changed China: Power of the People*, Boulder, Colorado: Westview Press, 1996

This book provides an uncommon but important perspective on reform by focusing on the impact of rural inhabitants on the reform process. The author argues that it was the farmers rather than the central government who fueled and shaped reform in the Dengist era, noting that farmers on their own initiative created markets and rural industries, challenged the state's migration and population policies, and redefined women's roles.

Culture

Gilmartin, Christina K., Gail Hershatter, Lisa Rofel, and Tyrene White, editor, *Engendering*

China: Women, Culture, and the State, Cambridge, Massachusetts: Harvard University Press, 1994

This multi-disciplinary collection of essays on the changing identity and status of women in China is distinctive for its combining both Western and Chinese scholarly perspectives. Although the volume draws upon Chinese history of the past few centuries, some of the articles focus on the post-Mao era. The book includes a debate about the utility of Western feminist theory for Chinese women.

Jones, Andrew F., *Like a Knife: Ideology and Genre in Contemporary Chinese Popular Music*, Ithaca, New York: East Asia Program, Cornell University, 1992

Exploring the links between ideology and popular music, this book focuses on three contemporary genres: "popularized music" sanctioned and disseminated by the CCP, "popular music" that focuses on pleasure, and rock music that exists largely as an underground phenomenon. The author explores the historical roots of these genres and their significance for identity and ideology in contemporary China.

Kraus, Richard Curt, *Pianos and Politics in China: Middle-Class Ambitions and the Struggle Over Western Music*, New York: Oxford University Press, 1989

A well-written and interesting study of the politics of Western music in the Maoist era. The author uses this original topic as a window onto the cultural politics of the era, making it clear that Western classical music was not above the cultural battles of the era. He supplements his general discussion with detailed case studies of individual musicians' experiences during and after the Maoist era.

Lee, Chin-Chuan, editor, *China's Media, Media's China*, Boulder, Colorado: Westview Press, 1994

A collection of essays on various aspects of journalism in Greater China during the Dengist era that brings together Chinese and American perspectives. The articles explore such topics as the role media plays in state power over society as well as society's ability to voice dissent and opposition. The book includes a comparative dimension with discussion of Hong Kong and Taiwanese media as well as the US media's perspectives on China.

Potter, Sulamith Heins, and Jack M. Potter, *China's Peasants: The Anthropology of a Revolution*, Cambridge and New York: Cambridge University Press, 1990

A rich anthropological analysis of the impact of rural reforms on Zengbu Brigade in Guangdong province, spanning the late Maoist period to the early Dengist era (1978–85). Based on extensive fieldwork, the authors trace the breakup of communes and its impact on such issues as family and social relations, the power and influence of local officials, and the rise of materialist values.

Pye, Lucian W., *The Mandarin and the Cadre: China's Political Cultures*, Ann Arbor: Center for Chinese Studies, University of Michigan, 1988

A psychological account of political culture by a recognized cultural analyst. The author argues for the continuity of Chinese political thought and practice in the dynastic as well as the Maoist and Dengist eras.

Siu, Helen F., *Agents and Victims in South China: Accomplices in Rural Revolution*, New Haven, Connecticut: Yale University Press, 1989

Based on extensive anthropological fieldwork, this book focuses on the human aspects of changing state-local relations over the past century from the perspective of a Guangdong community. The author argues that communists substantially changed rural life but that this was made possible by local political entrepreneurs allying themselves with the state in order to secure their own agendas.

Tu, Wei-ming, editor, *The Living Tree: The Changing Meaning of Being Chinese Today*, Stanford, California: Stanford University Press, 1994

A thought-provoking collection of essays, most of which originally appeared in *Daedalus* (Spring 1991). The essays are joined by a common thematic concern of what it means to be Chinese and whether a culturally based identity can supplant one formerly crafted around the idea of China as "center." The essays tend to focus on intellectuals and overseas Chinese, with analysis ranging from academic to highly personal.

Tyson, James, and Ann Tyson, *Chinese Awakenings: Life Stories from the Unofficial China*, Boulder, Colorado: Westview Press, 1995

Two reporters for the *Christian Science Monitor* offer profiles of eight individuals they met while stationed in China, all of whom represent elements of contemporary society that official PRC sources either sanitize or ignore. Sympathetic toward their subjects, the authors are concurrently critical of the Chinese state.

Wasserstrom, Jeffrey N., and Elizabeth J. Perry, editor, *Popular Protest and Political Culture in Modern China: Learning from 1989*, Boulder, Colorado: Westview Press, 1992

This interdisciplinary collection of articles by leading scholars takes a somewhat different look at the events and significance of Tiananmen by focusing on the role that culture plays in political action.

Yang, Mayfair Mei-hui, *Gifts, Favors, and Banquets: The Art of Social Relationships in China*, Ithaca, New York: Cornell University Press, 1994

A sophisticated analysis of a pervasive social phenomenon in China–*guanxi*, or social connections–drawing upon postmodern theories and illustrated with examples from fieldwork conducted in the early 1980s and 1990s. The author argues that *guanxi* in the reform era serves as a force against state dominance by creating a realm of social activity autonomous from the state.

Zha, Jianying, *China Pop: How Soap Operas, Tabloids, and Bestsellers Are Transforming a Culture*, New York: New Press, 1995

A lively and somewhat irreverent look at contemporary cultural activities by both state and non-state actors. The author examines the tension between politics, artistic integrity, and making money in such domains as architecture, film, literature, and music.

Stephen B. Herschler is a Ph.D. candidate in the department of political science, University of Chicago.

Index

Index

Note: Numerals in bold indicate glossary entries